HTML
ESSENTIALS

Steve Callihan

EMCParadigm

Senior Editor	Christine Hurney
Editorial Assistant	Susan Capecchi
Production Team	Jim Patterson, Desiree Faulkner
Copy Editor	Julie McNamee
Cover and Text Designer	Jennifer Wreisner
Desktop Production	Desktop Solutions
Indexer	Larry Harrison

Publishing Management Team

George Provol, Publisher; Janice Johnson, Director of Product Development; Tony Galvin, Acquisitions Editor; Lori Landwer, Marketing Manager; Shelley Clubb, Electronic Design and Production Manager

Acknowledgements

The author and publisher wish to thank the following reviewers for their technical and academic assistance in testing exercises and assessing instruction:

- Velda James, Citrus College, Glendora, CA
- Jon Storslee, Ph.D., Paradise Valley Community College, Phoenix, AZ

Library of Congress Cataloging-in-Publication Data

Callihan, Steven E.
    HTML essentials / by Steve Callihan.
        p. cm.
    Includes index.
    ISBN 0-7638-1655-8
    1. HTML (Document markup language) I. Title.

    QA76.76.H94 C33 2004
    005.7'2--dc21

                  2002033884

Text ISBN: 0-7638-1655-8
Product Number: 01583

HTML
ESSENTIALS

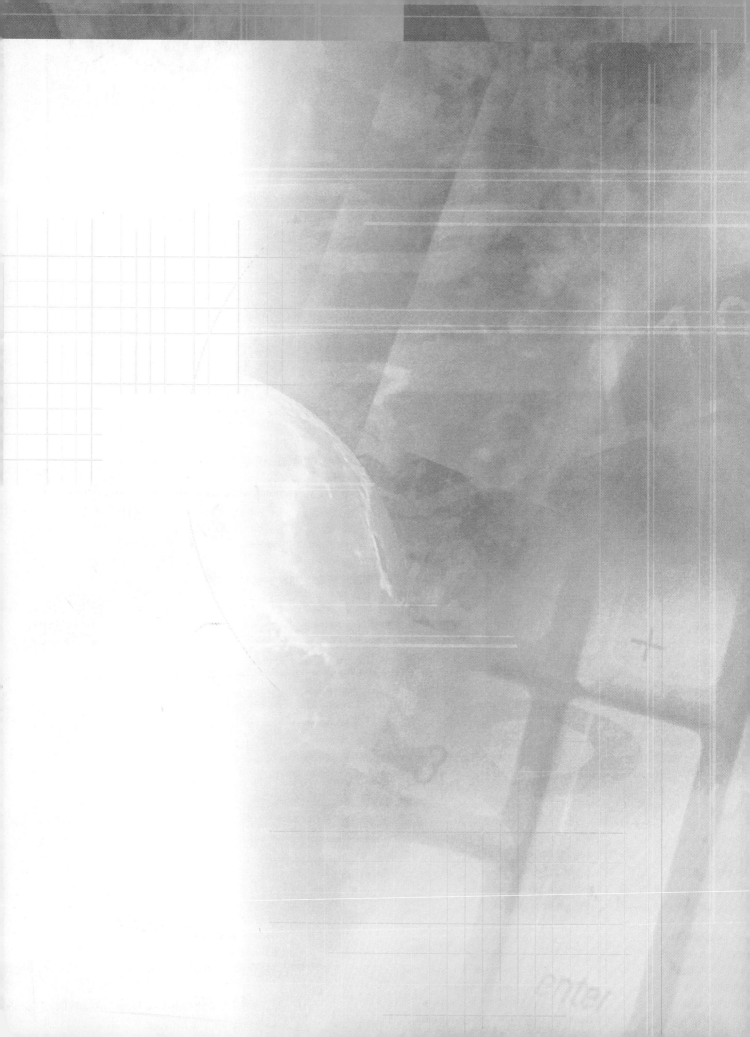

Contents

Chapter 2

Chapter 3

Chapter 4

Chapter 6

Chapter 5

Chapter 7

Preface

In a short period of time, the Web has become a ubiquitous presence in the lives of many people, be they workers, students, business people, or even children. Today, many rely on the Web for research, communication, and entertainment.

HTML IS FOR EVERYONE

From the beginning, the Web was conceived as a two-way medium. Anyone who surfs the Web can also create and publish documents that others can surf. These Web sites are created using HTML, or *Hypertext Markup Language*. Many think HTML must be overly technical or too difficult for the average person to learn and master. From the beginning, however, HTML was conceived as a tool that anyone could use without a great deal of previous technical experience or know-how.

Graduated Learning Process

The chapters in this book break down the material covered and skills taught into logically consistent steps that move from basic to intermediate and then to advanced topics. In each chapter, the student develops new skills, which can then be applied to addressing more challenging examples in the next chapter, and so forth, with each chapter representing a higher step upon which the student can stand toward mastery of the subject.

Chapter work might take one to two class periods to complete, with review exercises, quizzes, online research, and independent projects requiring additional time. Examples, exercises, and projects can be done in class, in a computer lab, or at home. Students can break off at any time, save their work, and then later pick up where they left off, in the same or another place.

Special Features

This book is designed to make learning Web development with HTML both easy and productive by including these special features:

- **Downloadable Example Files.** These files are used to complete each chapter's examples and exercises and can be easily downloaded by the instructor or by students from this book's Internet Resource Center (IRC) at www.emcp.com/. Additional student resources and instructional support are also available at this book's IRC.

- **Differentiation of Action from Content.** This book makes it easy for students to differentiate between material included for understanding and material that should be acted upon. The in-context code examples enable the student to see and complete the tasks quickly and easily.
- **Notes, Tips, and Margin Hints.** These features highlight additional information the student might find useful or helpful in comprehending information or completing examples.
- **Trouble Spots.** Trouble Spots highlight points at which problems might occur and provide relevant advice and solutions.
- **Real-World Case Examples and Scenarios.** Examples and scenarios are used in each chapter to demonstrate topics, features, and methods.
- **Online Research and Extended Learning.** These opportunities are frequently referenced at relevant points within each chapter; margin icons call out the location of Web addresses within the text that can be accessed to find out more about different topics or subjects.
- **Chapter Summaries.** This feature summarizes the topics that should be comprehended and the skills that should be gained in each chapter.
- **Code Reviews.** This section reviews all elements, attributes, or other codes introduced in a chapter.
- **Online Quizzes.** These quizzes are available online at this book's IRC to check comprehension and retention of key topics and information. Students receive immediate feedback, highlighting areas in which further study or review might be helpful.
- **Review Exercises.** These exercises can be done by students who finish the chapter work early. Review exercises also can be completed during lab time or at home.
- **Projects.** Projects present real-world Web publishing projects that students can independently undertake or the instructor can assign to provide additional opportunities for, and practical experience in, applying the skills and knowledge gained in each chapter.
- **A Team Project.** This project follows the tutorial chapters and provides students with the opportunity to work together in teams to plan, produce, and publish a real-world Web publishing project.

WHAT THIS BOOK COVERS

This book covers all the essential features and capabilities of HTML:
- The Introduction includes background information and perspectives on the Internet, the Web, and HTML.
- Chapter 1, *Creating a Basic Web Page*, covers using the example files, using a text editor and a browser, and creating a Web page using common features such as headings, paragraph text, bulleted lists, hypertext links, and inline images.
- Chapter 2, *Working with Online Documents*, covers using bold and italic inline highlighting, superscripts and subscripts, numerical lists, non-keyboard characters, monospaced and preformatted text, and other key features commonly used in creating online documents.

- Chapter 3, *Working with Fonts, Colors, and Backgrounds*, covers using HTML and Cascading Style Sheets to control the size, color, and face of fonts; the color of text, links, and backgrounds; and background images.
- Chapter 4, *Working with Images and Other Media*, covers working with inline images in more depth, including floating images; designing an online picture gallery using thumbnail images and image links; using graphic rules, banners, and buttons; and learning about creating your own Web images. Adding GIF animations and embedding audio and video files are also covered. Copyright issues involved in using images, audio, and video in Web pages are also discussed.
- Chapter 5, *Working with Tables*, covers displaying and formatting tabular data arranged in rows and columns in Web pages, including importing and formatting an Excel worksheet, structuring and aligning HTML tables, controlling table appearance using HTML codes and styles, creating floating figure captions and indented icon link lists, formatting an online resume, and creating a two-column layout using tables.
- Chapter 6, *Working with Multi-Page Web Sites*, covers creating Web sites using frames, including creating two-column, two-row, and combination row-column framed Web sites; using an external style sheet to control the appearance of a multi-page Web site; using relative URLs to link to images and pages located in multiple folders; validating Web pages using the W3C HTML Validator; and publishing Web sites using an FTP program.
- Chapter 7, *Working with Forms*, covers using common form elements to elicit user feedback, including text boxes, radio buttons, check boxes, list menus, text area boxes, and submit and reset buttons; using mailto forms and handling and processing mailto form responses; using stock form-processing CGI scripts commonly provided by online presence providers; using colors and backgrounds to improve the appearance of forms; and using preformatted text and tables to vertically align form elements.
- The Appendixes contain additional reference information, including an HTML quick reference, a special characters chart, and a Web-safe colors chart.

Standards-Based Instruction

All instruction in this book is based on the official specifications and standards for HTML, XHTML, Cascading Style Sheets (CSS), JavaScript, the Document Object Model (DOM), and other covered technologies as established by the World Wide Web Consortium and other responsible standards-setting organizations. Non-standard or proprietary methods and techniques are presented in this book only when there is no corresponding standards-based method or technique to achieve an important or necessary result. Any non-standard or proprietary methods and techniques covered in this book are clearly identified as such.

It is important that students learn not merely what happens to work at the moment in current Web browsers, but what will continue to work in future Web browsers as well. There is no guarantee that non-standard methods and techniques will continue to be supported in the future.

Software Requirements

Although most of the figures in this book use screen captures taken on a Windows system, the execution of the examples, projects, and other assignments does not require system-specific software or facilities. The example files used in this book are available for download in Windows, Macintosh, or UNIX/Linux format from this book's Internet Resource Center at www.emcp.com/.

The only software required to complete this book's examples, assignments, and projects is a simple text editor and a relatively current graphical Web browser:

- **A text editor.** You do not need anything fancy to create HTML files, which are just straight text files. Most operating systems include text editors you can use, such as Windows Notepad or SimpleText on the Macintosh. More full-featured text editors can be downloaded and installed from the Web.

- **A graphical Web browser.** To preview and debug all the examples, assignments, and projects, you need a relatively current HTML 4-compatible graphical browser installed on your system. The examples have been tested in Microsoft Internet Explorer 6 for Windows, Microsoft Internet Explorer 5 for the Macintosh, Netscape 6, Opera 6, and Mozilla 1. Earlier versions of these browsers can be used, but they might not be able to preview all the examples.

- **A connection to the Internet.** You can create Web pages without being connected to the Web, but if you want to download additional software tools or Web art images, or want to publish projects you create on the Web, you will need an Internet connection. An Internet Resource Center (IRC) has also been created for this book that provides downloadable example files and many additional resources that complement and extend the material in the book.

No other software tools are required to create and preview this book's examples and assignments. Students, however, may choose to use optional software tools for creating individual and team projects, such as image editors, GIF animators, image map editors, image splicers, Java animation programs, and so on. Students also will need to use an FTP program if they want to publish Web pages or projects they create on the Web. Additional software tools that students can choose to employ will be discussed in more depth in the relevant chapters.

ABOUT THE AUTHOR

Steve Callihan has authored several books on Web design, HTML, Web animation, and Cascading Style Sheets; published articles on Web publishing in major computer magazines; and worked extensively as both a technical writer and desktop publisher, designing and producing hardware and software user documentation. He has more than 15 years experience as a team member, team leader, department supervisor, and independent contractor, working in a wide variety of computer document processing and production capacities.

Introduction

Before you start working with HTML, you should understand what HTML is and where it came from. HTML is a key aspect of the World Wide Web, which is an evolution of the Internet.

WHAT IS THE INTERNET?

How the Internet came to be is an interesting story. The Internet actually is rooted in the Cold War, in that the initial impetus to establish the network that was to eventually become the Internet was motivated by a desire to establish a communication system that could survive an atomic attack.

Following the launch of the Sputnik satellite by the Soviet Union in 1957, the U.S. Defense Department established the Advanced Research Projects Agency (ARPA) to develop the first U.S. satellite, which was launched 18 months later. Later, ARPA undertook a new challenge, establishing a communication system to command and control the U.S.'s ICBM missile system and strategic bomber fleet. In 1963, the Rand Corporation was asked by ARPA to conceptualize the design principles behind such a system, a primary requirement being the ability to survive and remain functioning after a nuclear attack.

The ARPAnet

The Rand Corporation responded that the system would need to have "no central authority" and would need to be designed from the beginning to "operate while in tatters." These two characteristics define the essence of what later was to become first the ARPAnet and then later the Internet: a communication system, or network, that has no central authority (that could be knocked out in nuclear strike) and operates in a condition of assumed unreliability (cities destroyed by nuclear blasts, telephone lines down). The irony, of course, is that what was to eventually become the anarchic Internet we know today, which even nation states are unable to control, had its roots in a severe case of Cold War paranoia.

The ARPAnet was commissioned by the Department of Defense in 1969, initially linking research centers at four universities involved in defense research (UCLA, Stanford, University of California at Santa Barbara, and the University of Utah). Within the next two years, the ARPAnet grew to 15 nodes (including MIT, Harvard, NASA/Ames, and others). By 1973, the ARPAnet had expanded to England and Norway.

A number of key technologies that are associated with the Internet were also developed in the early days of the ARPAnet. Telnet was introduced in 1972, standardizing the capability to dial in and log on to a computer on the network. FTP (File Transfer Protocol) was introduced in 1973, standardizing how files were transferred between computers on the network. The first network-wide e-mail system was established in 1977. Newsgroups (USENET) were introduced in 1979.

A Network of Networks

The problem initially faced by the founders of the Internet was that many different network topologies were in use. What would work to communicate with one network might not work with another network. The system needed a shared set of *protocols*, or agreed upon rules, by which these different networks could all communicate which each other.

It doesn't matter what kind of system or device is connected to the Internet—it only matters that systems or devices connected to the Internet speak the same language when sending and receiving data over the Internet. That language, in the form of a set of common protocols, is TCP/IP (Transmission Control Protocol/Internet Protocol), which was introduced in 1982. Thus was born a "network of networks," or an *Internet*.

TCP/IP

In 1982, the ARPAnet adopted *TCP/IP* (Transmission Control Protocol/Internet Protocol) as the standard set of rules for sending and receiving data across the network. Today, TCP/IP remains the key suite of protocols that enables the exchange of data over the Internet. TCP/IP actually comprises two different protocols:

- **TCP (Transmission Control Protocol).** Breaks the message down into smaller packets, which makes the transmission of larger files or messages across the network more efficient. Each packet is individually labeled, identifying its origin, destination, and position within the file. When the packets arrive at their destination, TCP checks the packets for errors, verifies that all the packets that belong to the file have arrived, and then reassembles them in the proper order to reconstitute the full file. If errors are found or a packet fails to arrive, a request is sent to the sender to resend the file.

- **IP (Internet Protocol).** At each node along the way, a *router* reads a packet's address and then, if the current node is not its destination, forwards it on toward its destination.

Any system, whether a network gateway, a mainframe computer, a Web server delivering content over the Web, or your own personal computer you use to dial in and connect to the Internet, uses TCP/IP to connect to and share information over the Internet (see Figure I.1).

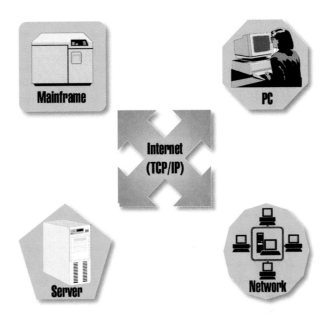

FIGURE I.1 • *The Internet uses a common language (TCP/IP) that connects systems and devices to share (send and receive) data between them.*

TCP has been compared with packing up the contents of your house and moving it across the country. The movers come in and pack everything up into boxes (or "packets"), which are then shipped across country. When they finally arrive at their destination, simply checking the shipment's manifest shows whether all the packets have arrived, or whether any have been lost along the way. The movers then unpack the packets, which then become the contents and furniture of your new house. This way of transferring data over a network is also called *packet switching*. For an illustration of how this works, see Figure I.2.

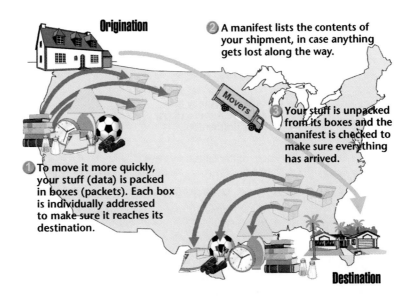

FIGURE I.2 • *Breaking data into smaller packets can speed its transmission to its destination.*

IP has been compared with sending a letter across the country. You place the letter in an envelope and as long as the address on the envelope is correct, barring mishaps, the letter should eventually be delivered safely to its address. A mail sorter doesn't have to know anything about the contents of the letter; a mere look at the zip code for the letter is sufficient to send the letter off in the right direction.

Over the Internet, the packets that compose a message might take different routes to get to the same destination. In other words, based upon changing traffic conditions, one packet might go from New York to Seattle by first going via St. Louis, San Francisco, and Portland, before finally arriving, safe and sound, in Seattle. Another packet, on the other hand, due to sudden congestion on the route to St. Louis, might go from New York to Seattle by following an entirely different route, traveling via Chicago, St. Paul, Missoula, and Spokane, before arriving in Seattle (see Figure I.3). On the Internet, if any packets that are part of a message fail to arrive (are lost along the way), the receiver of the message simply requests that the sender resend the message. After all the packets have arrived, they are reassembled into the full message, which is then read or executed.

The advantage of packet switching is that it makes it easier for multiple message streams to share the same network space. If only whole files, for instance, could be sent over the Internet, one large file could block other smaller files from getting through. Breaking messages and files—transmissions—into smaller packets is more efficient and much less prone to bottlenecks.

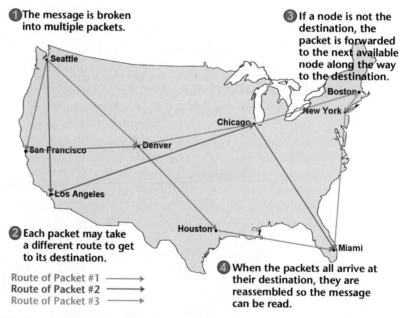

FIGURE I.3 • *When a file or message is broken down into packets, each packet can take a different route to get to its destination.*

NOTE

For TCP/IP, TCP (Transmission Control Protocol) defines the "packet," and IP (Internet Protocol) does the "switching" that routes the packets to their destination. You can think of TCP as boxcars in a train and IP as a train switch that moves the train from one track to another, except that in the case of TCP/IP, the individual boxcars could be switched onto different tracks.

One of the main points to remember about TCP/IP is that the essence of what makes up the Internet is not the wire, or the means of transmission, but the protocols that determine how information is sent, forwarded, and received over the wire. The Internet, in other words, is not the wires and connections (the hardware) that makes up the physical network, but rather the intelligence (or software) that directs and orders the traffic, or transmission stream, over the Internet. That directing and ordering intelligence is TCP/IP.

Thus, many and varied systems can be connected to the Internet. The only thing that matters is that they all use the same set of protocols—TCP/IP—to communicate with each other. When you dial in and connect to the Internet, you are connected to the Internet in exactly the same fashion as a whole network of computers might be connected at your local university, through TCP/IP.

The standardization upon TCP/IP as the common means for exchanging information across the network allowed the ARPAnet to grow and expand to eventually become the Internet we know today. In 1986, the National Science Foundation (NSF) formed the NSFNet, which initially linked five supercomputing centers to form the first high-speed backbone, running at what was then a blazing speed of 56 KBps. Unlike the ARPAnet, which linked together academic centers that were involved in defense research, the NSFNet opened up the network to the rest of the academic community, allowing anyone connected through a university to exchange information and ideas with anyone else who was also connected. Soon afterwards, the speed of the NSFNet backbone increased to 1.544 Mbps (called a "T1" connection). In 1990, the ARPAnet ended and was absorbed into the NSFNet. In the same year, the first commercial provider of dial-up access to the Internet, the World (world.std.com), came online, with many other ISPs (Internet Service Providers) coming along shortly after. The NSFNet finally became the full Internet, to which anyone could connect, that we know today.

In 1991, a new organization, the Internet Society, was founded in response to the growing internationalization of the Internet and the need to consolidate responsibility for establishing Internet infrastructure standards.

NOTE

Look at the Internet Society's site at **www.isoc.org/** for additional resources and information about the history and development of the Internet—just click on the Internet History link in the site's menu bar.

The Client-Server Model

TCP/IP enables the exchange of information and data over the Internet, but it does not, by itself, enable the distribution of services or the sharing of resources. Over a network, whether your local-area network (or LAN) or the Internet, this is done by means of a process by which computers make and respond to requests over the Internet, a process that is often referred to as the *client-server model*. A *client* is a computer that requests a service from another computer (a server). A *server* is a computer that responds to requests for services from another computer (a client).

A computer can be both a client and a server. A server is simply a computer operating on the Internet running software that enables it to function as a server. Besides Web servers, for instance, Gopher, FTP, e-mail, news, and other servers also function on the Internet. The same computer might function as a Web, FTP, and e-mail server, simply by running software that enables these functions. A server also can request a service from another server, in which case it is functioning as a client.

Most personal computers connected to the Internet are not running as servers, but only as clients—such computers are normally connected at a transmission speed of 56 KB or slower, which is just too slow to successfully function as a server, unless they are connected through DSL, ISDN, or some other form of broadband connection. Also, when you dial up to connect your computer to the Internet, most ISPs (Internet Service Providers) randomly assign an available *IP address*. An IP address is a series of numbers that uniquely identifies any computer (server or client) that is connected to the Internet. To be continually available as a server on the Internet, a computer needs to have the same permanent IP address during all the time it is connected to the Internet, and not a different IP address each time it is connected. You can think of an IP address as a street address: if you were to continually change your street address, nobody would be able to find you. They would be showing up looking for you where you were last, but not where you are.

You can think of the client-server model functioning much like a pizza delivery service. You, the client, feeling the irresistible urge for a three-cheese pizza with mushrooms and anchovies, call up the pizza delivery service, the server, and make your request: a 16-inch pizza with three cheeses (mozzarella, parmesan, and romano), mushrooms, and anchovies. As part of your request, you also tell the pizza order person what your address is, so the pizza delivery person can deliver it to your front door. The person taking your order confirms that they can supply the request. After the pizza is cooked according to your specification, it is loaded into a truck and rushed to your door, so you can eat it while it is still hot and steaming. Transactions occurring over the Internet happen in much the same manner, with a client requesting a service from a server, and then the server delivering the requested service to the client (see Figure I.4).

A client is simply software running on a computer. You should already be familiar with one client: your Web browser. Another term for a Web browser is a *user agent* (which might also encompass non-visual browsing agents as well, for instance). Web browsers aren't the only kind of clients that operate across the Internet. Other clients

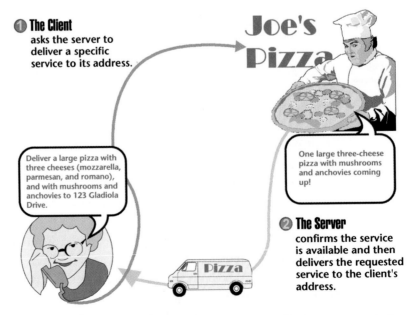

FIGURE I.4 • *The client-server model is similar to a pizza delivery system, in which a customer places an order for a pizza, specifying size and toppings, to be delivered to her door.*

include Gopher, WAIS, Archie, and FTP clients, for instance. In each case, these all work relatively the same: a Gopher client makes a request of a Gopher server or an FTP client makes a request of an FTP server, which then responds by delivering the service that is being requested by the client. A Web browser, on the other hand, can function as several different clients in one—functioning as a Gopher, FTP, or WAIS client, for instance. All it needs to know is the IP address on the Internet of the particular server to which it wants to make a request.

As you learn more about using HTML and other related technologies to create your own Web pages or sites, you also will find out about server-side and client-side applications and processes. A *server-side* application is a program or script that is run on a server, whereas a *client-side* application is downloaded to and executed by a client. An example of a server-side application is a script on a server that processes responses from online forms included in Web pages, directing those responses to an e-mail address, a folder location, or a database, for instance. A Web page is the most obvious example of a client-side application, in that the codes included within a Web page are first downloaded to a Web browser, to be executed, or parsed. JavaScript scripts and Cascading Style Sheets (CSS) are also first downloaded to a browser before they are executed.

WHAT IS THE WORLD WIDE WEB?

If the Internet is said to have begun with the formation of the ARPAnet around 1970, then it predates the *World Wide Web* ("the Web") by over 20 years. If the start of the Internet is dated, however, from the formation of the NSFNet, which came about in 1986, then it predates the World Wide Web by a mere 4 or 5 years. In fact, without the formation of the NSFNet, such a development as the Web could not have come about in the first place. NSFNet opened up the Internet to allow the participation of anyone connected through participating universities and research centers, which allowed the Web—the brainchild of an academic and scientist who was also connected to the Internet—to come to fruition.

The Inventor of the Web: Tim Berners-Lee

In 1989, a British scientist working at CERN (*Conseil European pour la Recherche Nucleaire* or European Organization for Nuclear Research) in Bern, Switzerland, made a radical proposal to facilitate the sharing and exchange of information and ideas between academics across the Internet. That scientist was Tim Berners-Lee and his radical proposal was for something he called "the World Wide Web." In his original proposal for the World Wide Web, Berners-Lee described it as "a wide area hypermedia information retrieval initiative aiming to give universal access to a large universe of documents." More recently, he provided an updated description and definition for the Web: "the universal space of all network-accessible information." He also has used the term "universal space" in online presentations to describe the nature and character of the Web. A close variant of this that Berners-Lee has published on the Web replaces "the universal space" with a somewhat less redundant phrase, "the universe."

NOTE

You can find CERN's home page at **www.cern.ch/**. To learn about CERN's role in the invention and early evolution of the Web, click the "general public" link, the Highlights link, and the World Wide Web link.

The Universal Medium

Another way of looking at the Web is as a universal medium. The Web, in other words, encompasses all media—print, radio, television, and so on—within a single universal medium. This is actually already implicit in the term "hypermedia" that Berners-Lee used in his initial description of the Web (hypertext and hypermedia are discussed in a later section, "The History of Hypertext").

The original focus of the Web was on the sharing and exchanging of textual information. Web documents are referred to as "pages" for that reason. The term *Web page*, however, is a bit of a misnomer, in that a document on the Web can be of virtually any length. It would be more accurate to refer to a Web document as a *Web scroll*, but somehow that just does not have the right ring.

The Original Purpose of the Web

As it was originally conceived, the Web was designed to facilitate the exchange of ideas and the sharing of information between individuals or groups, with little distinction between those who create and those who consume what was being exchanged and shared. From the beginning, it was intended that the Web would be a medium (or "information retrieval initiative") that would allow anyone to communicate with anyone. The initial participants on the Web were mostly academics and scientists, only because the Internet at the time of the introduction of the Web was still largely an academic affair. The first ISP, the World (world.std.com), made access to the Internet available outside of connected universities and other research facilities 1990, a year after the Berners-Lee's initial proposal for the formation of the Web. From the beginning, however, Berners-Lee's vision for the Web was one in which no group, community, or individuals held privileges over any other, with all having equal rights to not only consume, but also to originate and create, the content that composes the Web.

Thus, although the Web has evolved into much more than its initial vision, becoming both an entertainment medium and a platform for the distribution of commercial applications, programs, and services, the original vision of the Web as a "universal space" within which everyone could, and should, be able to communicate and interact with everyone else, remains at the heart of what the Web is and will continue to be.

In other words, on the Web, large-scale economic or political concerns, such as General Motors, Universal Studios, or the federal government, for instance, really have no greater privilege to conceptualize, produce, and distribute (or share) information, ideas, or even software products, across the Web than the plain ordinary individual. On the Web, all addresses are coequal; in other words, Joseph Schmoe's Web address of www.joseph-schmoe.com/, to cite an entirely fictional example, is just as easily reachable as Yahoo!'s Web address of www.yahoo.com/. Joe, of course, being just an ordinary guy, does not have the advertising budget of a Yahoo!, nor would the traffic limitations of his Web hosting account stand up to even a small fraction of the traffic Yahoo!

attracts, but anyone knowing his address should be able to reach his site just as quickly and easily as they can reach Yahoo! From that perspective, Yahoo!'s multi-billion dollar presence and Joseph Schmoe's presence on the Web (very much a shoestring affair) are equal. The same holds for a grandmother in Ireland, a schoolboy in France, or even a homeless person in Seattle—anyone with access to the Internet and the Web can be a creator and producer, not just a consumer, of content on the Web.

The World Wide Web Consortium

Although the World Wide Web was born at CERN in Switzerland, the fostering of a worldwide communication network was neither CERN's primary mission nor its mandate. In 1994, under the auspices of INRIA (the National Institute for Research in Computer Science and Controls, located in France), the World Wide Web Consortium (W3C) was formed in collaboration with the Laboratory of Computer Science at MIT (Massachusetts Institute of Technology) in the United States, where Berners-Lee took up a research position.

NOTE

You can find the W3C's home page at **www.w3.org/** (see Figure I.5). To find out about the W3C's work on the different HTML standards, just click the HTML link in the left sidebar.

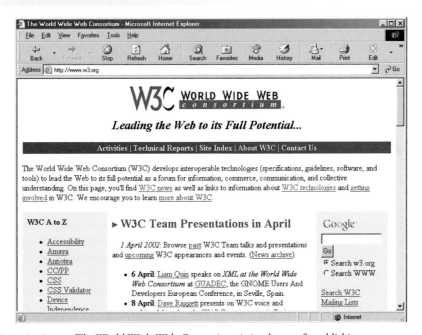

FIGURE I.5 • *The World Wide Web Consortium is in charge of establishing consensus on Web standards, including HTML.*

The W3C's stated mission is "to lead the Web to its fullest potential." The W3C is responsible for fostering and developing the specifications, guidelines, protocols, software, and tools that provide the standard foundation upon which the Web can stand and grow. Without the W3C, we might otherwise have ended up with a bevy of less-than-worldwide "webs," each based on separate proprietary protocols and accessed through different interfaces. As a standards-setting organization, the W3C is responsible for creating consensus among the various member organizations and vendors in the

W3C, forging a path forward that all agree they can follow. The W3C, in other words, is not a governing organization charged with enforcing dictates from some kind of elite council of technological elders, but rather simply establishes the forums and working groups within which organizations and vendors with a stake in the future development of the Web can come together and work out common agreements and commitments. The W3C is a bottom-up, "grass roots" organization that is run by and functions on the basis of consensus among its members, in other words, and not a top-down organization charged with enforcing rules and regulations. In fact, the W3C does not even refer to its specifications as "standards," but merely as "recommendations."

Basic Web Protocols

As is the case with the Internet, the Web is really nothing more than a set of agreed upon protocols and specifications. The essential protocols and specifications that comprise the Web are:

- **HTTP (HyperText Transfer Protocol).** This protocol formalizes the interchange (requests and responses) that occurs between Web-based clients (Web browsers, for instance) and Web-based servers (Web servers). All Web addresses, for instance, begin with "http://".

In this book, the "http://" is omitted from Web addresses referenced in order to lessen the chance that a Web address will take up more than the available space on a line. All current browsers allow you to omit "http://" when typing a Web address in their Address or Location bars. Non-HTTP URLs (such as FTP or Gopher URLs, for instance) still need to be typed in full.

- **HTML (Hypertext Markup Language).** This specification establishes the common language that allows for the universal exchange of information over the Web. HTML defines elements and attributes that facilitate the presentation of structured information and data. User agents (Web browsers, for instance) then interpret the HTML coding within the document to determine how it should be presented.
- **URL (Uniform Resource Locator).** For resources to be accessible over the Web, there must be a means by which they can be located. That means is provided by a URL, which defines the "Web address" of any resource on the Web. A URL specifies how a resource is to be accessed (the protocol), where the resource is located (the host server), and what the resource is (its path and name).
- **CGI (Common Gateway Interface).** This specification provides a common means by which Web server software running HTTP can interface with the host computer on which it is running. CGI allows server-side programs and scripts to be executed across the network. An example of this might be a CGI script written in Perl (a programming language common to UNIX servers) that processes requests sent from HTML forms embedded in Web documents.

An HTTP request, for instance, might use the following commands to ask a server to

- **GET** a particular document or file, providing the name and location of the file on that server.
- **SEARCH** for keywords within a particular document or subset of documents.
- Request only return documents created **SINCE** or **BEFORE** a particular date and/or time.
- Return a document's **HEAD** (header information), which allows Web browsers, or other client software, to compare the creation date of a cached copy of a document (residing on the browser's local machine) against the non-cached remote copy of the document (residing on the server). That way, if the remote copy has not been updated since the local copy was cached, the browser can just open and display the local copy, rather than having to download the entire remote copy.
- Identify the **USER**, the user's **HOST**, and the client software that is making the request so that requests can be logged and tracked.

After receiving a request, an HTTP server informs the client of the *status* of the requested resource or service. A server can signal back to a client the status of requests for resources or services in a variety of ways. For instance, a Web server might

- Respond that the request is a success (the document is present and available for delivery).
- Forward the client to a new address, if the resource has been moved.
- Inform the client that the document cannot be found (does not refer to a valid document path and name on the server).
- Inform the client that access to the document is not authorized, forwarding the client to a form for inputting a user name and password, for instance, or simply telling the client that access has been refused.
- Inform the client that the resource is not available due to a server error.
- Inform the client that the resource is temporarily unavailable and that the client might check back later.
- Tell the client that a keyword search of documents came up with no results.
- Tell the client the format on the server to which the requested document corresponds.

After the server signals back to the client, the client can then request that the server deliver the resource if it is available. The client also can go to a forwarded address and start the whole transaction over again, or simply relay the information to the user that the resource is not available for one reason or another and wait for the user to provide a different address to go to. The client also can decide to display a locally cached copy of the resource, if it is available.

HTTP is just one of several protocols used to exchange documents and information over the Internet. Other protocols that share the Internet with HTTP include FTP, Gopher, Archie, Telnet, and WAIS. All of these other protocols require server software that can respond to requests and deliver the requested resource, as well as client software that can communicate and interact with the specific server software.

NOTE

For links to resources on the Web that discuss the history of the Internet and the Web, see this Introduction's section on the IRC for this book at **www.emcp.com/**.

WHAT IS HTML?

The acronym HTML stands for Hypertext Markup Language. HTML was a key part of the original proposal for the Web. Without HTML, the Web would be much different than it is now. HTML was originally conceived as a subset of SGML (Standard Generalized Markup Language). SGML is the standard markup language used to prepare computer-generated documents for publishing on a printing press. HTML has a similar function, except it is used to prepare computer-generated documents for publishing on the Web.

HTML Documents Are ASCII Files

HTML documents are straight ASCII text documents. ASCII (American Standard Code for Information Interchange) defines a standard set of characters and control codes that are automatically recognized by almost all computer systems. The only exceptions are IBM's mainframe computer systems that use EBCDIC (Extended Binary Coded Decimal Information Code), a standard that predated ASCII. Because the standard ASCII codes are represented by 7-bit binary numbers (0000000 to 1111111), there are 128 standard ASCII codes. These include the alphabetic characters (a to z and A to Z), numbers (0 to 9), punctuation (period, comma, colon, semicolon, and so on), the space character, and various other commonly used characters (@, #, $, and so on). Also included are a number of control characters that command actions (tab, carriage return, line feed, backspace, delete, and so on).

NOTE

ASCII is also referred to as US-ASCII because it includes the "$" symbol for U.S. currency. It doesn't include any of the accented characters used by many European languages. Many international variants of ASCII have been developed; in UK-ASCII (BS 4730), for instance, the number symbol (#) is replaced by the British pound symbol (£).

ASCII text files can be read and written by simple text editors, such as Notepad on the Windows platform, SimpleText on the Macintosh platform, and vi (pronounced "vee eye") on the UNIX (or Linux) platform.

You do not need to know the ASCII codes, however, to create HTML files. In Chapter 1, *Creating a Basic Web Page*, you use a simple text editor to create an HTML file. A text editor has one purpose, to read and write ASCII text files. An ASCII text file is also sometimes referred to as a "plain" text file because it does not include any additional formatting codes (such as for bold, italics, indents, and so on) that a word processor might include in a word processing document. Text editors are also commonly used to read and write program code, which also does not require any formatting or extra characters.

HTML Is Not a Proprietary Format

HTML is not a proprietary document format, such as is the case with documents created by word processing programs, for instance. When you create a document in a word processing program, such as Microsoft Word or Corel WordPerfect, you can include all sorts of additional formatting and other characteristics that are invisibly coded beneath the surface. You might decide to bold a phrase, set a heading in a different font face or size, apply a color to a paragraph, set margins, create footnotes, add page numbers, and so on. You are limited only by the capabilities of the program you are using.

There is a penalty, however, for being able to format word processing documents in various and fancy ways—a word processing document will be much larger than an equivalent ASCII text file containing the same textual characters. On your local computer system, the difference in file sizes between the two formats is not very important because the speed of processing files locally renders the difference in file sizes as having a negligible effect on how fast a file is displayed or updated. For that reason, you undoubtedly use a word processor to create any documents you create for local use (or for sharing across your local network or via "sneakernet").

HTML documents, however, need to be transmitted across the Internet and the Web, which means they need to be no larger than is absolutely necessary. Using only ASCII codes to compose HTML documents achieves that. The choice of using ASCII for HTML files, in other words, is an important aspect of ensuring that HTML files can easily and quickly be transmitted and exchanged over the Internet and the Web. If a proprietary format had been used for HTML instead, the Internet traffic jams would have been much worse much earlier, and special software would have been required to interpret and read HTML documents.

HTML Is a Markup Language

Many people think HTML is a programming language because it is represented by an acronym. However, HTML is actually a *markup language*. The term *markup* originates from the world of printing and publishing. A formatter or designer would actually "mark up" the copy or layout, indicating how different elements should be printed. For instance, markup might be added to indicate that a heading at the top of the document should be printed in a bold 24-point Helvetica font. Other markup on the document might indicate color, margins, indents, leading, kerning, and so on. Back before mechanical or electronic typesetters, a person would then physically set the type for the document in the specified typefaces and sizes. Later, mechanical and electronic typesetting machines were invented that automated this process. Markup in an HTML file works in a somewhat similar fashion, with a Web browser functioning as a kind of typesetter.

With HTML, you mark up your textual copy to specify the structural elements that compose your document, such as headings, paragraphs, bulleted lists, bolding, italics, superscripts, and so on. A Web browser then interprets (or "parses") your markup code to appropriately display your document according to your instructions.

A primary difference between markup for printing and for the Web is that when designing a flyer, for instance, you already know the size of the media on which the flyer will be printed, whereas a Web page may be displayed on monitors of widely different sizes, at different resolutions, and using different default font-pitches. The actual dimensions of a Web page, in other words, are unknown and variable and might even have no dimensions at all, if presented through a Braille or speech browser, for instance. Because of this, the original philosophy of HTML has been to indicate what an element is, with the identity of the element indicating its function and structural import, rather than to try to describe what an element should look like.

HTML is based on SGML (Standard Generalized Markup Language). SGML is generally used to mark up electronic documents for processing, whether for printing on a printer or for display on a computer monitor. A desktop publisher, for instance, might use SGML conventions to identify (or tag) the different elements that compose an electronic document (whether a newsletter, a brochure, a calendar, a catalog, and so on). A separate program (a desktop publishing application such as PageMaker, Quark Express, or Ventura Publisher) then applies the formatting characteristics specified for the indicated elements.

HTML shares many common characteristics and features with SGML. Both are used to specify the hierarchical structure of a document in the form of elements and their attributes. An HTML standard is defined by means of a DTD (Document Type Definition), which originates from SGML. A DTD defines the elements, attributes, and other conventions that pertain to the processing of a specific type of document—an HTML file versus some other kind of file, such as some kind of DTP (Desktop Publishing) file that is intended for printing on a printing press, for instance. HTML is much simpler than SGML, however because it is intended for a specific purpose (specifying the structure of electronic documents for presentation over the Web), while SGML is intended to take into account any and all purposes that an electronic document might be used for.

Two other markup languages are also in use: XHTML (Extensible HyperText Markup Language) and XML (Extensible Markup Language). XHTML is a version of HTML that has been brought into conformance with XML. XML is intended to facilitate the presentation of structured data (database records, spreadsheets, catalogs, address books, financial transactions, bibliographies, or any data that can be given a structure). XML also makes possible the formulation of more specific markup languages, or modules, to be used for presenting documents and data over the Web—XHTML is, in fact, an XML module. Any individual or organization can formulate an XML-based markup language simply by publishing its DTD on the Web, as long as it is otherwise in conformance with XML. Other XML-based markup languages that have been or are being developed include MathML (Mathematical Markup Language), SMIL (Synchronized Multimedia Integration Language), RDF (Resource Description Framework), SVG (Scalable Vector Graphics), and XForms (Next-Generation Web Forms).

HTML Is a Client-Side Application

In its original conception at least, HTML markup was not intended to specify individual formatting characteristics. Rather, it was intended to specify only the structural aspects of a document, leaving the question of how the different elements in the document should be displayed entirely up to the Web browser (or other user agent used to interpret the HTML code). Thus, the idea was to specify only that an element was a level-one heading, for instance—a browser might then decide to display the heading in whatever typeface and font size it determined to be appropriate. As a result, the same HTML document might look different in different browsers because the browsers were free to determine on their own how different elements should be displayed.

Doing it this way enables HTML files to remain relatively small because information does not need to be included in the file to specify how a level-one heading is to be formatted. Rather, an element is simply marked up as being a level-one heading and the browser determines on its own how to display it.

This means that decisions about how a document is to be displayed do not have to be made until the document has been downloaded to the client (the Web browser). In other words, the load of determining formatting characteristics is assigned to the client (the local Web browser), while the server (the Web server) is only responsible for conveying the structural components of the documents to the client. This is referred to as a client-side application or process, in that instructions are downloaded and delivered to a client (your local Web browser, for instance) before they are executed. With a *server-side* application or process, on the other hand, a script or program located on the server might be executed (via CGI), with the results then downloaded and delivered to the client.

WHAT IS HYPERTEXT?

Besides being a markup language, HTML is a language that facilitates the dynamic and nonlinear interlinking of documents by means of *hypertext*. The prefix, *hyper-*, is from the Greek and is generally translated as meaning "over" or "above." *Hyper*text, thus, indicates an additional set of nonlinear and nonsequential relations or linkages that can be defined within and between textual documents, over and above the normal flow that a straight linear or sequential reading of a document's text would encompass. This is actually not an entirely new or radical idea. Regular books, for instance, include something similar to hypertext links—they are called cross-references, footnotes, and endnotes. With a book's cross-reference, however, you have to thumb through to the page that is being referenced to find the object of the cross-reference. With a footnote, you might have to put on your hat, coat, and shoes, head on down to the library, search through the catalog or shelves to retrieve the actual book, and then turn to the chapter and page being referenced.

With a hypertext link, however, you can immediately jump to the object of the link. That object might be another HTML document, a map or chart, a figure illustration, a section in another document, and so on. The object can be in the same file, in the same folder, in the same Web site, on the same server, or located anywhere else in the Web or on the Internet. A hypertext link, for instance, can jump to a location two-thirds down from the top of another HTML file that is located halfway around the World. Besides HTML files and locations within HTML files, other objects also can be linked, including images, audio files, animations, videos, and more. In fact, anything that has an address on the Internet can be linked to, including many Internet services that predate the Web but still continue to exist on the Internet along with the Web, including Gopher files, FTP directories, WAIS files, Archie databases, Veronica searches, and so on.

In July 1945, Vannevar Bush, who had been the head of the Office of Scientific Research and Development during World War II, wrote an article, "As We May Think," that was published in *Atlantic Monthly*. In the article, he made the earliest proposal for what might be interpreted as a hypertext system. He proposed a system called a *memex*, which he described as working along similar lines to the human brain, being characterized by the association of an "intricate web of trails."

NOTE — You can read Vannevar Bush's article, "As We May Think," online at the *Atlantic Monthly* site (**www.theatlantic.com/unbound/flashbks/computer/bushf.htm**).

Twenty years later, in 1965, Ted Nelson, a graduate student at Harvard, inspired by reading Vannevar Bush's article, coined the term *hypertext* and worked out the basic characteristics of what a hypertext system might be. Nelson described hypertext as being "nonsequential writing" in *Literary Machines*, a book that he self-published in 1974. He worked for many years on elaborating a full-fledged hypertext system that he called Zanadu, but which was never completed. Nelson also coined the term *hypermedia* to describe the nonsequential linking of different media, as well as another wonderfully apt term, the *docuverse*, which encompasses the universe of hypertext-linked documents.

Prior to the invention of the Web, a number of hypertext systems were implemented. The earliest was Xerox's NoteCards system created in 1985. The Owl Guide hypertext system was released in 1986, and Apple released the HyperCard system, created by Bill Atkinson, in 1987. Asymmetrix Toolbox, a clone of the HyperCard system, was later developed for Windows.

In 1989, Berners-Lee was directly influenced by Nelson's ideas when he formulated his concepts for the creation and formation of what soon became the World Wide Web. It is no accident that the term *hypermedia* is prominently featured in Berners-Lee's initial description of the Web as a "wide-area hypermedia information retrieval initiative." Nelson's term, *docuverse*, is also a very close analog for Berners-Lee's description of the Web as "the universal space of all network-accessible information." Figure I.6 provides a graphic illustration of how hypertext and hypermedia interact within the universal space, or docuverse, that they inscribe.

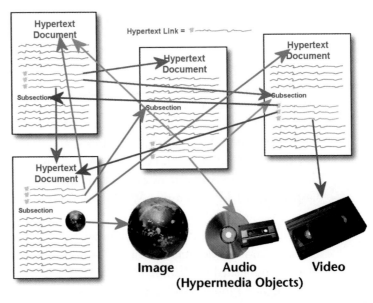

FIGURE I.6 • *A hypertext link can jump to another document, a subsection within a document, a hypermedia object (image, audio, video, animation, and so on), or any other object or resource that has an address on the Internet.*

NOTE For links to resources on the Web that discuss the history of hypertext, see this Introduction's section at the IRC for this book at **www.emcp.com/**.

HOW DID HTML EVOLVE?

Although Berners-Lee defined the original principles and specifications for HTML, HTML has undergone change. Many other individuals, organizations, companies, and factors have had a hand in determining what HTML was eventually to become.

The Original Version of HTML

HTML has evolved over time. Berners-Lee introduced the original version of HTML in 1989 along with the proposal for the formation of the World Wide Web. The original version of HTML provided for the following features:

- A document title.
- Heading elements used to structure an HTML document hierarchically.
- Standalone paragraph elements, but used as separators, not as containers, as in later versions of HTML. (There was no provision for adding line breaks, however.)
- Hypertext anchors (the A element) for creating hypertext links to documents or locations within documents.
- Bulleted and glossary lists, but not numbered lists.
- Non-keyboard character entities (such as for the copyright and registered symbols).
- An address block designator (the ADDRESS element).

NOTE To find out more about the original version of HTML at the W3C site at **www.w3.org/History/19921103-hypertext/hypertext/WWW/MarkUp/MarkUp.html**. Reading the earlier versions of HTML can be a great way to find out more about why HTML is what it is and how it has evolved and changed in response to the evolution and growth of the Internet and the Web.

HTML 2.0

The original version of HTML, although functional, was simple and missing many of the key features taken for granted by today's Web authors. A number of proposals were made for extending the original version of HTML, which as a group were generally referred to as "HTML+," but which were never formalized into a final recommendation (or standard).

   The first official new version of HTML, following the original version, was HTML 2.0, which was formalized as an official recommendation in 1995. HTML 2.0 added the following features:

- HTML, HEAD, and BODY elements, to provide a more explicit structure to an HTML document (specifying separate "header" and "body" sections within an HTML document).

- The paragraph element goes from being a standalone "separator" to being a container element, but with an implied ending.
- Display of inline images.
- Bold, italic, and monospace highlighting.
- Horizontal rules and line breaks.
- Numbered lists.
- Various other elements still in common use in HTML, including block quotes, preformatted text, metadata, HTML comment codes, and input forms.

NOTE — To find out more about HTML 2.0, you can read its specification at the W3C site at **www.w3.org/MarkUp/html-spec/**.

Vendor Extensions to HTML

Early on, browser vendors began adding their own extensions to HTML in response to the clear desire of authors and surfers for more richly formatted documents. For instance, the capability to display inline images in an HTML document was originally an extension to HTML created by the makers of the first widely distributed graphical Web browser, Mosaic. Many of these extensions to HTML are commonly referred to as "Netscape extensions" because the makers of the Netscape Navigator browser, the first widely distributed commercial Web browser, introduced them. Some of these extensions allowed authors of HTML documents to specify changes in font colors and sizes, as well as background colors and images, for instance. Later, Microsoft, when its Internet Explorer browser began to overtake the Netscape browser in popularity, introduced some of its own extensions to HTML, which are commonly referred to as "Microsoft extensions." Examples of Microsoft extensions include changing the typeface being used to display an element (using the FONT element's FACE attribute) and creating text that scrolls horizontally across the screen (the MARQUEE element).

Many of the extensions originally introduced as extensions to HTML have since been incorporated into the official specifications (or "standards") for HTML. Some extensions to HTML, however, remain as unofficial and proprietary extensions of HTML. For instance, a Netscape extension, the ability to specify blinking text, has not been incorporated into standard HTML. Microsoft's MARQUEE element has also never been incorporated into standard HTML.

HTML 3.2

After failing to come to consensus on a more comprehensive reformulation of HTML (the proposed HTML 3.0 specification), the W3C ended up approving a somewhat less ambitious proposal in January of 1997, which it termed HTML 3.2. This new HTML standard brought into the fold a number of extensions to HTML that had been introduced by Netscape, as well as several features that had originally been proposed as part of HTML 3.0:

- Variable font sizes and colors, text and link colors, and background colors and images
- Flowing text around images and image borders

- Tables for displaying data in rows and columns
- Horizontal alignment of document divisions (new), headings, paragraphs, and rules
- Superscripts and subscripts, strikethrough, and underlining
- Client-side image maps
- Scripts and styles (the latter, however, not implemented until HTML 4.0)

To find out more about HTML 3.2, you can read its specification at the W3C site at **www.w3.org/TR/REC-html32**.

HTML 4

Less than a year later, in December of 1997, the W3C recommended a new specification, HTML 4.0. HTML 4.0 included the following new features:

- Frames and inline frames
- Fully implemented style sheets
- Font typeface changes
- New form and table elements
- New text highlighting elements, including insertions and deletions, quotations, abbreviations, acronyms, and text spans
- Java applets and multimedia objects (not just inline images, but other hypermedia objects such as videos, animations, audio consoles, and so on)
- Triggering of scripts in response to mouse and user actions

The W3C has since come out with an HTML 4.01 recommendation. The HTML 4.01 recommendation is largely a fine-tuning of the HTML 4.0 specification. The W3C has announced that HTML 4.01 is the final version of HTML—there should be no new HTML elements or attributes added in the future. HTML 4.01 will remain a recommended specification, but future development will be focused in other related technologies (style sheets, scripting technologies, the document object model, as well as XHTML and XML). This is actually a good thing because it provides stability to what has been a tumultuous evolution—the HTML 4.01 you learn today should still be fully usable and an approved specification 5, 10, or even 20 years from now. Unlike many other technologies, you do not have to worry that what you learn today will become almost completely obsolete in the next 5 to 10 years.

To find out more about HTML 4.01, you can read its specification at the W3C site at **www.w3.org/TR/html4/**. For links to resources on the Web that discuss the history of HTML, see this Introduction's section at the IRC for this book at **www.emcp.com/**.

XML AND XHTML

The W3C recommended the XML 1.0 specification in February of 1998 and the XHTML 1.0 specification in January of 2000. The W3C describes XML as "a universal format for structured documents and data on the Web." Unlike HTML, XML does not possess a specific set of named elements and attributes, but allows authors to freely invent the elements and attributes that describe the structure of a document or data set. Elements and attributes can be created to take advantage of specific applications, or applications can be created to take advantage of specific element and attribute sets. XML, by itself, provides no formatting or display characteristics, but relies on style sheets to determine the presentation or appearance of an XML document.

XHTML, on the other hand, is an attempt to reformulate HTML as a conforming XML application. An XHTML document, however, is much closer to an HTML document in structure and function than it is to an XML document. XHTML adopts certain syntactical rules from XML, which account for most of the differences between HTML 4 and XHTML, but lacks the freedom to liberally create new elements and attributes that is present in XML. Like HTML 4, XHTML possesses a specific set of elements and attributes that possess specific meanings and functions: a <p> start tag signals the beginning of a paragraph element in both XHTML and HTML, but in XML might signal the beginning of a process, priority, practice, or just about anything that an author might determine the letter "p" to mean.

XHTML 1 possesses the ability to be further extended and modularized in ways not provided for in HTML 4. The main body of XHTML, apart from the differences in its syntactical rules and its ability to be further extended and modularized in the future, is simply HTML 4, so you need not worry that learning HTML 4 first will be a waste of time. In fact, having a good grasp of HTML 4 is essential if you later decide to also learn XHTML.

XHTML is just one of a family of new XML-based applications. Other XML-based applications include MathML (Mathematical Markup Language), SMIL (Synchronized Multimedia Integration Language), and RDF (Resource Description Framework). Additionally, XML is at the heart of a new W3C initiative called the Semantic Web, which proposes the creation of a layer of semantic relations on the Web, so that Web-based objects can be identified, not just by name and object type, but by meaning as well. A semantic meaning of "game" could be attached to a certain type of object (a game application), while a meaning of "tutorial" could be attached to another type of object (an educational application), and so on, which could help facilitate finding and identifying relevant data in what is otherwise threatening to become a haystack composed entirely of needles.

NOTE

Tim Berners-Lee, along with co-authors James Hendler and Ora Lassila, originally proposed the idea for the Semantic Web in an article published in the May 2001 issue of *Scientific American*. If you would like to read the article, it is available online at **www.sciam.com/issue.cfm?issueDate=May-01**. To find out about the current work being done to develop the Semantic Web, see the W3C's page on the Semantic Web at **www.w3.org/2001/sw/**.

THE IMPORTANCE OF WEB STANDARDS

Even though the W3C does not term its recommended specifications as being standards, the intent is clearly to arrive at a degree of agreement and consensus that can result in the establishment of a standard. For instance, browser vendors are members of the W3C and vote, along with other members, on whether proposed specifications should be formally recommended by the W3C. While the W3C has no power to force anyone to follow a recommendation, those who are expected to follow the recommendation, such as browser vendors, for instance, have been directly involved in formulating the recommendation and voted for its approval. The likelihood of their implementing the recommendation is therefore considerably enhanced. Only a broad-based implementation of a recommendation will cause it to become a "standard."

This brings up an important consideration for anyone who wants to produce HTML documents for wide distribution over the Web. Only by sticking to the agreed upon recommendations for HTML (the HTML "standards") can you be relatively assured that your documents will be reliably displayed not only in all current Web browsers, but in future Web browsers as well. Browser vendors are committed to supporting standard features in future browsers, but can drop non-standard ("proprietary") features at their whim. Netscape, for instance, supported a proprietary feature, the LAYER element, in its Navigator 4.x browsers, but has dropped support for it in its Netscape 6.x browsers. Netscape, however, is not at similar liberty to drop support for features that have been included in the recommended HTML specifications. By sticking to using only standard elements and attributes in your HTML documents, you help to ensure that your documents will remain *forward-compatible* with future browsers and user agents.

Does that mean you should never use non-standard (or proprietary) HTML codes? Not really. Sometimes, the only way to do a particular thing is by means of non-standard HTML codes. For instance, when creating a framed Web site, you cannot create absolutely "seamless" frames (with no visual indication of the separation between frames) using standard HTML that will work in all browsers. Thus, to have that effect, you must use non-standard HTML codes. All the same, you need to be aware that a cross-browser trick that works today may no longer work when a new generation of browsers arrives on the scene. This is a trade-off you may have to live with, however, if it is important to take advantage of a non-standard method to achieve a particular result.

If you are creating HTML documents for distribution over an intranet that is limited to users of your local network who all use the same browser, there should be no immediate harm in using proprietary extensions provided by that browser. When creating HTML documents for distribution across the Web, however, you should try to stick as much as possible to using standard HTML codes, except where there is absolutely no alternative other than to use a non-standard code.

In providing HTML instruction, this book stresses the importance of using standard HTML codes to create HTML documents. Only a few instances exist in which the added facility provided by a non-standard code might justify its use. Even so, you should carefully consider the possible impacts whenever you use a non-standard code. In the rare instances they are presented, this book clearly identifies any non-standard codes that are included in its examples, so you can decide for yourself whether you want to use them or not.

This book teaches the latest HTML standard, HTML 4.01. The W3C has stabilized the current element and attribute set that composes HTML 4.01, so what you learn this year will not be outmoded next year, as has frequently happened in the past. HTML 4.01 is also almost entirely incorporated into XHTML, forming an HTML core component that should remain largely unchanged as new extensions and modules are added to XHTML in the future.

NOTE For links to resources on the Web that discuss the importance of Web standards, see this Introduction's section at the IRC for this book at **www.emcp.com/**.

RELATED WEB TECHNOLOGIES

Additional client-side and server-side technologies have been developed over the years that are used as adjuncts to HTML. These include Cascading Style Sheets (CSS), JavaScript and other scripting languages (such as VBScript, for instance), the Document Object Model (DOM), the Java programming language, Server-Side Includes (SSI), Active Server Pages (ASP), Structured Query Language (SQL), Cold Fusion, PHP (PHP: Hypertext Preprocessor), Macromedia Flash, Wireless Application Protocol (WAP), Virtual Reality Modeling Language (VRML), Microsoft.NET, and more.

NOTE For links to resources on the Web describing many of the Web technologies that are used in conjunction with HTML, see this Introduction's section at the IRC for this book at **www.emcp.com/**.

WEB-BASED LEARNING ACTIVITIES

In this book's text, Find It icons in the margin highlight the Web addresses of additional resources you might find helpful or informative. To further extend your learning using the Web, you can

- Go back and visit any of the Web addresses highlighted in this Introduction that you have not yet visited. Look for additional resources and information that add to your understanding and knowledge of the Internet, the Web, and HTML. When you find a relevant page or site with information or resources you might want to access later, add it to your Favorites (in Internet Explorer) or your Bookmarks (in Netscape or Mozilla).
- Visit this book's Internet Resource Center at **www.emcp.com** to find additional Web addresses of resources that you can investigate and explore.
- Do further research a specific topic discussed in this Introduction. For instance, do further research on the Web on packet-switching networks, what they are, how they work, and so on. Compile your research into a report that can be shared with your fellow students. You can also team up with other students to create a class presentation on particular topic. Look for other topics mentioned in this introduction that you could further research and report upon.

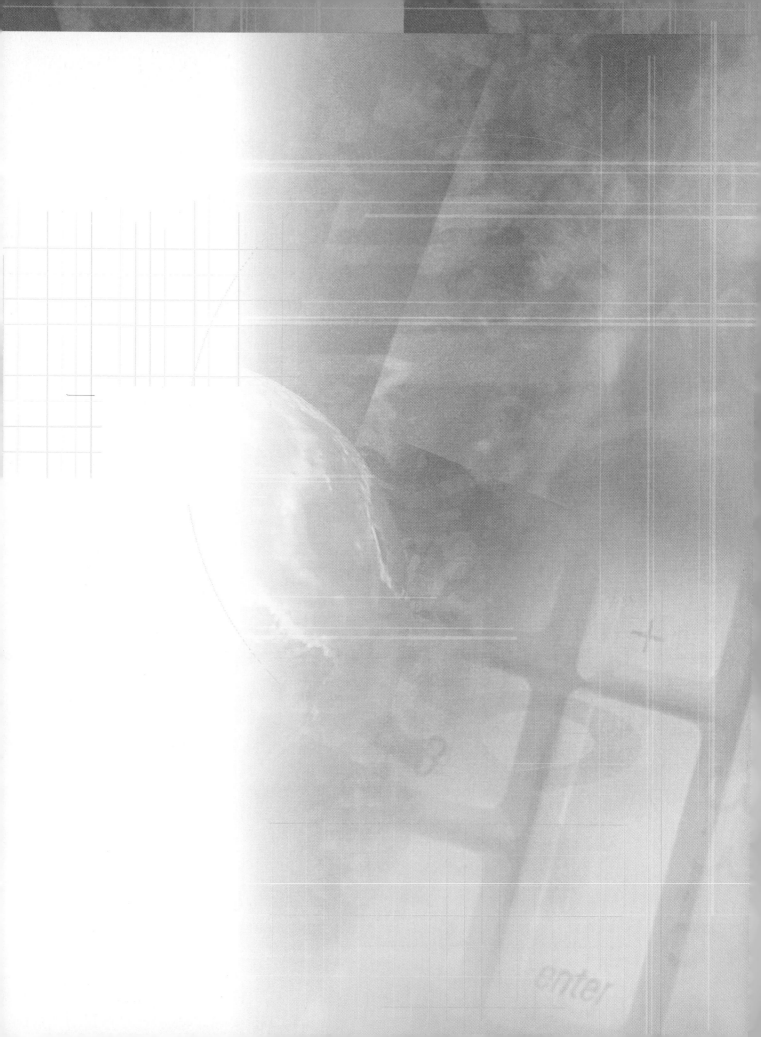

1

Creating a Basic Web Page

PERFORMANCE OBJECTIVES

After finishing this chapter, you should understand the basics involved in creating a typical Web page, including how to:
- Use your text editor and a graphical Web browser to create and preview your HTML files.
- Create your page's top-level elements.
- Use heading and paragraph elements to structure and create the base content for your page.
- Create hypertext links, lists, and link lists.
- Align elements horizontally on the page.
- Insert inline images in your page.
- Create an address block for your page.

Learning how to use HTML to create a Web page is similar to learning how to ride a bicycle. No amount of theorizing or reading about it is going to teach you how to ride, in other words. You just have to get on and ride, although some training wheels, and someone to grab the handlebars if you start to teeter after the training wheels come off, can definitely be helpful.

In this chapter, you learn how to use this book's example files, review basic HTML pointers, and create a basic Web page. You will not be doing anything particularly fancy, but you will use everything you learn in this chapter in virtually every Web page you create in the future.

USING THE EXAMPLE FILES

In this book's chapters, you use the author-prepared example files to complete the included tutorials and exercises. Your instructor might provide these to you or ask you to download them from the Web.

Downloading the Example Files

If your instructor provided the example files to you in a network folder, on a CD-R disc, or on floppy disks, skip to the next section. If your instructor wants you to download the example files, go to this book's Internet Resource Center (IRC) at the EMCParadigm

Web site at **www.emcp.com/**, click on College Division, and then click on the Internet Resource Centers link in the sidebar.

The example files are available for download in Windows, Macintosh, and Linux/UNIX formats, all as ZIP-formatted files. If you do not have software capable of expanding ZIP files installed on your computer, the following programs for Windows, the Macintosh, and Linux can be downloaded from the Web:

- WinZip at **www.winzip.com/** (shareware/Windows)
- Stuffit Expander at **www.stuffit.com/expander/** (freeware/Macintosh, Linux, and Windows)

For additional links to file-compression utilities you can download and use, visit this book's IRC at **www.emcp.com/** or the Tucows site at **www.tucows.com/**.

See this book's IRC for more pointers and tips on how to download the example files. Ask your instructor for additional help if you still have trouble successfully downloading and expanding them.

NOTE Although the example files for this book are available in Windows, Macintosh, and Linux/UNIX formats, this book only includes procedure steps, notes, tips, and cautions for using Windows or the Macintosh, which are more likely to be used in a classroom or computer lab.

Creating a Working Folder or a Working Disk

You can use a working folder on your computer or your network or you can use a working disk to work with this book's examples.

CREATING A WORKING FOLDER The easiest way to work with the examples is to create a working folder on the computer you are using or in your network folder. Your instructor will let you know whether you should use a working folder to do the examples and exercises.

If your instructor has provided the example files to you in a network folder or on a CD-R disk, or if you have downloaded and expanded the example files, you will find all of the example files available in an **HTML_Examples** folder. To create your working folder, you just need to copy the HTML_Examples folder and rename it as **My_HTML_Examples**:

- If using your network folder, copy the HTML_Examples folder to your network folder and rename it as your working folder.
- If using Windows, copy the HTML_Examples folder to the **My_Documents** folder and rename it as your working folder.
- If using a Macintosh, copy the HTML_Examples folder to your **Desktop** and rename it as your working folder.
- If using a Linux or other UNIX-based operating system, copy the HTML_Examples folder to your root folder or to any other folder where you are storing your data files and rename it as your working folder.

The My HTML Examples folder name for your working folder is just a suggestion. You can use any name you want for your working folder (**Gillian's_HTML_Examples**, for instance). In this book, this folder is referred to as "your working folder."

In your working folder, you will now find separate folders (**chap01**, **chap02**, and so on) that contain the example files for each chapter. When working on a chapter's examples and exercises, you need to save the files you create in that chapter's folder within your working folder.

If your instructor has provided the example files to you on floppy disks, you need to create and name your own working folder, and then copy the individual chapter files from the floppy disks into your working folder.

CREATING A WORKING DISK Your instructor might want you to create and work on a working disk. To create a working disk, you should have two formatted 3.5-inch floppy disks. From the example files provided by your instructor or that you have downloaded from this book's IRC, copy the example folder for the chapter you are working on. For this chapter, for instance, copy the **chap01** folder. Save any files you create while doing this chapter's examples or exercises in that folder. For each following chapter, copy its example folder to your working disk and save your work for that chapter in that folder. When you fill up your working disk, just copy the most recent chapter folder you are working in to a new working disk.

At the end of each work session, you should copy your working disk onto a second floppy disk. If your working disk becomes damaged or lost, you will have a backup.

If you need more help in using the example files, ask your instructor for assistance. You also can find additional help and instructions at the IRC at the EMCParadigm Web site.

When working with the example files and saving files you create, you might need to perform basic operations, such as copying, moving, renaming, deleting, or opening folders or files. You should already be familiar with these kinds of basic operations. If you are confused about how to complete a particular folder or file operation on the system you are using, ask your instructor for assistance.

UNDERSTANDING THE BASICS

Before you actually start creating an HTML file, it might be helpful to review some basic pointers about how an HTML file is organized and composed.

Tags, Elements, and Attributes

The *element* is the basic building block of an HTML document. Anything included within an HTML document is either an element or is contained within an element.

HTML uses codes called *tags* to delimit elements within an HTML document. For any element, a range of *attributes* can be set to further qualify the presentation or function of an element, some of which are required, while others are optional.

In HTML, you can set two different element types: a *container element* and an *empty element*.

CONTAINER ELEMENTS A container element brackets text (or other elements) between two tags, a *start tag* and an *end tag*, with the end tag distinguished from the start tag by a leading forward slash, like this:

```
<tagname>element content</tagname>
```

In this book, HTML code or other code that you need to key is printed in a magenta color. Code printed in a black color is presented for example purposes or for context and need not be keyed. You will be prompted later in this chapter when you need to run your text editor and start keying in any HTML codes.

For instance, the following is an example of setting a level-one heading element (a container element) using start and end tags:

```
<h1>This Is a Level-One Heading</h1>
```

In this case, the start of the container is *tagged* with a **<h1>** start tag, while its end is tagged with a **</h1>** end tag. Both start and end tags are enclosed inside of left and right angle-brackets (< and >), while in the end tag, the element name is preceded by a forward slash (/).

HTML elements are often loosely referred to as tags. It is important to stress, however, that an HTML element comprises both the tags that are used to mark the start and end of the element *and* anything that is enclosed within those two tags (see Figure 1.1).

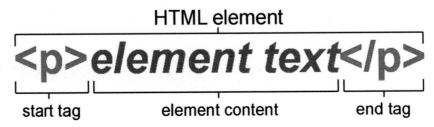

FIGURE 1.1 • *An HTML element is not only the tags (codes) used to delimit it, but everything in between as well.*

EMPTY ELEMENTS An empty element uses a single tag, without an end tag, and does not contain text or other elements. An empty element is also called a *standalone element*, because it stands on its own and does not bracket anything.

In the following example, the HR (Horizontal Rule) element, which is an empty element, indicates where a browser should draw a horizontal rule across the page:

```
<h1>This Is a Level-One Heading</h1>
<hr>
```

HTML does not have many empty elements; most HTML elements are container elements. Besides the HR element, some other empty elements that are frequently used include the IMG (Image) and BR (Line Break) elements.

You will also run into some instances where a container element will look like an empty element, with just a start tag, but no end tag. Rather, the element actually has an implied end tag, where the end of the element is implied by the start of a following element. (You will be alerted to this when such an element is first utilized in the examples.)

BLOCK AND INLINE ELEMENTS An HTML element that is contained in the body of an HTML document (in the BODY element) also can function as a *block element* or an *inline element*. Block elements are presented as separate blocks, starting on a new line with vertical spacing inserted above and below the element. Inline elements are presented "in a line" in the position where they are inserted, without starting a new line (and without any additional vertical spacing inserted above or below the element).

Nesting and Overlapping

Because an HTML document is organized in a hierarchical fashion, elements must always either bracket or be nested inside of other elements. You should never overlap elements in an HTML document. For instance, the following two examples apply both italics and bolding to text within an HTML document:

```
<b><i>bolded and italicized</i></b>
<i><b>italicized and bolded</b></i>
```

Both of these are correct—all that matters is that one be nested inside the other. On the other hand, here is an example of how you should not do it:

```
<b><i>bolded and italicized</b></i>
```

In this case, the B (Bold) element overlaps the I (Italic) element, which might confuse a browser about what should be nested inside of what.

Attributes and Attribute Values

In HTML elements, attributes can be used to further specify the presentation or function of an element. An attribute has two parts, the name of the attribute and its value, which are included in an HTML element in the following manner:

```
attribute="value"
```

The following example shows a series of attributes being applied to the IMG (Image) element:

```
<img src="myimage.jpg" height="200" width="150">
```

In HTML, you are free not to quote an attribute value as long as it contains only letters (a–z and A–Z), digits (0–9), hyphens, periods, underscores, and colons. The W3C recommends, however, that all attribute values be quoted.

Case-Insensitivity

In HTML, both element and attribute names are case-insensitive. Both of the following lines of code are perfectly valid, for instance:

```
<img src="myimage.jpg" height="200" width="150">
<IMG SRC="myimage.jpg" HEIGHT="200" WIDTH="150">
```

In this book, element and attribute names included in code examples are all presented in lowercase. Part of the reason for this is that XHTML, unlike HTML, is case-sensitive— XHTML requires that all element and attribute names be lowercased. Following the same rule in your HTML documents will make your task much easier if you ever decide you need to convert any of them to XHTML.

CASE EXAMPLE: CREATING A PERSONAL WEB PAGE

To gain experience creating a basic Web page, you will create one of the most common pages found on the Web: a *personal Web page*. A personal Web page might include information about a person's life, family, and other interests, for instance. It might provide further details about a person's educational, professional, or career background and involvements. It might also focus on particular interests or hobbies that the person creating the page might have. In other words, a personal page can include just about anything under the sun that is related to the person creating the page.

Johnny Watson is a college student who wants to create his own personal Web page. He does not yet know a lot about HTML, so he wants to keep things simple. He has two primary interests—sports and gardening—that he wants to feature in his page, although he wants to include other information, too. Soon to be graduating, he wants to include links to his biography and his resume. He also wants to share links to his favorite sports and gardening Web sites, and to Web pages created by his friends.

RUNNING YOUR TEXT EDITOR

You will be using a text editor to create, edit, and save your HTML documents. If using Windows, you can use Notepad. If using the Macintosh, you can use SimpleText.

Windows. In Windows 95, 98, and higher, to run Notepad, click the Start button and select Programs, Accessories, and Notepad. In Windows XP without the Classic Desktop theme selected, you need to select All Programs before you select the Programs option.

For a shortcut for running Notepad, click the Start button, select Run, key **notepad**, and press Enter.

TROUBLE *spot*

Word Wrap is turned off by default in Windows Notepad. That is fine for writing program code, but when creating and editing HTML documents, you want Word Wrap turned on. To turn Word Wrap on in Notepad in all versions of Windows except Windows XP, select Edit and Word Wrap; in Windows XP, select Format and Word Wrap. When Word Wrap is on, a checkmark is displayed next to the Word Wrap option.

If you are using Windows 95, you will need to turn Word Wrap on each time you run Notepad. If you are using Windows 98 or any other later version of Windows, Word Wrap in Notepad remains turned on until you turn it off.

Macintosh. To run SimpleText for OS 8 and higher, double-click on the Macintosh HD icon, the Applications folder, and the SimpleText program icon. (Mac OS X users can find SimpleText in their folder of OS 9 applications.) If you cannot find the SimpleText program in the Applications folder, use the Finder to search for its location. (Select File, Find, and then search for **simpletext**.)

Users of earlier versions of the Macintosh OS (OS 7 or earlier) can use the TeachText text editor to edit and save HTML files.

Users of Macintosh OS X can also use TextEdit, which is included in the Applications folder, to edit and save HTML files. Note, however, that TextEdit defaults to saving files in RTF (Rich Text Format), so you need to first select Format, then Make Plain Text, when creating and saving an HTML file. To turn on word wrap, select Format, then Wrap to Page.

Other Platforms. If you are using a platform other than Windows or Macintosh, you should still be able to do the examples, exercises, and assignments included in this book. See your system documentation or help system to find out how to run any text editor that is included with your system's software. You also can download text editors for many platforms, including Linux, OS/2, BeOS, and QNX, from Tucows at **www.tucows.com/**.

STARTING YOUR PAGE

For this example, you will be creating an HTML file from scratch. You do not need to open an example file to get started. Just key the indicated example codes directly into your text editor's window. Any text that you need to key is displayed within a code example in a magenta font.

Let any long lines wrap—you do not need to insert a hard return at the end of every line in the example codes. Additional leading is inserted between code blocks to indicate where you need to insert a hard return.

Starting with the Top-Level Elements

The HTML, HEAD, and BODY elements specify the top-level hierarchy of a Web page. The HTML element identifies that the document is an HTML document, while the HEAD and BODY elements are nested inside the HTML element.

Key the following codes into your text editor's window to create the top-level elements for your page:

```
<html>
<head>
</head>
<body>
</body>
</html>
```

In the HEAD element you will be including elements that define characteristics of the document, such as a title, a style sheet, meta data elements that describe the document, and so on.

In the BODY element you will be including elements that will be displayed in a browser, such as headings, paragraphs, lists, and so on. Because you have not yet included anything in the BODY element, opening your document in a browser at this point would just display a blank browser window. I will prompt you later when you should run your browser to check out the visual results of your work.

The specifications for HTML make including the start and end tags for the HTML, HEAD, and BODY elements optional. If you leave out the tags for these elements, the elements will still be there; they are implied, rather than absent. The original version of HTML (from 1992) did not even include HTML, HEAD, or BODY elements. When first learning HTML, it is a good idea to include these elements to help clarify how an HTML document is structured and organized.

Creating a Title for Your Page

The TITLE element is a required element that is nested inside the HEAD element. Every HTML document should have a TITLE element (even if you choose to omit the optional start and end tags for the HEAD element).

Add the following TITLE element to your HTML document:

```
<html>
<head>
<title>Johnny Watson's Home Page</title>
</head>
<body>
</body>
</html>
```

The content of the TITLE element is generally displayed in a browser's title bar. Including additional text in your title that summarizes the content of your page may improve the chances of your page being displayed, or cause it to be displayed earlier, in a search engine's list of search results. There is effectively no limit on the amount of text you can include in your title, but search engines vary on how much of an extended title content they will display or index. The Google search engine (**www.google.com/**), for instance, only displays up to 60 characters in a page's title.

Add additional text to your title that more specifically indicates the actual content of your page to make your title more informative and more likely to be found in a search engine's list of search responses. Because Johnny Watson's two favorite interests are sports and gardening, add additional text to the title to indicate that:

```
<html>
<head>
<title>Johnny Watson's Home Page: Sports and Gardening</title>
</head>
<body>
</body>
</html>
```

A number of other elements can be included in the HEAD element. These include the META, BASE, LINK, STYLE, SCRIPT, OBJECT, and ISINDEX elements. Because you are creating a basic Web page in this chapter, these other elements are not discussed at this point. You will learn about using the META element in Chapter 2, *Working with Online Documents*. For more information on the other HEAD elements, see Appendix A, *HTML Quick Reference*.

Saving a Starting Template

All HTML files start out the same. You can save your HTML file now as a template, so you can use it later to create additional HTML files without having to retype the same starting HTML elements every time.

Earlier in this chapter, you were prompted to create a working folder or disk to hold the HTML files you will be creating in this book. If you have not done that yet, return to "Using the Example Files" earlier in this chapter and follow the instructions that are given there.

Windows. Save your HTML document as a starting template, so you can reuse it later:

1. In Notepad, select File and Save. The My Documents folder should be displayed in the Save As dialog box.
2. If using a working folder (located in your My Documents folder), just double-click the folder to open it. If using a working disk, click on the Save in box and click the drive where your working disk is located. (If your working folder is located in your network folder, use the Save in box to navigate to the folder and open it.)
3. Click on the Save as type box and select All Files (*.*).
4. In the File name box, key a name for your starting template. For instance, you might key **start.html** as the file name. Click the Save button (or press the Enter key) to save your starting template.
5. Resave your HTML document under another name, so you will not overwrite your starting template. Select File and Save As, open your working folder or working disk, and then open the chap01 folder. Key **watson.html** as the file name (see Figure 1.2) and click Save.

FIGURE 1.2 • *The HTML document, watson.html, is to be saved in the chap01 folder.*

Windows. If you have display of known file extensions turned off and save an HTML file with Text Documents selected in the Save as type box, Windows tacks a hidden ".txt" file extension to the end of your file name. Thus, watson.html, for instance, would actually be saved as watson.html.txt. When you go to open this file, you will just see the "watson.html" part of the file name, since the .txt file extension is hidden. The file icon, however, will indicate it is a text file, rather than an HTML file. Internet Explorer will display this file as an HTML file, but all other browsers will treat it as a straight text file, displaying the raw HTML codes instead.

To avoid this problem and make working with files much easier in Windows, you should turn on the display of file extensions. On the Web, files are identified by their file extensions, so it is important that they be visible to you. To turn on display of file extensions, double-click My Computer on your Desktop, select View and Folder Options (or Tools and Folder Options in Windows XP), click the View tab, and uncheck the Hide file extensions for known file types (or similar) check box.

Turning on the display of file extension also can help reduce your vulnerability to e-mail viruses. Many e-mail viruses use a visible and a hidden file extension to fool you into thinking that a file is a type of file that is safe to open.

Macintosh. Save your HTML document as a starting template, so you can reuse it later:

1. In SimpleText, select File and Save. The contents of your Desktop should be displayed in the dialog box.
2. If using a working folder (located on your Desktop), just double-click it to open it. If using a working disk, insert the disk into your floppy disk drive (it should

automatically be opened in the Save dialog box). (If your working folder is located in your network folder, you can use the Network Browser, located on the Apple menu, to open any shared network drives.)

3. In the Save this document as box, key a name for your starting template. For instance, you might key **start.html** as the file name. Press Return (or the Enter key) or click the Save button to save your starting template.

4. Resave your HTML document under another name, so you will not overwrite your starting template. Select File and Save As, open your working folder or working disk, and then open the chap01 folder. Key **watson.html** as the file name and click the Save button.

When saving an HTML file, do *not* include any spaces in the file name. Although this is allowed in both Windows and the Macintosh, it is not allowed on a UNIX server (and most Web servers run UNIX). More recent UNIX Web servers will substitute the space character's escape code (**%20**) for spaces in folder and file names, but any link to the file would also have to reduplicate the escape character in place of the space, or the link will not work. Other UNIX Web servers will simply generate a "file not found" or other error when encountering spaces in folder or file names. Substitute underscores (_) for spaces, if necessary.

Also, always add the file extension **.html** (or **.htm**) to any HTML file that you save (even if working on the Mac, which does not use file extensions to identify the file type). Internet Explorer will display an HTML file without the file extension as an HTML file, but other browsers will treat it as a straight text file and simply display the raw HTML codes.

ADDING A LEVEL-ONE HEADING

HTML includes six heading-level elements (H1, H2, H3, and so on) that can be used to create headings. Generally, only one H1 heading is included, at the top of the BODY element, functioning as a heading, or title, for the whole document. The other heading elements are then used to indicate sections and subsections within a document.

Unlike the content of the TITLE element, which is only displayed on a browser's title bar, the content of the H1 element is displayed within the browser window and serves as the displayable title for the document.

Edit the H1 element as shown here to include keywords in the level-one heading:

```
<html>
<head>
<title>Johnny Watson's Home Page: Sports and Gardening</title>
</head>
<body>
<h1>Sports, Gardening, and Other Interests</h1>
</body>
</html>
```

PREVIEWING YOUR WORK

To preview your work while creating the document examples that are presented in each chapter, you need to have your HTML document open in both your text editor and your browser. You should frequently switch between your text editor and your browser, saving your work in your text editor and then refreshing the display of your document in your browser.

Previewing Your HTML Document in Your Browser

Now that you have added something to your HTML document that will be displayed within a browser's window, you should preview your results in your browser.

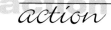

Save your document and then open it in your browser, so you can see your results for yourself:

1. Resave **watson.html**. In Windows Notepad or SimpleText on the Macintosh, select File and Save to resave your document. In SimpleText, you also can press Command+S to resave your document.

Although you can press Ctrl+S to resave a document in most Windows applications, that will not work in Windows Notepad. In Windows Notepad, you need to select File, then Save to resave your document.

2. Run your browser. You do not need to connect to the Internet to preview a local file, so if you are prompted to connect or if your dialer starts to dial up your connection, just click the Cancel button. Depending upon which browser you are using, your browser might generate an error message, saying it is unable to open its default start page; just click OK.
3. Open **watson.html** in your browser. The steps for doing this can vary between browsers, and even between different versions of the same browser.
   In Internet Explorer 6 for Windows, for instance, select File, Open, and click the Browse button; in Netscape 6 for Windows, select File, Open Page, and click the Choose File button; in Internet Explorer 5 and Netscape 6 for the Macintosh, select File and Open File.
4. Next, open your working folder or working disk, open the folder for the chapter (chap01) you are working in, and then open **watson.html**. Figure 1.3 shows watson.html opened in a Web browser.

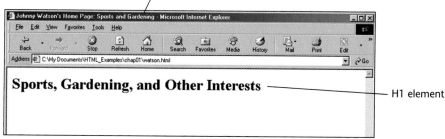

FIGURE 1.3 • *The HTML document, watson.html, is opened in a Web browser.*

Alternatively, you can open a local HTML file in your browser by dragging it from its folder and dropping it in your browser's window. You will need to arrange your HTML file's open folder and your browser's window so you can drag your file from one and drop it in to the other. Whether this is easier than just using the File menu, however, is debatable.

You also can press the keyboard shortcut Ctrl+R in Windows or Command+R on the Macintosh to refresh your page in your browser.

As you add more example code to your HTML document, do not just rely on the figures to show you what your results should look like. Instead, use the figures as prompts to save your HTML document in your text editor and switch over to your browser. Just click the Refresh (or Reload) button in your browser to refresh the display of your page.

Hopping between Your Text Editor and Your Browser

Both Windows and the Macintosh support similar shortcut key combinations that you can use to quickly hop back and forth between your text editor and your browser.

Practice hopping back and forth between your text editor and your browser:

Windows. Hold down the Alt key and tap the Tab key to cycle through the icons for any open applications. Release the Alt key when the icon for the application you want to hop to is highlighted to bring its window to the foreground. You also can just press Alt+Tab once to jump to the previously opened application window.

Macintosh. Hold down the Command key and tap the Tab key to cycle through any open application windows. Release the Command key when the application window you want to hop to is displayed.

Stopping and Restarting Your Work

Depending on your learning style and computer experience, the amount of time required to complete this chapter's examples and exercises varies. It is not how fast you learn HTML that matters, but how well you learn it, so do not feel that you have to rush to complete a chapter within any specific time frame. You can stop at any point within a chapter, save your work, and then pick up where you left off at another time or location.

Follow these steps to resume work on a chapter's examples and exercises at home or in a computer lab, for instance:

1. In your text editor, save your HTML file in the chapter folder in which you are working.
2. Copy the chapter folder you are working in (the chap01 folder for Chapter 1) to a formatted 3.5-inch floppy disk.
3. Take the floppy disk to any other location where you want to resume working on a chapter's examples or exercises. In the new location, just run your text editor, select File, then Open, and reopen the HTML file you are working on.

Windows. When opening a file in Notepad, the Open dialog box defaults to displaying only text files (with a .txt extension). To see HTML files (with a .html extension), you need to first select All Files (*.*) in the Files of type box.

WRITING AN INTRODUCTORY PARAGRAPH

The P (Paragraph) element is used to tag regular text paragraphs in an HTML document. An HTML document should contain no untagged text.

Using an introductory paragraph in an HTML document allows you to include additional keywords that search engines and Web directories can index, improving the chances of visitors finding your page.

Add the following introductory paragraph to your HTML document (see Figure 1.4):

```
<body>
<h1>Sports, Gardening, and Other Interests</h1>
<p>Welcome to my home page! My name is Johnny Watson and I'm a
big nut about two things: sports and gardening! You may think
that is an odd combination, but they really have more things in
common than you might suppose. First they are both largely
outside activities: I enjoy participating in, rather than just
watching, sports, for one thing. When the weather is bad, there
can be an indoor component to both activities. I enjoy following
some of my favorite teams on TV, while watering my indoor
plants at the same time!</p>
</body>
</html>
```

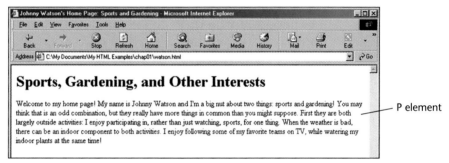

— P element

FIGURE 1.4 • *An introductory paragraph can both describe your page and include keywords that search engines and Web directories can use to index your page.*

NOTE

Beginning HTML authors often think they can just insert multiple empty P elements to add vertical spacing within a Web page. That will not work. Browsers completely ignore multiple empty P elements in an HTML document. In Chapter 2, you will learn how to use the PRE element, which is the only element in which nested spaces, tabs, and returns are displayed and can be used to insert vertical spacing within an HTML document (by nesting two or more returns).

SPACING, TABS, AND RETURNS

Web browsers ignore any spacing, tabs, and hard returns you insert into an HTML document. You can use these to make your document's raw codes easier to read and interpret visually.

Insert hard returns where ¶ characters are shown and insert spaces where · characters are shown:

```
<html>
<head>
¶
···<title>Johnny Watson's Home Page: Sports and Gardening</title>
¶
```

```
</head>
<body>
¶
...<h1>Sports, Gardening, and Other Interests</h1>
¶
...<p>Welcome to my home page! My name is Johnny Watson and I'm
a big nut about two things: sports and gardening! You may think
that is an odd combination, but they really have more things in
common than you might suppose. First they are both largely
outside activities: I enjoy participating in, rather than just
watching, sports, for one thing. When the weather is bad, there
can be an indoor component to both activities. I enjoy following
some of my favorite teams on TV, while watering my indoor plants
at the same time!</p>
¶
</body>
</html>
```

You also can use tabs, instead of three spaces, to indent the first line of nested elements within your text editor.

To test this yourself, save your HTML file in your text editor (select File, Save), switch over to your Web browser, and refresh the display of your page by clicking the Refresh (or Reload) button. You should not see any change in your page, which should still look like Figure 1.4. That is because spaces, tabs, and hard returns, while visible in your text editor, should have no effect when displayed in a Web browser.

INSERTING COMMENTS

You can annotate your HTML document by inserting comments, which can be helpful if you or someone else has to revise your document at a later date, for instance. Later you might not remember why you did something a certain way, but a comment can remind you.

In HTML, bracket anything you want to include as a comment within <!-- and --> codes. Any text or codes included within these two codes can be read within your text editor, but will not be displayed in a browser.

Test using HTML comments in your document:

1. Add the following HTML comments to your document:

```
<body>
<!--Top-level heading for document-->
    <h1>Sports, Gardening, and Other Interests</h1>
<!--Introductory paragraph-->
    <p>Welcome to my home page! My name is Johnny Watson and I'm
a big nut about two things: sports and gardening! You may think
that is an odd combination, but they really have more things in
common than you might suppose. First they are both largely
outside activities: I enjoy participating in, rather than just
watching, sports, for one thing. When the weather is bad, there
can be an indoor component to both activities. I enjoy following
some of my favorite teams on TV, while watering my indoor
plants at the same time!</p>
```

2. Select File, then Save to save your document, switch over to your Web browser, and refresh the display of your page by clicking the Refresh (or Reload) button.

After refreshing the display of your page, you should not see any change in your page, which should still look like Figure 1.4, since HTML comment codes and any text or other elements contained within them, although visible in your text editor, have no effect when displayed in a Web browser.

Although you can nest both text and HTML elements inside HTML comment codes, you cannot nest an HTML comment inside another HTML comment.

You also should make sure that any HTML comment codes you add to your document are properly nested and not overlapping any elements. When commenting out an element's start tag, make sure that its corresponding end tag, if it has one, is also commented out.

CREATING A HYPERTEXT LINK

In HTML, the A (Anchor) element is used to add hypertext links to Web pages. Hypertext links can be added anywhere you can add text within an HTML document.

Johnny Watson wants to link the word "sports" in the first sentence of his introductory paragraph to his favorite sports-related Web site.

Add the following codes to link the word "sports" to ESPN.com:

```
Welcome to my home page! My name is Johnny Watson and I'm a big
nut about two things: <a href="http://www.espn.com/">sports</a>
and gardening!
```

Johnny Watson also wants to link the word "gardening" in his introductory paragraph's first sentence to his favorite gardening site.

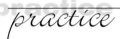

To get some practice creating a hypertext link on your own, follow the previous example of linking the word "sports" to the ESPN Web site, but this time link the word "gardening" in the same sentence to the BBC's Lifestyle/Gardening site, using **http://www.bbc.co.uk/gardening/** as the value of the HREF attribute.

You should have now inserted two inline hypertext links, linking the words "sports" and "gardening" to actual sites that exist on the Web (see Figure 1.5).

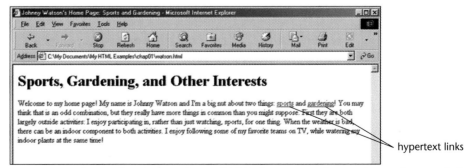

FIGURE 1.5 • *Any word or phrase within an HTML document can be turned into a hypertext link.*

If you are connected to the Internet, you can test any links you create on your local machine, without having to publish your page to the Web.

Test the "sports" and "gardening" links you just created:

1. If not already connected, run your dialer and connect to the Internet.
2. Save your document in your text editor, switch to your browser, and refresh the display of your page.
3. Click the "sports" and "gardening" links to test them. Your browser should jump to the ESPN site and the BBC gardening site, respectively. Click your browser's Back button to return to your example page.

A common error when creating hypertext links is to leave off the second quotation mark that encloses the A element's HREF value. This omission causes most browsers to simply ignore anything that follows because it is considered to still be part of the HREF value, until a following A element start tag is encountered. This can result in a single word, a whole paragraph, or even the rest of a page not being displayed. Figure 1.6 shows what this looks like in a browser.

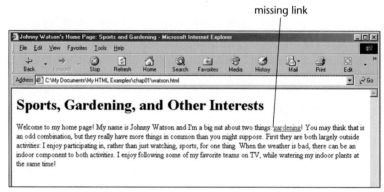

FIGURE 1.6 • *Leaving off a following quote in a hypertext link can cause following text to disappear.*

Other common errors when creating hypertext links include leaving off the closing > character of the A element's start tag and leaving out the / character in the A element's end tag. Browsers may react to either of these errors by considering all following text to be part of the same hypertext link (and underlining it), until another A element is encountered.

These link examples illustrate that you can turn any word (or phrase) within an HTML document into a hypertext link. Additionally, if Johnny Watson also had created a biography page for himself, he could have linked his name to that page.

The A element must include either an HREF (Hypertext Reference) attribute or a NAME attribute. To create a hypertext link, you use the HREF attribute. The NAME attribute is used for targeting a location within an HTML document that can be jumped to via a hypertext link—you will learn about doing that in Chapter 2.

The HREF attribute references the Web address, or *URL* (*Uniform Resource Locator*), of an object or resource on the Web. For an explanation of the different components that make up a URL, see the "What Is a URL?" sidebar later in this chapter.

In this chapter's code examples, two types of URLs are used: *absolute URLs* that point to locations on the Web and file names. When you use just a file name to link to a file, you are telling a browser that the linked file is located in the same folder as the linking file. A URL that only references a file name is actually a form of a *relative URL*. A relative URL states the position of the linked object *relative to* the location of the linking file (with just a file name, for instance, indicating that both the linked and the linking files are located in the same folder). You also can use relative URLs to link to files located in other folders within your own site. For a full explanation of how to use relative URLs in your Web pages, see the "Using Relative URLs" sidebar in Chapter 6, *Creating Multi-Page Web Sites*.

Links are generally displayed in a browser as blue underlined type (as shown previously in Figure 1.6), while links to sites you have already visited are generally colored purple.

For a graphical illustration of the different parts that compose a hypertext link, see Figure 1.7.

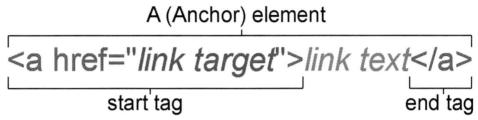

FIGURE 1.7 • *A hypertext link is composed of several parts.*

ADDING A NEW SECTION

As was stressed earlier, an HTML document is structured hierarchically. Heading-level elements are generally used to indicate the hierarchical structure of a document, with an H1 element marking the document heading, H2 elements marking major section headings, and H3 elements marking subsection headings within major sections. If an additional heading level is required, an H4 element can mark subsection headings within other subsections. Six heading-level elements are available, from the largest (H1) to the smallest (H6). Of these, only the four largest are normally used because the two smallest (H5 and H6) are displayed in font sizes that are smaller than the default paragraph text font.

To see this for yourself, look at the HTML document included with this chapter's example files, which shows all six heading-level elements in relation to the default paragraph text. Just open **headings.html** in your browser from the chap01 folder (see Figure 1.8).

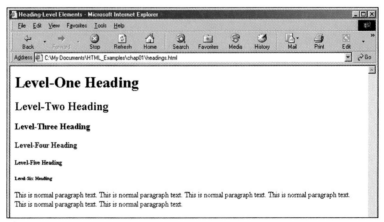

FIGURE 1.8 • *Six different heading-level elements are available, but only four are as large as or larger than normal paragraph text.*

Johnny Watson wants to add a list of links to his page linking to both local Web pages, such as his biography and resume, and to other Web pages that are located at other sites on the Web. He also wants to include his link list inside its own section, with an H2 element heading the section and a following text paragraph introducing the list of links.

What Is a URL?

The Web forms a space (a "universal space," as Tim Berners-Lee puts it) through which users ("surfers") can navigate to find information, objects, or other resources. To locate something, however, that something must have a discreet and unique location and identity. On the Web, a *Uniform Resource Locator* (URL) identifies the location and identity of any object. An object's URL is also commonly referred to as a *Web address*. A URL can be divided into the following functional parts:

- **Scheme.** A URL's scheme identifies the service (and protocol) being requested. For a URL linking to an object located on a Web server, `http:` specifies that HyperText Transfer Protocol (HTTP) be used to transfer the requested object. Any other valid URL scheme can be used (`ftp:`, `gopher:`, `telnet:`, and so on). A double forward-slash (`//`) following the scheme indicates it is a hierarchically structured service (organized in folders and subfolders). For instance, Web servers and FTP servers organize the documents and objects they contain in folders (and subfolders) and thus require the double forward-slash following their URL's scheme: `http://www.yahoo.com/` or `ftp://ftp.netscape.com/`, for instance. On the other hand, USENET news servers and e-mail addresses are not hierarchically organized and thus should not have the double-slash following the scheme (`news:comp.infosystems.www.authoring.html` or `mailto:peterpiper@picklepicker.com`, for instance).

- **Host (IP Number or Alias/Domain Name).** Every device connected to the Internet has an IP (Internet Protocol) number that uniquely identifies it (221.196.64.21, for instance). In place of an IP number, the combination of an *alias* and a *domain name* also can be used, which is how most people connect to servers on the Web. An alias is a prefix to a domain name that stands for (is an alias for) a resource located within that domain. It precedes, rather than follows, the domain name because it is not a hierarchically located object under that domain, but rather is an alias for such an object. The most commonly

 Add a level-two heading and a following paragraph element (remove the horizontal spacing and the HTML comments that you inserted previously; see Figure 1.9):

```
<p>Welcome to my home page! My name is Johnny Watson and I'm a big
nut about two things: <a href="http://www.espn.com/">sports</a>
and <a href="http://www.bbc.co.uk/gardening/">gardening</a>! You
may think that is an odd combination, but they really have more
things in common than you might suppose. First they are both
largely outside activities: I enjoy participating in, rather than
just watching, sports, for one thing. When the weather is bad,
there can be an indoor component to both activities. I enjoy
following some of my favorite teams on TV, while watering my
indoor plants at the same time!</p>
<h2>Biography, Interests, and Friends</h2>
<p>In the following list, I've included links to biographical
and career info, resources focused on topics that I'm especially
interested in, and pages that have been created by friends of
mine:</p>
```

used URL alias on the Web is www (as in `http://www.altavista.com/`). Not all Web addresses use a www alias. For instance, `http://maps.yahoo.com/`, uses an alias, maps, to point to the location of the Yahoo! Maps home page within the yahoo.com domain. A domain name, such as yahoo.com, on the other hand, is a unique name that identifies a resource on the Internet and the Web.

- **Port Number (Optional).** A port number is included in a URL only if a server is using a port number other than the default: `http://www.somehost.org:81/`, for instance. The default port number for a Web server is 80, whereas the default port number for an FTP server is 21; generally, you should only have to include a port number in your own URLs if your hosting server requires it (a rarity).

- **Resource Path.** If the linked object is not located in the host's root folder, the resource path specifies the folder path to the object's location. For instance, `http://www.somehost.org/users/jwatson/` specifies that the URL's object is located in the **jwatson** folder, which is located in the **users** folder, which is itself located in the root folder of www.somehost.org.

- **Object.** The object of a URL is the actual file that is being linked to. For instance, `http://www.somehost.org/users/jwatson/watson.html` specifies that the object of the URL is a file named watson.html. Note, however, that a Web server administrator can specify a default file name, usually index.html, which is implied if an object file name is not included in a URL. This file is often called an *index page*. Thus, `http://www.somehost.org/users/jwatson/` and `http://www.somehost.org/users/jwatson/index.html` may represent the same URL. Other default file names also can be used (index.htm, default.html, welcome.html, or main.html, for instance), but index.html is by far the most commonly used.

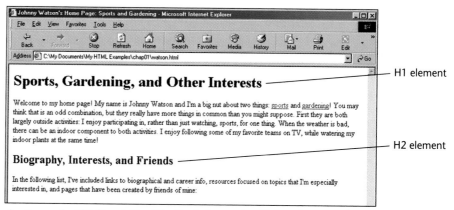

FIGURE 1.9 • *An H2 (Level-Two Heading) element is added to the page, along with a following text paragraph.*

Creating a Bulleted List

You can add two basic kinds of lists to an HTML document: *bulleted lists* and *numbered lists*. A bulleted list is also called an *unordered list* and is created using the UL (Unordered List) element; a numbered list is also called an *ordered list* and is created using the OL (Ordered List) element. In this section, you will add a bulleted list to your HTML document.

To create a bulleted list, you use two HTML elements: a UL element brackets the list as a whole, indicating that it is a bulleted (or unordered) list, while LI (List Item) elements indicate the individual items that are included in the list.

Use the UL and LI elements to create a bulleted list, following the introductory paragraph you added previously (see Figure 1.10):

```
<h2>Biography, Interests, and Friends</h2>
<p>In the following list, I've included links to biographical
and career info, resources focused on topics that I'm especially
interested in, and pages that have been created by friends of
mine:</p>
<ul>
<li>My biography
<li>My resume
<li>Get the latest sports scores
<li>Get indoor gardening tips and advice
<li>My friend Joe's site
<li>My friend Jane's site
</ul>
```

Biography, Interests, and Friends

In the following list, I've included links to biographical and career info, resources focused on topics that I'm especially interested in, and pages that have been created by friends of mine:

unordered list ———

- My biography
- My resume
- Get the latest sports scores
- Get indoor gardening tips and advice
- My friend Joe's site
- My friend Jane's site

FIGURE 1.10 • *A series of bulleted list items are added to the page.*

That is all you have to do to create a bulleted (or unordered) list. Lists are simple to create and add to your Web pages, so do not hesitate to use them.

Notice that the LI element, used to create a list item, has no end tag. The LI element is not an empty element, but its end tag is implied, either by the start of a following LI element or by the end of the list.

TROUBLE *spot*

Including the P element end tag (**</p>**) is also optional in all versions of HTML. In many instances, however, this omission can cause problems or produce differing results in different browsers—for that reason, you should always add the end tag at the end of your paragraph elements.

Creating a Link List

After you have created a bulleted list, you only need to add the links to create a link list (or list of hypertext links).

Create a link list and test it in your browser:

1. Create a link list by nesting the list item text within hypertext links (see Figure 1.11):

```
<ul>
<li><a href="mybio.html">My biography</a>
<li><a href="myresume.html">My resume</a>
<li><a href="http://www.usatoday.com/sports/scores.htm">Get the
latest sports scores</a>
```

```
<li><a href="http://www.about-house-plants.com/">Get indoor
gardening tips and advice</a>
<li><a href="http://www.blank.com/jshmoe/">My friend Joe's site</a>
<li><a href="http://www.wherever.com/jdoe/homepage.html">My friend
Jane's site</a>
</ul>
```

Biography, Interests, and Friends

In the following list, I've included links to biographical and career info, resources focused on topics that I'm especially interested in, and pages that have been created by friends of mine:

link list —
- My biography
- My resume
- Get the latest sports scores
- Get indoor gardening tips and advice
- My friend Joe's site
- My friend Jane's site

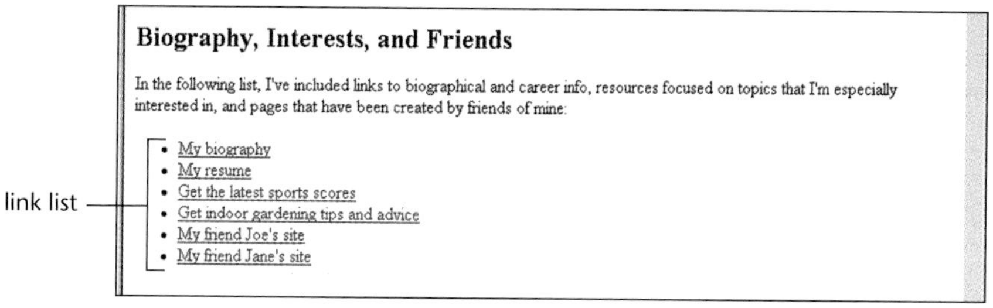

FIGURE 1.11 • *A link list is just a list with links.*

2. Save your file, switch over to your browser, and refresh the display of your page.
3. Test the biography and resume links. Dummy example pages are included with the example files that should display in your browser when you click on the links. Click the Back button to return to your example page.
4. The next two links are to actual sites on the Web; test them if you are connected. The last two links, however, to Joe's and Jane's sites, are fictional links that should not connect to anything—test either one to find out what happens when the object of a link does not exist.

In Windows and on the Macintosh, file and folder names are case-insensitive. However, on a UNIX computer, file and folder names are case-sensitive. For example, on a UNIX computer the file names MyPage.html and mypage.html actually represent two different file names.

This UNIX naming convention matters because most Internet Web servers are UNIX servers. If you find that links that worked on your local Windows or Macintosh machine suddenly stop working after you transfer your Web page files to a Web server, the problem might be due to the case-sensitivity of file and folder names on a UNIX server. To avoid the problem, make sure that file and folder names included in your URLs match the actual file and folder names *exactly*.

The same holds true for absolute URLs that link to sites located on the Web. Although domain names are case-insensitive, any folder or file names may be case-sensitive—so whenever you include an absolute URL in your page, make sure that you include it exactly as it is given (including any uppercase characters).

Linking Etiquette

At one time it was considered proper *netiquette* to request permission before linking to someone else's page. That was because unwanted traffic could easily push a page or site beyond its traffic allowance, when such allowances were much smaller than they are now. If running a major site, you should still request permission to link to a smaller site for that very reason. In general, especially when linking to a site's front page, you should not feel constrained to ask permission to link. These days most people want all the links they can get. However, if someone requests that you not link to their page, especially if it is a personal or family page, it is only good manners to comply.

Even linking to a page within someone else's site should not be a problem, as long as you properly identify both the site and page you are linking to. It is the responsibility of the Web author to code a site's pages so that the home or front page can easily be reached from any page within the site. The basic nature of hypertext and the Web, as enunciated in the visions of Ted Nelson and Tim Berners-Lee, is that any page can be linked to from any other page. Without links, there would be no Web, after all. Links are what make the Web valuable.

If using frames, however, you should not link to another's page so that it is displayed within a frame within your site without first getting permission. Always include `target="_blank"` or `target="_top"` in your link's A element when linking within a framed page to an external site or page, so the page will be displayed outside of your frame. You will learn about using frames in Chapter 6.

On the other hand, some authors design pages to be displayed only within a frame in their own site. If at all possible, you should try to link to the page containing the frame, rather than simply the page within the frame. Where this is not possible, you might include a link to the site's front page, along with a link to their framed page.

It is, however, unethical to link to someone else's images or other media files without permission, whether using the A, IMG, EMBED, or OBJECT elements, because doing so can significantly increase someone else's traffic, which they have to pay for. Such linking on the Web is usually considered to be a form of theft (stealing someone else's bandwidth). Instead, you should always link to the site or page where the image or other media file is located, rather than directly to the file. If the image or media file is the only content of a page, you should link to a page that links to that page, has content that identifies the site, and provides a link to its front page.

Gathering URLs

If you later want to create your own list of hypertext links, you will need to gather the URLs and other link information you want to use. You can gather URLs for use in your Web pages in several ways:

- **While Surfing.** Open the page you want to create a link to in your browser, click and drag to highlight the contents of the Address (or Location) box, and press Ctrl+C (Windows) or Command+C (Macintosh). Press Ctrl+V (Windows) or Command+V (Macintosh) to paste the URL into your text editor. Copy and paste the level-one heading content to use it as your link text.
- **Copying a Link.** Just right-click on the link (on the Macintosh, hold down the Ctrl key and click) and select to copy the link. The actual menu option varies from browser to browser: Copy Shortcut, Copy Target, Copy Link Address, Copy Link Location, and so on.
- **From Internet Explorer Favorites.** Open your Favorites in the Explorer bar (select View, Explorer Bar, and Favorites). Locate a favorite you want to use, right-click on it (on the Mac, hold down the Ctrl key and click), and select Properties. Copy the contents of the URL box and paste it into your text editor. For the link text, you can type in the name of the Favorite (or any other text you want to use).
- **From Netscape or Mozilla Bookmarks.** In Netscape 6, select Bookmarks and Manage Bookmarks. Find the Web page you want to link to, right-click on it (on the Macintosh, hold down the Ctrl key and click), and select Properties. Copy the contents of the Location box and paste it into your text editor; copy the contents of the Name box and paste it to use it as the link text.

HORIZONTALLY ALIGNING HEADINGS, PARAGRAPHS, AND DIVISIONS

So far, all of the elements you have added to your example page are left-aligned (horizontally aligned with the left margin). That is because left-alignment is the default horizontal alignment for block elements, except for the CENTER element.

Using the ALIGN Attribute

You can use the ALIGN attribute to center, right-align, left-align, or justify text contained in a number of block elements, including heading level and paragraph elements. You only need to explicitly set left-alignment for a block element if a different horizontal alignment has been set for it, by being nested inside of a CENTER element, or inside of a center- or right-aligned DIV element, for instance.

Right-align the level-one heading, justify the text paragraphs, and center the level-two heading (see Figure 1.12):

```
<h1 align="right">Sports, Gardening, and Other Interests</h1>
<p align="justify">Welcome to my home page! My name is Johnny
Watson and I'm a big nut about two things: <a
href="http://www.espn.com/">sports</a> and <a
href="http://www.bbc.co.uk/gardening/">gardening</a>! You may
think that is an odd combination, but they really have more
things in common than you might suppose. First they are both
largely outside activities: I enjoy participating in, rather than
just watching, sports, for one thing. When the weather is bad,
there can be an indoor component to both activities. I enjoy
following some of my favorite teams on TV, while watering my
indoor plants at the same time!</p>
<h2 align="center">Biography, Interests, and Friends</h2>
<p align="justify">In the following list, I've included links to
biographical and career info, resources focused on topics that
I'm especially interested in, and pages that have been created
by friends of mine:</p>
```

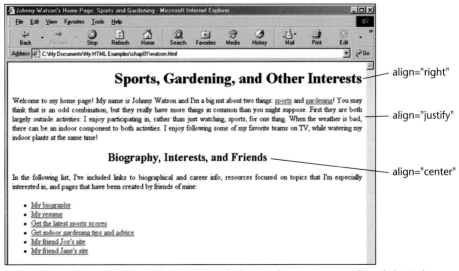

FIGURE 1.12 • *The H1 element is right-aligned, the H2 element is centered, and the P elements are justified.*

Using the DIV Element

You cannot use the ALIGN attribute to horizontally align the UL (or OL) element. You can, however, horizontally align a list by nesting it inside a centered or right-aligned DIV (Division) element. The DIV element is used to delineate a division within a document. Any element that can be nested in the BODY element can also be nested in a DIV element.

Center the link list by nesting it inside a center-aligned division (see Figure 1.13):

```
<div align="center">
<ul>
<li><a href="mybio.html">My biography</a>
<li><a href="myresume.html">My resume</a>
<li><a href="http://www.usatoday.com/sports/scores.htm">Get the
latest sports scores</a>
<li><a href="http://www.about-house-plants.com/">Get indoor
gardening tips and advice</a>
<li><a href="http://www.blank.com/jshmoe/">My friend Joe's
site</a>
<li><a href="http://www.wherever.com/jdoe/homepage.html">My
friend Jane's site</a>
</ul>
</div>
```

centered DIV element ————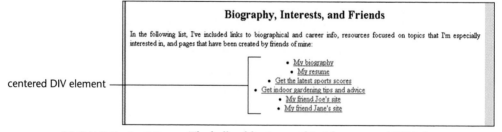

FIGURE 1.13 • *The bulleted list is nested inside a centered DIV element.*

By itself, a DIV element has no formatting. Using HTML alone, you can only change the horizontal alignment of text or other elements nested in a DIV element. To apply additional formatting directly to a DIV element, you need to use styles. You will learn about using styles in Chapter 3, *Working with Fonts, Colors, and Backgrounds*.

INSERTING AN INLINE IMAGE

The IMG (Image) element is used to insert an *inline image* in an HTML document. The IMG element is an inline element and not a block element. When you insert an inline image, it is displayed in the position—in the middle of a line of text, for instance—where it is inserted. The IMG element is also an empty (or standalone) element.

An example *banner image*, banner.gif, is included with the example files for this chapter. A banner image is an image that is displayed along the top of a Web page and thus is normally wider than it is high. A logo image is similar to a banner image and is also displayed at the top of a Web page, but is usually of relatively equal height and width.

Image formats other than GIF (Compuserve Graphics Interchange Format) can be used to insert inline images, including JPEG (Joint Photographic Experts Group) and PNG (Portable Network Graphics) graphic formats. GIF, JPEG, and PNG images are compressed; non-compressed image formats, such as TIF or BMP, should not be inserted as inline images. Differences between image formats and how to decide which image format is best to use in a given situation are discussed in Chapter 4, *Working with Images and Other Media*.

action

Remove the H1 element's right-alignment and then use the IMG element to insert a banner image as an inline image at the top of the page (see Figure 1.14):

```
<p><img src="banner.gif"></p>
<h1 align="right">Sports, Gardening, and Other Interests</h1>
```

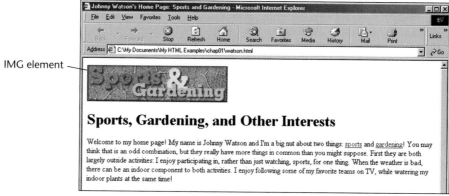

IMG element

FIGURE 1.14 • *A banner image can add visual appeal to a Web page.*

In the IMG element, the SRC (Source) attribute specifies the URL of the image file that is to be inserted into the HTML document. This attribute works just like the HREF attribute in the A element. To specify an image file that is located in the same folder as the HTML file in which it is to be inserted, you just need to specify the image's file name.

Notice in the code example that the IMG element is nested inside a P element. That is because the IMG element is an inline element and should not be nested directly inside the BODY element. An inline element should always be nested inside a block element.

TROUBLE
spot

Alternatively, you can nest the banner image at the start of the level-one heading, with a line break providing vertical separation between the image and the following heading text:

```
<h1><img src="banner.gif"><br>Sports, Gardening, and Other
Interests</h1>
```

Nesting in this way adds less vertical spacing between the inline image and the following heading text than nesting the inline image in a separate P element. Use of the BR (Break) element to add a line break is discussed later in this chapter, in the "Creating an Address Block" section.

Horizontally Aligning an Inline Image

Because the IMG element is an inline element, you cannot directly align it horizontally relative to the page. Instead, you must nest it inside a block element that is horizontally aligned.

Center the inline image by nesting it inside the centered paragraph element (see Figure 1.15):

```
<p align="center"><img src="banner.gif"></p>
<h1 align="center">Sports, Gardening, and Other Interests</h1>
```

FIGURE 1.15 • *Nesting it in a centered paragraph centers the inline image.*

Using the CENTER Element

Alternatively, you also can use the CENTER element to center nested text or other elements. In HTML 4, the CENTER element is considered a shortcut for a center-aligned DIV element. Current browsers should treat **<center>element content</center>** as equivalent to **<div align="center">element content</div>**.

Remove the **align="center"** attribute from both the P element and the following H1 element, and then nest both elements within a CENTER element:

```
<center>
<p align="center"><img src="banner.gif"></p>
<h1 align="center">Sports, Gardening, and Other Interests</h1>
</center>
```

When you view this in your browser, the result should be identical to using the ALIGN attribute to center the P and H1 elements (refer to Figure 1.15). Because the CENTER element was originally a Netscape extension, it has been around longer than the DIV element, which was introduced with HTML 3.2. Thus, older browsers that are not HTML 3.2-compliant might support the CENTER element, but not the DIV element. For that reason, you might want to use the CENTER element, rather than a DIV element, when you want to center nested text or other elements.

Including Alternative Text

Not everyone uses a graphical Web browser to access Web pages. Some surfers still use text browsers, such as Lynx, which cannot display images. Individuals with visual impairments may use a Braille browser or a speech browser to access Web pages. Inclusion of alternative text for images is required for Web pages created for government organizations and agencies, which must comply with the Americans with Disabilities Act (ADA). Schools, libraries, businesses, or other entities that accommodate the public may have their own policies that mandate the inclusion of alternative text in Web pages, as well as other requirements, to ensure accessibility.

If you only include an SRC attribute in an IMG element, users of text-only or non-visual browsers may have a hard time identifying what the import of your image is or even that it is an image. Other surfers might be accessing your page through a Web-enabled cell-phone display, for instance, that shows only the text in your page, but not the images. Figure 1.16 shows watson.html as it is displayed in Lynx, a text-only browser.

To make it easier for anyone using these alternative means to access a Web page, you should include an ALT (Alternative Text) attribute in your IMG elements to further identify your image.

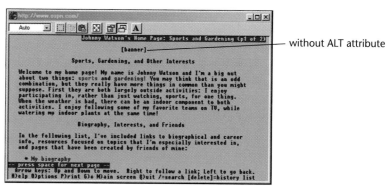
— without ALT attribute

FIGURE 1.16 • *When viewing a Web page in Lynx, a text-only browser, a user might have difficulty identifying that an image is an image or what its function or content is.*

Use the ALT attribute to add alternative text to the IMG element's start tag, indicating the function and content of the image:

```
<center>
<p><img src="banner.gif" alt="Banner Image: Sports & Gardening"></p>
<h1>Sports, Gardening, and Other Interests</h1>
</center>
```

As shown in Figure 1.17, the inline image is now more helpfully identified in Lynx.

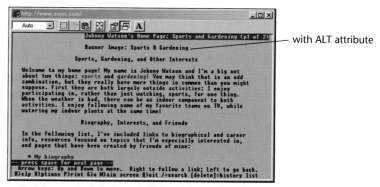
— with ALT attribute

FIGURE 1.17 • *Alternative text helps users of text-only or non-visual browsers to identify the function and content of images used in your Web pages.*

N O T E — You can download versions of Lynx for Windows, UNIX, and Macintosh at **lynx.browser.org**/. To open a local HTML file in Lynx, just press the G key to select G(o); type a standard URL for a local file, replacing any spaces in folder names with the **%20** escape sequence; and press the Enter key. The following is an example of a standard local URL:

```
file:///C:/My%20Documents/My%20HTML%20Docs/mypage.html
```

Some people also surf the Web with the display of graphics turned off in their browsers because they can find and access information on the Web faster by just downloading text and not the accompanying images. If you do not include alternative text in your images, these surfers will be presented with an image icon, but with no information to help them interpret the function or content of your image.

N O T E — For additional information and resources on Web design accessibility issues, see the Blindness Resource Center's "Access to the Internet and Web" site at **www.nyise.org/access.htm**.

Accessibility is an important issue in Web design, so look for additional comments, notes, and tips in the remainder of this book that highlight measures you can take to make your own Web designs accessible to everyone.

Specifying an Image's Height and Width

Whenever you include an inline image in your page, you should specify its dimensions. That way, browsers can allocate display space for your image before it has been completely downloaded, which can allow the remainder of the page to be displayed quicker. The HEIGHT and WIDTH attributes are used in the IMG element to set the dimensions, in pixels, of an inline image.

action — Add HEIGHT and WIDTH attributes to the IMG element that specify the actual dimensions of the image:

```
<p><img src="banner.gif" alt="Banner Image: Sports & Gardening"
height="75" width="300"></p>
```

In most cases, you should not use the HEIGHT and WIDTH attributes to change the dimensions of an inline image, but should use these attributes to specify the actual dimensions of the image. Instead of resizing an image in the browser, you should open it in your image editor and resize it there. Reducing the size of an image in a browser is a waste of bandwidth because the full-size image still must be downloaded over the Internet. Increasing the size of an image in a browser might magnify any image flaws or deficiencies.

CREATING AN ADDRESS BLOCK

In HTML, the ADDRESS element is used to create an *address block* within your page. The address block should identify the author or owner of a page and provide a means for visitors to provide feedback. Most often, the address block is inserted at the bottom of the page.

 Use the ADDRESS element to add an address block to the example document that contains the author's name and e-mail address:

```
<address>
Johnny Watson<br>
E-mail: jwatson@whatnot.com
</address>
</body>
</html>
```

TROUBLE spot

Spam is unsolicited and unwanted e-mail messages. Spammers use spiders (or robots) to crawl the Web looking for e-mail addresses listed in Web pages. Including your e-mail address in your Web page might expose you to more spam than you are already receiving.

One option is to sign up for a free *Web-mail* (Web-based e-mail) address and include it in your Web pages to provide visitors a way to contact you or give you feedback. A Web-mail account is accessed through a Web site's address using your browser, rather than through a mail server using a mail program (such as Outlook Express, for instance) that you may have installed on your computer. If your Web-mail address starts to get spammed too much, just dump it and sign up for another Web mail address and use it instead, editing your pages to include the new address. Most Web-mail accounts limit the amount of space available to store messages (anywhere from 1Mb - 4Mb), so you should delete messages after you have read them, or move them to your own hard drive. You can then only let close friends and relatives know your permanent e-mail address, which should help limit the amount of spam sent to that address.

For a comprehensive listing of free Web-mail providers, just go to Yahoo! and do a search on **free e-mail**.

Most browsers display text nested in an ADDRESS block in an italic font. Nothing in the HTML specifications, however, dictates that text in an ADDRESS element should be italicized. Some earlier browsers do not italicize address block text and nothing compels future browsers to do so, either.

 Nest the text in the address block inside an I (Italic) element to insure that every browser italicizes it:

```
<address><i>
Johnny Watson<br>
E-mail: jwatson@whatnot.com
</i></address>
```

Inserting a Line Break

You might notice in the previous example that a BR (Break) element is used. This element, as its name implies, is used to insert a line break. The BR element is an empty element that is useful for causing a break in a line when you do not want additional vertical spacing added, like the spacing that is automatically added between paragraph elements. It also can be used to demarcate the ends of lines in the stanzas of a poem, for instance.

Although current browsers generally support it, using multiple BR elements to create vertical blank space within an HTML document generally should be avoided. The HTML 4 specifications do not specify at all how multiple BR elements should be treated in browsers. Earlier HTML specifications stated that multiple BR elements should be collapsed to a single BR element and that may be how they are treated in some browsers. To add vertical blank space within an HTML document, you should use either the PRE (Preformatted) element or styles. You will learn about using the PRE element in Chapter 2 and about styles in Chapter 3.

Adding a Horizontal Rule

To help demarcate your address block from the remainder of your document's body, you can use the HR (Horizontal Rule) element as a separator. The HR element is an empty element that draws a horizontal line between the margins of the page.

Insert an HR element to separate the address block from the rest of the page (see Figure 1.18):

```
<hr>
<address><i>
Johnny Watson<br>
```

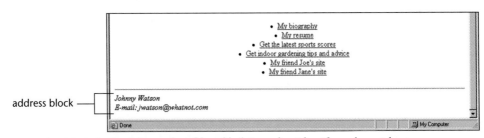

address block

FIGURE 1.18 • *An address block is used to identify, and provide a means to contact, the author or owner of a Web page.*

Linking to Your E-Mail Address

You can use a special form of URL to link to your e-mail address. This type of URL is commonly referred to as a *mailto address*. A link to a mailto address is created the same way you create a link to a regular Web address, except that mailto: is used as the URL scheme, instead of http:// and an e-mail address is used instead of a domain name address.

Add the following codes to turn Johnny Watson's e-mail address into a mailto link (see Figure 1.19):

```
Johnny Watson<br>
E-mail: <a
href="mailto:jwatson@whatnot.com">jwatson@whatnot.com</a>
```

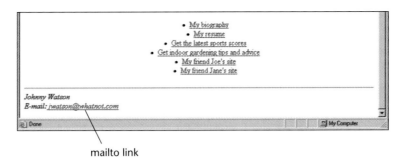

mailto link

F I G U R E   1 . 1 9   •   *You can use a mailto address to link to your e-mail address.*

A mailto link provides a convenient and easy way for visitors to your page to give you feedback by sending you an e-mail message. Not everyone can use a mailto link, however. Users of the Netscape and Mozilla browsers can, as long as they have installed the e-mail programs that come with those browsers and configured them to send mail. Users of Internet Explorer 5 or 6, however, need to install Outlook Express and configure it to send mail and then configure Internet Explorer to use that e-mail program as its default e-mail program (select Tools, Internet Options, click the Programs tab, and select Outlook Express as the e-mail client), before they can use a mailto link.

Because not everyone can use a mailto link, it is important to always include your e-mail address *both* as the mailto URL and as the link text, for instance:

```
<a href="mailto:your@address.com">your@address.com</a>
```

That way, if someone cannot use your mailto link, they can still click and drag to copy your e-mail address and then paste it into their e-mail program's mail composition window.

Horizontally Aligning Your Address Block

The content of the ADDRESS element is left-aligned by default. However, as is the case with the UL element, the ALIGN attribute cannot be used to horizontally align the content of the ADDRESS element. To horizontally align the content of your ADDRESS element, you need to nest it inside a CENTER element or a horizontally aligned DIV element.

Center the content of the ADDRESS element by nesting it in a CENTER element (see Figure 1.20):

```
<hr>
<center>
<address><i>
Johnny Watson<br>
E-mail: <a
href="mailto:jwatson@whatnot.com">jwatson@whatnot.com</a>
</i></address>
</center>
```

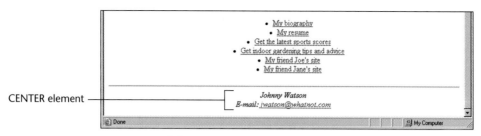

CENTER element

FIGURE 1.20 • *For a different look, you can center your address block.*

Including Other Items in the Address Block

You can include other things in your address block. If you are representing a business, you could include your toll-free number, fax number, and so on. You can include a link to your home page, for instance—this can be a good thing to do, even if the current page is your home page, because it lets others know that it is your home page. Some authors like to include the date when the page was created or last updated, as well.

Another option is simply to include a link in your address block to a contact page. This can be helpful if you have multiple e-mail contacts, phone numbers, and so on, especially if you need to update them frequently. If you use a link to a contact page, you will only need to update that page if you need to make a change, rather than updating your address block on every page.

CHAPTER SUMMARY

In this chapter, you set up your working folder or working disk, learned how to use the example files, reviewed basic HTML pointers, and created a basic Web page. You should now be familiar with many of the most commonly used HTML elements, including the top-level elements of an HTML document and the elements used to create headings, paragraphs, unordered (bulleted) lists, hypertext anchors, inline images, horizontal rules, line breaks, and address elements.

Code Review

HTML element	Contains all other elements within an HTML document.
HEAD element	Contains any elements used to provide "header information" about a document that is not displayed in a browser window.
BODY element	Contains any elements that compose the "body" of an HTML document and that are directly displayed within a browser window.
TITLE element	A required element within the HEAD element that specifies the title of the document. The title is not displayed within a browser window, but is displayed on a browser's title bar.
H1 element	A level-one heading (or displayable title) that is displayed in a browser's window.
H2 element	A level-two heading that marks the beginning of a major section within an HTML document. The H3 and H4 elements can be used to mark further subsection levels.
P element	Contains paragraph text that is included in an HTML file. There should be no untagged text within an HTML document.
HTML comments	Anything nested between `<!--` and `-->` is not displayed in a browser.
A element	When used in conjunction with the HREF attribute, specifies that included text or elements operate as a hypertext anchor (or link).
HREF attribute	Within an A element, specifies the URL of a linked object.
UL element	A bulleted list (or unordered list).
LI element	List items that are included within a list.
ALIGN attribute	Used in the H1, H2, P, DIV, and ADDRESS elements, among others, to horizontally align their content on the page.
DIV element	Defines a document division, which can contain any other "body" elements.
CENTER element	A shortcut for `<div align="center">`*division content* `</div>` centers nested inline content.
IMG element	An inline image in an HTML document.
SRC attribute	Specifies the URL of an image to be displayed.
ALT attribute	Provides alternative text that can be displayed in place of an image.
HEIGHT attribute	Specifies the actual vertical dimension of an image in pixels.
WIDTH attribute	Specifies the actual horizontal dimension of an image in pixels.

ADDRESS element	Specifies an address block within an HTML document, in which the author or owner is identified and a means for feedback is provided.
HR element	Creates a horizontal rule that can be used as a separator in an HTML document.
BR element	Inserts a line break inside another element.

ONLINE QUIZ

Go to this text's IRC at **www.emcp.com/** and take the online self-check quiz for this chapter.

REVIEW EXERCISES

This section provides hands-on practice exercises to reinforce your understanding of the information and material included within this chapter. Save **watson.html** under another file name (**watson_practice.html**, for instance) and then use the new document to practice using the elements, attributes, and other features that were covered in this chapter:

1. Combine H2 or H3 elements with paragraph elements to add additional sections or subsections to your HTML document. Type dummy text for the paragraphs, if you wish—the main thing is to experiment with how heading and paragraph elements work, without worrying about the actual content.

2. Practice using the HTML comment codes (<!-- and -->). Do not worry at this point whether the comments you add help to annotate your code or not—the idea is to just get practice inserting comments, so feel free to use dummy text to create the comments.

3. Experiment using the ALIGN attribute to center, right-align, or justify headings, paragraphs, and divisions (DIV elements). Experiment using the CENTER element to center nested text and elements.

4. Practice creating additional in-context hypertext links. Look for additional words or phrases that can be turned into hypertext links. For instance, turn the word "weather" into a link to the Weather Channel (**www.weather.com/**). Look for or add other words or phrases that you can turn into in-context hypertext links to related sites you have discovered on the Web.

5. In the link list, add additional link items that link to sites on the Web. For instance, do research on the Web to find the URLs for any of the following: a major newspaper (Washington Post, Los Angeles Times, Chicago Tribune, and so on), a TV or cable news outlet (ABC News, PBS News, BBC News, and so on), a friend's Web site, or any other links you want to try creating.

WEB-BASED LEARNING ACTIVITIES

In this book's text, Find It icons inserted in the margin highlight the Web addresses of additional resources you might find helpful or informative. To further extend your learning using the Web, you can:

- Go back and visit any of the Web addresses highlighted in this chapter that you have not yet visited. Look for additional resources and information that add to your understanding and knowledge of the material covered in this chapter. When you find a relevant page or site with information or resources you might want to access later, add it to your Favorites (in Internet Explorer) or your Bookmarks (in Netscape or Mozilla).

- Visit this book's Internet Resource Center at **www.emcp.com/** to find additional Web addresses of resources related to the material covered in this chapter that you can further investigate and explore.

- Further research a specific topic introduced in this chapter. For instance, do further research on different text editors that are available for your platform (Windows, Macintosh, or UNIX). Create a catalog or database of the different features offered by different text editors (search and replace, spell checker, macros, and so on). Note whether the program is free to use or requires a registration fee for continued use (some programs are free for educational use). Download some text editors and write a report or review that can be shared with your fellow students. Individually, or teamed up with other students, provide an onscreen demonstration of how some different text editors work.

- It was stressed in this chapter that you should not use copyrighted images in your Web pages. You will find links to additional resources on this issue at this book's IRC. Use those resources, or other resources you can discover through Yahoo!, Google, or Altavista, to further research the issue of the use of copyrighted material (or images) on the Web. Discover at least three sources of public domain images that you are free to use. Write a report on this issue that can be shared with your fellow students.

PROJECTS

These projects can be done either in class, in a computer lab, or at home. Use the skills learned in this chapter to create any of the following projects.

Project 1. Create your own personal Web page.

Plan, write, and create your own personal Web page:

1. Plan and write the content of your personal page, including content to be used for a title, level-one heading, and introductory paragraph.

2. Gather any URLs, site names, or titles, and accompanying descriptive text you want to use in creating hypertext links, to be used either in-context or in a link list. Remember that any word or phrase in an HTML document can be a link, so look for opportunities to create interesting links to other sites or resources on the Web.

3. At the bottom of your text document, type the text you want to use as your address block. At minimum, type your name and an e-mail address. *Note: See the caution earlier, however, about the danger of exposing your e-mail address to spammers.* Use a dummy e-mail address here, if you like, or you can sign up for a free Web mail address that you can use.

4. Optionally, gather any JPEG or GIF images you want to include as inline images. Scan a snapshot of yourself, for instance, in the image-editing software that came with your scanner, and resize the image (keep it under 500 pixels wide, and 250 pixels wide is not too small for a personal snapshot). (You do not need to include any images, and you also do not need to include more than one, so you should not go overboard adding images at this stage.)

5. Tag your file with HTML tags to define the HTML elements of your page. Create your top-level elements (HTML, HEAD, TITLE, and BODY). Tag the level-one heading and any paragraphs. Tag any sublevel headings, bulleted lists, hypertext links, and your address block (inserting line breaks where needed). Insert any GIF or JPEG image you want to include as an inline image (adding HEIGHT and WIDTH attributes and alternative text).

Project 2. Create a topical Web page.

Plan, write, and create a basic Web page based on a topic you are interested in or know something about. Follow the directions given previously for creating a personal Web page, but substitute text and links (and any images you want to use) focused on the topic you want to present (instead of on yourself).

Project 3. Create a Web page for a club or organization.

Do you belong to or participate in a club or organization that does not yet have its own Web page? Create a Web page that includes a description of the club or organization, a list of its activities, and an e-mail link that visitors can use to find out about joining or contributing. Include a link list to other related clubs, organizations, and sites.

CHAPTER

2

Working with Online Documents

PERFORMANCE OBJECTIVES

In this chapter, you will learn to add features and execute formatting tasks that are common to a broad selection of online documents, including how to:

- Add a DocType declaration to identify the HTML version and compatibility level of your document.
- Use the META element to add a document description, a list of keywords, and other meta data.
- Add emphasis, such as bolding, italics, and underlining to text.
- Format quotations, citations, and definitions.
- Create superscripted footnote and endnote links.
- Insert copyright, register, and trademark symbols.
- Create a document menu (table of contents).
- Use monospaced highlighting.
- Work with numerical lists.
- Use preformatted text.

In Chapter 1, *Creating a Basic Web Page*, you learned how to create a simple personal Web page. In this chapter, you will learn more about how you can use HTML to format online documents, including creating an online academic paper, a frequently asked questions (FAQ) page, and online technical documentation.

USING THE EXAMPLE FILES

If you have created a working folder for storing files you create, you will find the example files for this chapter located in the **chap02** folder within your working folder. You should save any HTML files you create in this chapter in that folder.

If you have created a working disk, you should copy the chap02 folder to your working disk from the HTML_Examples folder that you or your instructor downloaded from this book's Internet Resource Center, or from a CD-R disc or floppy disk provided by your instructor. You should be able to include your work from both Chapter 1 and Chapter 2 on the same working disk. Ask your instructor for assistance if you do not know where you can find the HTML_Examples folder or how to copy the chap02 folder. You should save any HTML file you create in this chapter in the chap02 folder that you have copied to your working disk.

CASE EXAMPLE: FORMATTING AN ONLINE ACADEMIC PAPER

Increasingly, both students and teachers are choosing to publish academic papers and essays online, rather than just in paper form. Publishing a paper online can be a great way to get feedback and to stimulate discussion on a topic or position. In this exercise, you will add formatting to an example academic paper that is included with this book's example files.

Crystal Porter is a junior in college majoring in sociology. She is writing a paper titled "Commerce and Civilization" for her "Origins of Civilization" class. In this paper, she is arguing for commerce as a root cause, rather than simply a consequence, of the transition from simpler and more primitive "folk societies" to more complex urbanized civilizations.

Crystal wants to format her online document so that it looks and works like a regular academic paper that she would print out on a printer. However, she also wants to take advantage of some of the additional facilities afforded by HTML, such as using hypertext links to connect footnote numbers with their respective footnote text.

Although still in draft form and incomplete, she wants to put the paper online to start getting feedback from her professor and fellow students while she is still writing the paper.

Opening an HTML File in Your Text Editor

In this case example, you will be working with an example file, acad_paper_ex.html, which has been created for you. If using a working folder, you will find this file in the chap02 folder located inside your working folder. If you are using a working disk and have not already copied the chap02 folder (from the example disk or folder provided by your instructor) to your working disk, you need to do that to start working with the case example.

Open **acad_paper_ex.html** in your text editor:
1. Run your text editor (Notepad or SimpleText, for instance).
2. Select File, Open, and then open your working folder (My HTML Examples, or whatever you named it).

If you created your working folder in My Documents (Windows) or on your Desktop (Macintosh), you should just have to double-click on your working folder to open it.

If you created your working folder in your network folder, you need to navigate to and open that folder in your text editor's Open dialog box. In Windows, for instance, click on the Look in box to go to and open your network folder, and then open your working folder.

If you are using a working disk, you need to navigate to and open your floppy disk drive where your working disk is inserted. In Windows, for instance, click on the Look in box to go to and open your floppy disk drive.

3. If you are using Windows, click on the Files of type box and select All Files (*.*); otherwise, you will not be able to see files with other than a .txt extension.
4. With your working folder open, double-click the **chap02** folder to open it, and then double-click **acad_paper_ex.html**.

Windows. If you are using Windows version 98 or later, the display of file extensions for known file types is turned off by default. If you have not turned on the display of these file extensions, you will not be able to see the file extensions for most file types when lists of files are displayed on your system. For instance, when opening "acad_paper_ex.html," you will only see "acad_paper_ex" displayed as the file name, with only the file icon helping to identify the file type.

The file extension is actually there—it is just hidden. Besides making working with files a lot easier, turning on the display of file extensions can help protect you against e-mail viruses, which often use hidden file extensions to try to fool recipients into clicking on a link that activates a virus. If you have not turned on display of file extensions, see the Trouble Spot under "Saving a Starting Template" in Chapter 1 for directions on how to do that.

Saving and Previewing Your HTML File

To avoid overwriting the example file, you can resave it under another name. That way, you can use it as a reference point, or backtrack to the beginning and start over fresh, if you need to.

1. Select File, Save As, and resave the example file as **acad_paper.html** in the chap02 folder in your working folder or working disk.
2. Run your browser (or switch over to it if it is already open) and open **acad_paper.html** from the chap02 folder in your working folder or disk. (If you are unclear about how to open a local HTML file in your browser, see "Previewing Your HTML Document in Your Browser" in Chapter 1.)

When working through this chapter's examples, be sure to frequently save your HTML file, switch over to your browser, refresh the display of your Web page, and then test and debug the example code you have created. Use the screen captures in this chapter's figures as prompts to switch over to your browser to check out the results of your work for yourself, rather than simply depending upon the figures to show you how your code should look.

DECLARING THE DOCUMENT TYPE

According to the HTML 4.01 specification, a valid HTML document should declare the version of HTML that is used in the document. This is done by inserting a special code, a *Document Type Declaration* (or *DocType declaration*), at the top of the document, above the HTML element. The DocType declaration specifies the HTML version used in a document and the level of conformance being enforced.

Understanding Conformance Levels

The W3C has defined three different conformance levels for HTML 4 and XHTML 1:
- **Strict.** Disallows any deprecated or frameset elements or attributes and is intended for use with browsers that fully implement the HTML 4.01 standard.

- **Transitional (or "loose").** Allows deprecated elements or attributes and is intended for use in pages that use elements and attributes that have been deprecated in HTML 4.01.
- **Frameset.** Allows both deprecated and frameset elements or attributes and is intended for use in pages that use the FRAMESET element, the FRAME element, and other related elements or attributes to create framed Web sites.

Deprecation means that you are either discouraged from using an element or attribute, which has been superceded by newer elements or attributes, for instance, or encouraged to use an alternative. For instance, several elements and attributes have been deprecated in HTML 4 and XHTML 1 in favor of using Cascading Style Sheets (CSS) to achieve similar or superior results. Deprecated elements and attributes are perfectly legal in HTML 4 and XHTML 1 and you are free to use them. You will learn more about deprecated elements and attributes, and about using styles to achieve similar or superior results in Chapter 3, *Working with Fonts, Colors, and Backgrounds*.

Frameset element refers to the FRAMESET, FRAME, and NOFRAMES elements that are used to create a framed Web page. A page containing frameset elements is often referred to as a *frameset page*. You will learn more about using frames in Chapter 6, *Working with Multi-Page Web Sites*.

Following are three examples of DocType declarations that can be included in an HTML document to specify conformance to the strict, transitional, or frameset definitions for HTML 4.01:

```
<!DOCTYPE HTML PUBLIC "-//W3C//DTD HTML 4.01//EN"
  "http://www.w3.org/TR/html4/strict.dtd">

<!DOCTYPE HTML PUBLIC "-//W3C//DTD HTML 4.01 Transitional//EN"
  "http://www.w3.org/TR/html4/loose.dtd">

<!DOCTYPE HTML PUBLIC "-//W3C//DTD HTML 4.01 Frameset//EN"
  "http://www.w3.org/TR/html4/frameset.dtd">
```

Unless you are creating a frameset page, you should stick to declaring your Web pages as conforming to the transitional definition for HTML 4.01. You should only declare it as conforming to the strict definition for HTML 4.01 if it contains no deprecated or frameset elements or attributes.

Generally, a browser will not care if you slip up on this, but if you try to validate your page using the W3C's *HTML Validator*, you will likely get an error if you have declared your document to be in conformance with the transitional definition for HTML 4.01 and a TARGET attribute is included in it. You will learn more about validating your Web pages in Chapter 6.

Understanding DocType Switching

The newest browsers, such as Internet Explorer 6 and Netscape 6, however, use the DocType declaration to do *DocType switching*. Based on the DocType declaration included in your document, a newer browser can run in either of two modes: *standards mode* or *quirks mode.* In standards mode, current HTML standards are strictly adhered to, even if that will cause problems when displaying a page that was coded to take advantage of the non-standard quirks of an earlier browser version. In quirks mode, earlier non-standard quirks are reduplicated, even if that will cause problems when displaying a page that was coded to be standards-compliant.

If you use any of the previously listed DocType declarations in your document, browsers that do DocType switching should switch to using standards mode. If you omit a DocType declaration, such browsers will default to using quirks mode. DocType declarations other than those previously listed might also trigger quirks mode. When you are just using straight HTML, whether a browser is running in standards or quirks mode should not make much, if any, difference. It can make a difference, however, if you are using styles, scripts, or dynamic HTML features in your document. For links to additional resources on the Web that discuss DocType declarations and DocType switching, see this book's IRC at **www.emcp.com/**.

Adding a DocType Declaration

The DocType declaration is inserted at the top of an HTML document, above the HTML element.

Insert a DocType declaration declaring that your HTML document is compatible with the transitional definition for HTML 4.01:

```
<!DOCTYPE HTML PUBLIC "-//W3C//DTD HTML 4.01 Transitional//EN"
"http://www.w3.org/TR/html4/loose.dtd">
<html>
<head>
```

USING META ELEMENTS

The META (Meta Data) element is an empty element that allows authors to include *meta data* in their HTML documents. Meta data is information that is about, or describes, a document, rather than content that is displayed in a document. META elements are inserted in a document's HEAD element.

Specifying the Document's Character Set

As the Web becomes more and more of a global phenomenon, pages are being published in many languages, many of which do not use the Latin-based alphabet used by Western European languages (such as Chinese and Japanese, for instance). Because of this, the specific character set being used in a document is a much more important issue than it once was (when virtually all Web pages were published in English). If you try to display a page originating from China or Japan and square blank boxes appear where text characters would normally be, the character set being assumed by your browser (most likely ISO 8859-1) does not match the character set being used by the page you are trying to access.

Also, you are required to specify your document's character set when validating an HTML document using the W3C's HTML Validator. The W3C recommends that Web authors specifically declare their document's character set.

You declare your document's character set by inserting it as meta data in your document's HEAD element. This should be inserted ahead of any other element within the HEAD element.

Insert the following META element at the start of your document's HEAD element to declare that your document is using the ISO 8859-1 character set (used by most Western European languages, including English):

```
<head>
<meta http-equiv="Content-Type" content="text/html; charset=ISO-8859-1">
<title>Commerce and Civilization by Crystal Porter</title>
```

The various ins and outs of using different character sets can get complex. See Appendix B, *Special Characters Chart*, for all of the displayable characters included in the ISO 8859-1 character set, as well as a discussion of using other character sets or Unicode characters in your HTML documents. For links to resources on the Web that discuss using the ISO 8859-1 and other character sets, see this book's IRC at **www.emcp.com/**.

Including a Description and Keyword List

Probably the two most common uses of the META element are to include a description of your page and a list of keywords that are related to the content of your page. Many search engines use these META elements when listing or indexing your site. These kinds of META elements are included in an HTML document using the following general format:

```
<meta name="meta data name" content="meta data content">
```

Add a META element below your document's TITLE element that provides a description of the document's content:

```
<title>Commerce and Civilization by Crystal Porter</title>
<meta name="description" content="Discussion of the impact of
commerce on the development of civilization, contrasting folk
and urban societies, and debating the role of trade and commerce
in the transition between the two.">
</head>
```

Search engines and Web directories that support the use of META elements might display your META element description, instead of the initial text of your document, in a list of search responses. This can be useful, for instance, if the initial text of your document does not provide a good description or is short on information about your document. A good META element description makes it more likely that someone interested in a document such as yours will actually click on its link in a search engine list, rather than pass on to the next link.

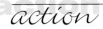

Add a META element below the one you just added that provides a list of keywords a search engine might use in indexing your document:

```
<title>Commerce and Civilization by Crystal Porter</title>
<meta name="description" content="Discussion of the impact of
commerce on the development of civilization, contrasting folk and
urban societies, and debating the role of trade and commerce in
the transition between the two.">
<meta name="keywords" content="civilization, society, societies,
culture, higher societies, folk society, folk societies,
sociology, primitive, tribal, urban, egypt, sumeria, trade,
commerce, import, export, market, generalist, specialist">
</head>
```

Search engines and directories that support use of the META element can use your keyword list to help index your document. This can increase the likelihood that someone doing a search on any of the keywords you have listed will be able to find your document. For links to resources on the Web that further discuss these and other uses of the META element, see this book's IRC at **www.emcp.com/**.

ADDING INLINE HIGHLIGHTING

Bold and italic often are used to add highlighting and emphasis to text within a document. HTML includes a number of inline elements that can be used to add bolding or italics to an HTML document.

Using the I and B Elements

The I (Italic) and B (Bold) elements are used to add italic or bold highlighting to enclosed text. They are sometimes referred to as *literal* elements because they literally specify a display characteristic, italics or bolding.

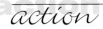

Use the I and B elements to apply italics and bolding to the example text:
1. Use the I element to italicize the included text (see Figure 2.1):

```
<p>Civilizations have often been referred to as <i>advanced
societies</i>, in contrast to less developed societies.
```

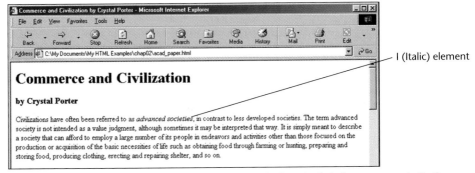

FIGURE 2.1 • *A Web browser displays text tagged with the I (Italic) element in an italic font.*

2. Use the B element to create bolded lead-in headings for the first two items in the bulleted list (see Figure 2.2):

```
<ul>
<li><b>Geographical expansion.</b> A civilization occupies a
relatively wide expanse of territory.
<li><b>Population growth and concentration.</b> A civilization
requires sufficient population and sufficient population density
to be able to employ large numbers of individuals in activities
with no direct economic return. These individuals include those
involved in government, ceremonial activities, art, philosophy,
and scientific inquiry.
```

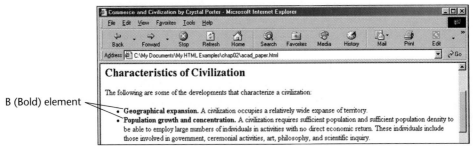

B (Bold) element

FIGURE 2.2 • *A Web browser displays text tagged with the B (Bold) element in a bold font.*

Using the EM and the STRONG Elements

The EM (Emphasis) and STRONG (Strong Emphasis) elements are used to emphasize or strongly emphasize enclosed text. They are inline elements and are sometimes referred to as *logical* elements because they specify a logical display characteristic, emphasis or strong emphasis, rather than a literal one (italics or bolding). In a graphical Web browser, an EM element is displayed in an italic font, while a STRONG element is displayed in a bold font.

It is customary in publications to use italics to emphasize book, journal, or magazine titles, rather than set them in quotes. In HTML, you can use either the I or the EM element to italicize (or emphasize) these kinds of text strings.

Use the EM and STRONG elements to add emphasis and strong emphasis to the example document:

1. Use the EM element to emphasize the journal and book titles included in the following example (see Figure 2.3):

```
<h2>Distinguishing Between Folk and Urban Societies</h2>
<p>In an article published in the <em>American Journal of
Sociology</em>, Robert Redfield described the more primitive and
pre-urbanized state of society as forming "folk societies."(1)
John A. Wilson, in <em>The Culture of Ancient Egypt</em>,
summarizes Redfield's conclusions in the following manner:</p>
```

Text label pointing to image: E (Emphasis) element

FIGURE 2.3 • *A Web browser displays text tagged with the EM element in an italic font.*

2. Use the STRONG element to add stronger emphasis. Scroll down to the bottom part of the document and insert the following codes where indicated to strongly emphasize the included text (see Figure 2.4):

```
<hr>
<p><strong>Notes</strong></p>
<p>
1. Robert Redfield, "The Folk Society," American Journal of
Sociology, LII (1947), pp. 293-308.<br>
```

STRONG (Strong Emphasis) element

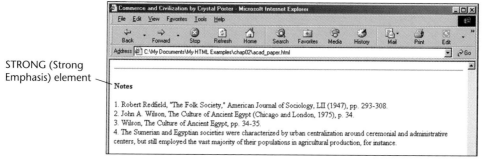

FIGURE 2.4 • *A Web browser displays text tagged with the STRONG element in a bold font.*

Whether you use logical or literal highlighting elements to apply italics to your Web pages is up to you; all graphical browsers, at least, treat the I and EM elements and the B and STRONG elements as interchangeable. The I and B elements are more economical and easier to type. The logical character of the EM and STRONG elements, however, still holds when the presentation media is not a visual media. In a speech browser, for instance, emphasized text might be preceded and followed by a pause and expressed through a somewhat louder voice, while strongly emphasized text might be expressed through both a louder and deeper voice.

Creating Bold Italic Highlighting

You can create text that is both italicized and bolded by nesting an I and a B element. It does not matter which is nested inside of which; just do not overlap them. You can also nest an EM and a STRONG element to get the same bold italic text. You can even nest an I and a STRONG element, or an EM and a B element, to get bold italic text.

Nest the STRONG element you defined in the last code example inside of an EM element (see Figure 2.5):

```
<p><em><strong>Notes</strong></em></p>
<p>
1. Robert Redfield, "The Folk Society," American Journal of
Sociology, LII (1947), pp. 293-308.<br>
```

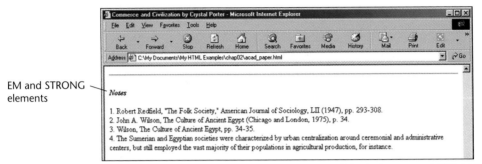

EM and STRONG elements

FIGURE 2.5 • *A Web browser displays text tagged with both the EM and STRONG elements in a bold italic font.*

Using Underlining

The U (Underline) element is an HTML 4 element that can be used to apply underlining to text in an HTML document.

Use the U element to underline the same text you previously tagged with the STRONG and EM elements (see Figure 2.6):

```
<hr>
<p><em><strong><u>Notes</u></strong></em></p>
```

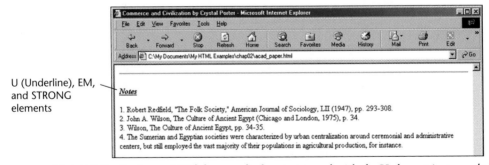

U (Underline), EM, and STRONG elements

FIGURE 2.6 • *A Web browser displays text tagged with the U element in an underlined font.*

The U element was not included in versions of HTML prior to HTML 4, so some earlier browsers do not support it. Some Web authors also avoid using the U element because underlined text is too easily confused with a hypertext link, which also is usually displayed in an underlined font. Underlining in a computer document is also somewhat of an anachronism, dating back to when early computer displays and printers lacked the capability to produce an italic font. Underlining was also commonly used in typewritten documents to indicate emphasis when using a typewriter lacking an italic font. Because modern displays and printers have no problem producing italics, there is little reason to use underlined text in a Web page. The U element is also deprecated in HTML 4.01, in favor of using styles or the DEL (Delete) element to produce an underlined font.

So far you have only marked up some of the instances in the example file where the I (Italics), B (Bold), EM (Emphasis), STRONG (Strong Emphasis), and U (Underline) elements could be used to further mark up the document for display on the Web. To gain more practice, look for other places in the document where you can use these elements. For instance:

- The I element was used to italicize a phrase that benefited from being so highlighted in the text. Look for other instances within the document's text paragraphs where you might use the I element.
- The B element was used to bold the lead-in phrases of the first two bulleted list items. Use the B element to bold the remaining lead-in phrases in the bulleted list.
- The EM element was used to emphasize (and thus italicize) the titles of a journal and a book. Look for other journal or book titles in the footnote items at the bottom of the document and use the EM element to emphasize those titles as well.

WORKING WITH QUOTATIONS

Crystal's paper includes two extended quotations. For print publications, the general rule is that any quote that is four lines or longer should be formatted as a block quote (as a separate text block indented from the margins). In HTML, the BLOCKQUOTE element is used to tag a block of text as a block quote.

action

Nest the indicated paragraph inside of a BLOCKQUOTE element to format it as a block quote and delete the quotation marks, since block quotes do not need to be quoted (see Figure 2.7):

```
<h2>Distinguishing Between Folk and Urban Societies</h2>
<p>In an article published in the <em>American Journal of
Sociology</em>, Robert Redfield described the more primitive and
pre-urbanized state of society as forming "folk societies."(1)
John A. Wilson, in <em>The Culture of Ancient Egypt</em>,
summarizes Redfield's conclusions in the following manner:</p>

<blockquote><p>"This ideal folk society is homogenous, small,
and has a strong sense of community. It is nonliterate, and its
economy is one of self-sufficiency rather than of buying and
selling. In general, the ties of family provide the community.
The society is deeply rooted in religious belief and custom, and
relations are personal, so that the secular and impersonal have
not yet come into being. The behavior of such a society is
strongly traditional, so that there is no encouragement to
speculation or to experimentation, since sanctified tradition
has provided all the answers. Such a folk society could exist
as a pure culture only if the conditions of its maintenance and
security from disturbance were assured."(2)</p></blockquote>
```

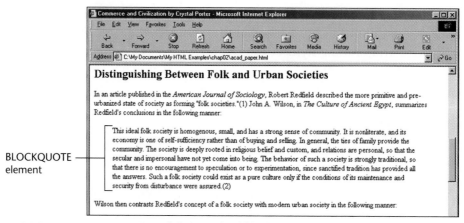

FIGURE 2.7 • *Extended quotes should be formatted as block quotes.*

Nesting Paragraphs in Block Quotes

In the example, you nested a P element, rather than raw text, within a BLOCKQUOTE element. This is not required by the transitional and frameset versions of HTML 4.01 or XHTML 1.0, which allow both block and inline elements to be nested directly inside of a BLOCKQUOTE element. The strict versions of HTML 4.01 and XHTML 1.0, however, only allow block elements to be nested directly inside of a BLOCKQUOTE element.

Nesting P elements (or other block elements) instead of raw text inside of a BLOCK-QUOTE element is a good idea, nonetheless. Nesting P elements, for one thing, lets you include more than one paragraph of text in a block quote. An additional consideration comes into play when using styles, in which case a P element and raw text nested inside of a BLOCKQUOTE element might differ in their display characteristics if the styles for the P and BLOCKQUOTE elements are not identically defined.

Nesting Other Block Elements in Block Quotes

Besides paragraph elements, you can nest any other block element inside of a BLOCK-QUOTE element that can be nested inside of the BODY element. Some Web authors take advantage of this capability to indent a whole page by nesting all of the other BODY elements within a BLOCKQUOTE element. Although using the BLOCKQUOTE element in this manner—purely as a formatting device—is legal in all versions of HTML, you might decide against it for a couple of good reasons.

The first reason is that using the BLOCKQUOTE element purely as a formatting device violates the meaning and purpose of the BLOCKQUOTE element, which is to present a block of quoted text—users of non-visual user agents, such as a Braille browser or speech browser, for instance, might be confused by BLOCKQUOTES that are used for purposes other than quoting blocks of text. The second reason is that the level of support for Cascading Style Sheets in current browsers provides a much better means for effecting margin changes for elements in HTML documents.

Just a little further down in the document, another paragraph is enclosed within quotation marks. Delete the quotation marks and then use the BLOCKQUOTE element to turn that paragraph into a block quote also.

MARKING REVISIONS

HTML includes a number of elements that can be used to mark up insertions or deletions within an HTML document.

Using the DEL and INS Elements

The DEL (Delete) and INS (Insert) elements let you mark deletions and insertions within an HTML document. Browsers that support these inline elements display deletions as strikethrough text and insertions as underlined text.

Cynthia wants to display deletions and insertions as she revises her online paper.

Use the INS and DEL elements to mark insertions and deletions in the following example text (see Figure 2.8):

```
<p><ins>As described</ins><del>Admittedly</del>, these
characteristics of folk societies and urban societies
<ins>place</ins><del>situate</del> them as extremes at either
end of a<ins>n overall</ins> continuum<ins> that is defined by
society in all of its forms</ins>. However, in reality,
societies tend to contain characteristics of both of these
societ<ins>al</ins><del>y</del> types. For example, most
societies have both generalists and specialists, but in a
community considered to be a folk society, generalists
predominate. In a community considered to be an urban society,
specialists predominate at least in rank, if not necessarily
always in numbers.(4)</p>

<h2>Commerce as a <ins>Cause of</ins><del>Means Toward</del>
Urbanization</h2>
```

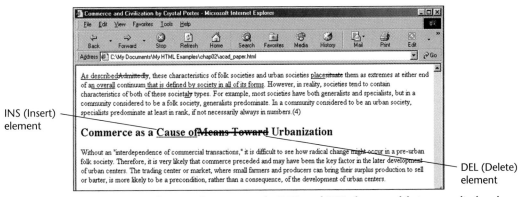

FIGURE 2.8 • *In a browser that supports the DEL and INS elements, deletions are displayed as strikethrough text, while insertions are displayed as underlined text.*

One of the main drawbacks of using the DEL and INS elements is lack of support in earlier browsers. As with the Q element, these elements do not degrade gracefully in non-supporting browsers, with both deletions and insertions indistinguishably displayed as normal text in those browsers. In Chapter 3, you will learn some methods you can use to redirect or alert visitors using browsers that do not comply with the latest HTML standards.

tip

Cascading Style Sheets provide a rather neat trick that can be done with deleted text. Setting a style property of **display: none** for the DEL element causes nested text not to be displayed in browsers that support this. For instance, the following style might be defined in the document's HEAD element:

```
<title>Commerce and Civilization by Crystal Porter</title>
<style type="text/css">
del { display: none }
</style>
</head>
```

The result of this in a supporting browser is that the deleted text is not displayed, while the inserted text is still displayed as underlined (see Figure 2.9).

INS element only

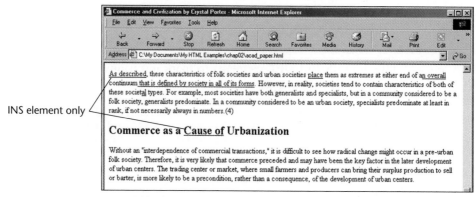

FIGURE 2.9 • *When the display of deletions (DEL elements) is turned off using CSS, a supporting browser displays only the insertions (INS elements).*

Striking Out Text

HTML provides two additional inline elements that can create strikeout text: the STRIKE and S elements. The STRIKE element had a long history as a Netscape extension before it was included in HTML 3.2. The S element was proposed for the failed HTML 3.0 proposal, but was not included in standard HTML until HTML 4.0, primarily because it is more concise than the STRIKE element. Both of these elements are deprecated in HTML 4.01, in favor of using the DEL element or styles to achieve similar or better results.

All the same, of all the elements that are displayed as strikeout text, the STRIKE element is still the most universally supported, particularly by older browsers. So, if you just want to display strikeout text, using the STRIKE element is a better choice than using the S element.

CREATING FOOTNOTES AND ENDNOTES

Footnotes or endnotes are often needed in academic papers. In this section, you learn how to incorporate both footnotes and endnotes in an online document, including how to superscript note numbers and create hypertext footnote and endnote links.

Superscripting Note Numbers

Note numbers are superscripted in documents. In HTML, the SUP (Superscript) element is used to superscript text. Example note numbers are already included in the example document.

Find the first note number and use the SUP element to superscript it, as shown here (see Figure 2.10):

```
<h2>Distinguishing Between Folk and Urban Societies</h2>
<p>In an article published in the <em>American Journal of
Sociology</em>, Robert Redfield described the more primitive and
pre-urbanized state of society as forming "folk
societies."<sup>(1)</sup> John A. Wilson, in <em>The Culture of
Ancient Egypt</em>, summarizes Redfield's conclusions in the
following manner:</p>
```

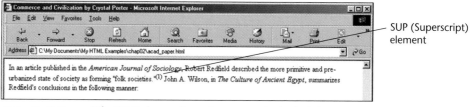

FIGURE 2.10 • *The SUP element is used to superscript included text.*

Notice in the example that the superscripted note number is enclosed within parentheses. The primary reason for doing this is to avoid *ungraceful degradation* in non-supporting browsers or in browsers, such as text browsers, that cannot display superscripted text. In those browsers, an unsuperscripted note number would be displayed immediately following the preceding text, displaying **text1**, instead of **text[1]**, for instance.

An element or attribute is not determined to ungracefully degrade merely because it produces an unexpected or unpleasant visual effect in a browser. The effect is only deemed ungraceful degradation if it also makes accessing or understanding the content of the element or document more difficult or impossible.

Three additional footnote numbers (within parentheses) are included in the example document. Find each additional footnote number and use the SUP element to superscript the number and the surrounding parentheses.

Although not included in the current example, just as you can use the SUP element to superscript nested text, you also can use the SUB (Subscript) element to subscript nested text. For instance, to format the chemical formula of water you might do this:

```
H<sub>(2)</sub>0
```

This should then display in a browser as $H_{(2)}0$, for instance.

Besides simply formatting superscripted note numbers, you can turn them into hypertext links that will jump from the note number to a footnote located at the bottom of the page.

When creating a hypertext link that jumps to a location within a document, you need to create two separate anchor elements (A elements): a destination anchor that marks the location in the document that you want to jump to and a linking anchor (or jump link) that links to the destination anchor.

CREATING A DESTINATION ANCHOR A destination anchor marks a location within a document to which a hypertext link can jump. A destination anchor is created using the A element, but with a NAME attribute, instead of an HREF element. A destination anchor is also sometimes referred to as a named anchor, for that reason. A destination anchor is created in the following general format:

```
<a name="anchorname"></a>
```

Each destination anchor you create within your document must have a unique name. If you create two destination anchors that have the same name, a browser will not be able to decide which one it should jump to and, therefore, will not jump anywhere.

You can find several example footnotes at the bottom of the example document.

Add a destination anchor to mark the location of the first footnote:

```
<hr>
<p><em><strong><u>Notes</u></strong></em></p>
<p>
<a name="note1"></a>1. Robert Redfield, "The Folk Society,"
<em>American Journal of Sociology</em>, LII (1947), pp. 293-
308.<br>
```

Notice that the destination anchor you inserted is not bracketing anything. That is fine because this element is not tagging any text for presentation; it is merely marking a location.

CREATING A FOOTNOTE LINK Now that you have created a destination anchor, you can create a hypertext link that will jump to the location you have marked. A jump link that jumps to another location in a document is created in the following general format:

```
<a href="#anchorname">link text</a>
```

The # character and the following *anchorname* string together also are referred to as a *fragment identifier*. The *anchorname* specifies the name of the destination anchor to which the link will jump.

Create a jump link that jumps from a note number in the text to a footnote at the bottom of the document:

1. Return to the first note number that you previously superscripted and apply the following codes to turn it into a jump link (see Figure 2.11):

```
<h2>Distinguishing Between Folk and Urban Societies</h2>
<p>In an article published in the <em>American Journal of
Sociology</em>, Robert Redfield described the more primitive and
pre-urbanized state of society as forming "folk
societies."<sup><a href="#note1">(1)</a></sup> John A. Wilson,
in <em>The Culture of Ancient Egypt</em>, summarizes Redfield's
conclusions in the following manner:</p>
```

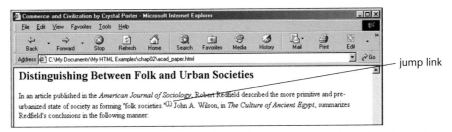

jump link

FIGURE 2.11 • *The superscripted note number has been turned into a jump link that, when
clicked on, will jump to the specified destination anchor.*

2. Save your document, switch over to your browser, refresh the display of your page,
   and then click on the **(1)** note link. Your browser should jump to the first footnote
   at the bottom of the page (see Figure 2.12).

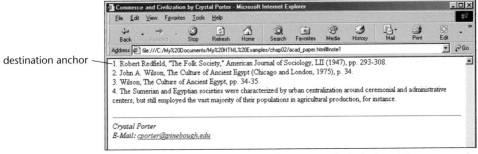

destination anchor

FIGURE 2.12 • *A note at the bottom of a page can be linked with its corresponding note
number in the body of the document.*

At the bottom of the BODY element, a PRE (Preformatted Text) element has been inserted
that contains 30 hard returns. The reason for doing this is to add vertical spacing at the bottom of the document, so that when a hypertext footnote link jumps to one of the footnotes
at the bottom of the page, the footnote will be displayed at the top of the browser window,
rather than partway down in the window. The PRE element can be used for this because it
is the only element that does not ignore nested hard returns. Alternatively, a style could be
used to add additional margin space at the bottom of the page.

CREATING A RETURN LINK Visitors can just click the browser's Back button to
return to the location they were at before clicking a hypertext link. It is not a bad idea,
however, to provide a more explicit means by which visitors can return to their previous
position within the document. You can do this by creating another link that jumps the
other way, from the end of a footnote back up to its corresponding note number in the
document's text.

   An anchor element can include both an HREF and a NAME attribute, so you do not
have to create a separate destination anchor next to the jump link you created previously.
By including both HREF and NAME attributes in an A element's start tag, you can create
an anchor element that can serve as both a jump link and as a destination anchor.

Create a hypertext link that jumps back up from the footnote to its corresponding note number in the text:

1. Edit the hypertext note link you previously created, giving it a unique name using the NAME attribute:

```
<p>In an article published in the <em>American Journal of
Sociology</em>, Robert Redfield described the more primitive and
pre-urbanized state of society as forming "folk
societies."<sup><a href="#note1" name="return1">(1)</a></sup>
John A. Wilson, in <em>The Culture of Ancient Egypt</em>,
summarizes Redfield's conclusions in the following manner:</p>
```

2. Scroll back down to the list of footnotes at the bottom of the document body. At the end of the first footnote, create a jump link that will jump back to the note number link that you just named (see Figure 2.13):

```
<p><em><strong><u>Notes</u></strong></em></p>
<p>
<a name="note1"></a>1. Robert Redfield, "The Folk Society,"
<em>American Journal of Sociology</em>, LII (1947), pp. 293-308.
<a href="#return1">[Return]</a><br>
```

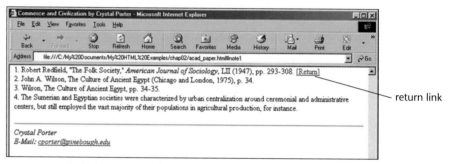

return link

FIGURE 2.13 • *Including a return link following a footnote provides visitors with an explicit means to return to their previous location in the document.*

3. Save your file, switch over to your browser, refresh the display of your page, and click on the **[Return]** link at the end of the first footnote. Your browser should jump back to the first note number (see Figure 2.14).

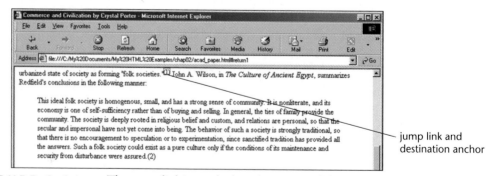

jump link and destination anchor

FIGURE 2.14 • *The return link jumps back to the position of the note number.*

The easiest way to keep jump links and destination anchors straight in your mind is to remember these simple differences between the two:

- A jump link always includes an HREF attribute with a fragment identifier (beginning with a # character) that identifies the name of the destination anchor it jumps to (for example: **href="#anchorname"**).

- A destination anchor (or named anchor) includes a NAME attribute (*not* beginning with a # character) that identifies (or names) it, so it can be targeted by a jump link (for example: `name="anchorname"`).

TROUBLE spot

Fragment identifiers and anchor names are case-sensitive. Whatever you specify as the name of a destination anchor must be duplicated exactly, including any uppercase characters, in the fragment identifier used to jump to it. In other words, if you specify `name="note1"` as the name of a destination anchor, then `href="#note1"` must be used in the corresponding jump link, and not `href="#Note1"` or `href="#NOTE1"`.

practice

So far, you have created one hypertext note link (a jump link) that jumps from the first note number in the document to the first footnote listed at the bottom of the page (marked by a destination anchor). Using that experience as a guide, do the same for the three remaining note numbers and footnotes:

1. Create the destination anchors that mark the location of the remaining three footnotes at the foot of the page. Using the A element's NAME attribute, give each one a unique name (**note2**, **note3**, and **note4**).
2. Find each of the remaining note numbers in the document (they are the same note numbers, surrounded by parentheses, that you superscripted earlier). Turn each note number (and surrounding parentheses) into a jump link by nesting it inside of an A element with an HREF attribute targeting the name of the destination anchor you want it to jump to (**#note2**, **#note3**, and **#note4**).
3. In your browser, test each of the links you have created.

You also previously created a return link at the end of the first footnote that jumps back up to the corresponding note number in the document's text. Using that experience as a guide, create return links at the end of the other three footnotes:

1. Find the three remaining note numbers. In the jump links you created for them, use the NAME attribute to give each one a unique name (**return2**, **return3**, and **return4**). These anchor elements now serve as both jump links and destination anchors.
2. Use the A element's HREF attribute to create return links at the end of the remaining footnotes that jump back up to the corresponding note numbers. For the HREF attribute value, use fragment identifiers that target the names of the destination anchors you want to return to (**#return2**, **#return3**, and **#return4**).
3. In your browser, test each of the return links you have created.

CREATING A FOOTNOTE SEPARATOR LINE In the example text, an HR (Horizontal Rule) element is inserted above the footnotes to create a separator line between them and the rest of the document's text. An HR element, however, draws a line all the way across the page, while in printed documents with footnotes, a footnote separator line is usually drawn only part of the way across the page. By using the HR element's WIDTH, SIZE, ALIGN, and NOSHADE attributes, you can alter the dimensions, position, and appearance of a horizontal rule.

action Create a footnote separator line:

1. Reduce the width of the horizontal rule to 150 pixels and set left-alignment, as shown in the following example code (see Figure 2.15):

```
<hr width="150" align="left">
<p><em><strong><u>Notes</u></strong></em></p>
<p>
<a name="note1"></a>1. Robert Redfield, "The Folk Society,"
<em>American Journal of Sociology</em>, LII (1947), pp. 293-308.
<a href="#return1">[Return]</a><br>
```

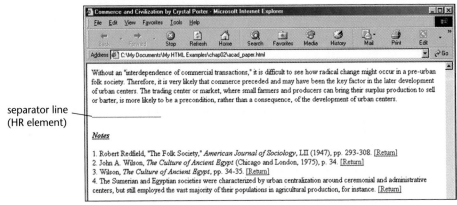

separator line
(HR element)

FIGURE 2.15 • *The horizontal rule is set to 150 pixels wide and left-aligned.*

NOTE

You also can set the width of a horizontal rule using a percentage value. For instance, **width="25%"** would set the width of the horizontal rule to 25 percent of the width of the browser window.

To right-align the horizontal rule, insert **align="right"**. Horizontal rules are center-aligned by default.

2. To create a thinner footnote separator, set the size of the rule to 1 pixel and turn off 3-D shading (see Figure 2.16):

```
<hr width="150" align="left" size="1" noshade>
<p><em><strong><u>Notes</u></strong></em></p>
<p>
<a name="note1"></a>1. Robert Redfield, "The Folk Society,"
<em>American Journal of Sociology</em>, LII (1947), pp. 293-308.
<a href="#return1">[Return]</a><br>
```

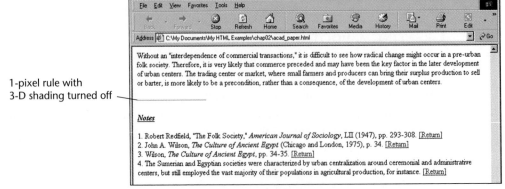

1-pixel rule with
3-D shading turned off

FIGURE 2.16 • *The size (height) of the horizontal rule is set to 1 pixel and 3-D shading is turned off.*

The NOSHADE attribute can be confusing. You might assume, for instance, that it is used to fill the horizontal rule with a shade. In fact, it is just the opposite. With the NOSHADE attribute present, some browsers fill the interior of the rule with a gray tone, whereas others fill it with black. When NOSHADE is absent, browsers fill the interior of the rule with white, while adding a variable amount of "shading" to the sides of the rule to provide relief against the page's background.

To test this, increase the size of a horizontal rule (`size="6"` and then view it in your browser with the NOSHADE attribute both present and absent.

All of these attributes are deprecated in HTML 4.01 in favor of using styles to achieve similar or better results. Standalone attributes are also illegal in XHTML. If used in an XHTML document, you would need to insert **noshade="noshade"** instead of just **noshade**.

If you want to reduce the amount of vertical spacing following a horizontal rule, you can nest the HR element within a following block element. This trick works in all major browsers. You can try it out for yourself if you wish.

action

Insert a P start tag in front of the HR element and delete the following P start tag (see Figure 2.17):

```
<p><hr width="150" align="left" size="1" noshade>
<p><em><strong><u>Notes</u></strong></em></p>
```

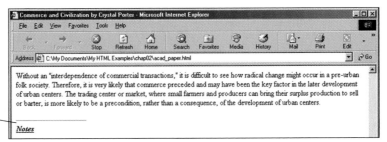

vertical spacing reduced by nesting HR element inside of P element

FIGURE 2.17 • *A quirk supported by most browsers reduces the vertical spacing following a horizontal rule when it is nested inside of a following block element.*

You should be aware that this is not standard HTML, in that an HR element is a block element and thus should not be nested inside of a P element. According to the standard, an HR element should terminate a preceding P element, with an implied end tag assumed for the P element, which would also then leave the following text ("Note") as untagged raw text (with an end tag, but no start tag). That the implied termination of the P element would also render it as an empty P element (which browsers should entirely ignore), only adds to the soup of non-standard features included in this trick. This trick is also not very friendly to text browsers or non-visual browsers, which might not know what to make of a horizontal rule nested inside of a P element.

Your document will also, of course, not be a valid HTML 4.01 document if you use this trick and will generate an error if you try to validate it using the W3C's HTML Validator. The only way to achieve this effect using valid HTML 4.01 code is to use a style. Styles (in the form of Cascading Style Sheets, or CSS) are used to specify formatting (or "styling") for HTML elements. Styles can be included in documents using style sheets (using the STYLE element) or they can be inserted inline within document elements (using the STYLE attribute).

Use an inline style in the following paragraph to reduce the element's top margin space (see Figure 2.18):

```
<p><hr width="150" align="left" size="1" noshade>
<p style="margin-top: -0.25em">
<em><strong><u>Notes</u></strong></em></p>
```

vertical spacing
reduced by an inline
style in P element

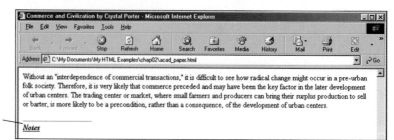

FIGURE 2.18 • *You can use a style to decrease the amount of vertical spacing following the HR element.*

This has the effect of eliminating any top margin set by the P element, while reducing the bottom margin set by the HR element by a quarter of an em (or one quarter of the current line height). It is not important that you understand styles in any depth at this point (nor what an em is, for that matter). It is important to understand, however, that when creating HTML documents, there are often ways to achieve effects that are supported by browsers but which are not part of the HTML standard (HTML 4.01). Often, the only way to achieve these effects in a standard fashion is by using styles. The use of styles will be discussed in more depth in Chapter 3 where the use of styles to specify font sizes, colors, and faces will be introduced.

Creating Endnote Links

In a published article or book, the only difference between footnotes and endnotes is that footnotes are listed at the bottom of a page and endnotes are listed at the end of an article or chapter (or possibly at the end of a book). A Web page, of course, is a single page of indeterminate length, so the foot and the end of the document are really the same. When working in HTML, endnotes are generally grouped in a separate document, whereas footnotes are displayed at the foot of the current document.

You might want to consider using endnotes, rather than footnotes, if you have many notes in your document or they include an extensive amount of text. If you only have a handful of relatively brief notes, then you might want to consider using footnotes.

You link to an endnote in the same way that you link to any location in another document. You create such a link in the following fashion:

```
<a href="url#anchorname">link text</a>
```

In the example, *url* stands for the object file that is targeted by the link, which can be just a file name (if the name of the file you are linking to is located in the same folder), an absolute Web address (**http://www.yourhost.com/yourfolder/yourpage.html**), or a relative Web address that points to a file located in your own site (**yoursubfolder/ yourpage.html**). See "Using Relative URLs" in Chapter 6 for guidance on using relative URLs.

When working with Web pages, endnotes are generally grouped in their own separate document. You might want to do this, for instance, if you have a lot of notes that need to be listed, and for the sake of brevity or design, you do not want to display them at the foot of your page. You might also want to group notes from a collection of documents (or chapters) in a single file, which can then be referenced from those documents (these notes would function like endnotes at the end of a book, for instance).

This example uses an endnotes_ex.html example file that is included with the other example files for this chapter (in the chap02 folder). In creating the following example, you will be instructed to open endnotes_ex.html in your text editor and resave it as endnotes.html in the chap02 folder in your working folder or disk.

Edit the jump links for the note numbers so they also point to the name of the file containing the endnotes (endnotes.html):

1. Locate the first note number link and, in the HREF element, insert the name of the file that will contain the endnotes (endnotes.html) in front of the fragment identifier (#note1):

```
<h2>Distinguishing Between Folk and Urban Societies</h2>
<p>In an article published in the <em>American Journal of Sociology
</em>, Robert Redfield described the more primitive and pre-
urbanized state of society as forming "folk societies."<sup><a
href="endnotes.html#note1" name="return1">(1)</a></sup> John A.
Wilson, in <em>The Culture of Ancient Egypt</em>, summarizes
Redfield's conclusions in the following manner:</p>
```

2. Do the same with the three other note number links you have created, so they each also point to endnotes.html. Resave your file.
3. Run a second copy of your text editor and open **endnotes_ex.html** from the chap02 folder in your working folder. (If using a text editor that lets you open multiple windows, just open endnotes_ex.html in a separate window.)
4. Resave **endnotes_ex.html** in the chap02 folder as **endnotes.html**, so you will not overwrite the original example file.

NOTE

In viewing the example file in your text editor, you will notice that the endnotes in endnotes.html are identical to the footnotes in your other document, including the destination anchors and return links you added to your footnotes. This demonstrates that you can link to a location within any document anywhere, even halfway around the world, as long as a destination anchor marks it.

5. Edit the return links, so they target your academic paper's file name (if you resaved your document under a different file name, substitute that file name in the following code). Resave your file.

```
<p>
<a name="note1"></a>1. Robert Redfield, "The Folk Society,"
American Journal of Sociology, LII (1947), pp. 293-308. <a
href="acad_paper.html#return1">[Return]</a><br>
<a name="note2"></a>2. John A. Wilson, The Culture of Ancient
Egypt (Chicago and London, 1975), p. 34. <a
href="acad_paper.html#return2">[Return]</a><br>
<a name="note3"></a>3. Wilson, The Culture of Ancient Egypt, pp.
34-35. <a href="acad_paper.html#return3">[Return]</a><br>
```

```
<a name="note4"></a>4. The Sumerian and Egyptian societies were
characterized by urban centralization around ceremonial and
administrative centers, but still employed the vast majority of
their populations in agricultural production, for instance. <a
href="acad_paper.html#return4">[Return]</a>
</p>
```

6. Switch to your browser and refresh the display of your page (it should still be displaying your academic paper). Find the first note number link and click on it. Your browser should open endnotes.html and jump down to the position of the first endnote (see Figure 2.19).

destination anchor

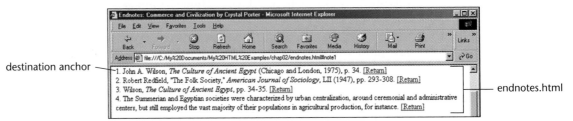

endnotes.html

FIGURE 2.19 • *Note links can be created that jump to a list of endnotes grouped in a separate file.*

7. Click the [**Return**] link at the end of the first endnote. Your browser should reopen your academic paper's file and return to the note number link that you just jumped from. You also can click the Back button to do the same thing.

8. Test the remaining note number links. They should each jump to endnotes.html, displaying the corresponding endnote at the top of the browser window.

NOTE

The endnotes.html example file also includes a PRE element containing multiple hard returns at the bottom of the page to help ensure that the endnotes are displayed at the top of the browser window when they are jumped to. The actual number of returns needed to cause this can vary depending upon the length of the page and the width and height of the browser's viewport.

INSERTING A COPYRIGHT SYMBOL

If you publish original material on the Web, you might want others to understand that your material is copyrighted and not part of the public domain. Including a copyright notice will not necessarily stop someone else from copying and reusing your material, but it will at least put them on notice that it is illegal for them to do so.

The copyright symbol is not included on your keyboard, so you have to use a special means to insert it into your page. To insert a non-keyboard character (sometimes called a "special character") in your document, you use an *entity code*, in the form of either a *numerical entity code* or a *named entity code*.

A numerical entity code identifies a character by its numerical position in the ISO 8859-1 character set and is inserted in this general format:

```
&#entitynumber;
```

The HTML specifications list many entity names that can be used to reference many special characters. A name entity code is inserted in this general format:

```
&entityname;
```

For instance, the copyright symbol's numerical entity code is `&#169;`, whereas its named entity code is `&copy;`.

action

Use the named entity code for the copyright symbol to add a copyright notice at the bottom of your example document (see Figure 2.20):

```
<hr>
<address>
Crystal Porter<br>
E-Mail: <a
href="mailto:cporter@pinebough.edu">cporter@pinebough.edu</a><br>
</address>
<p>&copy; Copyright 2003 by Crystal Porter. All rights
reserved.</p>
```

copyright symbol
(©)

FIGURE 2.20 • *You can insert a copyright symbol by inserting its named entity code.*

NOTE

Including a copyright notice on your page is not required to protect your copyright; under current copyright law, anything you create is automatically copyrighted. You are also not required to register your copyright. Including a copyright notice on your work, however, puts others on notice that your work is copyrighted and strengthens your case against someone who infringes on your copyright. Registering your copyright makes you eligible to receive statutory damages of as much as $100,000. For links to resources on the Web that discuss copyrights, go to this book's IRC at **www.emcp.com**/.

You also can use the copyright symbol's numerical entity code to insert it into your document. Just replace `&copy;` with `&#169;`.

Although many named entity codes are allowed by the HTML specifications, some earlier browsers, such as versions of Netscape Navigator prior to Version 4.75, might not recognize many of them. This is a case of ungraceful degradation because the raw code is displayed instead of the character in a non-supporting browser, as shown in Figure 2.21.

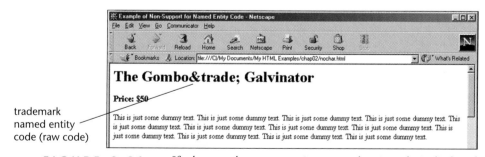

trademark
named entity
code (raw code)

FIGURE 2.21 • *If a browser does not recognize a named entity code, it displays the raw code.*

In Figure 2.21, the raw code of the named entity code of the trademark symbol is shown, as displayed in Netscape Navigator 4.75. Later in this chapter, including a trademark symbol is covered in the "Inserting the Registered and Trademark Symbols" section.

Because named entity codes do not degrade gracefully in non-supporting browsers, you should only use named entity codes to insert the characters shown in Table 2.1, and use numerical entity codes to insert all other characters.

TABLE 2.1 • *Named Entity Codes Supported by Versions of Netscape Earlier than 4.75*

Description	Named Entity Code	Character/Symbol
Copyright	&copy;	©
Registered	&reg;	®
Left Angle	&lt;	<
Right Angle	&gt;	>
Ampersand	&amp;	&
Double-quote	&quot;	"
Most accented characters	À, Õ, and ä for instance	À, Ô, and ä, for instance

You do not generally have to substitute entity codes for left angle, right angle, ampersand, or double-quote characters, except where they are part of an HTML code that you want to display "as is" in a Web page. For instance, to display `<img src="myimage.jpg">` as it appears, rather than as it is parsed by a browser, you would include the following in an HTML document:

```
&lt;img src=&quot;myimage.jpg&quot;&gt;
```

Even among the accented characters, a number of these characters cannot be displayed on a Macintosh even when using a numerical entity code, because they are not included in the Macintosh's native character set. For full details on which accented characters have this problem, see Appendix B.

Do not use keyboard shortcuts, or Window's Character Map or the Macintosh's Key Caps, to insert non-keyboard characters into an HTML document. Different systems might have different characters included at different locations in their native character sets, meaning that what displays as one character on one system might be displayed as an entirely different character on another system. Always use HTML entity codes to insert non-keyboard characters into HTML documents. See Appendix B for a listing of non-keyboard characters that can be included in an HTML document and their respective entity codes.

CASE EXAMPLE: CREATING A FREQUENTLY ASKED QUESTIONS PAGE

A frequently asked questions (or FAQ) page is one of the most common types of pages that can be found on the Web. On the Web, you can find FAQ pages on just about every topic or subject. Most FAQ pages are organized as a series of questions and answers, with a menu at the top of the page to make it easier to find the answer to a particular question.

Eddie Lopez is a support technician at CD Bunson Burners, Inc., which manufactures multi-drive CD-R recording systems. He has been given the task of creating a frequently asked questions (FAQ) page that compiles answers to questions that are frequently asked by customers. While compiling the questions and answers, Eddie noticed that a menu system at the top of the page would make it easier for users to find the particular question for which they are seeking an answer.

This example uses the cdr-faq_ex.html example file that is included with the other example files for this chapter (in the chap02 folder).

To start using the example file for this case example:
1. Open **cdr-faq_ex.html** in your text editor from the chap02 folder within your working folder or disk.
2. Resave your document as **cdr-faq.html** in the chap02 folder.
3. Open **cdr-faq.html** in your browser from the chap02 folder.

If you need more help opening and resaving an HTML file in your text editor, see "Opening an HTML File in Your Text Editor" earlier in this chapter. If you need more help opening an HTML file in your Web browser, see "Saving and Previewing Your HTML File" earlier in this chapter.

Many of the HTML codes have already been added to this example document. You will be adding codes to the example document to help demonstrate a variety of different features, including creating a document menu (or table of contents), making text bigger or smaller, creating multi-level numbered lists, inserting registered and trademark symbols, and using monospaced text to format input, output, and program code.

CREATING A DOCUMENT MENU

A document menu presents a list of links at the top of a document that jump to corresponding section headings within a longer, multi-part document. A document menu is also called a table of contents.

HTML actually provides three different elements—the UL, MENU, and DIR elements—that can be used to create a bulleted menu. Browsers have always displayed lists created using the MENU and DIR elements exactly the same as lists created using the UL element. As a result, the W3C has deprecated both the MENU and DIR elements and now strongly recommends that Web authors use the UL element instead.

Creating the Menu Links

A bulleted list is already included at the top of the example document. You just have to add the links to turn it into a menu. The menu links you will be creating work the same as the note links you created in the previous case example, except that they link to document sections, instead of to footnotes at the bottom of the page.

Add the following codes to turn the text in the list items into hypertext links (or jump links) that will jump to locations in your document (see Figure 2.22):

```
<h3>CD Bunson Burners, Inc.</h3>
<h1>CD-R Frequently Asked Questions</h1>

<ul>
<li><a href="#quest1">What is CD-R?</a>
<li><a href="#quest2">What is the difference between CD-R and
CD-ROM?</a>
```

```
<li><a href="#quest3">How long is a CD-R disc?</a>
<li><a href="#quest4">How do I back up an audio CD?</a>
<li><a href="#quest5">Can I batch process recording jobs?</a>
</ul>
```

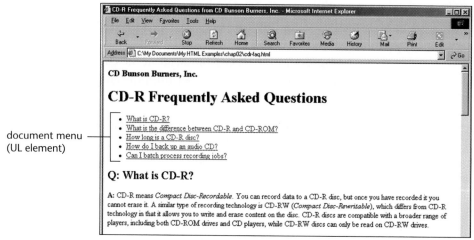

FIGURE 2.22 • *A document menu makes it easier to access the different parts of a longer document.*

Inserting the Destination Anchors

Before your menu links will work, destination anchors need to be inserted to mark the locations to which the menu links are going to jump.

The questions in the document are formatted as level-two headings (H2 elements). For the menu links to be able to jump to them, they need to be marked with named destination anchors.

action

Insert the destination anchor that marks the first question and answer section and then test the link that jumps to it to make sure it works:

1. Scroll down to the first H2 element and insert a destination anchor that will be jumped to from the first menu link:

```
<h2><a name="quest1"></a>Q: What is CD-R?</h2>
<p><b>A:</b> CD-R means <i>Compact Disc-Recordable</i>. You can
record data to a CD-R disc, but once you have recorded it you
cannot erase it.
```

2. Save your file in your text editor, switch over to your browser, and refresh the display of your page. Click on the first menu link to test it. Your browser should jump down to the position of the destination anchor you inserted, displaying the first question and answer at the top of the browser window (see Figure 2.23).

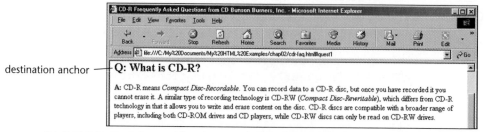

FIGURE 2.23 • *After the menu link is clicked on, a browser jumps to the location of the corresponding named destination anchor.*

3. Create the other destination anchors. Using the first destination anchor you created as a guide, insert destination anchors that mark the locations of the other question and answer sections. Name these destination anchors so they match the anchor names that are used in the menu links (**quest2**, **quest3**, **quest4**, and **quest5**).

4. Save your file, switch over to your browser and refresh your page, and then test the other links in your menu. For instance, click on the third menu link ("How long is a CD-R disc?"); your browser should jump down to the third question and answer section (see Figure 2.24).

destination anchor ⟶

FIGURE 2.24 • *After the third menu link is clicked, the browser jumps to the third question and answer section.*

Creating Return Links

Whenever you create a menu that jumps to different sections within an HTML document, you should also add links at the end of each section that will return a visitor to the menu. These links are similar to the return links you added at the end of the footnotes in the previous case example, except they all return to the same destination anchor.

Add a destination anchor at the top of the document menu and then create the return links that jump back up to it:

1. Add a destination anchor at the top of your menu that your return links can jump back to:

```
<ul><a name="menu"></a>
<li><a href="#quest1">What is CD-R?</a>
<li><a href="#quest2">What is the difference between CD-R and
CD-ROM?</a>
```

2. Create the return link following the first question and answer section (see Figure 2.25):

```
<h2><a name="quest1"></a>Q: What is CD-R?</h2>
<p><b>A:</b> CD-R means <i>Compact Disc-Recordable</i>. You can
record data to a CD-R disc, but once you have recorded it you
cannot erase it. A similar type of recording technology is CD-RW
(<i>Compact Disc-Rewritable</i>), which differs from CD-R
technology in that it allows you to write and erase content on
the disc. CD-R discs are compatible with a broader range of
players, including both CD-ROM drives and CD players, while CD-
RW discs can only be read on CD-RW drives.</p>
<p>Return to the <a href="#menu">Menu</a>.</p>
```

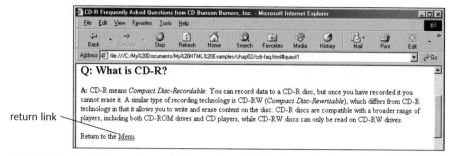

FIGURE 2.25 • *Return links can be added that jump back to a document menu.*

3. Copy the return link you just created and paste it in following the other question and answer sections to create the other return links. All of your return links are identical because they all jump back to the same destination anchor.

4. Test your return links in your browser. Figure 2.26 shows a browser window after a return link has jumped back to the document menu.

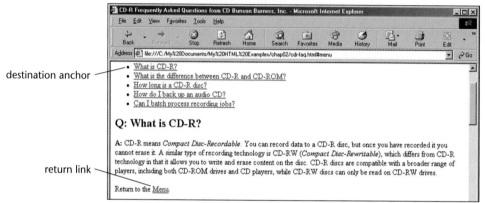

FIGURE 2.26 • *After a return link is clicked on, a visitor is returned to the top of the document menu.*

MAKING BIGGER AND SMALLER TEXT

The BIG and SMALL elements are used to increase or decrease the size of nested text. You can also increase and decrease the size of text using the FONT element. You should be aware, however, that while the FONT element is deprecated in HTML 4.01, the BIG and SMALL elements are not. Use of the FONT element to control font sizes and the issue of deprecation are covered in more detail in Chapter 3.

Making Text Bigger

In the example file, increasing the size of the "Q:" and "A:" text strings that precede each question and answer can help the reader identify them.

Use the BIG element to increase the size of the "Q:" and "A:" text strings for the first question and answer (see Figure 2.27):

```
<h2><a name="quest1"></a><big>Q:</big> What is CD-R?</h2>
<p><b><big>A:</big></b> CD-R means <i>Compact Disc-
Recordable</i>.
```

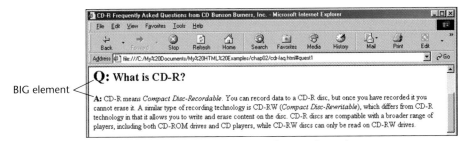

BIG element

FIGURE 2.27 • *The BIG element increases the size of nested text.*

You also can nest multiple BIG elements to further increase the size of nested text.

action

Nest the "A:" text string within another BIG element to further increase its size (see Figure 2.28):

```
<h2><a name="quest1"></a><big>Q:</big> What is CD-R?</h2>
<p><b><big><big>A:</big></big></b> CD-R means <i>Compact Disc-
Recordable</i>.
```

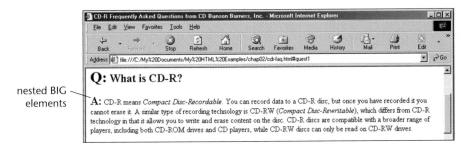

nested BIG
elements

FIGURE 2.28 • *Two BIG elements increase the size of nested text even more.*

You can nest up to four BIG elements to increase the text size (more than four nested BIG elements will not further increase the text size). That is because HTML only provides for seven font sizes, only four of which are larger than the default paragraph font size. Text in heading-level elements can be increased even fewer times—the size of text can be increased once in an H1 element, twice in an H2 element, three times in an H3 element, and so on. You will learn more about setting font sizes in Chapter 3.

practice

Use the BIG element to increase the "Q:" and "A:" text strings for the other four question and answer sections. Be sure you nest the two BIG elements used to increase the size of the "A:" text strings inside of the B element's start and end tags, rather than overlap them.

Making Text Smaller

In some situations, you might want to make text smaller. For example, you might not want certain text to be as noticeable as the other text on your page, while still being legible.

Use the SMALL element to decrease the size of the copyright statement at the bottom of the page (see Figure 2.29):

```
<p><small>&copy; Copyright 2003 by CD Bunson Burners, Inc. All
rights reserved.</small></p>
</body>
```

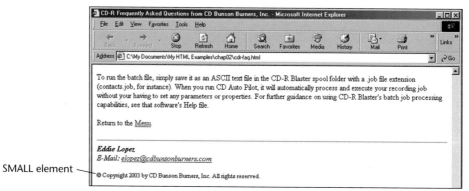

SMALL element

FIGURE 2.29 • *The SMALL element decreases the size of nested text.*

Generally, it is not a good idea to nest SMALL elements to decrease the size of text even further, because doing so might render the nested text unreadable on some systems.

USING NUMBERED LISTS

The FAQ includes one answer that provides instructional steps formatted as numbered lists. Technical documents often include numbered instructional steps. In HTML, the OL (Ordered List) element is used to create a numbered list.

In the example document, one question and answer section contains instructions formatted as separate paragraphs instead of numbered steps. The paragraphs are marked by single **<p>** start tags, without corresponding end tags, which is legal in HTML, since including end tags for paragraph elements, although generally advisable, is not required. You will be deleting the **<p>** start tags anyway, so leaving off the end tags just means you do not have to delete them as well. You create a numbered list in exactly the same way you created a bulleted list in the previous chapter, except you use an OL element, rather than a UL element.

Delete the **<p>** start tags and use the OL and LI elements to create a numbered list (see Figure 2.30):

```
<h3>Create an Image File:</h3>
<ol>
<li><p>Click the Start button and select Programs, Adaptec Easy
CD Creator 4, and Create CD.
<li><p>Click the Audio CD button.
<li><p>Insert the audio CD you want to copy in your CD-ROM or
CD-R drive. Click on the first track to highlight it. Hold down
the Shift key and click on the last track to highlight all of
the tracks. Click the Add button on the Toolbar.
<li><p>Select File, then Create CD Image. Change to the folder
where you save your image files (or you can create a folder for
this) and then save your image file, ending the file name with
a .cif file extension. For instance, type myimage.cif as the
name of your image file.
```

```
<li><p>The message "CD created successfully" will be displayed
when the image file has been successfully created. Click the OK
button.
</ol>
```

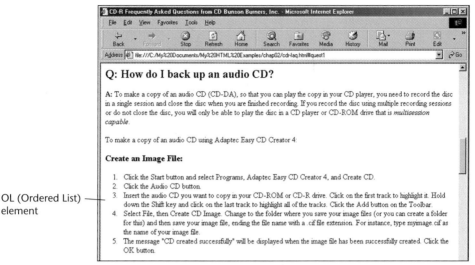

OL (Ordered List)
element

FIGURE 2.30 • *The OL element is used in combination with the LI element to format a numbered list.*

practice

The next two H3 elements ("Select Recording Options" and "Select Advanced Options") are also followed by paragraphs that can be turned into numbered lists. To gain more practice creating numbered lists, use the OL and LI elements to turn paragraphs following those headings into numbered list items as well.

Creating Multi-Level Numbered Lists

If you nest bulleted lists inside each other, a browser automatically changes the bullet type for each nested list level. Nesting numbered lists inside each other does not work in the same way; each nested list level still has the same number type (Arabic numerals).

The TYPE attribute is used in the UL or OL elements to change the bullet or number type, respectively. The OL element's TYPE attribute takes the following values: **I** (uppercase Roman), **i** (lowercase Roman), **A** (uppercase alphabetic), **a** (lowercase alphabetic), and **1** (Arabic numerals).

action

Change the H3 elements into list items in an ordered list and then set an uppercase alphabetic number type for the list:

1. Nest all of the H3 elements (and following numbered steps) inside an OL element, and then change the H3 elements into LI elements:

```
<ol>
<li><h3>Create an Image File:</h3>
<ol>
<li>Click on the Start button and select Programs, Adaptec Easy
CD Creator 4, and Create CD.

[...]
```

```
<li><h3>Select Recording Options:</h3>
<ol>
<li>Insert a blank (unrecorded) CD-R disc in your CD-R drive.

[...]

<li><h3>Select Advanced Options:</h3>
<ol>
<li>If the Advanced options are not displayed, click the
Advanced button.

[...]

<li>The message "CD created successfully" will be displayed when
the image file has been successfully recorded to the CD-R disc.
Click the OK button.
</ol>
</ol>
```

2. Use the TYPE attribute in the OL element to specify that it should be numbered using uppercase alphabetic characters (see Figure 2.31):

```
<ol type="A">
<li>Create an Image File:
<ol>
<li>Click on the Start button and select Programs, Adaptec Easy
CD Creator 4, and Create CD.
```

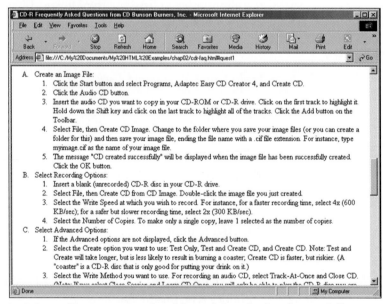

FIGURE 2.31 • *You can nest numbered lists inside each other that use different numbering schemes.*

Adding Vertical Spacing between List Items

By default, browsers do not add extra vertical spacing above or below list items (in the OL or UL elements). When creating instructional steps, however, it is nice to include a little more air in the list. One way to do that is to insert two BR (Line Break) elements at the end of the list items.

Add two BR elements at the end of all the LI elements in your nested OL elements:

1. Insert two BR elements at the end of the following LI elements (at the end of the first list item in the top-level list and the first nested list, respectively):

```
<ol type="A">
<li>Create an Image File:<br><br>
<ol>
<li>Click on the Start button and select Programs, Adaptec Easy
CD Creator 4, and Create CD.<br><br>
```

2. Insert double BR elements at the end of all the other LI elements in the numbered lists (see Figure 2.32).

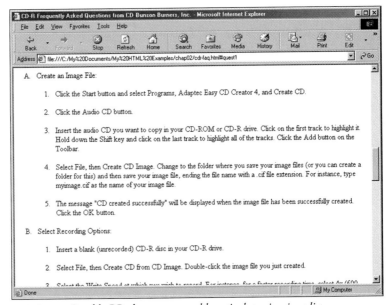

FIGURE 2.32 • *Double BR elements can add vertical spacing in a list.*

This works because browsers have traditionally added vertical space when more than one BR element is combined. Earlier HTML standards seemed to imply that multiple BR elements should be collapsed to a single BR element, but the browser vendors ignored that injunction. The current specifications for HTML and XHTML do not define any specific behavior for multiple BR elements, so you cannot rely on this working in all browsers. Inserting multiple BR elements, however, also cannot be considered to be non-standard, at least according to the latest HTML specifications, as long as they are nested inside of a block element. If some browser does not support inserting multiple BR elements, little harm is done, however, because less space between list items just means they will be more closely spaced in those browsers.

There are only two other alternatives for adding vertical spacing between list items: inserting a PRE element containing one or more hard returns between the list items (hard returns are preserved when nested in a PRE element) and using a style to set a top margin for the list items.

INSERTING THE REGISTERED AND TRADEMARK SYMBOLS

Earlier, in the academic paper example, you learned how to insert the entity code for the copyright symbol. The named entity code for the registered symbol was also mentioned, although no example was given. Another common symbol that you may want to include in an HTML document is the trademark symbol.

The named entity code for the registered symbol (**®**) is supported by both current and earlier browsers. The named entity code for the trademark symbol (**™**), however, while supported in current browsers, is not supported in Netscape Navigator prior to version 4.75 and should be avoided.

Complicating matters somewhat, in the ISO 8859-1 character set, the trademark symbol is listed outside of the range of displayable characters, among the "unused characters," which means that it is not a legal character that should be included in an HTML document, even when inserted using its numerical entity code (**™**). In practice, however, the trademark symbol's numerical entity code works in Windows, Macintosh, and UNIX browsers, but since it is not a legal character, there is no guarantee that it will display on every possible system.

The only standard way to insert a trademark symbol that should display in most current browsers is to insert it as a Unicode character (**™**). As its name implies, Unicode is a universal character set that aims ultimately to include all characters that are used in every language. As it stands, Unicode includes many thousands more characters than the ISO 8859-1 character set.

Eddie Lopez's boss told him to insert trademark or registered symbols wherever required.

Insert the registered and trademark symbols as shown in the following example (see Figure 2.33):

```
<h2><a name="quest4"><big>Q:</big> How do I back up an audio
CD?</h2>
<p><b><big><big>A:</big></big></b> To make a copy of an audio CD
(CD-DA), so that you can play the copy in your CD player, you
need to record the disc in a single session and close the disc
when you are finished recording. If you record the disc using
multiple recording sessions or do not close the disc, you will
only be able to play the disc in a CD player or CD-ROM drive
that is <i>multisession capable</i>.</p>
<p>To make a copy of an audio CD using Adaptec&reg; Easy CD
Creator&#8482; 4:</p>
```

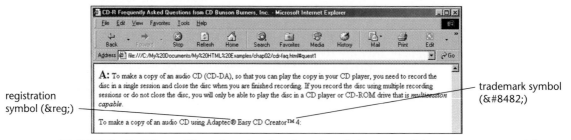

FIGURE 2.33 • *The registered and trademark symbols are two of the more common special characters that can be displayed on a Web page.*

The main problem with using the Unicode trademark symbol, however, is that it does not display in all browsers. It displays in the Netscape Navigator 4 browsers for Windows and the Macintosh, which is a big plus, but it does not display in the same browser versions for the X-Windows platform (UNIX).

If it is important to include a trademark symbol that can be displayed by all browsers (your lawyers, for instance, might insist that it be used wherever required within any corporate documents), even in non-graphical browsers, you do have an alternative. You can include a trademark symbol in a Web page by parenthesizing and superscripting the "tm" letter pair: `<sup>(tm)</sup>`. This is the same, somewhat ungraceful workaround that you used before to get around the problem of superscripted note numbers in browsers that do not support superscripting.

For more information about the ISO 8859-1 and Unicode character sets, see Appendix B.

USING MONOSPACED TEXT

HTML provides a number of elements that cause text to be displayed in a *monospaced* font. In a monospaced font, also called a *fixed-pitch* font, all characters, including letters, numbers, punctuation marks, and even spaces, are the same width, taking up exactly the same amount of horizontal space. When monospaced text is displayed in a Web page, most computer systems default to a Courier font (Courier New on a Windows system or Courier on a Macintosh system). By contrast, text in other non-monospaced elements is displayed in a *proportional* font, such as Times New Roman or Times Roman, for instance, in which each character may have a different (or "proportional") width.

Monospaced text is most common in technical documents, where it is generally used to represent different kinds of computer-generated text and to distinguish it from other surrounding text that is purely informational (rather than representational).

In HTML, the TT (Teletype) element is a generic element for producing monospaced text. The name of the element comes from a device, the *teletype*, which was used for both input and output on mainframes and minicomputers before the introduction of computer monitors using cathode ray tubes. The teletype was both a typewriter and a printer, which is why the TT element is a generic monospaced element that can be used to highlight both input and output text. Timothy Berners-Lee, and many others who helped pioneer the formation of the Web, worked with teletypes both as computer science students and later on the job, which is undoubtedly how the teletype element got its name in the first place. Bill Gates and Paul Allen, the founders of Microsoft, first learned how to program on a teletype at Lakeside Prep School in Seattle. (To read more about Bill Gates' early computer learning experiences, see "William H. Gates III: Before Microsoft" by John Mirick at **ei.cs.vt.edu/~history/Gates.Mirick.html**.) Perhaps to accommodate younger users who have never heard of nor seen a teletype, the TT element is sometimes referred to as the "typewriter text" element.

HTML provides other elements that are intended for marking up more specific types of monospaced text. These include the KBD (Keyboard), CODE (Program Code), and SAMP (Sample Code) elements. Many Web authors just stick to using the TT element for producing monospaced text, since none of these other elements display any differently than a TT element. A non-visual browser, such as a speech browser, might distinguish between a TT and a KBD element, with the KBD element indicating that nested text is input text (rather than output text). A style sheet can also be used to specify additional unique formatting to distinguish these elements, causing a KBD element to be displayed in both a monospaced and a bold font, for instance. You also can nest a B element inside a KBD element to achieve the same effect (although you also could nest the B element inside a TT element, for that matter, to indicate input text).

action

Use the TT element to highlight screen labels (options, buttons, and so on), the KBD element in combination with the B element to highlight keyboard input, and the SAMP element to highlight computer output (and replace the quotation marks), as shown here (see Figure 2.34):

```
<li>Select <tt>File</tt>, then <tt>Create CD Image</tt>. Change
to the folder where you save your image files (or you can
create a folder for this) and then save your image file, ending
the file name with a .cif file extension. For instance, type
<kbd><b>myimage.cif</b></kbd>, as the name of your image
file.<br><br>
<li>The message <samp>CD created successfully</samp> will be
displayed when the image file has been successfully created.
Click the <tt>OK</tt> button.<br><br>
```

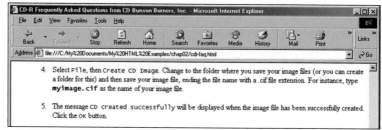

FIGURE 2.34 • *The TT, KBD, and SAMP elements are all displayed in a monospaced font.*

You also might want to display strings or blocks of computer code as monospaced text. The CODE element is an inline element, the purpose of which is to display strings of computer code. By inserting BR elements at the end of lines, the CODE element also can be used to display short blocks of computer code.

action

Format the example document's listing of a computer batch file in a monospaced font using the CODE element (the BR elements have already been inserted for you), as shown here (see Figure 2.35):

```
<p><code>[CD-R Blaster Job]<br>
Job Name = Contact Database<br>
Image File = F:\contacts.cif<br>
Label File = F:\Label templates\contacts.lbl<br>
Merge File = F:\contacts.mrg<br>
Type = Disk-At-Once<br>
Session = Single<br>
Disk = Close<br>
Number of Discs = 20<br>
Verify Type = None<br>
CRC32 = FFFFFFFF<br>
Serialize = No<br>
Serial Number Field = 1<br>
Serial Number Start = 123<br>
Serial Number Step = 1</code></p>
```

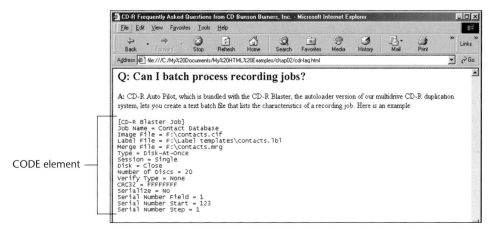

CODE element ──

FIGURE 2.35 • *The CODE element is also displayed in a monospaced font.*

For formatting longer blocks of programming code, however, you might want to use the PRE (Preformatted Text) element, which also preserves any hard returns, spaces, or tabs that have been used to visually organize the code. The PRE element can be used to format any text that you want to display "as is" (that is, as "preformatted").

action

Nest the code text inside a PRE element and space out the text following the "=" character to form a second column:

1. Nest the code text inside a PRE element and delete the tags for the P, BR, and CODE elements:

```
<pre>
<p><code>[CD-R Blaster Job]<br>
Job Name = Contact Database<br>
Image File = F:\contacts.cif<br>
Label File = F:\Label templates\contacts.lbl<br>
Merge File = F:\contacts.mrg<br>
Type = Disk-At-Once<br>
Session = Single<br>
Disk = Close<br>
Number of Discs = 20<br>
Verify Type = None<br>
CRC32 = FFFFFFFF<br>
Serialize = No<br>
Serial Number Field = 1<br>
Serial Number Start = 123<br>
Serial Number Step = 1</code></p>
</pre>
```

2. To complete the next step, the text used to display the code text inside the PRE element must be displayed in your text editor using a monospaced font. If using SimpleText on the Macintosh, click and drag to highlight the code text, and then select Font and Courier New (or Courier). (If using Notepad, your text is displayed in a monospaced font by default.)

3. Insert spaces (shown by dot characters) following the "=" characters so that a second, left-aligned column is formed (see Figure 2.36):

```
<pre>
[CD-R Blaster Job]
Job Name = ············Contact Database
Image File = ··········F:\contacts.cif
Label File = ··········F:\Label templates\contacts.lbl
Merge File = ··········F:\contacts.mrg
Type = ················Disk-At-Once
Session = ·············Single
Disk = ················Close
Number of Discs = ·····20
Verify Type = ·········None
CRC32 = ···············FFFFFFFF
Serialize = ···········No
Serial Number Field = ···1
Serial Number Start = ···123
Serial Number Step = ····1
</pre>
```

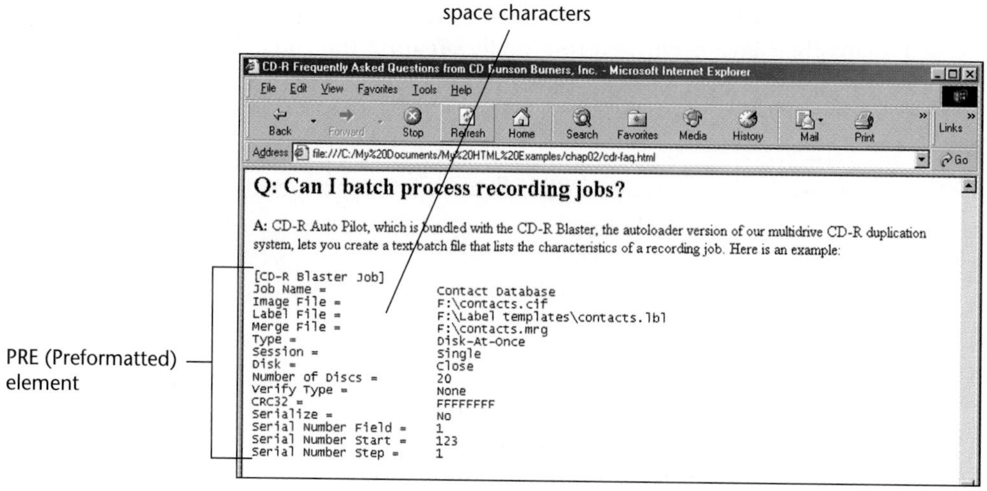

space characters

PRE (Preformatted) element

FIGURE 2.36 • *The PRE element displays a block of text in a monospaced font, while preserving any included spaces, tabs, or hard returns.*

CHAPTER SUMMARY

You should now be familiar with many of the HTML features and elements that are commonly used in creating and formatting online documents, including adding DocType declarations, META elements, inline highlighting (italics, bolding, underlining, monospacing, and so on), commonly used special characters (copyright, registered, and trademark), superscripted notes, hypertext note links, big and small text, and document menus.

Code Review

DocType declaration	Specifies the version of HTML (or XHTML) that the document is compatible with.
META element	Standalone element that is used to include meta data in an HTML document's HEAD element.
I and B elements	Literal inline elements for displaying italics and bolding.
EM and STRONG elements	Logical inline elements for adding emphasis (normally displayed as italics and bolding).
U element	Inline element that applies underlining to a text string (deprecated).
BLOCKQUOTE element	Specifies that a text block is to be formatted as a block quote, indented in from the margins.
DEL element	Specifies that nested text is a deletion.
INS element	Specifies that nested text is an insertion.
STRIKE element	Specifies strikeout text (deprecated).
S element	A more concise, but less universally supported element that specifies strikeout text (also deprecated).
SUP element	Inline element that superscripts a nested character or characters.
SUB element	Inline element that subscripts a nested character or characters.
NAME attribute	Used in the A (Anchor) element to create a destination anchor that can be jumped to from a hypertext link (or jump link).
WIDTH attribute	Used in the HR (Horizontal Rule) element to set the width of the rule (either in pixels or as a percentage).
ALIGN attribute	Used in the HR element to left-align or right-align a rule when the width of the rule is less than the width of the page (center alignment is the default).
SIZE attribute	Used in the HR element to specify the height of a horizontal rule in pixels.
© and ®	Named entity codes for the copyright and registered symbols.
&#8482;	Unicode numerical entity code for the trademark symbol.
BIG and SMALL elements	Increases and decreases the size of a text string.
OL element	Creates an ordered list (or numbered list).

TYPE attribute	Used with the OL or UL elements to change the number or bullet type that is displayed for the list.
TT element	The Teletype element, a generic element that can be used wherever a monospaced text string is desired.
KBD element	The Keyboard element, which can be used to indicate keyboard input (normally displayed in a monospaced font).
SAMP element	The Sample element, which can be used to indicate sample text or output (normally displayed in a monospaced font).
CODE element	Can be used to indicate program or script code (normally displayed in a monospaced font).
PRE element	The Preformatted Text element used to display a text block with all spaces, tabs, and hard returns displayed rather than ignored (normally displayed in a monospaced font).

ONLINE QUIZ

Go to this text's IRC at **www.emcp.com/** and take the online self-check quiz for this chapter.

REVIEW EXERCISES

This section provides some hands-on practice exercises to reinforce the information and material included within this and the previous chapter.

Save **acad_paper.html** and **cdr-faq.html** under new file names (**paper_practice.html** or **faq_practice.html**, for instance) and then use the new documents to practice using the elements, attributes, and other features that were covered in this chapter.

1. In either document (or both), delete the META element description and keyword list in the HEAD element and create a new description and keyword list based on the actual topic and content of the document. Do not use the description and keyword list provided in the chapter, but write your own from scratch.

2. Look for additional instances in both case example documents where you can apply any of the inline highlighting elements (I, B, EM, STRONG, U, and TT).

3. Find a poem that you like and format it using the BLOCKQUOTE element. Do not worry about context or realism; this is merely to get some practice formatting poetry as a block quote. Write an introductory paragraph that cites the poem and its author and then insert the poem as a block quote. For a single-stanza poem, nest the entire poem within a paragraph element; for a multi-stanza poem, nest the stanzas inside paragraph elements. Insert line breaks at the end of the individual verse lines.

4. In the academic paper document, add a fifth note number (following the other four note numbers). Do not worry about it being related to the text where you insert it; this is just for practice. Superscript the note number. Create a mock fifth footnote at the bottom of the page (following the other footnotes). Finally, turn the superscripted note number into a hypertext link (a jump link) that jumps to a destination anchor that marks the location of the corresponding footnote. Create a return link that jumps back from the end of the footnote to the corresponding note number in the document text.

5. In the CD-R FAQ document, create a mock question and answer section. Do not worry about it relating to CD-R; any question and answer will do. Format it exactly like the other question and answer sections. Finally, add a new option to the document menu (using the question as the link text) that jumps to your new question and answer section. Add a return link below the question and answer section that jumps back up to the document menu.

6. In the CD-R FAQ document, add a mock nested number list following any of the answer sections. Do not worry about the content; use dummy text if you wish. Just make sure that you create a numbered list that has at least three levels of nested lists (including a list nested in a list that is nested in a list, in other words). Use the OL element's TYPE attribute to assign a different number-type (or letter-type) to each level of nested list. Use any of these values: **I** (uppercase Roman), **i** (lowercase Roman), **A** (uppercase alphabetic), **a** (lowercase alphabetic), **1** (Arabic numerals).

7. Experiment further with using the BIG and SMALL elements. Do not worry about context or content. The point is to see what the BIG and SMALL element will do when applied in different circumstances. Try nesting up to four BIG elements to get even bigger text. Try nesting multiple instances of SMALL elements, just to see in your browser why you should not nest SMALL elements.

8. In either document, experiment with using the HR element's WIDTH, SIZE, ALIGN, and NOSHADE attributes. Try different combinations and then check them out in your browser.

9. In the CD-R FAQ document, experiment further with inserting non-keyboard characters. Look for any additional instances in the document where you think a copyright, registered, or trademark symbol might be appropriate, or write additional example text of your own. Use named entity codes referenced in the chapter to insert the copyright and registered symbols. Use the Unicode numerical entity code referenced in the chapter to insert the trademark symbol. Alternatively, insert a trademark symbol that can be viewed in all browsers, by using the somewhat inelegant solution mentioned in the chapter to insert a trademark symbol by super-scripting a parenthesized "tm" text string.

10. In either document, experiment with creating a nested bulleted list. Using dummy text, if you wish, create a nested bulleted list with at least three nested levels. A browser automatically displays different bullet characters for different nested bullet list levels, in this sequence, corresponding to the TYPE attributes that assign bullet-types: disc, circle, and square. Using these TYPE attribute values, assign bullet types to each nested bullet level that are different than the default sequence.

WEB-BASED LEARNING ACTIVITIES

In this book's text, Find It icons inserted in the margin highlight the Web addresses of additional resources you might find helpful or informative. To further extend your learning using the Web, you can:

- Go back and visit any of the Web addresses highlighted in this chapter that you have not yet visited. Look for additional resources and information that add to your understanding and knowledge of the material covered in this chapter. When you find a relevant page or site with information or resources you may want to access later, add it to your Favorites (in Internet Explorer) or your Bookmarks (in Netscape or Mozilla).

- Visit this book's Internet Resource Center at **www.emcp.com/** to find additional Web addresses of resources related to the material covered in this chapter that you can further investigate and explore.
- Further research a specific topic introduced in this chapter. For instance, do research on using DocType declarations or META elements within Web pages. Compile your research into a report that can be shared with your fellow students. You also can team up with other students to create a class presentation on a particular topic.

PROJECTS

These projects can be done in class, in a computer lab, or at home. Use the skills you have developed in this and the previous chapter to create any of the following projects.

Project 1. Format a paper or essay you have authored as an online document.

Take the lessons learned in this chapter and apply them to formatting a paper or essay that you have written so it can be displayed as an online document. Some guidelines for completing this assignment follow:

1. In your word processor, save your paper or essay under another name as a text file in this chapter's folder (chap02). For instance, you might save it as mypaper.html. (*Note: Do not save your paper or essay as an HTML file in your word processor—that is likely to generate a bunch of unnecessary and redundant HTML codes, sometimes referred to as spaghetti code.*)
2. Using the example online paper you created in this chapter, in your text editor, tag the text file you saved with the appropriate HTML elements, including the top-level HTML elements, a title element, heading elements, paragraph elements, bulleted or numbered list elements, block quote elements, and so on. No untagged text should be nested directly inside your BODY element. Optionally, also add a DocType declaration and META elements specifying your document's character set, a description of your page, and a list of keywords.
3. Scan your document's text for any special characters or symbols that have been carried over from your word processing document. Replace them with appropriate entity codes (see Appendix B) or type a substitute (replacing an *e* character with a grave accent, for instance, with a simple *e* character).
4. Look for instances in your original word processing document where you included italicized, bolded, or underlined text. Tag the same text in your text file using the I and B elements (or the EM and STRONG elements). Decide whether you want to carry over any underlined text—a better solution may be to simply format underlined text as italicized text.
5. Look for instances where you have included footnotes in your document. Use the SUP element to superscript footnote numbers and create hypertext links that jump to any footnotes listed at the bottom of your page.
6. Use the ADDRESS element to create an address block at the bottom of your page's BODY element. At minimum, type your name and an e-mail address. Sign up for a free Web-mail address that you can use here, if you do not want to expose your regular e-mail address to spammers.

Project 2. Create a Frequently Asked Questions page.

Using the FAQ page you worked with in this chapter as an example, create an FAQ page on a topic or subject about which you have some expertise. Create a list of questions and then write answers to them. Create a menu at the top of the page (listing only the questions) that uses hypertext links to jump to the corresponding question and answer sections. Insert loop-back links following each question and answer section that loop back to the menu. Add an address block to the bottom of your page.

Project 3. Write instruction steps for a computer or application procedure you are familiar with.

Create a Web page that features instruction steps that will give you an opportunity to use the TT, KBD, SAMP, CODE, and PRE elements in appropriate circumstances, as well as the I and B (or EM and STRONG) elements.

Project 4. Create a poetry page.

If you write poetry, create a Web page to show off your poems. Insert the poems inside block quote elements to indent them from the margin. Nest stanzas inside paragraph elements and insert BR elements to break the verse lines. Use any other elements or attributes you have learned to use.

CHAPTER

3

Working with Fonts, Colors, and Backgrounds

PERFORMANCE OBJECTIVES

In this chapter, you learn how to change the appearance of your Web page by using different fonts, colors, and backgrounds, including how to:

- Change the size and face of fonts for elements and text.
- Change the color of fonts, text, and links.
- Use background colors and images in Web pages.
- Set element backgrounds using styles.

In the first two chapters, you learned how to use basic and common features of HTML to create typical Web pages. In this chapter, you will learn how to change the appearance of your Web pages by changing font sizes and faces, applying color changes to fonts and links, and using background colors and images.

USING THE EXAMPLE FILES

If you have created a working folder for storing files you create, you will find the example files for this chapter located in the **chap03** folder within your working folder. You should save any HTML files you create in this chapter in that folder.

If you have created a working disk, you should copy the chap03 folder to your working disk from the **HTML_Examples** folder that you or your instructor downloaded from this book's Internet Resource Center (IRC), or from a CD-R disc or floppy disk provided by your instructor. If the working disc you used in previous chapters is getting full, create a new one. Ask your instructor for assistance if you do not know the location of the HTML_Examples folder or how to copy the chap03 folder. You should save any HTML file you create in this chapter in the chap03 folder that you have copied to your working disk.

CASE EXAMPLE: UPDATING THE APPEARANCE OF A PERSONAL WEB PAGE

In this example, you revise the personal Web page you created in Chapter 1, *Creating a Basic Web Page*, by using fonts, colors, and backgrounds to make it more attractive and visually appealing.

Johnny Watson made some changes to his personal Web page, adding a DocType statement, a META element declaring the character set his page uses, and two other META elements that provide a description and keyword list that search engines and directories can use to index or list his page. He also made a few other minor changes to the text in his page, but not to the HTML codes. His friends like the content and links he included in his page, but have commented that it might look better if he varied the size and face of his fonts and incorporated colors and backgrounds into his page's design. When Johnny Watson first created his personal Web page, he was still learning HTML and had not learned yet how to make font or color changes. He has since learned more about using these features and wants to apply them to update the appearance of his personal Web page.

To get started working with this example:

1. Run your text editor and open **watson2_ex.html** from the chap03 folder in your working folder or working disk.
2. Save watson2_ex.html as **watson2.html** in the chap03 folder.
3. Run your browser and open **watson2.html** from the chap03 folder.

If you need more guidance on opening and saving an HTML file in your text editor and opening and previewing it in your Web browser, see "Opening an HTML File in Your Text Editor" and "Saving and Previewing Your HTML File" in Chapter 2, *Working with Online Documents*.

CHANGING FONT SIZES

In HTML, the FONT element can be used to change the appearance of nested text, including the size, color, and face of the font in which text is displayed. In this section, you will focus on the first of these features, changing the size of the font used to display nested text. In the FONT element, the SIZE attribute is used to change the size of nested text.

Using Absolute Font Sizes

The FONT element's SIZE attribute enables you to specify seven different absolute font sizes, by using an integer value from 1 to 7. An absolute font size will not change, even if the default base font size is changed. For instance, the following sets an absolute font size of 5 for the nested text:

```
<font size="5">nested text</font>
```

Figure 3.1 shows the seven font sizes in relation to the default sizes of a level-one heading and paragraph text.

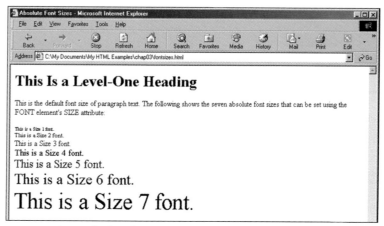

FIGURE 3.1 • *Seven absolute font sizes can be set in HTML.*

NOTE

The HTML file shown in Figure 3.1 is available with the example files for this chapter. To look for yourself, open **fontsizes.html** in your browser from the chap03 folder. After viewing it, click the Back button to return to watson2.html in your browser.

As shown in Figure 3.1, two of the font sizes (sizes 1 and 2) are smaller than the default size of paragraph text, one (size 3) is the same size, and four (sizes 4 through 7) are larger.

Johnny Watson discovered that by using the FONT element he can set a font size that is one size larger than the default font size of a level-one heading. He decided to take advantage of this to increase the size of the initial letters in each word of his level-one heading.

Use the FONT element's SIZE attribute to increase the initial letters in the level-one heading to size 7 (see Figure 3.2):

```
<h1><font size="7">S</font>ports, <font size="7">G</font>ardening,
and <font size="7">O</font>ther <font size="7">I</font>nterests</h1>
```

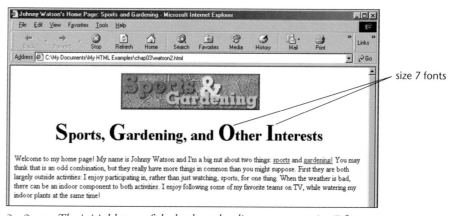

size 7 fonts

FIGURE 3.2 • *The initial letters of the level-one heading are set to a size 7 font.*

Johnny liked the result of increasing the size of the initial letters in his level-one heading so much, he decided to do the same with his level-two heading.

 Use the FONT element's SIZE attribute to increase the initial letters in the level-two heading to size 6 (see Figure 3.3):

```
<h2 align="center"><font size="6">B</font>iography, <font
size="6">I</font>nterests, and <font
size="6">F</font>riends</h2>
```

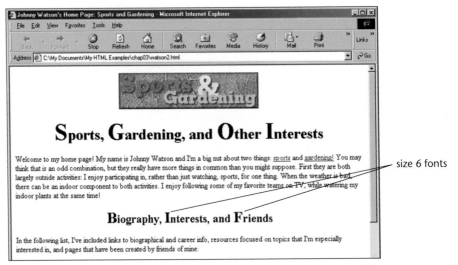

FIGURE 3.3 • *The initial letters of the level-two heading are set to a size 6 font.*

Using Relative Font Sizes

Alternatively, you can set font sizes relative to the default base font size. Relative font sizes are adjusted, up or down, if the default base font size is increased or decreased. A relative font size is indicated by a "+" or "-" character in front of the SIZE attribute integer value. For instance, the following increases the font size of text one size above the base font size:

```
<font size="+1">nested text</font>
```

Johnny wants to increase the font size of the two in-context hypertext links that are in his introductory paragraph. He has decided to try using relative font size changes to do this.

 Set relative font sizes that will increase the size of text nested inside of the two hypertext links in the introductory paragraph (see Figure 3.4):

```
<p>Welcome to my home page! My name is Johnny Watson and I'm a
big nut about two things: <a href="http://www.espn.com/"><font
size="+1">sports</font></a> and <a
href="http://www.bbc.co.uk/gardening/"><font
size="+1">gardening!</font></a>
```

FIGURE 3.4 • *A relative font size increases the size of text relative to the default base font size.*

In the previous chapter, you used the BIG and SMALL elements to increase and decrease the size of nested text. At first glance, a BIG element and a FONT element with a `size="+1"` attribute seem to do the same thing, but that is not true.

A BIG element increases the font size of nested text relative to the font size of the current element. A FONT element with a `size="+1"` attribute increases the size of nested text one size relative to the base font size.

action

Add the following text and codes to the example page (temporarily) to see this for yourself (see Figure 3.5):

```
<h1><font size="7">S</font>ports, <font
size="7">G</font>ardening, and <font size="7">O</font>ther <font
size="7">I</font>nterests</h1>
<h2>by <big>Johnny</big> <font size="+1">Watson</font></h2>
</center>
```

When you are finished viewing the example in your browser, delete the text and codes you just added.

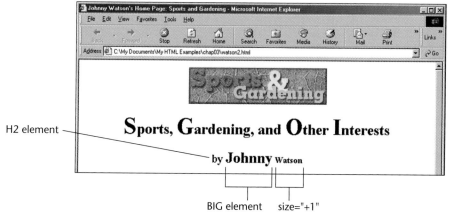

H2 element

BIG element   size="+1"

FIGURE 3.5 • *A relative font size increases the size of text relative to the base font size.*

As the callout for Figure 3.5 indicates, a BIG element changes the size of nested text relative to the font size of the element in which it is nested (the H2 element, in this case). A relative font size, on the other hand, changes the size of nested text relative to the size of the base font (the default size of the P or LI elements, for instance).

Changing the Base Font Size

The BASEFONT element is an empty element that changes the base font size for any following text. Among current major browsers, only Internet Explorer and Netscape support the BASEFONT element. The Mozilla and Opera browsers completely ignore it.

action

Test what changing the base font size looks like in your browser (if using Internet Explorer or Netscape):

1. Use the BASEFONT element to increase the size of the base font one size (see Figure 3.6):

```
<body>
<basefont size="4">
```

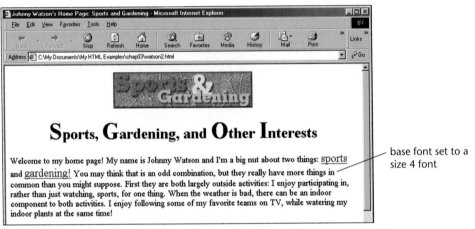

base font set to a size 4 font

FIGURE 3.6 • *The BASEFONT element is used to change the base font size in browsers that support it.*

2. After viewing the effect of the BASEFONT element on your page in your browser, delete the BASEFONT element you just set.

NOTE

Later in this chapter, in "Controlling Fonts, Colors, and Backgrounds Using Styles," you will learn how to use styles to change the font size of paragraph and other body text elements.

CHANGING THE FONT FACE

The FONT element's FACE attribute lets you specify a font face (or typeface) or a comma-delimited list of font faces to be used in displaying nested text.

Understanding Font Realities

You might see some neat font on the Web and think you would like to use that font in your Web page. You download and install it, reference it in your Web page, and it works! You publish your page to the Web and then ask all your friends to check out your page, adding as your final words, "Be sure to check out the snazzy font I'm using!" One by one, however, your friends report that all they can see is the same font that is displayed on almost every Web page (Times New Roman or Times).

The problem is that your friends, unlike yourself, have not downloaded and installed the font you are using, and thus do not have it available on their systems. For a font to be displayed in a Web page using the FONT element's FACE attribute, it must be available on a user's system. Just because a particular font is available on your system does not mean that others will have the same font available on their systems, and no one font is guaranteed to be available on all systems. When specifying fonts for display in your Web page, you need to stick with specifying the most commonly available fonts, avoiding less commonly available fonts you may have installed on your system or can download from the Web. See "Specifying a Font List" a little later in this chapter for a rundown on some of the more commonly available fonts.

Specifying a Single Font Face

To specify that a particular font face, if available, should be used to display an element, you specify the name of the font as the value for the FACE attribute.

To add some visual variety to his page, Johnny Watson wants to change the look of his heading-level elements by displaying them using a sans serif font. He has decided to use the Arial font because it is one of the more common sans serif fonts. He understands that the Arial font may not be available on every system, but is willing to have a serif font displayed instead on systems that do not have the Arial font because that does not cause any accessibility problems.

He has also removed the font size changes he added earlier to his level-one and level-two headings to get a cleaner, less busy look.

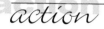

Use the FONT element to specify that the level-one and level-two heading elements should be displayed in an Arial font, if available:

1. Delete the font size changes that you added earlier and set a single FONT element that sets an Arial font for the H1 element.

```
<h1><font face="Arial">Sports, Gardening, and Other
Interests</font></h1>
```

2. Do the same for the H2 element (see Figure 3.7):

```
<h2 align="center"><font face="Arial">Biography, Interests, and
Friends</font></h2>
```

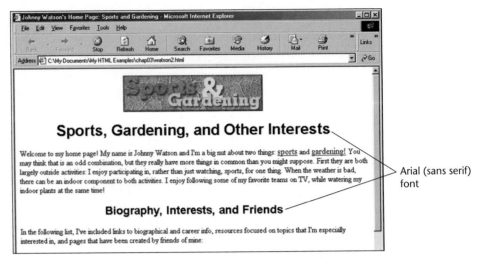

FIGURE 3.7 • *Using a sans serif font for headings can add visual variety to a page.*

The FONT element is an inline element and thus should always be nested inside of a block element and should not have block elements nested inside of it. For instance, you should *not* apply a font face change to the H2 element like this:

```
<font face="Arial"><h2>Biography, Interests, and
Friends</h2></font>
```

Specifying a Font List

The problem with only specifying a single font face is that there are many systems that may not have that font installed. The Arial font is a TrueType font that should be present on every Windows system, but many Macintosh and UNIX users might not have that font. To get around that problem, HTML enables you to specify a comma-delimited list of fonts. The second listed font can be displayed if the first font is not available, the third listed font if the second font is not available, and so on.

Johnny Watson wants to specify a list of fonts, rather than just a single font, to increase the chances that one of the listed fonts will be available on a user's system.

Specify a list of fonts to be used to display the level-one and level-two headings:

1. Specify a list of fonts for the H1 element:

```
<h1><font face="Arial, Geneva, Helvetica">Sports, Gardening, and
Other Interests</font></h1>
```

2. Make the same change for the H2 element.

Because some Macintosh and UNIX systems only have PostScript fonts available, it is a good idea to include a PostScript font in a font list.

The Geneva font is a sans serif TrueType font often available on Macintosh systems, whereas the Helvetica font is an Adobe PostScript font that should be available on most Macintosh and UNIX systems.

TROUBLE *spot*

Some browsers treat font-face names as case-sensitive. When specifying font-face names, you should type them using any initial uppercase characters that are included in the font-face name. For instance, you should type **Arial** and not **arial** as the FACE attribute value.

Current Windows browsers ignore most PostScript fonts in a font list. Internet Explorer 6 and the Opera browser display Courier, a PostScript font, but completely ignore Helvetica, as well as any other PostScript fonts, displaying the default text font (usually a serif font) instead. Netscape 4 and 6, as well as the Mozilla browser, substitute Arial for Helvetica and Courier New for Courier, but ignore any other PostScript fonts.

Microsoft provides a selection of Web core fonts that Windows, Macintosh, and UNIX/Linux users can download and install if they are not already available on their systems. You can download any these fonts from **www.microsoft.com/typography/fontpack/default.htm**. Fonts included are Andale Mono, Arial, Arial Black, Comic Sans MS, Courier New, Georgia, Impact, Times New Roman, TrebuchetMS, Verdana, and Webdings (Windows only). UNIX/Linux users can download the Windows versions of these fonts (which are available as self-extracting archives). For additional links to font resources on the Web, see this chapter's section at this book's IRC at **www.emcp.com/**.

Table 3.1 shows the names of some of the most commonly available fonts for Windows, the Macintosh, or UNIX/Linux systems.

TABLE 3.1 • *Fonts Commonly Available on Different Systems*

System	Should Be Available	May Be Available
Windows	Arial, Courier New, and Times New Roman	Andale Mono, Arial Black, Century Gothic, Comic Sans MS, Georgia, Impact, Marlett, Monotype.com, Tahoma, Trebuchet MS, and Verdana
Macintosh	Times, Helvetica, Courier, and Palatino (PostScript fonts)	Arial, Arial Black, Charcoal, Chicago, Comic Sans MS, Courier New, Espy Sans, Gadget, Geneva, Georgia, Impact, Minion Web, Monaco, New York, Sand, Techno, Textile, Times New Roman, Trebuchet MS, and Verdana (TrueType fonts)
UNIX/Linux	Times, Helvetica, Courier, and Palatino (PostScript fonts)	Charter, Charter BT, Lucida, LucidaTypewriter, New Century Schoolbook, and Utopia (UNIX/Linux user can also download and install Microsoft's Web core fonts)

You cannot rely on any one font being available on all systems. Any font face you specify using the FONT element's FACE attribute is a suggestion only that may or may not be displayed on someone else's system. To maximize the chance that a particular font will be available on a user's system, you should stick to specifying Arial and Helvetica sans serif fonts, Times New Roman and Times serif fonts, and Courier New and Courier mono-spaced fonts.

You should also realize when using uncommon fonts that different fonts can have the same name. Thus, the Carumba font installed on your system might be an entirely different font than the Carumba font installed on someone else's system. This is another good reason to stick to using only commonly available fonts in your Web pages.

Different fonts of the same size can have different *x-heights*. The x-height is the height of the lowercase letters in a font (the height of the lowercase "x"). A font with a larger x-height will take up more horizontal space on a line than another font of the same size, but with a smaller x-height. Figure 3.8 shows a series of different fonts specified for the H2 element. (To check this out for yourself, open **fontfaces.html** in your browser from the chap03 folder.) Notice that the amount of horizontal space occupied by these fonts varies, even though they are the same size and contain the same text. When specifying a list of fonts, be aware that, while your preferred font (Arial, for instance) may not cause an H1 heading to wrap, another font in your font list with a larger x-height (Verdana, for instance) may cause the heading to wrap to a second line.

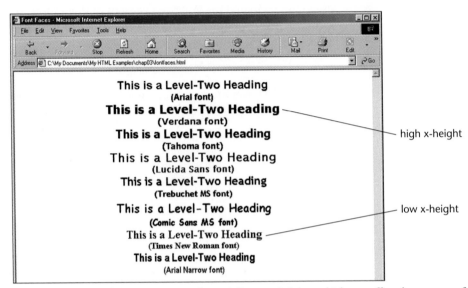

FIGURE 3.8 • *Fonts of the same size can have different x-heights, which can affect the amount of horizontal space the fonts take up.*

Specifying a Generic Font-Family Name

The Cascading Style Sheets specification includes a list of generic font-family names that can be used to refer to generic classes of fonts. These font-family names are serif, sans-serif, monospace, cursive, and fantasy. Current browsers also support these generic font-family names when using the FONT element's FACE attribute, although earlier browsers generally do not support them. Because generic font-family names used with the FACE attribute might not be supported by earlier browsers and are not part of the HTML 4.01 specification, you should include a generic font-family name only at the end of a font list as a stop-gap in case none of your listed fonts are available on a user's system.

Johnny Watson discovered that most current browsers also support using a generic font-family name in a list of font names for the FACE attribute. He has decided to include the sans-serif generic font-family name in his font list to increase the chances that a browser will display a sans serif, rather than a serif font.

Include a generic font-family name at the end of the document's font lists to increase the chances of a sans serif font being displayed on a user's system:

1. Add a generic font-family name, sans-serif, to the end of the font list for the H1 element:

```
<h1><font face="Arial, Geneva, Helvetica, sans-serif">Sports,
Gardening, and Other Interests</font></h1>
```

2. Make the same change for the H2 element.

Of the generic font-family names, only the serif, sans-serif, and monospace names are consistently supported by browsers. Browsers that support using these names generally display a Times New Roman or Times font when a serif generic font-family name is specified, Arial or Helvetica when a sans-serif generic font-family name is specified, and Courier New or Courier when a monospace generic font-family name is specified. The other generic font-family names are inconsistently supported by browsers and should be avoided.

Using Sans Serif and Serif Fonts

Most browsers use a serif font for displaying text, generally some variant of Times or Times New Roman. The Times font is so named because it was first used to print columnar text in the London Times newspaper. A serif font, such as is used in this book's paragraph text, has strokes (serifs) that accentuate the ends of the letterforms, whereas a sans serif font, such as is used in this book's headings, lacks any accentuating strokes. Serifs make larger amounts of text displayed in a smaller-sized font, such as paragraph text, for instance, easier to read and scan because the serifs guide your eyes along as you read. For that reason, books and newspapers generally use a serif font for body text that needs to be read for content, and a sans serif font only in headings and display type.

Designers, on the other hand, often use sans serif fonts in advertising copy, especially where the text also serves as a design element, but also to create a contrast with serif fonts used in a magazine's text columns. Some magazines have gone to printing body text in a sans serif font, to give their pages a look they consider more modern and stylish; when that is done, however, the space between the text lines, called the leading, is usually also increased to help make the sans serif body text easier to read.

Web page designers also sometimes opt for using sans serif fonts for body text (paragraph text), for much the same reasons print designers do, because it gives their pages more of a "designed" (and less "bookish") look. This is fine in a shorter page, such as Johnny Watson's personal page, which contains less than two screens worth of text, but if you are presenting larger amounts of text that need to be read for comprehension, a serif font is probably the better choice. Crystal Porter, for instance, would not want to present her online academic paper in a sans serif font, not simply because that is what is expected, but also because it would make her text more difficult to read and comprehend.

action Compare reading the text of the *Declaration of Independence* in a serif and a sans serif font:

1. Open **textcompare.html** in your browser from the chap03 folder (see Figure 3.9).

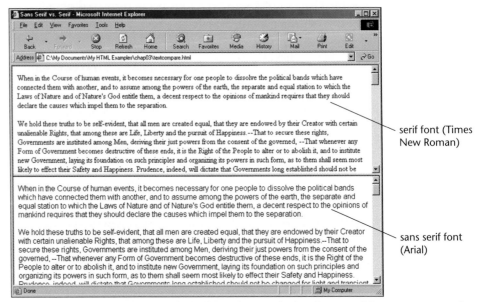

FIGURE 3.9 • *According to one school of thought, text displayed in a serif font is easier to read and comprehend than text displayed in a sans serif font.*

2. The two versions are displayed in separate frames. Read the text in each frame. You can grab the divider line between the two frames with the mouse pointer and pull it up or down to display more text in either frame.

3. Understanding that you are making an entirely subjective and unscientific judgment, make a note in your book next to Figure 3.9 indicating which of the two fonts you feel is the most readable.

NOTE

To find out more about readability and comprehension issues related to using serif and sans serif fonts, you can read Wendy Priestly's article, "Instructional typographies using desktop publishing techniques to produce effective learning and training materials," available online at **cleo.murdoch.edu.au/gen/aset/ajet/ajet7/su91p153.html**. See the section for this chapter at this book's IRC at **www.emcp.com/** for additional links to resources on typography and the Web.

WORKING WITH COLORS

The FONT element's COLOR attribute is used to specify a foreground color to be displayed for nested text. Font colors can be assigned by using either color names or hexadecimal color codes.

Using Color Names

These are the 16 standard color names that can be used as values for the FONT element's COLOR attribute: white, black, gray, silver, white, maroon, red, fuchsia, green, lime, olive, yellow, navy, blue, teal, and aqua. These color names are derived from the 16 colors available on a 16-color VGA display.

Johnny Watson's friends told him that, other than his banner graphic, his page is a drab affair that could stand to be touched up with a little color. Johnny learned that he can use the FONT element's COLOR attribute to specify any of 16 standard color names.

action

Use the FONT element's COLOR attribute to assign foreground colors to the text nested inside the H1 and H2 elements:

1. Specify that text nested inside the H1 element should be displayed in a blue color:

```
<h1><font color="blue" face="Arial, Geneva, Helvetica, sans-
serif">Sports, Gardening, and Other Interests</font></h1>
```

2. Specify that text nested inside the H2 element should be displayed in a red color:

```
<h2 align="center"><font color="red" face="Arial, Geneva,
Helvetica, sans-serif">Biography, Interests, and
Friends</font></h2>
```

As shown in Figure 3.10, the text nested inside the H1 element is now displayed in a blue color and the text nested inside the H2 element is now displayed in a red color.

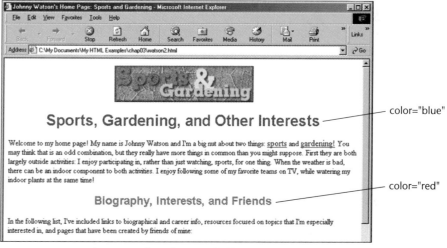

FIGURE 3.10 • *A Web page need not be a purely black-and-white affair.*

An example file, colornames.html, is included in the chap02 folder with the other example files for this chapter. You can open and view **colornames.html** in your browser, as shown in Figure 3.11.

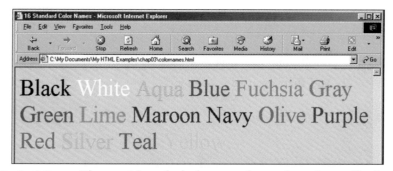

FIGURE 3.11 • *There are 16 standard color names that can be used to specify colors in Web pages.*

Most current browsers actually support many more than the standard 16 color names specified in the HTML 4 specifications. There are 140 color names that date back to the beginnings of the Web—they were part of the X-Windows system under UNIX. Many current browsers still recognize these same color names. The main problem with using these color names, however, is that the same color name may correspond to different colors on different systems. You will also likely get an error message if you try to validate your page's HTML if it contains any of these non-standard color names. Also, not all current browsers support all of these color names, which means that you could end up displaying a foreground color that is supported against a background color that is not supported, for instance.

You do not need to use non-standard color names, however, to make use of a much wider selection of colors in your Web pages. Any of the non-standard color names can also be specified using a hexadecimal RGB code, which all browsers that recognize colors support.

Using Hexadecimal RGB Codes

The 16 color names are admittedly somewhat limiting. You might have noticed that there is no "orange" color name, even though there are "green" and "purple" color names. That is because the original 16-color VGA display did not include an orange color, but derived it from combining two different colors (red and yellow). To display a different color than those specified by the standard 16 color names, you can use a *hexadecimal RGB code*. A hexadecimal RGB code states the RGB (red-green-blue) values for a color in hexadecimal numbers, in the following format:

```
color="#rrggbb"
```

The hash character (#) indicates that the following six characters correspond to three hexadecimal color values (*rr*, *gg*, and *bb*) that together represent a specific RGB color value.

The U.K. keyboard for the Macintosh does not have the "#" (hash) character at the Shift+3 position, but has the "£" (British pound) symbol instead. To insert the "#" character using a U.K. keyboard, just press Option+3 (or Alt+3).

The hexadecimal numbering system uses a 16-number base (0, 1, 2, 3, 4, 5, 6, 7, 8, 9, A, B, C, D, E, and F), as opposed to the 10-number base that forms the decimal numbering system. Programmers tend to prefer using hexadecimal numbers because up to 256 numerical values can be stated using only 2 characters, while using a decimal numbering system 3 digits are required. Table 3.2 shows the 16 hexadecimal numbers and their decimal equivalents.

TABLE 3.2 • *The 16 Hexadecimal Base Numbers and Their Decimal Equivalents*

Hex = Dec	Hex = Dec	Hex = Dec	Hex = Dec
0 = 0	4 = 4	8 = 8	C = 12
1 = 1	5 = 5	9 = 9	D = 13
2 = 2	6 = 6	A = 10	E = 14
3 = 3	7 = 7	B = 11	F = 15

To derive the decimal value of a hexadecimal number, just apply the following formula:

$$(h^1 \times 16) + h^2 = d$$

The variable h^1 corresponds to the decimal value of the first hexadecimal digit, h^2 corresponds to the decimal value of the second hexadecimal digit (as shown previously in Table 3.2), and d equals the number's decimal value. In other words, the decimal value of AD (where the hexadecimal numbers A and D are equal to decimal values of 10 and 13, respectively) can be calculated in this fashion:

$$(10 \times 16) + 13 = 173$$

By using hexadecimal RGB codes, you can set 256 different values for each RGB color component, meaning that a total of 16,777,216 (16.7 million) separate colors ($256 \times 256 \times 256$) can be set using hexadecimal RGB codes.

tip

A number of sites on the Web list the hexadecimal codes for the non-standard color names supported by most current browsers. Although you should not use the color names, you can use them to identify a particular color that you like, and then use its listed hexadecimal code to apply it to your Web page. Thus, instead of using the non-standard DarkGoldenRod color name to specify a gold-like color, just use its hexadecimal equivalent (#b8860b). There are many sites on the Web that provide color charts that show the non-standard color names along with their corresponding hexadecimal RGB codes. See this chapter's section at this book's IRC at **www.emcp.com/** for a selection of links to where you can find color charts, color pickers, and other color resources.

Use hexadecimal RGB codes to change the colors of the level-one and level-two heading elements:

1. Use the hexadecimal RGB code, **#b8860b**, to change the color of the level-one heading to a color corresponding to the non-standard "DarkGoldenRod" color:

```
<h1><font color="#b8860b" face="Arial, Geneva, Helvetica, sans-serif">Sports, Gardening, and Other Interests</font></h1>
```

2. Use the hexadecimal RGB code, **#2e8b57**, to change the color of the level-two heading to a color corresponding to the non-standard "SeaGreen" color (see Figure 3.12):

```
<h2 align="center"><font color="#2e8b57" face="Arial, Geneva, Helvetica, sans-serif">Biography, Interests, and Friends</font></h2>
```

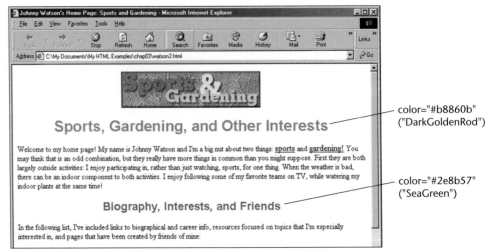

color="#b8860b"
("DarkGoldenRod")

color="#2e8b57"
("SeaGreen")

FIGURE 3.12 • *Use hexadecimal color codes to set colors other than those specified by the 16 standard color names.*

A common mistake when setting colors using hexadecimal RGB codes is to omit the # character at the start of the code. Internet Explorer actually lets you get away with doing this, but most other browsers will not display your color if the # character is missing.

Using Web-Safe Colors

Not everyone is surfing the Web on a system that can display colors from a palette of 16.7 million colors (also known as a True Color palette). Some users are still using graphic cards or monitors that limit them to 256 or fewer colors. For these users, if a specified color is not available on their system, their system uses *dithering* to approximate the color. Dithering is the adjustment of the colors in adjacent pixels so that they appear to the eye to be a single color. When successful, dithering realistically reproduces a color that is not otherwise available; when unsuccessful, it produces a noticeably splotchy or speckled color that may only remotely resemble the desired color.

An option for dealing with such users is to use only colors from *the Web-safe palette*. The Web-safe palette is also sometimes called the Netscape palette, because Netscape originally introduced it. The Web-safe palette has 216 colors that are guaranteed to be displayable on virtually all computer systems without having to be dithered. The Web-safe palette is composed entirely of colors with hexadecimal RGB codes that include only these hexadecimal numbers: 00, 33, 66, 99, CC, and FF. For instance, the hexadecimal RGB code of #996600 produces a color that is somewhat darker than the "DarkGoldenRod" color used previously, but which still produces a recognizably "gold" color.

action

Use the #996600 hexadecimal code to apply a Web-safe "gold" color to the H1 element (see Figure 3.13):

```
<h1><font color="#996600" face="Arial, Geneva, Helvetica, sans-
serif">Sports, Gardening, and Other Interests</font></h1>
```

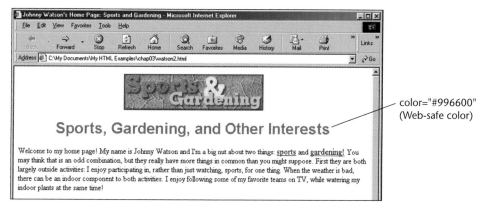

color="#996600"
(Web-safe color)

FIGURE 3.13 • *A Web-safe RGB color, including only the 00, 33, 66, 99, CC, or FF hexadecimal numerical values, will not be dithered on a 256-color system.*

practice

Appendix C, *Web-Safe Colors Chart*, shows all the Web-safe colors along with the hexadecimal RGB codes you need to use to apply them to your Web pages. Using the chart, choose a Web-safe color and apply it to your document's H2 element. Be sure to check out the result in your browser. If you do not like how your first choice looks, try another one. Experiment with setting different Web-safe colors for your H1 element as well. Repeat until you are satisfied with your choices of Web-safe colors for the H2 and H1 elements.

You can also find an HTML file, **colorchart.html**, included with the example files for this chapter in the chap03 folder that you can open in your browser. It shows all of the Web-safe colors along with their corresponding hexadecimal RGB codes.

Setting Text, Link, and Background Colors

The BODY element's TEXT, LINK, VLINK, ALINK, and BGCOLOR attributes enable you to set colors for your page's text, unvisited links, visited links, activated links, and the background. Unvisited and visited links connect to sites you have not visited and sites you have already visited. An activated link's color is displayed when the mouse is held down on a link.

action

Use a combination of color names and hexadecimal RGB codes to set colors for text, links, and the page background (see Figure 3.14):

```
<body text="navy" link="#ff6600" vlink="#996699" alink="blue"
bgcolor="#ffffcc">
```

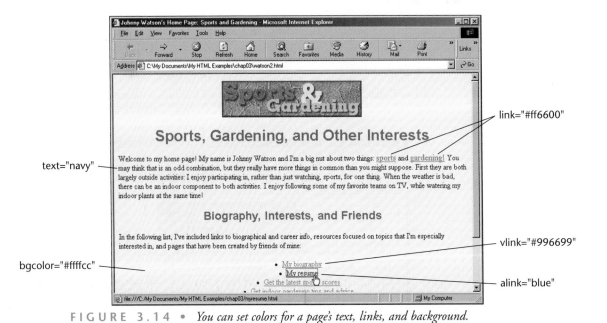

FIGURE 3.14 • *You can set colors for a page's text, links, and background.*

Whenever you set a foreground color for your page's text, you should also set a background color as well, if only a white color. That is because browsers let users also set foreground and background colors in their browser preferences. If you only set the foreground color, your foreground color could clash or lack contrast with a user's background color. You could even end up with navy blue text displayed against a navy blue background.

Although most browsers default to a white background color when they are installed, that is not universally the case. The Mosaic browser, for instance, defaults to a gray background color, as does Netscape Navigator 4 for the Macintosh. If you want to insure that your page's background is displayed as white, you should insert a **bgcolor="white"** attribute in the BODY element.

You also should be mindful when setting foreground and background colors that some people have color-vision deficiencies that make it difficult to distinguish between certain color combinations. About ten percent of males have some form of color-vision deficiency. Some people see red text as yellow text, for instance, while others may have trouble distinguishing between red and green. Others may see blue text as yellow text.

Make sure that you have sufficient tonal contrast between foreground and background colors in your pages in order to assist people with color-vision deficiencies. Do not rely simply on a color contrast, especially between red and green, to distinguish foreground and background colors. Visit this chapter's section at this book's IRC at **www.emcp.com/** for links to resources where you can learn more about color blindness and other accessibility issues related to the use of color in Web sites.

USING A BACKGROUND IMAGE

The BODY element's BACKGROUND attribute lets you assign a background image to your page. Using a background image can add to the visual appeal of your page; however, it also can make your page more difficult to access and read, if the image is busy or high contrast, or if its colors clash or do not provide sufficient contrast with your page's foreground and link colors. An example background image, **back_light.jpg**, is included with this chapter's example files.

Displaying a Background Image

The BODY element's BACKGROUND attribute is used to display a background image in a Web page. Its value is a URL or file name of an image, which can be any of the same kinds of image formats that are normally used for displaying inline images, including JPEG (.jpg), GIF (.gif), and PNG (.png) images. A background image is normally a smaller image, often less than 100 pixels wide or high, which is then tiled to fill a browser's background.

Use the BODY element's BACKGROUND attribute to assign a background image to your page (see Figure 3.15):

```
<body text="navy" link="#ff6600" vlink="#996699" alink="blue"
bgcolor="#ffffcc" background="back_light.jpg">
```

background=
"back_light.jpg"

FIGURE 3.15 • *A carefully chosen background image can further enhance the appearance of a Web page.*

Notice that both a background color and a background image are specified for the BODY element. That is because some users surf the Web with the display of graphics turned off to speed up access to Web pages over a slow connection. By specifying a background color that is close in color to your background image, you can insure that such users will still see your intended foreground-background color combination. This is especially important when displaying light text against a dark background image, which could end up displaying light text against a white background if the background image is not displayed.

Creating Your Own Background Images

Some image editors, such as Jasc Software's Paint Shop Pro and Ulead PhotoImpact, include features that allow you to create your own seamless background images. In Paint Shop Pro, for instance, select the area you want to convert to a seamless pattern, select Selections, and then select Convert to Seamless Pattern.

Even if your image editor does not support creating background images, you can still create your own seamless background image from scratch, if you like. Select or crop an image that you want to use. For instance, you might want to select and crop a section of cloudy sky from a photograph of a sunset. To turn the cropped image into a seamless background:

1. Select or create an image (Image A) that you want to use and size it to 50×50 pixels. Open a second image (Image B) that is sized at 100×100 pixels. Copy and paste Image A into the upper-left corner of Image B.

2. Flip Image A horizontally, so that what was on the left is now on the right, and vice versa. Copy and paste this image into the upper-right corner of Image B.

3. Using the mirrored image you created in step 2, flip Image A vertically, so that what was the top is now the bottom, and vice versa. Copy and paste this image into the lower-right corner of Image B.

4. Using the mirrored image you created in step 3, flip Image A horizontally, so that what was on the left is now on the right, and vice versa. Copy and paste this image into the lower-left corner of Image B (see Figure 3.16.)

5. Optionally, resize Image B to a smaller size (75×75 pixels, for instance) and then save it as a JPEG image (as myback.jpg, for instance).

The result is that myback.jpg matches up on all four sides, creating a seamless background tile (see Figure 3.17.)

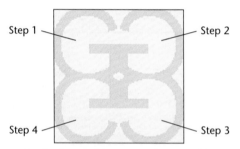

FIGURE 3.16 • *A seamless background image can be created by mirroring an image horizontally and vertically.*

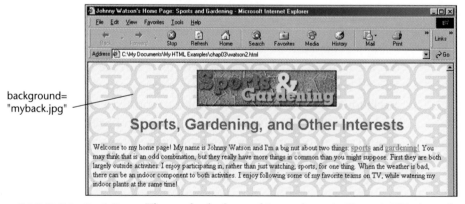

FIGURE 3.17 • *The seamless background image shown in Figure 3.16 is shown here displayed in a Web page.*

CONTROLLING FONTS, COLORS, AND BACKGROUNDS USING STYLES

The FONT and BASEFONT elements, as well as the BODY element's TEXT, LINK, VLINK, ALINK, BGCOLOR, and BACKGROUND attributes, have been depreciated in HTML 4.01 and XHTML 1.0 in favor of using Cascading Style Sheets (CSS) to achieve similar or better results. The primary reason for this is to provide for improved accessibility by separating appearance and presentation from structure and content. Deprecated elements and attributes are entirely legal, as long as you declare your document to conform to the transitional or frameset definitions of HTML 4.01 or XHTML 1.0.

The W3C, however, in the HTML 4 and 4.01 specification, advises the following: "In general, authors should use style sheets to achieve stylistic and formatting effects rather than HTML presentational attributes." All current browsers provide sufficient support for CSS to enable the design of colorful and attractive Web pages without the use of deprecated elements and attributes.

Government agencies, educational institutions, non-profit organizations, or larger companies may also decide on their own to require the use of styles in place of deprecated elements and attributes, in order to help ensure that documents they publish on the Web are accessible to all and compliant, not only with the letter, but also with the spirit of the Americans with Disabilities Act (ADA). Many of these agencies, organizations, and companies have subscribed to the W3C's Web Accessibility Initiative (WAI), which mandates the use of styles in place of deprecated elements and attributes in Web pages. Screen readers, for instance, used by individuals with visual impairments, can easily ignore any CSS styling added to a page while conveying the page's structure and content as indicated by its HTML coding. Separating appearance from content is a much more difficult task, however, if HTML elements and attributes are also being used to determine a page's visual presentation and appearance.

The main difficulty in implementing CSS in Web pages is not with early browsers that do not support CSS (such as Internet Explorer 2 or Netscape 3), in that they completely ignore any CSS styles included in a page, but with more recent browsers that support CSS, but do it badly (such as Internet Explorer 3 or Netscape 4). Many Web designers choose to continue to use deprecated elements and attributes, rather than implement styles, because of the backward-compatibility issues that the use of styles pose.

For these reasons, anyone contemplating a career in Web design should be proficient in the use of both deprecated elements and attributes (for creating documents that maximize backward-compatibility) and in the use of CSS styles (for creating documents that maximize accessibility).

The purpose of this section is not to teach you everything you need to know about using styles, but to provide you with examples of and some hands-on experience with using styles in place of deprecated elements and attributes to control fonts, colors, and backgrounds. It also directs you to some solutions for dealing with earlier browsers with poor support for CSS.

Save your current file so you can reference it later and then resave it under another file name for doing this section's examples:

1. In your text editor, first save **watson2.html** (File, Save) to keep any changes you have made to that file.
2. Resave watson2.html as **watson3.html** in the chap03 folder.
3. Open **watson3.html** in your browser from the chap03 folder.

Later, you can refer to your finished version of watson2.html to refresh your understanding of using the FONT element to set font changes and your finished version of watson3.html to refresh your understanding of using styles to set font changes.

Understanding Why the FONT and BASEFONT Elements Are Deprecated

The FONT and BASEFONT elements, along with the BODY element's TEXT, LINK, VLINK, ALINK, BGCOLOR, and BACKGROUND attributes, were originally introduced as unofficial extensions to HTML by Netscape, later adopted by other browsers, and finally officially included in HTML 3.2. These elements were introduced in response to a demand for HTML features that provided Web designers with more control over the visual appearance of Web pages than was possible in HTML 2, the standard version of HTML at the time. Little thought was taken at the time, however, over how these and other presentational HTML elements might impact the accessibility of HTML documents for individuals with visual disabilities. For instance, size and color changes made using the FONT and BASEFONT elements can prevent users with visual disabilities from setting their own font size and color preferences, making pages less accessible, or even inaccessible, to such users. A user with visual acuity problems, for instance, might need to set white as the text color and black as the background color in order to gain sufficient contrast to read the text, but be foreclosed from doing so because a Web author has chosen instead to specify font colors for text and other elements using the FONT element or BODY element attributes that control the color of text, links, and the page background. Another user with poor eyesight might need to increase the size of the default font size in order to read a page's text, but be foreclosed from doing so by a Web designer using the FONT and BASEFONT elements to dictate at which size text and other elements in a page must be displayed. The result is that the Web author might be pleased with the visual appearance of the page, but at the cost of denying individuals with visual impairments the ability to access the page's content.

NOTE This section provides a brief explanation of using styles to set font characteristics within an HTML document, but does not provide any extended discussion of the syntax and rules that govern the use of CSS. To learn more about the use of CSS in broader and different contexts than are presented in this section, see the W3C's CSS site at **www.w3.org/Style/CSS/**. Also, see this book's IRC at **www.emcp.com/** for additional resources on using styles in your HTML documents.

Changing Font Sizes Using Styles

You can use a style to change the size of the font used to display any element. This can be done using either an inline style or a style sheet. Font sizes set using styles are generally set using pixels or ems.

SETTING FONT SIZES USING PIXELS The term *pixel* is short for *picture element*. A computer's graphical display is composed entirely of pixels, with the total number of pixels determined by the resolution of the display. Common screen resolutions include 640 × 480 pixels, 800 × 600 pixels, 1024 × 768 pixels, 1152 × 864 pixels, and 1280 × 1024 pixels. Generally, the larger the monitor, the higher the screen resolution it will support. The screen grabs for most of the figures in this book were captured at a screen resolution of 800 × 600 pixels. Instead of using the BASEFONT element (which is not supported by all current browsers) to set the base font size, you can use an inline style set in the BODY element to set its font size to 18 pixels.

 Set the font size of the BODY element to 18 pixels:

1. Delete the BODY element attributes you set earlier:

```
<body text="navy" link="#ff6600" vlink="#006699" alink="blue"
bgcolor="#ffffcc" background="back_light.jpg">
```

2. Set an inline style, using the STYLE attribute, in the BODY element that sets its font size to 18 pixels (see Figure 3.18):

```
<body style="font-size: 18px">
```

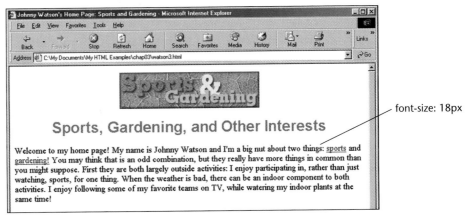

FIGURE 3.18 • *The size of body text is set to 18 pixels.*

Alternatively, you can also use a style sheet to set style properties for the BODY or other elements:

```
<style type="text/css">
body { font-size: 18px; }
</style>
</head>
```

In most browsers, the result of using a style to set the font size of the BODY element to 18 pixels should look the same as setting a size 4 font using the BASEFONT element because a size 4 font usually has a size of 18 pixels (although nothing in the HTML specifications dictates that a size 4 font must have a size of 18 pixels). This assumes, however, that a user has not increased the size of the browser's text font to make it more visible, which also would increase the size of a size 4 font.

TROUBLE *spot*

A major problem with using pixel measurements to set font sizes for the BODY element or other body text elements (P, LI, BLOCKQUOTE, ADDRESS, and so on) is that users are no longer able to adjust their own default font size in their browser preferences or user style sheets. A person with a visual handicap might increase the default font size of text to 32 pixels, for instance, to make it more readable. For such a user, a font size of 18 pixels would actually reduce, rather than increase, the size of their text font, rendering it less readable or even possibly unreadable. Setting font sizes using the FONT or BASEFONT elements causes the same problem because it locks in a specific font size in pixels.

A better solution that insures that your Web pages are accessible to everyone is to use em measurements to set font sizes for the body text elements (but not for the BODY element). Em measurements scale relative to any font size preferences a user might set. Using em measurements is covered in the next section, "Setting Font Sizes Using Ems."

The best solution of all, however, might be to simply leave the font size of the BODY element and other body text elements (P, BLOCKQUOTE, LI, and so on) unchanged, allowing users to determine the right font size they need to be using.

SETTING FONT SIZES USING EMS Setting font sizes using ems allows your font sizes to scale relative to user preferences. In CSS, nested elements are related to each other as a parent to a child. A *parent element* is an element that brackets another element, whereas a *child element* is an element that is nested inside another element. A child element can inherit style properties that are set for its parent element.

A font size of one em for an element is one times the size of (or the same size as) that element's parent element. For instance, if a font size of 1.1 ems is set for the P element, that is 1.1 times the size of the BODY element's font size (where the BODY element is the parent of the P element).

Setting a font size for the BODY element using a style is generally frowned upon because users in some browsers, such as Internet Explorer 6 for Windows, can set their own font size for the BODY element using a user-defined style sheet. If an author also sets the font size of the BODY element, that can conflict with the user's preferred body text size. If you want to increase the size of body text elements (P, BLOCKQUOTE, LI, ADDRESS, and so on), you should set sizes for those elements, rather than for the BODY element.

Delete the inline style you set in the BODY element and add a style sheet that sets the font size of the P, LI, and ADDRESS elements to 1.1 ems (see Figure 3.19):

```
<style type="text/css">
p, li, address { font-size: 1.1em; }
</style>
</head>
<body style="font-size: 18px">
```

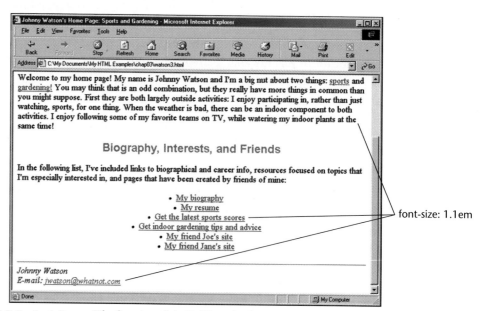

FIGURE 3.19 • *The font size of the P, LI, and ADDRESS elements is set to 1.1 ems.*

TROUBLE *spot* — A common error when typing styles within a style sheet is to type regular parentheses, "(" and ")", rather than squiggly brackets, "{" and "}".

An example style sheet file, **bigfont.css**, is included with this chapter's example files. If you are using Internet Explorer 6 for Windows, you can specify it as a user-defined style sheet to see what happens when a user employs a user-defined style sheet to increase their browser's default font size.

action

Internet Explorer 6 for Windows Only. Specify a user-defined style sheet that increases the browser's base font size to 32 pixels:

1. Select Tools, Internet Options, and click the Accessibility button (in the lower-right corner of the dialog box).
2. Check the Format documents using my style sheet check box, and then click the Browse button.
3. Open your working folder or working disk, and then open this chapter's folder (**chap03**). Double-click **bigfont.css** to open it.
4. Click OK twice to return to the document window. As shown in Figure 3.20, notice that the page's BODY text is now 1.1 times the size of the user-defined font size of 32 pixels, or 35 pixels. Also notice that the two links ("sports" and "gardening"), which have relative font sizes set using the FONT element's SIZE attribute, have not scaled in relation to the user-defined font size preference.

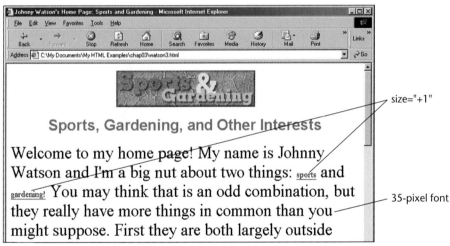

FIGURE 3.20 • *The BODY text is set to a size of 1.1 times a 32-pixel base font size set in a user-defined style sheet.*

5. For the time being, leave bigfont.css selected as a user-defined style sheet in Internet Explorer 6 (you will turn it off in the next section).

SETTING FONT SIZES USING THE SPAN ELEMENT Previously, in Chapter 1, you set relative font sizes for the "sport" and "gardening" in-context links. As shown in Figure 3.20, when a user increases his preferred font size, the relative font sizes do not scale relative to the user's preferred font size. To have the size of those links also scale relative to a user's preferred font size, you need to use styles to set a font size with an em measurement.

The SPAN element is a generic inline element that, by itself, has no display characteristics. By combining it with the CLASS attribute, which allows you to apply styles to a separate class of elements, you can create as many custom inline elements as you want.

Replace the FONT elements that are nested inside the "sports" and "gardening" anchor elements with SPAN elements that set the font size to 1.1 ems:

1. Delete the FONT elements that were set previously and add SPAN elements with **class="link"** attributes:

```
<p>Welcome to my home page! My name is Johnny Watson and I'm a
big nut about two things: <a href="http://www.espn.com/"><span
class="link">sports</span></a> and <a
href="http://www.bbc.co.uk/gardening/"><span
class="link">gardening!</span></a>
```

2. Add a style to the style sheet that applies a font size of 1.1 ems to SPAN elements belonging to the "link" class (see Figure 3.21):

```
<style type="text/css">
p, li, address { font-size: 1.1em; }
span.link { font-size: 1.1em; }
</style>
</head>
```

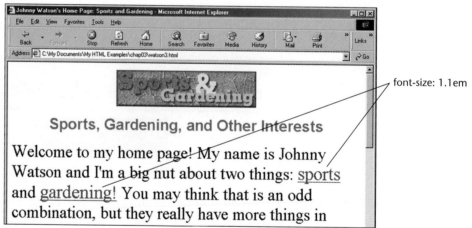

font-size: 1.1em

FIGURE 3.21 • *The size of the "sports" and "gardening" links now scale relative to a user's preferences.*

In a style rule, the "." character indicates that the following text references the name of an element class. The ".link" text in the style specifies that the style is to be applied only to SPAN elements with a **class="link"** attribute. The ".link" text also can be listed by itself, without the preceding "span" element reference, in which case the style can be applied to any element, and not just the SPAN element, that has a **class="link"** attribute.

As shown previously in Figure 3.21, the "sports" and "gardening" link sizes are now scaled relative to the font size of the SPAN elements' parent element (the P element). Each link is now 1.1 times the size of the P element's text, which in turn is 1.1 times the size of the BODY element's font size. If you previously set a user-defined style sheet in Internet Explorer 6 for Windows, you should now turn it off.

Internet Explorer 6 for Windows. Turn off the user-defined style sheet you set previously:

1. Select Tools, Internet Options, and click the Accessibility button.
2. Uncheck the Format documents using my style sheet check box. Click OK twice to return to the document window.

UNDERSTANDING COMPATIBILITY ISSUES WITH FONT SIZES USING EMS

All current browsers handle setting font sizes using ems just fine. Browsers that do not support styles, or that have styles turned off, completely ignore the font size changes. Earlier browsers that only partially support CSS might have problems with em measurements that can impact the readability of your page, however. Internet Explorer 3.x, for instance, treats one em as equal to one pixel, meaning that a font size measurement of 1.1 ems would cause paragraph text in that browser to be displayed in a 1.1-pixel font, rendering the text completely illegible.

NOTE

The Web Standards Project's Browser Upgrade Campaign at **www.webstandards.org/upgrade/** provides a number of ways to deal with older browsers with poor support for current Web standards. Just click on the "Developer Tips" link to find out about easy-to-implement methods for alerting users of older browsers that they need to upgrade their browsers.

Web Standard's DOM Sniff Method, for instance, uses a simple JavaScript script that automatically redirects users of Internet Explorer 3.x, Netscape Navigator 4.x, and other less than standards-compliant browsers to the Web address shown in the previous paragraph. You also can use it to direct users to a browser-upgrade page that you have created as part of your own site.

For a somewhat less radical solution (which does not risk losing visitors), the site also provides an Invisible Object Method. This method displays an alert at the top of the page to users of browsers that are less than standards-compliant. Such users are alerted that the page they are viewing would look much better in a standards-compliant browser, while providing a link they can use to find out how to upgrade their browser.

Use the Web Standards Project's Invisible Object Method to alert users of less than standards-compliant browsers that they need to upgrade their browsers:

1. Create a style that turns off the display of elements belonging to the "oops" class and add an IFRAME element to the top of the BODY element belonging to that class:

```
<style type="text/css">
p, li, address { font-size: 1.1em; }
span.link { font-size: 1.1em; }
.oops { display: none; }
</style>
</head>
<body>
<iframe class="oops">
<center><font size="5" color="maroon">This site will look much
better in a browser that supports <a
href="http://www.webstandards.org/upgrade/"
title="Download a browser that complies with Web standards.">
Web standards</a>,<br>but it is accessible to any browser
or Internet device.</font>
```

```
</center>
<hr>
</iframe>
```

2. Save your document. If you have a version of Netscape 4 installed on your computer, open **watson3.html** in that browser. You will see the content of the IFRAME element you added in step 1 displayed at the top of the page (see Figure 3.22). If you refresh the display of the page in a browser that supports the display property, the IFRAME element will be invisible.

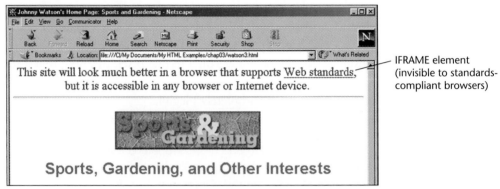

IFRAME element (invisible to standards-compliant browsers)

F I G U R E   3 . 2 2   •   *By using the Web Standards Project's Invisible Object Method, you can alert users of less than standards-compliant browsers, such as Netscape Navigator 4, as shown here, that they need to upgrade their browsers.*

3. If viewing the page in Netscape 4, click on the "Web standards" link. (If using a browser that supports the display property, use the Address or Location box to go to www.webstandards.org/upgrade/.) If connected to the Internet, you will be taken to the Web Standard Project's Browser Upgrade Campaign page (see Figure 3.23).

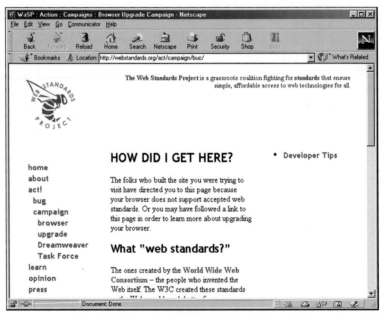

F I G U R E   3 . 2 3   •   *After clicking on the "Web standards" link in a browser that displays the IFRAME "oops" alert, a user is taken to the Web Standards Project's Browser Upgrade Campaign page.*

To find out more about using the DOM Sniff and Invisible Object methods, click on the Developer Tips link in the Browser Upgrade Campaign page. To find links to where users can upgrade their browsers, on the same page, scroll down to the "What can I do?" section.

The Invisible Object method works in two ways. First, any browser that does not recognize the `display: none` style property displays the alert message; in browsers that do recognize it, the message is invisible. Netscape 4, however, which has poor support for CSS, does recognize the `display: none` style property, but does not recognize the IFRAME (Inline Frame) element; because Netscape 4 does not recognize the IFRAME element, it also ignores the `display: none` style property that is assigned to it.

To cause this alert to display in Internet Explorer 3, but not in Netscape Navigator 4, just apply the `class="oops"` attribute to any standard element other than the IFRAME element that contains the alert text. If you do, however, be sure to test your page out in Netscape Navigator 4 to make sure that it displays your page in an acceptable manner.

TROUBLE spot
Reducing the font size of body text elements (P, LI, BLOCKQUOTE, ADDRESS, and so on) can affect the legibility of body text for some users, depending on their system or browser font settings. If you must decrease the font size for body text in a page you are creating, reduce it only slightly using an em measurement and not a pixel measurement, in conjunction with one of the Browser Upgrade Initiative's methods for dealing with earlier browsers that have trouble with em measurements. Here is an example of reducing the size of body text elements:

```
p, li, blockquote, address { font-size: .9em; }
</style>
```

As mentioned previously, you should not set this directly for the BODY element, since that is more likely to conflict with a user's own font-size setting in a user-defined style sheet. By setting it in the body text elements, the font-size will scale relative to a user's font-size set for the BODY element.

When setting CSS font sizes for documents to be displayed on the Web, you should use either pixels or ems. Other measuring units, such as inches (in), centimeters (cm), millimeters (mm), points (pt), or picas (pc), should never be used when setting font sizes for display on the Web. That is because they are absolute measurements that have no meaning relative to a Web page, the size and dimensions of which are always indeterminate.

TROUBLE spot
Use of points (pt) is to be avoided especially when specifying measurements in CSS. That is because, while points and pixels are equivalent by default on a Macintosh system, they are not equivalent on a Windows system, because of the different default dot pitches at which fonts are displayed on those systems (72 dpi on the Macintosh and 96 dpi in Windows). The result is that text set in an 8-point font, for instance, which is legible on a Windows browser, will be illegible on a Macintosh browser that does not readjust font sizes to match the Windows display.

Specifying Font Families Using Styles

Authors must be careful when setting font sizes using styles because of the poor support for font measurements using ems in early CSS-supporting browsers, and accessibility issues involved in specifying font measurements in pixels. The only real problem with specifying font families using styles, however, is non-support in earlier browsers that do not support the use of styles (but might support the use of the FONT element's FACE attribute).

When specifying font families using styles, you use the same font names you used when specifying font-face names using the FONT element's FACE attribute.

Set a style that specifies a list of font families to be used in displaying the H1 and H2 elements:

1. Delete the FONT element that was previously nested in the H1 element:

```
<h1><del>font color="#996600" face="Arial, Geneva, Helvetica, sans-serif"></del>Sports, Gardening, and Other Interests<del></font></del></h1>
```

2. Make the same deletion in your document's H2 element.
3. Add the following style to your page's style sheet (see Figure 3.24):

```
<style type="text/css">
p, blockquote, li, address { font-size: 1.1em; }
span.link { font-size: 1.1em; }
.oops { display: none; }
h1, h2 { font-family: Arial, Geneva, Helvetica, sans-serif; }
</style>
</head>
```

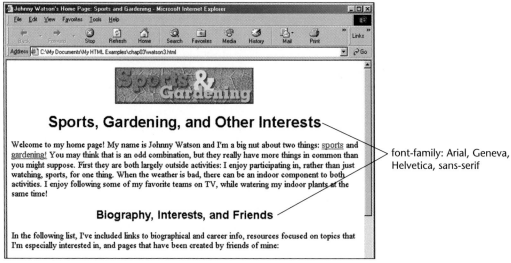

FIGURE 3.24 • *A single style causes the H1 and H2 elements to be displayed in an Arial font on systems that have that font available.*

Notice in the previous example that the H1 and H2 elements are both included in the same style. By using a comma-delimited list of element names, you can group elements to which you want to apply the same style.

USING STYLES AND THE FONT ELEMENT TOGETHER To catch both browsers that support styles and browsers that only support the FONT element's FACE attribute, you can combine using inline styles and the FONT element. You cannot do that by applying a style to an element while nesting a FONT element within that element, however, because the formatting of the nested element (the FONT element) takes precedence. Nothing in the HTML or CSS specifications, however, forbids using a style within the FONT element (as long as you are declaring your document to be in conformance with the transitional version of HTML 4.01). For instance, in the following code example, browsers that support styles will ignore the FACE attribute, while browsers that support the FACE attribute, but not styles, will ignore the STYLE attribute:

```
<h1><font style="font-family: Arial, Geneva, Helvetica, sans-
serif" face="Arial, Geneva, Helvetica, sans-serif">Sports,
Gardening, and Other Interests</font></h1>
```

In CSS, font-family names are officially case-insensitive. However, because some computer systems might separately dictate case-sensitive font names, font-family names used in styles should be treated as though they were case-sensitive, with all uppercase and lowercase letters typed in exactly as shown.

QUOTING FONT-FAMILY NAMES THAT INCLUDE SPACES When specifying font-family names using styles, any font names with spaces in them must be quoted. For instance, in the following example, the font-family name of Comic Sans MS needs to be quoted because there are spaces in the font-family name:

```
<h1 style="font-family: 'Comic Sans MS', Arial, Geneva,
Helvetica, sans-serif">Sports, Gardening, and Other
Interests</font></h1>
```

Single quotes are used because double quotes are already being used around the STYLE attribute. When specifying a font-family name with spaces in it in a style sheet, double quotes can be used:

```
<style type="text/css">
h1 { font-family: "Comic Sans MS", Arial, Geneva, Helvetica,
sans-serif; }
</style>
```

Setting Colors Using Styles

You also can set the foreground color of elements using styles. You use the same 16 standard color names or hexadecimal RGB codes that you used previously to specify colors using the FONT element's COLOR attribute.

Use styles to specify different colors for the H1 and H2 elements (see Figure 3.25):

```
h1, h2 { font-family: Arial, Geneva, Helvetica, sans-serif; }
h1 { color: #996600; background: transparent; }
h2 { color: #2e8b57; background: transparent; }
</style>
```

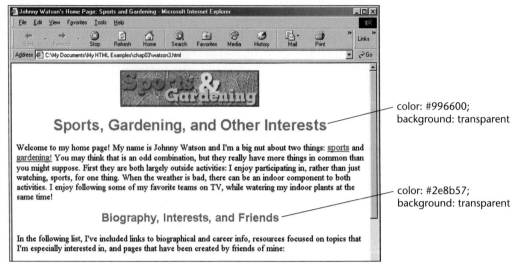

color: #996600;
background: transparent

color: #2e8b57;
background: transparent

FIGURE 3.25 • *Different colors are set for the H1 and H2 elements using styles.*

NOTE

As shown in the previous example, you can specify a series of style properties that can be applied to a specific style element. A style element and the properties that are assigned to it are referred to as a *style rule*. Semicolons are used to separate style properties within a style rule.

TROUBLE *spot*

A common error when typing styles is to type a colon where a semicolon is called for, or vice versa. Another common error is to type a regular opening or closing parenthesis, rather than an opening or closing squiggly bracket ("{" or "}"), before or after a style rule's properties. Also, if your style is not nested inside of a properly formed STYLE element (starting with `<style type="text/css">` and ending with `</style>`), it might not be displayed. If you find that a style is not working, check to make sure you have not made any of these errors.

tip

Notice that a transparent background is also specified for the H1 and H2 style rules. Whenever you specify a foreground color using styles, you usually should also specify a background color, if only as transparent. The reason for this is that a user might be using a user-defined style sheet that assigns foreground and background colors to the H1 and H2 elements—if you only set a foreground color, it could end up being displayed against a user's background color. You could end up with yellow text against a yellow background, for instance, or red text against a green background that someone who has red-green color-blindness might have difficulty reading.

Setting Text, Link, and Background Colors Using Styles

The BODY element's TEXT, LINK, VLINK, ALINK, and BGCOLOR attributes also are deprecated in HTML 4.01 in favor of using styles to achieve similar or better results. Alternatively, you can control the display characteristics of your page's text, link, and background colors using only styles.

action

Use styles to control text, link, and background colors:

1. Delete the SPAN elements you earlier nested inside the "sports" and "gardening" links:

```
<p>Welcome to my home page! My name is Johnny Watson and I'm a
big nut about two things: <a href="http://www.espn.com/"><span
class="link">sports</span></a> and <a
href="http://www.bbc.co.uk/gardening/"><span
class="link">gardening!</span></a>
```

2. Set styles that specify foreground and background colors for text and links (see Figure 3.26):

```
<style type="text/css">
body { color: navy; background: #ffffcc; }
p, blockquote, li, address { font-size: 1.1em; }
span.link { font-size: 1.1em; }
.oops { display: none; }
h1, h2 { font-family: Arial, Geneva, Helvetica, sans-serif; }
h1 { color: #996600; background: transparent; }
h2 { color: #2e8b57; background: transparent; }
a:link { color: #ff6600; background: transparent; }
a:visited { color: #996699; background: transparent; }
a:hover { color: green; background: transparent; }
a:active { color: blue; background: transparent; }
</style>
</head>
```

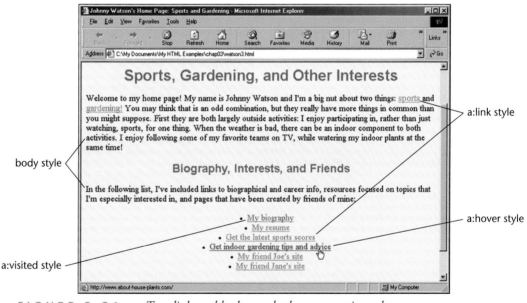

FIGURE 3.26 • *Text, link, and background colors are set using styles.*

This example reproduces the color scheme you set previously using the FONT element and the BODY element attributes, with the exception of the "hover" link style that controls the color of a link when the mouse pointer hovers over it. The "hover" link style can be set only using styles. The "active" link style is not shown in the figure since "hover" and "active" cannot be displayed at the same time. The a:link, a:visited, a:hover, and a:active style elements are a special class of style elements referred to as *anchor pseudo-classes* in CSS.

When using the anchor pseudo-classes to set link properties, you should always list the a:hover and a:active pseudo-classes after the a:link and a:visited pseudo-classes. If you do not, the hover and activated link states will not be displayed. You can list the a:hover and a:active pseudo-classes in whichever order you like; if you list a:hover after a:active, for instance, the activated state will not be visible when the mouse pointer is held down on the link.

In Internet Explorer, however, the activated state still will be visible after the user clicks the Back button to return to the page. To stop the activated state from being visibly displayed at all, just insert a:active before a:hover in the style sheet and set it to the same color as a:visited. Another option is to set a:link, a:visited, and a:active to the same color, while setting a:hover to a different color.

Setting a Background Image Using a Style

The final touch you need to add now is a background image.

action

Add a background image to your style sheet that will display behind the BODY element (see Figure 3.27):

```
<style type="text/css">
body { color: navy; background: #ffffcc; url(back_light.jpg); }
```

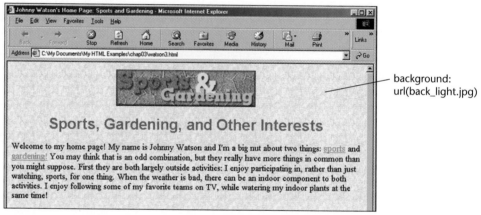

background: url(back_light.jpg)

FIGURE 3.27 • *A background image is set using a style.*

When specifying a background image URL in a style, be sure to surround it with regular parentheses ("(" and ")") and not squiggly brackets ("{" and "}"). As with setting a background image using a BODY element attribute, when setting a background image using a style, you should always specify a background color that is similar to your background image's coloration because some users surf the Web with the display of graphics turned off.

SPECIFYING A BACKGROUND IMAGE To make a more dramatic statement, you can use a dark background image. To do this, you must adjust your page's foreground colors so they provide proper contrast, as well as the background color you have specified. A dark background image, back_dark.jpg, is included with the other example files in the chap03 folder.

Set a dark background image and reset your page's foreground and background colors to match (see Figure 3.28):

```
<style type="text/css">
body { color: #ffffcc; background: navy url(back_dark.jpg); }
p, li, address { font-size: 1.1em; }
span.link { font-size: 1.1em; }
.oops { display: none; }
h1, h2 { font-family: Arial, Geneva, Helvetica, sans-serif; }
h1 { color: #ffcc33; background: transparent; }
h2 { color: #99ccff; background: transparent; }
a:link { color: #33ffcc; background: transparent; }
a:visited { color: #00cccc; background: transparent; }
a:hover { color: yellow; background: transparent; }
a:active { color: aqua; background: transparent; }
</style>
```

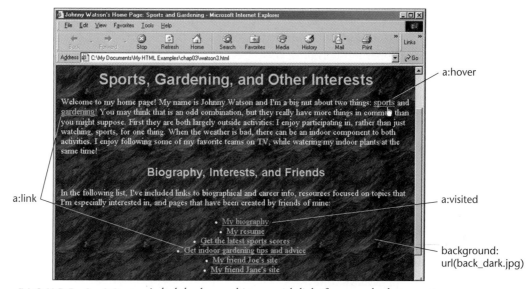

FIGURE 3.28 • *A dark background image with light foreground colors can give a page a more dramatic look.*

When printing a Web page, most browsers do not print background colors or images, which can result in light-colored text being printed against a white background. If displaying white text against a dark background, the result can be white text against a white background (or no visible text, in other words). One way to deal with this problem is to create and link to a "printer-ready" version of your page that substitutes dark text against a white background.

NOTE

Computer systems often do not come with good software utilities for viewing graphic files. When choosing a background image to use in a Web page, it helps to easily view, and possibly open and edit, any background images that you have available. For links to some freeware and shareware image viewers you can download, see this chapter's section at this book's IRC at **www.emcp.com**/. For additional links to freeware and shareware image viewers that you can download and use with Windows, the Macintosh, and other platforms, go to Tucows at **www.tucows.com**/.

USING OTHER BACKGROUND PROPERTIES There are a number of other background properties you can set using styles. The background-attachment, background-repeat, and background-position properties can be used to vary how a background image displays in a browser.

The background-attachment property specifies whether the background image is fixed relative to the browser window or scrolls along with the page. The default value is **scroll**, which causes the background to scroll along with the page. A **fixed** value, on the other hand, causes the background image to remained fixed relative to the browser window (so the document text scrolls within the browser window, but the background image remains fixed).

The background-repeat property specifies whether the background image is to be repeated (or tiled) and whether it should be repeated vertically or horizontally. The default value is **repeat**, which caused a background image to be tiled both vertically and horizontally within the browser background. The **repeat-y** value causes the background image to be repeated vertically only, while a **repeat-x** value causes it to be repeated horizontally only. The **no-repeat** value causes the background image to be displayed only once (not tiled). The no-repeat value is usually used in conjunction with the background-position property (otherwise the background image is displayed, untiled, in the upper left corner of the page).

The background-position property specifies the position of a non-tiled background image. Percentage or length (pixels or ems) can be used to space the background image in from the top left corner of a page or element's padding area. If only one value is given, it is assumed that only the horizontal position of the background image is being set. If two values are given, the first is used to set the horizontal position and the second to set the vertical position. The keywords of **left**, **center**, and **right** can also be used to set the horizontal position of the background image, while the keywords of **top**, **middle**, and **bottom** can be used to set the background image's vertical position. The keyword values cannot be combined with the percentage or length values. Here are some possible styles that could be set using these properties:

```
body {
background-image: url("backimg.jpg");
background-attach: fixed;
background-repeat: no-repeat;
background-position: 50% 50%;
}
```

or

```
body {
background-image: url("backimg.jpg");
background-repeat: repeat-y;
background-position: center;
}
```

or

```
body {
background-image: url("backimg.jpg");
background-repeat: no-repeat;
background-position: 50% 100px;
}
```

You can also use the background property to set all background properties at once. For instance:

```
body { color: #ffffcc; background: navy url("watermark.gif") no-
repeat fixed 50% 50%; }
```

When vertically positioning a non-tiled background image, using a percentage value or a keyword value (middle or bottom), some browsers position the background image relative to the browser window, while others position it relative to the length of the document. To insure that your watermark background image will always be displayed the same distance from the top of the page in all browsers that support this feature, set a specific length amount from the top of the page.

Creating Rollover Links

Using CSS, you also can set a background color or background image for specific elements. By using this capability with the a:hover pseudo-class, you can create a "rollover" effect that is displayed when the mouse pointer is passed over a link. A rollover effect generally refers to a dramatic change, often a flipping of color values, for an object or element that results in response to a user interaction. Using rollover links is one way to increase the interactivity of your page.

 Create a rollover link:

1. Set contrasting foreground and background colors for the a:hover pseudo-class, to create a rollover effect for your page's links:

```
a:hover { color: red; background: yellow; }
a:active { color: aqua; background: transparent; }
```

2. In your browser, pass the mouse pointer over a link to activate the rollover effect (see Figure 3.29).

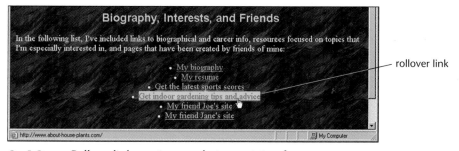

FIGURE 3.29 • *Rollover links can increase the interactivity of your page.*

Turning Link Underlining Off

Using styles, you also can turn off the underline that is displayed under a hypertext link. Be careful when doing this, however, because it can cause some surfers not to recognize that a link is a link. In some circumstances turning off this feature can be useful and effective. Using rollover links is one of those circumstances because the user will already have recognized that the link is a link before passing the mouse over it.

Turn the underlining off for the a:hover pseudo-class (see Figure 3.30):

```
a:hover { color: red; background: yellow; text-decoration: none; }
```

underlining turned off
(text-decoration: none)

FIGURE 3.30 • *A rollover link is one circumstance in which turning off the underlining of a
link is appropriate.*

Using Downloadable Fonts

The CSS2 specification includes a feature called the @font-face rule, which can be used
to specify the name of a font to be downloaded from the Web. When this feature is used,
a browser is supposed to look first to determine whether the specified font or a close
match is available on a user's computer; if the font or a close match is not available, the
browser can download the font from a URL specified by the author.

Of current browsers, only Internet Explorer (Version 4 and above) supports displaying
downloadable fonts. Netscape Navigator 4 earlier supported a different format for downloadable fonts, but Netscape 6 (up to Version 6.22) does not include support for
downloadable fonts.

To make a downloadable font available to users of Internet Explorer 4 and above, you
need to convert a TrueType font into an Embedded Open Type (EOT) font. A free tool,
Microsoft WEFT (Web Embedding Fonts Tool), is available from Microsoft—you can
find out more about WEFT at **www.microsoft.com/typography/web/embedding/weft2/**.

The following is a simple example of an @font-face rule that can be included in a style
sheet to specify an EOT font as available for download:

```
@font-face {
    font-family: Christmas;
    font-style: normal;
    font-weight: bold;
    src: url("http://www.someserver.com/somefonts/Christmas.eot");
    }
h1 { font-family: Christmas.eot; }
```

Although you can provide most TrueType fonts for download with a Web page using
WEFT and EOT font files, the TrueType font format allows embedding permissions to be
set to no embedding. The WEFT utility reports the permissions for any local TrueType
fonts installed on a Windows system.

Be aware, however, that using embedded fonts in a Web page can significantly increase the
amount of time required for that page to display. Before opting to use a downloadable font,
consider whether achieving a specific look for some users (of Internet Explorer 4 and above)
is worth the additional time required to download and display the page.

In this chapter, you have just barely scratched the surface of using styles within Web pages. Following are some online resources that provide more information about using styles in Web pages:

- The W3C's CSS site: **www.w3.org/Style/CSS/**
- The Web Design Group's Guide to CSS: **www.htmlhelp.com/reference/css/**
- The HTML Writers Guild CSS FAQ: **www.hwg.org/resources/faqs/cssFAQ.html**
- Web Review.com's Style Sheet Reference Guide: **www.webreview.com/style/**
- The CSS Pointers Group: **www.css.nu/**
- Visit the newsgroup: **comp.infosystems.www.authoring.stylesheets**

CHAPTER SUMMARY

You should now be familiar with using both HTML and CSS to control fonts, colors, and backgrounds in Web pages you create. You should know how to set absolute and relative font sizes, specify font-face names and font lists, apply colors using the 16 standard color names and hexadecimal RGB codes, use Web-safe colors in your pages, set foreground and background colors, use background images, set CSS font sizes using pixels and ems, use the SPAN element to create your own custom inline elements, and create interactive rollover links. You also should be aware of accessibility concerns that can arise when setting fonts, colors, and backgrounds in Web pages.

Code Review

FONT element	Specifies the font size, color, or face for an element. Deprecated in HTML 4.
SIZE attribute	In the FONT element, specifies the font size for an element. You can set seven absolute font sizes (1 to 7), or relative font sizes (+1 or -1, for instance).
FACE attribute	In the FONT element, specifies the font face of an element, in the form of a font-face name or font list.
COLOR attribute	In the FONT element, specifies the foreground color of nested text. Colors can be specified using any of the 16 standard color names or hexadecimal RGB codes.
BASEFONT element	An empty element that specifies font characteristics for the base font, with changes taking effect at the position where the element is inserted. Earlier browsers recognize only the SIZE attribute. The Opera and Mozilla browsers ignore it. Deprecated in HTML 4.
TEXT attribute	In the BODY element, sets the color of body text.
LINK attribute	In the BODY element, sets the color of unvisited links.
VLINK attribute	In the BODY element, sets the color of visited links.
ALINK attribute	In the BODY element, sets the color of activated links.
BGCOLOR attribute	In the BODY element, sets a background color for a page.
BACKGROUND attribute	In the BODY element, sets a background image for a page.
STYLE element	Element in the document head that specifies nested text in a style sheet.
STYLE attribute	Used to insert an inline style within an element's start tag.
font-size property	In CSS, sets the font size of an element.
SPAN element	A generic inline element that has no formatting characteristics of its own, but which can be used to create custom inline elements by using styles.
CLASS attribute	Assigns an element to a class. Any styles assigned to the class are then applied to the element.
display property	Style property that can be used to turn the display of an element off and on in supporting browsers.
IFRAME element	Specifies that nested text is to be formatted as an inline frame.
font-family property	In CSS, specifies a specific or generic font-family name or a font-family list.

color property	In CSS, specifies the foreground color of an element, using a color name or hexadecimal RGB code.
background property	In CSS, specifies a background color or background image for an element.
a:link	In CSS, an anchor pseudo-class that specifies the properties of an unvisited link.
a:visited	In CSS, an anchor pseudo-class that specifies the properties of a visited link.
a:hover	In CSS, an anchor pseudo-class that specifies the properties of a link when the mouse pointer is hovering over it.
a:active	In CSS, an anchor pseudo-class that specifies the properties of an activated link.
@font-face rule	In CSS, can specify a downloadable font.

ONLINE QUIZ

Go to this text's IRC at **www.emcp.com/** and take the online self-check quiz for this chapter.

REVIEW EXERCISES

This section provides some hands-on practice exercises to reinforce the information and material included within this and previous chapters.

Save **watson2.html** and **watson3.html** under new file names (**watson2_practice.html** and **watson3_practice.html**, for instance) and then use the new documents to practice using the elements, attributes, styles, and other features that were covered in this chapter.

1. In the first practice document (watson2_practice.html, or whatever file name you gave it), further experiment with using the FONT element's SIZE attribute to set font sizes. Practice setting both absolute and relative font sizes.

2. In the first practice document, further experiment with using the FONT element's FACE attribute to set font faces. Try specifying some of the other fonts that are available on your own system, just to see what they look like. If you are not sure which fonts are available on your system, you should be able to find a list of available fonts in your word processing program. Realize, however, that if users do not have the font you specify available on their systems, they will not be able to see the font you specify. For that reason, you should provide alternative fonts in your list of fonts that are more likely to be available on another's system.

3. In the first practice document, experiment with just specifying a sans-serif generic font-family name as the value of the FONT element's FACE attribute. See whether you can identify which specific font your browser defaults to when displaying a sans serif font. (Hint: Compare it with a list of fonts displayed in your word processor or other software that shows you what the fonts on your system look like.)

4. In the first practice document, experiment further with using the 16 standard color names to set font colors. Experiment with using all the standard color names except for black and white in setting colors for the H1 and H2 elements, as well as for the two in-context links included in the introductory paragraph. Make a note of which of the 16 standard colors you do and do not like and why.

5. In the first practice document, experiment further with using hexadecimal RGB codes to set colors. Use one of the links provided in the chapter to find a resource listing the hexadecimal RGB codes for the 140 or so non-standard color names. Use those codes to set colors using the FONT element's COLOR attribute and the BODY element's TEXT, LINK, VLINK, ALINK, and BGCOLOR attributes. Try to find at least three different color schemes that you think are both attractive and readable, with at least one of the three featuring light text displayed against a dark background color. Save each scheme as a separate file (**watson2_color1.html**, **watson2_color2.html**, **watson2_color3.html**). Ask at least two of your classmates to judge which one of the three schemes they like the best and which one they like the least. Try to find out what they like or do not like about the color schemes you have created.

6. Do the same as in exercise 5, but add using background images into the mix. You can find additional background images that you can use in the **art** folder included with this book's example files. See also this book's IRC at **www.emcp.com/** for links to resources where you can find and download background images on the Web.

7. In the second practice document (watson3_practice.html, or whatever file name you gave it), further experiment with using styles to set font sizes, using both pixels and ems.

8. In the second practice document, further experiment with using styles to specify font-family names to be used to display different elements.

9. In the second practice document, experiment further with using the 16 standard color names and hexadecimal RGB codes with styles to set colors. Create at least three color schemes for your page, using only styles to control foreground colors and background colors, with at least one of the three featuring light text displayed against a dark background color. Ask at least two of your classmates to judge which one of the three schemes they like the best and which one they like the least. Try to find out what they like or do not like about the color schemes you have created.

10. Do the same as in exercise 9, but add using background images into the mix. You can find additional background images that you can use in the **art** folder included with this book's example files. See also this book's IRC at **www.emcp.com/** for links to resources where you can find and download background images on the Web.

WEB-BASED LEARNING ACTIVITIES

In this book's text, Find It icons inserted in the margin highlight the Web addresses of additional resources you might find helpful or informative. To extend your learning using the Web, you can:

- Go back and visit any of the Web addresses highlighted in this chapter that you have not yet visited. Look for additional resources and information that add to your understanding and knowledge of the material covered in this chapter. When you find a relevant page or site with information or resources you might want to access later, add it to your Favorites (in Internet Explorer) or your Bookmarks (in Netscape or Mozilla).

- Visit this book's IRC at **www.emcp.com/** to find additional Web addresses of resources related to the material covered in this chapter that you can further investigate and explore.

- Further research a specific topic introduced in this chapter. For instance, do further research on the readability of serif versus sans serif fonts or the problems those with different forms of color-blindness can have viewing different color combinations on the Web.
- A good image viewer can make working with background images and other clip art much easier. Visit this chapter's section at this book's IRC at **www.emcp.com/** to see a listing of image viewers you can download. See Tucows at **www.tucows.com/** for additional freeware and shareware image-viewing utilities that are available for your platform. Download several and test them. Ask your instructor if you can give a demonstration to your fellow classmates of the best image-viewing software you have discovered.

PROJECTS

These projects can be done either in class, in a computer lab, or at home. Use the skills you have developed in this and the previous chapters to create any of the following projects.

Project 1. Update the appearance of a personal Web page using fonts, colors, and backgrounds.

If you created your own personal Web page as a project at the end of Chapter 1, apply the lessons learned in this chapter to update the appearance of your personal page, using the FONT element's SIZE, FACE, and COLOR attributes and the BODY element's TEXT, LINK, VLINK, ALINK, BGCOLOR, and BACKGROUND attributes. Experiment with using different color schemes and background images, until you find the combination you like best. You can find additional background images you can use in the **art** folder included with this book's example files. Also, see this book's IRC for links to where you can find additional background images on the Web that you can download and use in your Web pages.

Project 2. Update the appearance of a personal Web page using styles.

If you created your own personal Web page as a project at the end of Chapter 1, apply the lessons learned in this chapter to update the appearance of your personal page, using only styles (without using the FONT element's SIZE, FACE, and COLOR attributes or the BODY element's TEXT, LINK, VLINK, ALINK, BGCOLOR, and BACKGROUND attributes). Experiment with using different color schemes and background images, until you find the combination you like best. Pay special attention to making your page accessible to visitors with visual handicaps, by using em measurements for font sizes and avoiding color combinations that can cause difficulties for users with different forms of color-blindness, for instance. If using em measurements, be sure to also use one of the methods provided by the Web Standards Project to redirect or alert users of earlier, less than CSS-compliant Web browsers.

Project 3. Update the appearance of a topical Web page using fonts, colors, and backgrounds.

If you created a topical page as a project at the end of Chapter 1, apply the lessons learned in this chapter to update the appearance of your personal page, using the FONT element's

SIZE, FACE, and COLOR attributes and the BODY element's TEXT, LINK, VLINK, ALINK, BGCOLOR, and BACKGROUND attributes. See the guidelines for Project 1 for more details.

Project 4. Update the appearance of a topical Web page using styles.

If you created a topical page as a project at the end of Chapter 1, apply the lessons learned in this chapter to update the appearance of your topical page, using only styles. See the guidelines for Project 2 for more details.

Project 5. Update the appearance of a page you created for a club or organization.

If you created a page for a club or organization at the end of Chapter 1, apply the lessons learned in this chapter to update the appearance of that page, using either HTML elements and attributes or styles to control fonts, colors, and backgrounds. See the guidelines for Projects 1 and 2 for more details.

Project 6. Create a new Web page from scratch that uses fonts, colors, and backgrounds.

Create any kind of new page from scratch: a personal page, a topical page, a page for a club or organization, or a page created for any other purpose. If you are not sure what kind of page you want to create, look on the Web for examples that you can try to emulate. Apply the lessons learned in this chapter or previous chapters to create an effective and visually attractive page featuring font size, face, and color changes, combined with a background color or background image. Try to combine features learned in this chapter with features learned in earlier chapters. For instance, you might combine a document menu that jumps to subsections within a document, as was demonstrated in Chapter 2, with rollover links, as was demonstrated in this chapter.

Working with Images and Other Media

PERFORMANCE OBJECTIVES

In this chapter, you will learn to use inline images and other media to enhance the presentation and functionality of your Web pages, including how to:

- Flow text and other elements around a floating image.
- Create a thumbnail image gallery.
- Use graphic rules, banners, and buttons.
- Create GIF and JPEG Web graphics.
- Work with Web-safe and optimized color palettes.
- Create interlaced and transparent GIF images.
- Use and create GIF animations.
- Embed sound and video.

In Chapter 1, *Creating a Basic Web Page*, you learned how to include an inline image in an HTML document using the IMG element. In this chapter, you will learn much more about working with and using images and other media in HTML documents.

The original version of HTML had no means for including images. As has often happened in HTML, the market perceived a deficit, and supplied it. The IMG element was actually the first unofficial extension to HTML, supported by the first widely available graphical browser, the Mosaic browser.

The old adage that a picture is worth a thousand words is proven true by how the deft usage of carefully chosen images augments and supplements the textual content of a page. In fact, an image or a group of images can even stand by itself as the main content of a page.

USING THE EXAMPLE FILES

If you created a working folder for storing files you create, you will find the example files for this chapter located in the **chap04** folder within your working folder. Save any HTML files you create in this chapter in that folder.

If you created a working disk, you should copy the chap04 folder to your working disk from the **HTML_Examples** folder that you or your instructor downloaded from this book's Internet Resource Center (IRC). Ask your instructor for assistance if you need help copying the chap04 folder. Save any HTML files you create in this chapter in the chap04 folder on your working disk.

CASE EXAMPLE: CREATING A REPORT WITH FLOATING IMAGES

In this example, you will create a report on the history of NASA's Project Mercury space program to place a manned space vehicle into orbit around the earth. To supplement the textual content of the report, you will include actual NASA photographs at key points, which are included with the example files for this chapter.

> *Shirley Johnson is a science major who is particularly interested in astronomy and space exploration. For a class, she is writing a report on the history of the Project Mercury space program, which placed the first American, John Glenn, into orbit around the earth.*
>
> *Shirley has already done quite a bit of work developing her page. She has written the report text, set up a document menu that jumps to sections within the report, created note links that jump to footnotes at the bottom of the page, and set up the colors, fonts, and backgrounds she wants to use. For the background, she created her own seamless background image, taken from one of NASA's photographs of a star cluster in outer space.*

To get started working with this example:

1. Run your text editor and open **mercury_ex.html** from the chap04 folder in your working folder or working disk.
2. Save mercury_ex.html as **mercury.html** in the chap04 folder.
3. Run your browser and open **mercury.html** from the chap04 folder (see Figure 4.1).

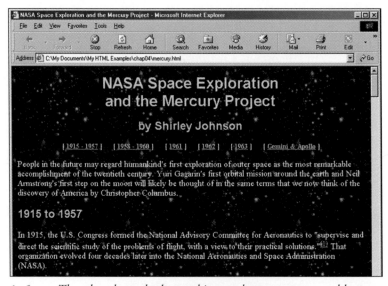

FIGURE 4.1 • *The color scheme, background image, document menu, and hypertext note links have already been created for mercury.html.*

This chapter uses a number of image files that are included with this chapter's example files in the chap04 folder. Any HTML files you create in this chapter must be saved in the same folder in which the example graphic files for this chapter are located; otherwise, the example graphics will not display when you preview the HTML files in your browser.

FLOATING IMAGES

You added an inline image to an HTML document in Chapter 1, but nested it by itself inside an otherwise empty P element, which added vertical spacing above and below the image, separating it from other elements. You had to do that because an IMG element is an inline element that is displayed in a line at the point at which it is inserted and, as such, does not insert line breaks or vertical spacing above or below an image.

Shirley decided to illustrate her report by using actual NASA photographs that are available online. She researched NASA's copyright and reproduction guidelines and discovered that most of NASA's photographs are not copyrighted, so she is free to use them for non-commercial or educational purposes.

action

Insert an inline image at the start of a paragraph containing text (see Figure 4.2):

```
<h2><a name="sect1"></a>1915 to 1957</h2>
<p>In 1915, the U.S. Congress formed the National Advisory
Committee for Aeronautics to "supervise and direct the
scientific study of the problems of flight, with a view to
their practical solutions."<sup><a href="#note1"
name="return1">(1)</a></sup> That organization evolved four
decades later into the National Aeronautics and Space
Administration (NASA).</p>
<p><img src="atlas_mercury.jpg" alt="Atlas rocket with Mercury
spacecraft" width="175" height="238">The Atlas rocket launch
vehicle, which lifted John Glenn into orbit, began being used
following World War II. Its initial test occurred in
1948.<sup><a href="#note2" name="return2">(2)</a></sup> The
first launch was not attempted until June 11, 1957, however,
just four months prior to the launching of the Sputnik I.
Unfortunately, the first Atlas launch ended with the missile
exploding at 10,000 feet. A second Atlas test launch also ended
in failure on September 25, 1957. It was not until January 10,
1958, that the Atlas rocket was successfully launched.</p>
```

Setting WIDTH and HEIGHT attributes for inline images can speed up display of the rest of the page, since the browser can allocate space for images before they have finished downloading.

inline image (non-floating)

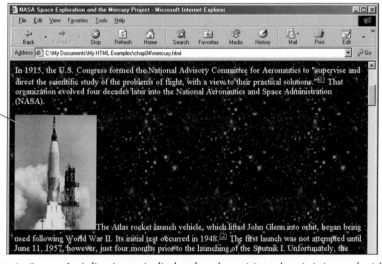

FIGURE 4.2 • *An inline image is displayed at the position where it is inserted within a line.*

Flowing Text around a Left-Aligned Image

The IMG element's ALIGN attribute has two different functions. It can be used to vertically align an image relative to the line of text it is inserted on (you will learn how to do that later in this chapter). ALIGN also can be used to float an image to the left or right margin and cause following text or elements to flow around the image.

Set the inline image you just added so that it floats to the left margin, with following text and elements flowing around the right side of the image (see Figure 4.3):

```
<p><img src="atlas_mercury.jpg" align="left" alt="Atlas rocket
with Mercury spacecraft" width="175" height="238">The Atlas
rocket launch vehicle, which lifted John Glenn into orbit, began
being used following World War II.
```

left floating image
(align="left")

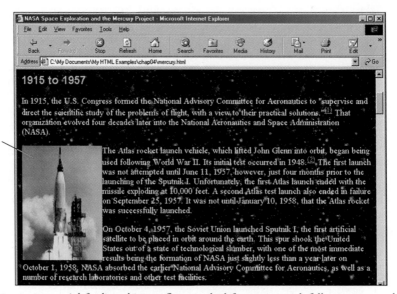

FIGURE 4.3 • *A left-aligned image floats to the left margin, with following text and elements flowing around the right side of the image.*

Setting Horizontal Spacing

The only problem with the floating image is that no horizontal spacing separates it from the flowing text. The IMG element's HSPACE attribute lets you set horizontal spacing that will be added on each side of the image.

Add 10 pixels of horizontal spacing to the inline image (see Figure 4.4):

```
<p><img src="atlas_mercury.jpg" align="left" hspace="10"
alt="Atlas rocket with Mercury spacecraft" width="175"
height="238">The Atlas rocket launch vehicle, which lifted John
Glenn into orbit, began being used following World War II.
```

horizontal spacing (hspace="10")

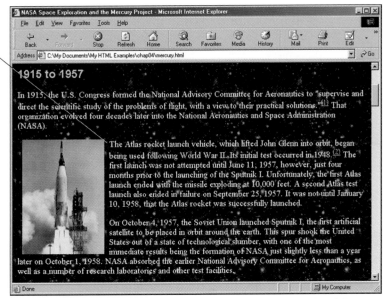

FIGURE 4.4 • *Ten pixels of horizontal spacing are added to both sides of the image.*

HINT

Use the VSPACE attribute, which works the same as the HSPACE attribute, to add vertical spacing above and below an inline image.

As shown in Figure 4.4, any horizontal spacing you add to the image is added to both sides of the image.

Flowing Text around a Right-Aligned Image

You also can float an image to the right margin, with following text and elements flowing around the left side of the image.

Insert a right-aligned inline image with 10 pixels of horizontal spacing set (see Figure 4.5):

```
<h2><a name="sect2"></a>1958 to 1960</h2>
<p>In June, 1958, the initial specifications were established for
what was to become the Project Mercury manned spacecraft. On
November 5, the Space Task Group was formed to implement a manned
satellite program; on November 26, the manned satellite program
was officially designated as Project Mercury.</p>
<p><img src="astronauts.jpg" align="right" hspace="10" alt="The
seven original Mercury astronauts" width="200"
height="197">Project Mercury was approved on October 7, 1958,
which led to the first orbital flight by an American astronaut,
John Glenn, in the "Friendship 7" spacecraft, about three years
and four months later, on February 20, 1962.</p>
```

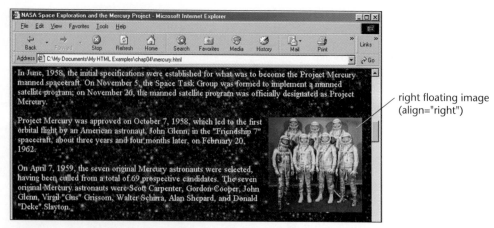

right floating image
(align="right")

FIGURE 4.5 • *A right-aligned image with 10 pixels of horizontal spacing is added to the page.*

Notice that an ALT attribute is included in both IMG elements you have added so far. Adding an ALT element to any inline image you include in a Web page informs someone using a non-visual browser, such as a Braille or speech browser, of the content or purpose of the image. In some, although not all, browsers, the content of the ALT attribute is displayed when the mouse is passed over the image (see Figure 4.6).

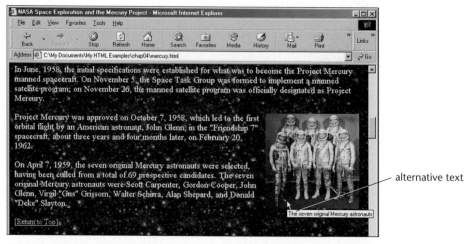

alternative text

FIGURE 4.6 • *Some browsers display the content of the ALT attribute when the mouse pointer is passed over an image.*

Flowing Text between Two Images

You also can flow text between a left-aligned and a right-aligned image.

Add both a left-aligned and a right-aligned image at the same location within the page (see Figure 4.7):

```
<h2><a name="sect3"></a>1961</h2>
<p><img src="chimp_ham.jpg" align="left" hspace="10" alt="Ham, the
first chimpanzee to go into outer space" width="175"
height="211"><img src="glenn_grissom_shepard.jpg" align="right"
hspace="10" alt="John Glenn, Virgil Grissom, and Alan Shepard in
front of the Redstone rocket" width="191" height="211">On January
31, 1961, a Redstone rocket launched a Mercury space vehicle from
Cape Canaveral with Ham, a 37-pound chimpanzee, as its passenger
```

in a suborbital flight. Ham survived the flight in good shape, but when he was shown the space vehicle again later, made clear he wanted no part of it. On February 1, John Glenn, Virgil Grissom, and Alan Shepard were selected to train for the first manned space flight.</p>

left floating image (align="left")

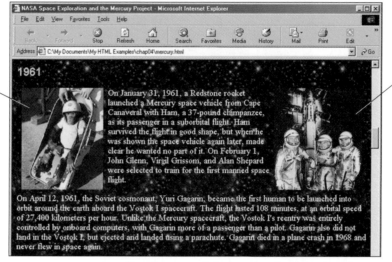

right floating image (align="right")

FIGURE 4.7 • *Text flows between a left-aligned and a right-aligned image.*

Overlapping Floating Images

You also can overlap floating images, so that text first flows just around the right side of the first image, then between both images, and finally just around the left side of the second image.

Move the second image down, so the two floating images overlap (see Figure 4.8):

```
<h2><a name="sect3"></a>1961</h2>
<p><img src="chimp_ham.jpg" align="left" hspace="10" alt="Ham, the
first chimpanzee to go into outer space" width="175"
height="211"><img src="glenn_grissom_shepard.jpg" align="right"
hspace="10" alt="John Glenn, Virgil Grissom, and Alan Shepard in
front of the Redstone rocket" width="191" height="211">On January
31, 1961, a Redstone rocket launched a Mercury space vehicle from
Cape Canaveral with Ham, a 37-pound chimpanzee, as its passenger
in a suborbital flight. Ham survived the flight in good shape,
but when he was shown the space vehicle again later, made clear
he wanted no part of it. <img src="glenn_grissom_shepard.jpg"
align="right" hspace="10" alt="John Glenn, Virgil Grissom, and
Alan Shepard in front of the Redstone rocket" width="191"
height="211">On February 1, John Glenn, Virgil Grissom, and Alan
Shepard were selected to train for the first manned space
flight.</p>
```

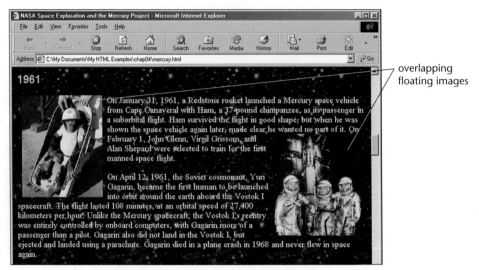

overlapping floating images

FIGURE 4.8 • *You can overlap a left-aligned and a right-aligned image.*

Practicing Using Floating Images

You should now have a good understanding of left-aligning and right-aligning inline images, as well as of flowing text between floating images and overlapping left-aligned and right-aligned images. A number of additional example graphics are included with this chapter's example files that you can use to get more practice using floating images.

Using the previous examples of inserting left-aligned and right-aligned images as a guide, insert additional floating images at appropriate points within the document. Be sure to specify the actual height and width of the images, add horizontal spacing, and include alternative text that describes the image. The following are some images included with the example images for this chapter that you can use:

- **alan_shepard.jpg** Close-up view of Astronaut Alan Shepard in his pressure suit for the first manned Mercury suborbital flight (MR-3). Width: 175; height: 201.
- **mercurylaunch.jpg** Launch of the Mercury-Atlas 6 mission that put John Glenn into orbit around the earth. Width: 200; height: 214.
- **glenn_orbit.jpg** View of earth taken by Astronaut John Glenn during his space flight. Width: 200; height: 153.
- **john_glenn.jpg** Astronaut John Glenn poses in Mercury Space Suit. Width: 175; height: 199.
- **schirra_splash_down.jpg** Navy frogman secures tow line to Sigma 7 flotation collar. Width: 200; height: 184.
- **white_eva.jpg** Astronaut Edward White during first EVA performed during Gemini 4 space flight. Width: 200; height: 171.
- **flagonmoon.jpg** Astronaut Edwin Aldrin poses for photograph beside deployed U.S. flag (Apollo 11 landing on moon). Width: 200; height: 171.
- **earth_apollo17.jpg** View of the Earth seen by the Apollo 17 crew traveling toward the moon. Width: 200; height: 192.

VIEWING IMAGES

When you are choosing an image to use, it helps to view it first. Windows users can use My Computer to view images. Just double-click the My Computer icon on your desktop and then locate and double-click on any image file. If the image format is recognized by Windows, the image is displayed in the left side panel (see Figure 4.9).

image file icon

preview image

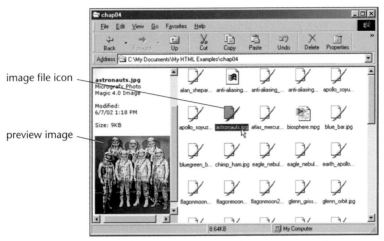

FIGURE 4.9 • *Windows users can use My Computer to see what an image looks like.*

You also can open an image in a Web browser, if it is a GIF, JPEG, or PNG image. Just open it as you would open a local HTML file (select All Files to see non-HTML files). Many image editors, such as Jasc Paint Shop Pro or Ulead PhotoImpact, also allow you to view a thumbnail gallery of all the images in a particular folder. Many image-viewing utilities are also available on the Web that let you view thumbnail galleries (see Figure 4.10). Following are some image viewers that you can download from the Web:

- CoffeeCup Free Viewer Plus at **www.coffeecup.com/viewer/** (freeware/Windows)
- XnView at **www.xnview.com/** (freeware/Windows, Macintosh, and Linux)
- ACDSee Classic at **www.acdsystems.com/English/Products/Other/ACDSeeClassic/** (Windows)
- Quick and Dirty Image Viewer at **www.epicware.com/** (freeware/Mac OS X)

HINT

For additional links to image viewers you can download and use, see this chapter's section at the IRC for this book at **www.emcp.com/** or visit the Tucows site at **www.tucows.com/**.

preview image

thumbnail image

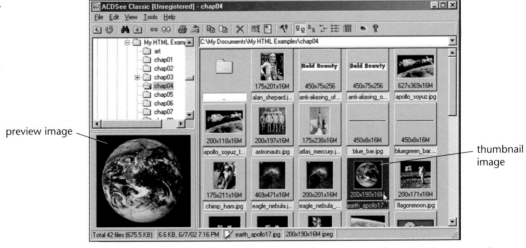

FIGURE 4.10 • *A thumbnail image viewer can make working with multiple images much easier.*

CASE EXAMPLE: CREATING AN ONLINE PICTURE GALLERY

A common way to present images on the Web is in an online picture gallery. Web authors might choose to display many different kinds of images in an online picture gallery, including personal snapshots, vacation photos, photographic artworks, paintings, drawings, sculptures, and so on.

Images can be presented as a gallery in many ways as well. One common way is to use left-aligned and right-aligned images in conjunction with caption text that describes the images. Additionally, online picture galleries usually use thumbnail images that link to fuller-sized images that can be viewed in a separate window. This method maximizes the number of images that can be shown on a gallery page, while keeping the size of the page as small as possible.

In addition to creating her online report on the Mercury spaceflight program, Shirley Johnson decided to create an online picture gallery of NASA space exploration images. Shirley already has a good start on her online gallery. She created her color scheme, set a background image, inserted images she wants to use, and wrote headings and captions for the gallery images.

To get started working with this example, from the chap04 folder, open **spacegallery_ex.html** in your text editor and resave it as **spacegallery.html** in the same folder. Open **spacegallery.html** in your browser (see Figure 4.11).

FIGURE 4.11 • *The color scheme, background image, images, headings, and captions are already set.*

CREATING A FLOWING LEFT-RIGHT GALLERY LAYOUT

To create this example you alternate left-aligned and right-aligned floating images, with headings and captions flowing around the images. You also set up the floating images to function as hypertext links to larger-sized versions of the images.

Floating the Gallery Images

Starting out, the gallery images are just inserted as regular inline images. You can float an image to either the left or right margin, but you need to be careful that following floating images do not also flow around the image. The BR (Break) element's CLEAR attribute lets you stop following text or elements from flowing around a floating image.

Float the first image and use the BR element's CLEAR attribute to stop following elements from flowing around the image (see Figure 4.12):

```
<hr>
<h2><img align="left" hspace="10" src="spacecapsules_th.jpg"
width="200" height="166" alt="Mercury, Gemini, and Apollo
spacecraft."> Mercury, Gemini, and Apollo Spacecraft</h2>
<p>The Mercury spacecraft carried one pilot, the Gemini
spacecraft carried two crew members, and the Apollo spacecraft
carried three crew members.<br clear="all"></p>

<hr>
<h2><img align="right" hspace="10" src="flagonmoon2_th.jpg"
width="200" height="169" alt="Astronaut Edwin Aldrin posing next
to U.S. flag on the moon.">U.S. Flag and Edwin "Buzz" Aldrin on
the Moon</h2>
<p>The Lunar Module "Eagle" is on the left. You can see the
footprints of the astronauts on the surface of the moon. The
picture was taken by Neil Armstrong on July 20, 1969.<br
clear="all"></p>
```

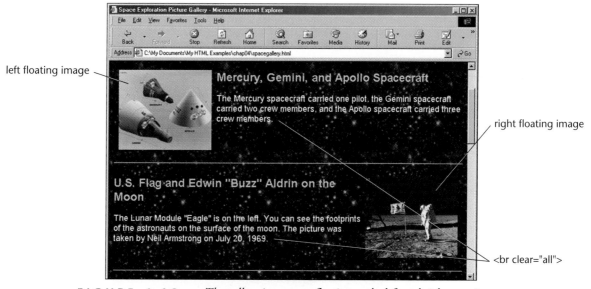

FIGURE 4.12 • *The gallery images are floating at the left and right margins.*

The CLEAR attribute value of **all** in the BR element causes following text or elements to clear any floating image. You also can set a CLEAR attribute value of **left** or **right**, which causes following text or elements to clear a left-aligned or right-aligned floating image, respectively.

Four more images are included in the online gallery. Using the first two images that have already been set up as floating images, do the same with the remaining images in the gallery. Alternate the image float from the left to the right and use BR elements with a `clear="all"` attribute at the end of the caption text to stop following text or elements from also flowing around the images.

Creating Image Links

An *image link* is an image that also functions as a hypertext link. To create an image link, you nest an inline image inside a hypertext link. An image link need not link to another image. It can link to any object that has an address on the Web.

A smaller-sized image that links to a larger-sized image is sometimes called a *thumbnail* image. For that reason, in the example file, the smaller-sized images have a "_th" at the end of their file names, while the larger-sized images do not have "_th" at the end of their file names.

Set up the first two floating images as image links:

1. Bracket the first two floating images with hypertext links that link to the corresponding fuller-sized images (see Figure 4.13):

```
<hr>
<h2><a href="spacecapsules.jpg"><img align="left" hspace="10"
src="spacecapsules_th.jpg" width="200" height="166"
alt="Mercury, Gemini, and Apollo spacecraft."></a>Mercury,
Gemini, and Apollo Spacecraft</h2>
<p>The Mercury spacecraft carried one pilot, the Gemini
spacecraft carried two crew members, and the Apollo spacecraft
carried three crew members.<br clear="all"></p>

<hr>
<h2><a href="flagonmoon2.jpg"><img align="right" hspace="10"
src="flagonmoon2_th.jpg" width="200" height="169" alt="Astronaut
Edwin Aldrin posing next to U.S. flag on the moon."></a>U.S.
Flag and Edwin "Buzz" Aldrin on the Moon</h2>
```

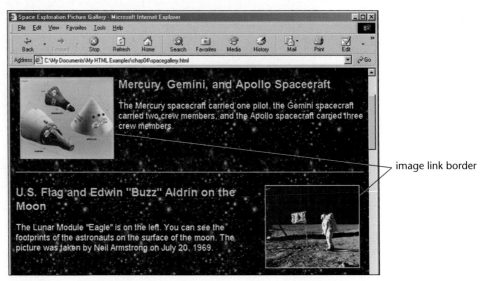

FIGURE 4.13 • *The first two floating images are set as image links.*

2. In your browser, click on the first image link to test it. The full-sized image should be displayed in the browser window (see Figure 4.14). Click your browser's Back button to return to the gallery page.

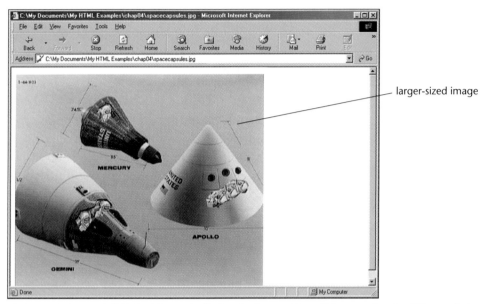
larger-sized image

FIGURE 4.14 • *A full-sized image is displayed when a visitor clicks on a thumbnail image link.*

When an image is set as an image link, a border is displayed around it. This border appears in whatever color is being displayed for unvisited and visited links, respectively, and serves the same function as the underline under a hypertext link.

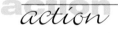

practice

Copy the first A element start tag, paste it in before the remaining floating images, and then edit the copies so they target the correct full-size images. Copy the A element end tag and paste it in following the remaining floating images.

Using the first two image links you created as a guide, also set the four remaining images as image links. Remember that the smaller-sized images have "_th" at the end of their file names, while the larger-sized images do not. After creating the image links, test each one in your browser.

CONTROLLING LINK TARGETS In the example, when you click on one of the image links, the object of the link is displayed in a browser window that replaces the current browser window. Some Web authors like to cause linked pages that are external to their own site to display in a second browser window, while the first browser window remains open in the background. They do this in order to keep visitors from simply taking an exit and never coming back. That way, when a visitor closes the second browser window, the first browser window should return to the foreground. The A element's TARGET attribute can be used to cause the object of a link to be displayed in a new browser window that does not replace the current browser window.

action

Cause the gallery's linked images to be displayed in a new browser window, rather than replacing the current browser window:

1. Insert a **target="_blank"** attribute in the first gallery image's link:

```
<h2><a href="spacecapsules.jpg" target="_blank"><img align="left"
hspace="10" src="spacecapsules_th.jpg" width="200" height="166"
alt="Mercury, Gemini, and Apollo spacecraft."></a>Mercury, Gemini,
and Apollo Spacecraft</h2>
```

2. Do the same for the other gallery images' links.
3. Test any of the image links. To return to the gallery page, close the new window that has been opened (click on the Close button in the upper-right corner).

To have the linked image display in the same browser window, rather than open a new browser window, substitute `target="_top"` for `target="_blank"`. A visitor then only has to click the Back button to return to the linking browser window.

TURNING OFF AN IMAGE LINK'S BORDER The introductory paragraph tells the visitor that the thumbnail images can be clicked on to view the full-size images. In this case, you can thus safely turn off the display of the image link border. You need to be careful, however, turning off image link borders, because visitors to your page might not be able to tell that an image link is a link if there is no border displayed around the image.

Turn off the image link borders:

1. Turn off the first image link border:

```
<h2><a href="spacecapsules.jpg" target="_blank"><img border="0"
align="left" hspace="10" src="spacecapsules_th.jpg" width="200"
height="166" alt="Mercury, Gemini, and Apollo
spacecraft."></a>Mercury, Gemini, and Apollo Spacecraft</h2>
```

2. Do the same for the other image links (see Figure 4.15).

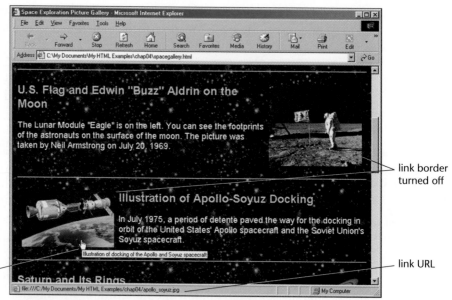

FIGURE 4.15 • *The image link borders are turned off.*

Although the image link borders are turned off, when a visitor passes the mouse pointer over one of the image links, as shown in Figure 4.15, the image still behaves as a link, with a "hand" cursor displayed over the image and the link URL displayed on the browser's status bar.

USING RULES, BANNERS, AND BUTTONS

Using graphic rules and banners can add visual appeal to your page, as well as give it more of a 3-D look.

Using Graphic Rules

A *graphic rule* is an image of variable width (usually 400 to 500 pixels in width), but which usually does not have a height of more than 5 to 10 pixels. Graphic rules are generally used as decorative separators and can be used in place of horizontal rules, giving your page a more colorful and 3-D look. An example graphic rule, **bluegreen_bar.jpg**, is included with this chapter's example files.

 Replace the HR element with a graphic rule:

1. Replace the first HR element with the example graphic rule:

```
<hr>
<p align="center"><img src="bluegreen_bar.jpg" height="8"
width="100%" alt="Horizontal separator"></p>
<h2><a href="spacecapsules.jpg" target="_blank"><img border="0"
align="left" hspace="10" src="spacecapsules_th.jpg" width="200"
height="166" alt="Mercury, Gemini, and Apollo
spacecraft."></a>Mercury, Gemini, and Apollo Spacecraft</h2>
```

2. Replace the remaining HR elements with the same example graphic rule (see Figure 4.16).

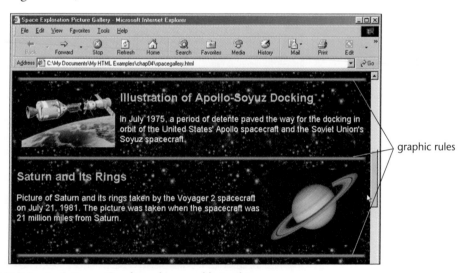

FIGURE 4.16 • *Graphic rules can add visual impact to a page.*

Notice that a percentage value (`width="100%"`) is used to set the width of the graphic rule. This is an exception to the general rule that you should specify the actual dimensions of an image and not a different size at which you want it to display. Varying the width of a graphic rule relative to the width of the browser window allows it to reduplicate the function of a horizontal rule (the width of which is also dynamically resized relative to the width of the browser window). This method also does not generally cause problems with image quality because a graphic rule's height is small (usually less than 10 pixels), so that increasing only its width is unlikely to magnify flaws within the image.

You can easily create your own graphic rules in your image editor. Most image editors allow you to add various effects to a graphic rule. The example graphic rule, for instance, was created in Paint Shop Pro, using its buttonize effect. A good width for a graphical rule is 450 pixels, which is short enough that it should not have its width reduced and is long enough that it should not undergo much distortion when being stretched to fill 100 percent of a browser's window.

Using a Transparent Banner Image

When displaying a background image, a banner image with one of its colors set to be transparent can make an effective visual impact. An example banner image with a transparent background color is included with this chapter's example files.

Add a banner image and turn off the display of the H1 element:

1. Add a style to the CENTER element that reduces the bottom margin of that element and then insert a banner image above the H1 element:

```
<center style="margin-bottom: -1em">
<p><img src="spacegallery.gif" width="450" height="75"
alt="Space Gallery Banner Image"></p>
<h1>Space Exploration Gallery</h1>
</center>
```

2. Edit the style sheet in the HEAD element to turn off display of the H1 element (see Figure 4.17):

```
h1 { color: aqua; background: transparent; display: none; }
```

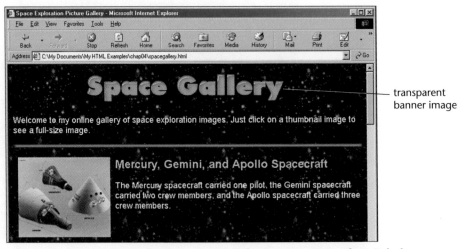

transparent banner image

FIGURE 4.17 • *A transparent banner image can help give a page more of a 3-D look.*

Notice in the example that the H1 element is left in the page, but with its display turned off (by the **display: none** style property), instead of simply being replaced by the banner image. The reason for this is that some search engines place special weight on the content of your H1 element when indexing your page, so it pays to leave it in, even though turning off its display.

Using Navigation Icons and Button Links

A *navigation icon* is an image that portrays an action a visitor can take by clicking on the image. For instance, a graphic of a house functioning as an image link conveys the idea that it is a link to the home page of the site or author. A left-pointing arrow conveys the idea that the link goes to the previous page, while a right-pointing arrow conveys that the link goes to the next page in a series of pages.

A button link is similar to a navigational icon because its design (with 3-D borders) conveys its function (that it can be clicked on), while its label conveys the action or result that will occur when a visitor clicks on the button.

Because they graphically indicate their function and purpose, it is customary to turn off the border of navigation icons and button links. An example button image, gobutton.gif, with the word "Go" as its label, is included with the other example files for this chapter.

action

Add an image link to the bottom of the page, below the address block, that uses a button link to link to Shirley Johnson's home page (see Figure 4.18):

```
</address>
<p align="center"><a href="home.html" style="text-decoration:
none"><img src="gobutton.gif" width="100" height="50" alt="Go
button" border="0" hspace="8" align="middle">to my Home
Page</a></p>
```

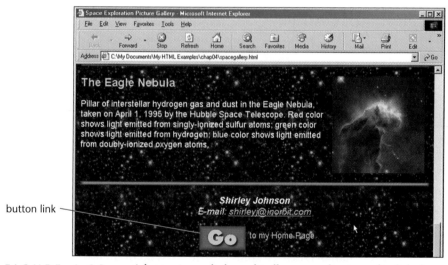

button link

FIGURE 4.18 • *A button image link graphically conveys that it can be clicked to go to an object or resource.*

Notice that the ALIGN attribute is used here to vertically align the image relative to the text line on which it is inserted—in this case, the middle of the image is aligned with the image's text line. You also can specify `align="top"` to align the top of the image relative to its text line. Bottom-alignment is the default. If you set top-, middle-, or bottom-alignment, you cannot also set left- or right-alignment. A style is also used to turn off underlining of the link to the right of the button.

The inline style in the A element, `text-decoration: none`, turns off the underline for the text following the button, which still functions as part of the link.

Finding Images on the Web

Many repositories of images are available on the Web. Always carefully read any terms of use that are posted relative to images you find on the Web (if you do not see a terms of use page, look for an FAQ page). Some images are true public domain images that you are free to use in any manner that you choose, either due to the lapsing of their copyright or a creator releasing them into the public domain. Many other images, however, are free to use only if you can satisfy the terms of use. Some images, for instance, are free for personal, non-commercial, or educational purposes, but not for commercial or for-profit purposes. Some providers also require a credit and a link back to their site if you use their images on your site.

A number of sites specifically provide clip art images that can be freely used by instructors and students in an educational environment. Many other Web art repositories allow free use of their art images for non-commercial or educational purposes. Following are some of these sources of clip art on the Web:

- Classroom Clipart at **www.classroomclipart.com/**
- Discovery School's Clip Art Gallery at **school.discovery.com/clipart/**
- Art Images for College Teaching (AICT) at **www.mcad.edu/AICT/**
- The Clip Art Connection at **www.clipartconnection.com/**
- GifArt.com at **www.gifart.com/**

HINT

For additional clip art resources, visit this book's IRC at **www.emcp.com/**.

CREATING YOUR OWN WEB IMAGES

You can create your own Web art images to give your page or site a unique or personalized appearance. To create your own Web art images, you need an image editor that can create and save GIF and JPEG images. A wide array of image editors can be used to create Web art images. If you do not already have an image editor you can use, here are some you can try out:

- **Adobe Photoshop (www.adobe.com/products/photoshop/).** The tool of choice preferred by many professional graphic designers (Windows and Macintosh).
- **Paint Shop Pro by Jasc Software (www.jasc.com/products/psp/).** A full-feature image editor that is both powerful and easy to use (Windows).
- **WebPainter by Totally Hip Software (www.totallyhip.com/).** A full-feature, but inexpensive, image editor (Windows and Macintosh).
- **Corel Draw Graphics Suite (www.corel.com/** for Windows and Macintosh; **www.linux.corel.com/** for Linux). Includes both Corel Draw and Corel PhotoPaint, either can be used to create Web graphics (Windows, Macintosh, and Linux).

HINT

For links to additional image editors and graphic utilities, see this chapter's section at the IRC for this book at **www.emcp.com/** or visit the Tucows site at **www.tucows.com/**.

Determining which Format: GIF or JPEG?

Beginning Web authors are often perplexed by which image format—GIF or JPEG—to use for displaying images on the Web. The GIF and JPEG image formats are different, so their relative strengths and weaknesses should determine which one you use to save a particular image.

The GIF image format works best for images that include line art, flat colors, and fewer than 256 colors. When such an image is saved as a GIF, it produces a smaller image, measured in bytes, than if the image is saved as a JPEG.

Photographs or other images with continuous tones or blends and with more than 256 colors should be saved as JPEG images. The exception to this rule is an image containing text. Buttons and banners with text as a prominent or primary feature, for instance, even if they contain color gradients and blends, should be saved as a GIF image because the JPEG image format, due to the kind of compression it applies, tends to blur sharp edges (such as the edges of letterforms) within an image.

For an image with a transparent background, you need to create a GIF image; JPEG images do not support transparency.

For images that contain both text and gradient blends, saving them as straight GIF images will likely produce undesirable dithering or banding effects within the image. *Dithering* is done by positioning pixels of different colors next to each other in order to simulate to the eye that a single color is present, which can result in a color with a speckled or mottled appearance that barely resembles the desired color. Without dithering, areas that use blends, gradients, or continuous tones might be displayed as a sequence of distinct color bands because only colors that are actually included in the palette can be displayed. Dithering is sometimes also referred to as *error diffusion*.

The answer to these problems is to save your GIF image using an optimized color palette, which contains only colors that are included within your image, rather than the standard GIF palette, which might contain many colors not included in your image.

Example graphics are included with this chapter's example files that show the same image saved as a JPEG image (with a 40-percent compression), an optimized GIF image, a non-optimized GIF image (with dithering), and a non-optimized GIF image (without dithering). To view these images in your browser, just open **image_compare.html** from the chap04 folder (see Figure 4.19).

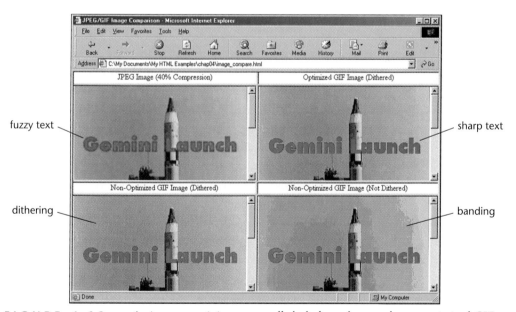

FIGURE 4.19 • *An image containing text usually looks best when saved as an optimized GIF image.*

The next section, "Creating GIF Images," provides more detailed directions on how to create optimized GIF images.

Creating GIF Images

The GIF image format was originally created by the CompuServe online service, to provide a means to exchange images over its network. GIF images use a form of compression and thus have smaller sizes in bytes than the same images saved in a non-compressed image format. Although GIF images were not originally designed for display on the Web, a number of basic methods and techniques have been created by Web authors that make using GIF images over the Web effective.

USING THE WEB-SAFE COLOR PALETTE In Chapter 3, *Working with Fonts, Colors, and Backgrounds*, you learned about using the *Web-safe color palette* to set HTML colors in Web pages. GIF images saved using the Web-safe color palette include only 216 colors that are included in all system palettes, which ensures that colors in the image will not be dithered on a system that is only able to display 256 colors. To ensure that everyone, regardless of the capabilities of their graphics card, sees the same image, you can save your image using the Web-safe (or browser-safe) color palette, rather than your system's default color palette. The system palettes for Windows and Macintosh are similar, but each contain colors not present in the other. Most full-feature image editors either default to saving GIF images using a Web-safe color palette, or allow you to select it as an option.

The problem with using the Web-safe palette, however, is that it only works well for images with relatively few colors or color gradations. Images that contain many colors that are not included in the Web-safe palette are likely to suffer considerably when saved using that palette. In other words, if you are concerned that some viewers of your image will see a lot of dithered colors, making sure that everyone sees a lot of dithered colors is hardly an optimum solution.

CREATING AN OPTIMIZED COLOR PALETTE Fewer and fewer users are accessing the Web using systems only capable of displaying 256 colors. As a Web author, you need to decide whether to design your site to make sure that a small minority of viewers have an optimal viewing experience, while limiting the visual appeal of your images to the vast majority of viewers. Increasingly, Web authors are choosing to focus their design efforts on the majority of viewers who are using true-color graphics cards (capable of displaying colors selected from a palette of 16.7 million colors).

GIF images, however, can only display up to 256 colors. When you save an image that has many more than 256 colors as a GIF image using the Web-safe palette, the image quality can suffer tremendously. Such images should be saved with an *optimized palette* (also called an *adaptive palette* in Photoshop). For instance, in Paint Shop Pro 7 for Windows, you create an optimized palette for an image like this:

1. Select Colors, Decrease Color Depth, and X Colors (4/8 bit).
2. For the Number of colors, select 216. Select the Optimized Median Cut radio button and the Reduce color bleeding check box. If you are not including a transparent color, select the Error diffusion radio button (otherwise, select the Nearest color radio button) (see Figure 4.20). Click OK.
3. Save your image as a CompuServe Graphics Interchange (*.gif) file.

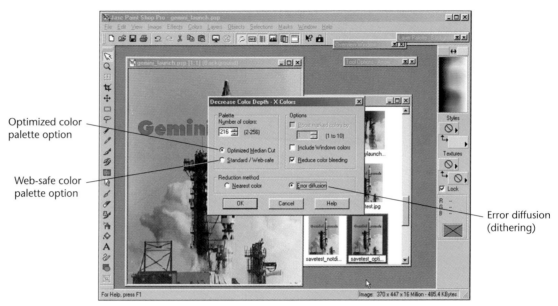

Optimized color palette option

Web-safe color palette option

Error diffusion (dithering)

NOTE

As shown in Figure 4.20, when creating an optimized color palette, you can choose 256 or fewer as the number of colors. The fewer colors you can select and still retain acceptable image quality, the fewer bytes the resulting image will consume.

If you are creating a GIF image with a transparent background color, choosing the Error diffusion radio button can result in the color of your background being diffused into more than one color. Because only one color can be defined as transparent, this can interfere with setting the background of your image as entirely transparent. If you want to set a transparent background, your choices are to either turn off error diffusion or refill your image's background later with a solid color.

Many image editors also include wizards that help automate the creation of optimized GIF images. These editors often let you see the results of different settings as you are using them.

USING TRANSPARENT GIF IMAGES An additional problem can occur when creating transparent GIF images that will be displayed against a non-white background in a Web page. If you include a text object that uses anti-aliasing, the edges of the curves and diagonals are blended with the image's background to give them a smoother appearance. If your image's background is white, the anti-aliasing blends to white; the problem occurs if you set the white background color of your image as transparent and then try to display it against a non-white background set in a Web page. Especially against a darker background color or image, the result will be a noticeable white "halo" around your text's letterforms, as shown in Figure 4.21. To see this for yourself, just open **anti-aliasing.html** in your browser from the chap04 folder. This also can be a problem with any other effect that blends a color into your image's background, such as a drop shadow effect, for instance.

FIGURE 4.21 • *Anti-aliasing can cause text in a transparent GIF image to display a white halo effect if created against a white background but displayed against a dark background.*

A workaround exists that allows you to use anti-aliasing in a transparent GIF image that you want to display against a Web page's non-white background. All you have to do is set the background color you want to be transparent within your image so that it closely matches the color of your Web page's background. You can do this by trying to match the color you want to use in your image editor with the background color displayed in your Web page, or you can make an exact match.

Paint Shop Pro 7 for Windows, in fact, lets you specify a color's hexadecimal RGB code (see Figure 4.22) when selecting a color, so all you have know is the corresponding hexadecimal RGB code for the background color that is used in your Web page to set an exactly matching color in your image. Just fill the background of your image with the selected color that you want to be transparent and then create your text object using anti-aliasing or a drop shadow effect on top of that color. The anti-aliasing or drop shadow effect will now blend to the new color, rather than to white.

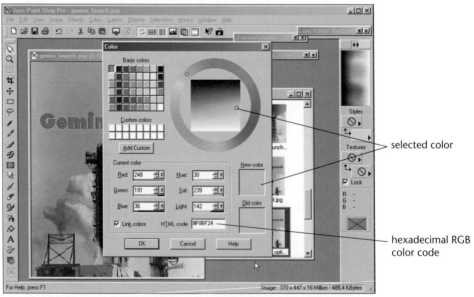

FIGURE 4.22 • *In Paint Shop Pro 7 for Windows, you can select a color based on its hexadecimal RGB code.*

A background image, however, can contain a number of colors. Most full-feature image editors contain an eye-dropper tool that lets you pick up a color from an image and set it as the color of your foreground or background swatch. Just open the background image in your image editor that you are using in your Web page, and then use its eye-dropper tool to assign a color included in the background image to the foreground color swatch. Figure 4.23 shows a color being picked up out of a background image using Paint Shop Pro 7's Dropper tool; with the mouse cursor hovering over the desired color, right-clicking assigns it to the foreground color swatch. The Flood Fill tool can then be used to fill an image's background with the selected color.

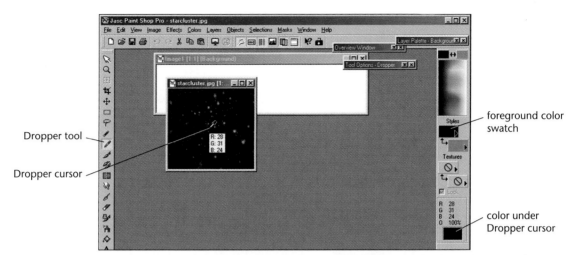

FIGURE 4.23 • *Paint Shop Pro 7's Dropper tool can pick up a color from a background image and assign it to the foreground color swatch.*

Picking the right color out of a background image to be used as a transparent background color in your image can take a little trial and error. Try to pick a color that is either the most prominent or one of the more common colors in the image.

USING INTERLACED GIF IMAGES *Interlacing* refers to displaying an image or display in more than one pass, with only some of the lines in the image or display appearing in any one pass. Earlier computer displays often used interlacing to display higher resolutions than they would otherwise be able to present, by displaying the odd lines in the display first, and then displaying the even lines. Interlacing in GIF images works in a somewhat similar fashion, except that four passes are used to display an interlaced GIF image, with the last two passes filling in progressively more lines than the first two passes. The result is that a viewer can start seeing what a downloaded interlaced GIF image will look like much sooner than with a non-interlaced GIF image.

Many visitors just click the Back button if they think a site's images are taking too long to display. By saving your GIF images as interlaced, you can give visitors to your site a much earlier indication of what the images will look like. When you save a GIF image, most image editors let you choose an option to save your image as interlaced.

Using JPEG Images

A photographic image or an image with a lot of colors or blends is best saved as a JPEG image. The exception to this rule is an image that includes text, which is best saved as an optimized GIF image because a JPEG image's compression method tends to blur and fuzz the edges of letterforms.

When you save a JPEG image, most image editors let you set a compression level for the image. The higher the compression level, the smaller the resulting file size will be. The smaller the file size, the quicker the image will download and display. Finding the right compression level for a JPEG image is a matter of finding the right balance between preserving image quality and saving bytes. Here is one way you can try to find the optimum compression level for an image:

1. Save your image as a JPEG with the lowest level of compression set, as **testimage1.jpg**, for instance. In most image editors, you can usually set the compression level for a JPEG image through an option in the Save dialog box. Figure 4.24 shows the compression level for a JPEG image being set in Paint Shop Pro for Windows.

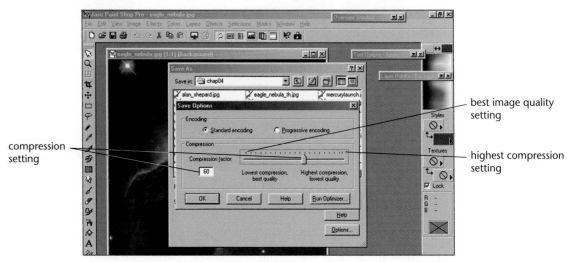

compression setting

best image quality setting

highest compression setting

FIGURE 4.24 • *When saving a JPEG image, the higher the compression level, the lower the image quality.*

2. Resave your image as a JPEG image at a compression level of 25 percent, as **testimage2.jpg**, for instance.
3. Repeat resaving your image, but at progressively higher compression levels, at 30 percent, 40 percent, 50 percent, and 60 percent, for instance. Save your images as **testimage3.jpg**, **testimage4.jpg**, and so on.
4. Close the original image and then open all the saved test images in your image editor. Position them side-by-side and compare the results. Use your image editor's zoom tool to get a closer look.
5. Compare the file sizes of the images. In Windows, for instance, in any Save or Open dialog box or in Windows Explorer, you can click the Details icon to display file details, including file sizes in kilobytes. In the Finder on the Macintosh, you can select View and choose to view the contents of a folder as a list, which displays the file size of each file (although you might need to scroll over to see it).
6. Identify which of the images provides you with the best balance of preserved image quality and savings in file size. That file represents the optimal compression settings for that particular image.

Realize, however, that some images can take much higher levels of compression than other images. The optimal level of compression can be different for each JPEG image you want to create. In general, however, you can usually compress JPEG images up to 20 to 30 percent without appreciable loss of image quality. Some images can take as much as a 50 percent compression, while others can take as high as 60 percent.

JPEG images use a *lossy* compression scheme. A lossy compression scheme results in bits in the image being thrown away, which means that a JPEG image cannot be uncompressed after it has been compressed. A *lossless* compression scheme, on the other hand, does not throw away bytes, which means that an image saved using such a scheme can later be uncompressed, with no bytes being lost. You should not store original images you create as JPEG images, but should save them in your image editor's proprietary format (PSD for Photoshop or PSP for Paint Shop Pro, for instance) or in an image format that uses a lossless compression scheme, such as PNG or TIFF.

Most image editors let you save a JPEG image as either a *standard* or a *progressive* JPEG image. A progressive JPEG image displays in a similar fashion to an interlaced GIF image, except that progressively higher resolutions of the image are displayed, starting with a low-resolution image. As with interlaced GIFs, viewers are able to see what the downloaded JPEG image will look like before it has completely downloaded. Earlier Web browsers, however, can have problems displaying progressive JPEG images. For that reason, many Web authors stick to just using standard JPEG images in their Web pages.

NOTE

Using the FONT element or styles, you are limited to displaying fonts that are available on a viewer's local computer. When creating your own Web images, however, you can use any font you have installed on your system, since you will be using them in a graphic instead of displaying them as part of your page's text. You can use a Dracula font, for instance, to create a banner graphic for your page if you have that font installed on your computer. For links to places on the Web where you can find and download fonts, see this chapter's section at the IRC for this book at **www.emcp.com/**. Before using a font, however, read the terms of use for copyright information and restrictions on use.

Using Other Image Formats

The PNG (Portable Network Graphics) image format has features in common with both GIF and JPEG images. Like GIF images, PNG images support transparency and interlacing. Although GIF images support only a single transparent color, PNG images can specify multiple transparent colors. Like JPEG images, PNG images support true-color images (up to a 48-bit palette as compared to up to a 24-bit palette for JPEGS). PNG images use a lossless compression scheme, rather than a lossy compression scheme, as is the case with JPEG images. Thus, although a PNG image can be uncompressed whereas a JPEG image cannot be uncompressed, the additional overhead required to encode every byte within the image means that the same image saved as a PNG image will likely be larger in bytes than if it were saved as a JPEG image.

Because earlier browsers and even some more recent browsers might not display PNG images, most Web authors still stick to using GIF and JPEG images. Eventually, PNG images are expected to replace GIF images on the Web, but not JPEG images. To find out more about the PNG image format, see the Portable Network Graphics site at **www.libpng.org/pub/png/**.

Another image format that shows a lot of promise is the SVG (Scalable Vector Graphics) format. Using SVG graphics, Web authors can create vector graphics and animations that will scale relative to a system's display. GIF and JPEG images are saved at fixed pixel dimensions, which do not scale relative to a system's display. To view SVG graphics, you can install the free Adobe SVG Viewer (for Windows or the Macintosh) at **www.adobe.com/svg/**.

Many other image formats are available, including BMP, WMF, TIFF, PCX, PICT, and more. Although these image formats are fine for using in a desktop publishing program where you only need to display them on your local computer and print them on your printer, they should not be used for display in a Web page.

Because Internet Explorer displays BMP images, many beginning Web authors mistakenly think that it is okay to use BMP images in Web pages. Many other browsers, such as Netscape Navigator, for instance, do not display BMP images. The BMP image format also does not use any compression, so images saved in that format can be many times larger than the same image saved as a GIF, JPEG, or PNG image. An image that has a size in the tens of kilobytes when saved as a JPEG image, for instance, can have a size of hundreds of kilobytes when saved as a BMP image. In other words, do not use BMP or WMF images in Web pages, even if you know everybody accessing your page will be using Internet Explorer.

USING ANIMATIONS

You can include media other than still graphics in a Web page. By adding animations to your pages, you can make them more dynamic and eye-catching than pages that include only still images (or no images at all).

Using GIF Animations

The GIF image format allows for the inclusion of multiple image frames within a single image. When displayed in a Web browser, the image frames within the image are displayed at a frame rate that can be set when the image is created. An example GIF animation, go_anim.gif, is included with this chapter's example files.

Replace the previous navigation icon at the bottom of the page with a GIF animation, go_anim.gif, set the image's vertical spacing to 5 pixels, and insert a BR element to move the following text below the image (see Figure 4.25):

```
</address>
<p align="center"><a href="home.html" style="text-decoration:
none"><img src="go_anim.gif" vspace="5" width="100" height="50"
alt="Go button" border="0" hspace="8" align="middle"><br>to my
Home Page</a></p>
```

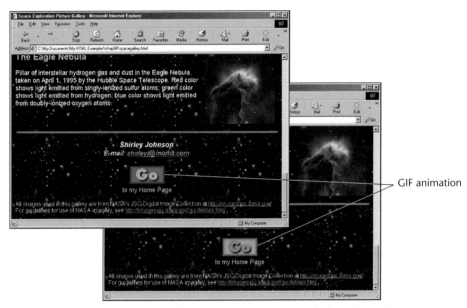

FIGURE 4.25 • *A GIF animation also can function as an image link and a navigation icon.*

Notice that a BR element is added that moves the following text below the GIF animation, and 5 pixels of vertical spacing is added to provide extra spacing between the animation and the following text. The `align="middle"` attribute is deleted because it has no effect with the following text moved below the image.

To create your own GIF animations, you need a GIF animation editor. Here are some GIF animation editors you can download and try:

- **Animation Shop (www.jasc.com/).** An excellent GIF animation editor included with Paint Shop Pro for Windows.
- **GIF Construction Set Professional (www.mindworkshop.com/alchemy/ gifcon.html).** A shareware GIF animation editor for Windows.
- **GIFfun (www.stone.com/GIFfun/).** A freeware GIF animation editor for the Macintosh.
- **Gifsicle (www.lcdf.org/~eddietwo/gifsicle/).** A freeware GIF animation utility for Linux.

For links to additional GIF animation editors, visit this chapter's section at the IRC for this book at **www.emcp.com/** or the Tucows site at **www.tucows.com/**.

Many GIF animation editors include animation wizards that make creating GIF animations as simple as selecting the images you want to use, the order in which you want them to appear, and the frame rate at which you want your animation to display. After you have created an animation, you can change the settings for individual frames, create transitions between frames, add and delete frames, preview the animation, and so on. Figure 4.26 shows go_anim.gif open in Animation Shop for Windows.

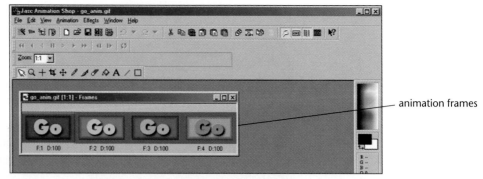

FIGURE 4.26 • *Using a GIF animation editor, you can create, edit, and preview your own GIF animations.*

GIF animations, although they can include multiple image frames, are still GIF images. The color palette used to display all the frames within a GIF animation is still limited to no more than 256 colors. The result is that some GIF images included in a GIF animation can suffer visually, due to additional dithering, for instance. Some GIF animators also let you import JPEG, PNG, or other true-color images that can suffer considerably from dithering when converted to GIF format within a GIF animation.

One way to try to fix this problem is to edit the individual images in your image editor and create optimized color palettes for each one that include only the minimal number of colors required to produce acceptable image quality. For instance, if you can reduce the total number of colors used by each image to 128 or 64 colors, you will reduce or eliminate the dithering that can result when the images are combined within a GIF animation.

File size is another issue to consider with GIF animations. For instance, a 4-frame GIF animation created in Animation Shop with the highest image quality settings produces an 8-KB (kilobyte) file, an 8-frame animation produces a 14-KB file, and a 16-frame animation produces a 27-KB file. If you add any transition effects between frames, that can add many additional frames to your animation, depending on the effect being used. Also, the more image frames you include in your animation, the more likely that individual images in your animation will be dithered. For these reasons, it is usually best to limit the number of frames included in a GIF animation; you would not want to include a 200-KB GIF animation in a Web page, for instance (a more reasonable size would be 30-KB to 50-KB, or less).

Using Other Animations

GIF animations are not the only kinds of animations that can be included in a Web page. Flash or Java animations can include many more effects than GIF animations. These types of animations can also do much more than just provide dynamic movement; they can create multimedia effects (animation, video, and audio effects) that interact with user actions or respond to events. Here are some software tools that can be used to create interactive Flash or Java animations for the Web:

- **Macromedia Flash for Windows or the Macintosh (www.macromedia.com/).** The program that introduced the Flash animation format.
- **Adobe LiveMotion (www.adobe.com/products/livemotion/).** Another full-feature Flash animation editor for Windows and the Macintosh.
- **CoffeeCup Firestarter (www.coffeecup.com/firestarter/).** A Flash animation editor for Windows that is much less expensive to purchase than Flash or LiveMotion.

For links to additional animation programs, see this chapter's section at the IRC for this book at **www.emcp.com/** or visit the Tucows site at **www.tucows.com/**.

- **AnFX (www.stepaheadsoftware.com/anfx.htm).** An inexpensive Java animation editor for Windows that lets you create interactive Java animations that conform to Sun's Java standard.

ADDING SOUND

You can add background sound that plays automatically when a Web page displays. An example WAV-format audio file, kennedy.wav is included with this chapter's example files.

Embedding Audio Files

The EMBED element is not actually a standard HTML element, but is an unofficial extension to HTML that was introduced by Netscape and is supported by most browsers.

PLAYING AN AUDIO FILE AUTOMATICALLY IN THE BACKGROUND You can embed an audio file that will play automatically in the background when the page is opened in a browser.

Add and test a WAV file that plays automatically in the background when the page is opened:

1. At the bottom of the page, use the EMBED element to insert an audio file that plays automatically in the background:

```
<p><embed src="kennedy.wav" autostart="true" loop="false"
width="2" height="2"></p>
</body>
```

2. Save your HTML file, switch to your browser, and click the Refresh (or Reload) button.

If your computer has a sound card and is otherwise configured to play WAV audio files, an audio file of President John F. Kennedy announcing the program to land a man on the moon will start playing in the background.

If the WAV file does not play in your browser, you may need to download and install a player or plug-in that will play WAV files. See this chapter's section at the IRC for this book at **www.emcp.com/** for a selection of audio/video players.

In the example, the `width="2"` and `height="2"` attribute values have the effect of hiding the WAV player console from view. These settings are necessary for the background sound to play in some versions of the QuickTime player, which will not play the audio file if the width and height are set to **0**. Because the 2-pixel × 2-pixel dimensions that are set might impact the formatting of the page if the EMBED element is inserted at the top of the page, it is inserted at the bottom of the page where it will have no impact on the page's formatting.

The **autostart="true"** attribute causes the audio file to start playing automatically as soon as it is finished downloading. The **loop="false"** attribute causes the audio file to only play once, rather than being looped indefinitely. Especially when hiding the player console, indefinitely looping an audio file that plays automatically in the background is strongly discouraged because users have no way of turning it off, except by accessing their system's audio volume controls. Because some visitors find audio annoying, you could also set **autostart="false"**, especially if the embedded audio is on your front page.

A common error is to specify a numerical value for the EMBED element's LOOP attribute, to specify a set number of loops, such as **loop="2"**, for instance. This causes varying results in different players, with some defaulting to looping the media file only once, while others loop it indefinitely. Always set either **true** or **false** as the LOOP attribute's value.

PLAYING AN AUDIO FILE AUTOMATICALLY IN THE FOREGROUND If you want to automatically play an indefinitely looping audio file, you should set the dimensions of the player console to make it is visible in the browser window, so users can turn off the audio if they wish.

Move the EMBED element from the bottom to the top of the page and edit it to cause the player console to be visible:

1. First, place HTML comment codes around the EMBED element that is already in the document (that way, you can go back to using it later, just by removing the comment codes):

```
<!--
<p><embed src="kennedy.wav" autostart="true" loop="false"
width="2" height="2"></p>
-->
</body>
```

2. Highlight and copy the EMBED element (but not the P element start and end tags).
3. Paste the EMBED element above the banner image's IMG element, as shown here:

```
<center style="margin-bottom: -1em">
<embed src="kennedy.wav" autostart="true" loop="false" width="2"
height="2">
<img src="spacegallery.gif" class="banner" width="450"
height="75" alt="Space Gallery Banner Image">
```

4. Edit the EMBED element to set an indefinite loop, specify width and height dimensions for the player console, and add a BR element:

```
<embed src="kennedy.wav" autostart="true" loop="true"
width="145" height="45"><br>
```

5. Save the document, switch over to your browser, and click the Refresh (or Reload) button (see Figure 4.27).

Stop button

player console
(EMBED element)

FIGURE 4.27 • *Displaying the player console on the page lets a user turn off the playing of a looping or long audio file.*

The width and height dimensions (145 and 45 pixels) are the minimum required to display the slider bar showing the progress of the playing of the audio file in the Windows Media player console. The player console displayed, however, depends upon which audio player is associated with WAV files. If that is the QuickTime player, for instance, then the QuickTime player console is displayed instead.

Even if you are not looping your audio file, you might want to display the player console, rather than hide it, if your audio file is longer than 10 to 15 seconds. That way, those who might be irritated by a background audio file playing can easily turn it off. Others might click the Back button as soon as they hear a background audio playing, especially if they are working in an office environment; if the player console is clearly visible and available, they can just as easily click the player console's Stop button.

USING THE **NOEMBED** ELEMENT   The NOEMBED element provides content that is displayed for visitors using browsers that do not support the EMBED element. The content of the NOEMBED element is generally a link that a visitor can click to play the media file.

Add a NOEMBED element that provides a link to the audio file if a visitor's browser doesn't support the EMBED element:

```
<embed src="kennedy.wav" autostart="true" loop="true" width="145"
height="45">
<noembed>Listen to <a
href="kennedy.wav">kennedy.wav.</a></noembed>
<br>
```

SPECIFYING A **PLUG-IN** PAGE   One problem with including audio in Web pages is that a user needs to have an appropriate player or plug-in to play the audio. The EMBED element's PLUGINSPLAYER attribute can be used to specify a URL for downloading an appropriate plug-in player for the audio format being played.

Use the PLUGINSPAGE attribute to specify the URL where the QuickTime player can be downloaded:

```
<embed src="kennedy.wav" autostart="true" loop="true"
width="145" height="45"
pluginspage="http://www.apple.com/quicktime/download/">
<noembed>Listen to <a
href="kennedy.wav">kennedy.wav.</a></noembed>
<br>
```

If a browser does not have the appropriate plug-in player to play a particular media file, it will present the URL provided by the PLUGINSPAGE attribute, so that the user can download a plug-in player capable of playing the media file.

Using the OBJECT Element to Insert Audio Files

The OBJECT element is a standard element included in HTML 4 that is intended as a generic means to insert objects into Web pages. An object might be an image, a sound file, a video, a Java applet, and so on. You can even embed an HTML file inside another HTML file as an object. The PARAM (Parameter) element can be nested inside the OBJECT element to set display, behavior, and other parameters.

PLAYING AN AUDIO FILE AUTOMATICALLY IN THE FOREGROUND Previously, you used the EMBED element to insert a WAV audio file that plays automatically when the page is opened. The same thing can be accomplished using the OBJECT element.

Comment out the EMBED element you added previously and then use the OBJECT element to automatically play and loop a WAV audio file with the player console displayed (see Figure 4.28):

```
<center style="margin-bottom: -1em">
<!--<embed src="kennedy.wav" autostart="true" loop="true"
width="145" height="45"
pluginspage="http://www.apple.com/quicktime/download/">
<noembed>Listen to <a
href="kennedy.wav">kennedy.wav.</a></noembed>
<br>
-->
<img src="spacegallery4.gif" class="banner" width"450" height="75"
alt="Space Gallery Banner Image"><br>
<object data="kennedy.wav" type="audio/wav" width="145"
height="45" vspace="5">
<param name="src" value="kennedy.wav">
<param name="autostart" value="true">
<param name="controller" value="true">
<param name="loop" value="true">
President Kennedy calling for landing a man on the moon.
</object>
<h1>Space Exploration Gallery</h1>
</center>
```

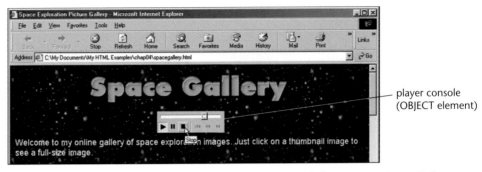

player console
(OBJECT element)

FIGURE 4.28 • *The OBJECT element, a standard HTML 4 element, is used to embed an audio file in a Web page.*

To not automatically play the audio file in the foreground, set a value of **false** for the **autostart** parameter. To listen to the audio file, the user must click the player console's Play button.

The OBJECT element's TYPE attribute specifies the MIME type (or content type) of an object file. MIME stands for *Multipurpose Internet Mail Extensions* and was originally devised to identify different e-mail attachments, but is now used more generally to identify files on the Internet. For instance, **audio/wav**, **image/gif**, and **text/css** are all MIME types for files that can be downloaded over the Web. MIME types have two parts, a type and a subtype, with **audio** specifying the type and **wav** specifying the subtype, for instance. Including the TYPE attribute in the OBJECT element is optional, but recommended; if a browser does not recognize the MIME type, it can simply not download the object.

Various additional attributes can be used with the OBJECT element. For a listing, see Appendix A, *HTML Quick Reference*. For further explanation of how to use the OBJECT element, see the W3C's HTML 4.01 specification at **www.w3.org/TR/html401/**.

PLAYING AN AUDIO FILE AUTOMATICALLY IN THE BACKGROUND You also can use the OBJECT element to automatically play an audio file in the background when a Web page is opened.

action

Use the OBJECT and PARAM elements to automatically play, but not loop, a WAV audio file with the player console hidden:

```
<object data="kennedy.wav" type="audio/wav" width="0" height="0"
vspace="5">
<param name="src" value="kennedy.wav">
<param name="autostart" value="true">
<param name="controller" value="true">
<param name="loop" value="true">
President Kennedy calling for landing a man on the moon.
</object>
```

Setting the width and height of the OBJECT element to **0** hides it from view. The **controller** parameter is deleted because it is not needed to display the player console. The **loop** parameter is also deleted to not loop the audio file (**value="false"** is the default value).

HANDLING EARLIER BROWSERS The main problem with using the OBJECT element is that earlier browsers might not support it. Netscape Navigator 4, for instance, does not support the OBJECT element. The EMBED element, although not a standard

HTML element, is more widely supported by earlier browsers that are not HTML 4-compliant.

When using the OBJECT element, you might want to use a method or technique for shielding or redirecting users of earlier browsers, such as those provided by the Web Standards Project's Browser Upgrade Initiative that was described in Chapter 3. You could also use a browser-sniffer JavaScript script to detect earlier browsers and redirect them to a different page.

Choosing Audio Formats

Many different audio formats can be used to play audio in a Web page. Some of the most commonly used audio formats are WAV, AIFF, MIDI, MP3, AU, and RealAudio. Table 4.1 shows many of the audio formats, along with their MIME types, that can be used in Web pages.

TABLE 4.1 • *Common Audio MIME Types*

Media Object	Extensions	MIME Types
AU (Sun/Next Audio format)	AU, SND	audio/basic
AIFF (Audio Interchange File Format)	AIF, AIFF, AIFC	audio/x-aiff
MIDI (Musical Instrument Digital Interface)	MID, MIDI, RMI	audio/mid
MPEG (Moving Picture Experts Group)	MPG, MPEG, MP2, MPE	audio/mpeg
MP3 audio	MP3	audio/mpeg3
RealAudio	RA	audio/x-realaudio
Windows (WAV) audio	WAV	audio/wav
Windows Media Audio file	WMA	audio/x-ms-wma

The WAV audio format is native to the Windows system, the AIFF format originated from the Macintosh, and the AU format originated from the Sun and Next computer platforms. The MIDI and MP3 formats are popular for playing music files.

ADDING VIDEO

You are not limited to including only still images or GIF animations in Web pages. Many video formats also can be inserted into a Web page using the EMBED or OBJECT elements. An example video file, biosphere.avi, is included with this chapter's example files.

Using the EMBED Element to Insert a Video

You can use the EMBED element to insert a video file in a Web page.

Embed a video file at the bottom of the page:
  1. Copy and paste the graphical rule at the bottom of your page, as shown here:

```
<p align="center"><img src="bluegreen_bar.jpg" height="8"
width="100%" alt="Horizontal separator"></p>
```

```
<p align="center"><img src="bluegreen_bar.jpg" height="8"
width="100%" alt="Horizontal separator"></p>
<address>
```

2. Use the EMBED element to insert a video file:

```
<p align="center"><img src="bluegreen_bar.jpg" height="8"
width="100%" alt="Horizontal separator"></p>
<center>
<h2>Earth Biosphere Animation from NASA</h2>
<p><embed src="biosphere.mpg" autostart="false" loop="true"
width="320" height="255"></p>
</center>
<p align="center"><img src="bluegreen_bar.jpg" height="8"
width="100%" alt="Horizontal separator"></p>
<address>
```

3. Save your file, switch over to your browser, and click the Refresh (or Reload) button.
4. If the video and player console are displayed, click the Play button to start the video (see Figure 4.29).

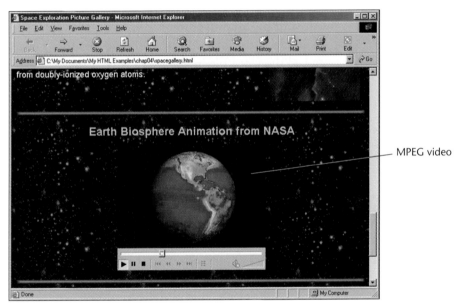

FIGURE 4.29 • *The embedded MPEG video file, biosphere.mpg, starts to play when the Play button is clicked.*

Depending on the browser you are using, how it is configured, and which players or plug-ins are installed, what you see on your system might differ from what is shown in Figure 4.29. If you have trouble playing video files in your browser, download and install the latest video players from Apple (**www.apple.com/quicktime/**), Real Networks (**www.real.com/realone/**), and Microsoft (**www.microsoft.com/windows/windowsmedia/**).

If after installing the QuickTime player, you are unable to view a video format in Internet Explorer, just reinstall all components of the Windows Media Player.

A visitor's browser, player, or plug-in settings also can affect the ability to view video files inserted in Web pages.

Using the OBJECT Element to Insert a Video

You also can use the OBJECT element to insert a video in a Web page.

Comment out the EMBED element and use the OBJECT element to insert an AVI video:

```
<!--
<p><embed src="biosphere.avi" autostart="false" loop="true"
width="320" height="255"></p>
-->
<p align="center"><object data="biosphere.avi" type="video/avi"
width="320" height="255" vspace="5">
<param name="src" value="biosphere.avi">
<param name="autoplay" value="false">
<param name="controller" value="true">
<param name="loop" value="false">
</object></p>
</center>
```

If your browser supports the OBJECT element, the result you see in your browser should look the same as when using the EMBED element (refer to Figure 4.29) to embed the video file in your Web page. Table 4.2 shows some of the more common video formats, along with their MIME types, that are used on the Web.

TABLE 4.2 • *Common Video MIME Types*

Media Object	Extensions	MIME Types
ASF (Advanced Streaming Format)	ASF	video/x-ms-asf
MPEG video	MPEG, MPG, MPE	video/mpeg
MPEG-2 video	MPV2, MP2V	video/mpeg2
QuickTime video	MOV, QT	video/quicktime
RealMedia meta file	RM, RAM	application/vnd.rn-realmedia
RealVideo	RV	video/vnd.rn-realvideo
Video for Windows (Audio/Video Interleave)	AVI	video/avi
Windows Media Video file	WMV	video/x-ms-wmv
VDOLive streaming video	VDO	video/vdo
Vivo streaming video	VIV	video/vnd.vivo

UNDERSTANDING COPYRIGHT ISSUES

A lot of images, audio clips, and video files can be downloaded easily from the Web, but that does not mean you are free to use them. Always make sure you have the right to use an image or other media file before you use it.

When using images or other media files from online sources, be sure to save any pages or documents that provide permission for usage or guidelines for fair or allowed usage of images or other media files. Also, the use of an image of a recognizable living person might require separate permission from that person. In its guidelines, for instance, NASA advises that images of such persons in its collection can be used without permission if for communicative purposes, rather than for commercial exploitation.

Additional considerations apply to musical copyrights, because a particular musical work's score (sheet music), arrangement, performance, recording, and sequencing might all be separately copyrighted. Both performance and distribution fees can be deemed due when offering copyrighted audio recordings for download over the Web.

If you are creating a commercial Web site, many sites on the Web offer access to images, music, and video for a membership or subscription fee. These media files are usually referred to as royalty-free, to distinguish them from public domain media files. To locate vendors of royalty-free images, music, or video files, search at AltaVista (**www.altavista.com/**) or Yahoo! (**www.yahoo.com/**) on the words "royalty free."

HINT

For links to additional resources on copyright issues as they apply to the Web, see this chapter's section at the IRC for this book at **www.emcp.com/**.

CHAPTER SUMMARY

You should now be familiar with using images and other media files in Web pages. When working with images, you should understand how to use floating images, image links, graphic rules, transparent banner images, navigation icons, button links, and GIF animations. You also should understand the differences between the GIF and JPEG image formats, including which format to use to save which kinds of images, how to optimize your GIF and JPEG images, and what transparent and interlaced GIFs are used for. You also should have experience using audio and video files in a Web page, including using both the EMBED element and the OBJECT element to play an audio file in the background, playing an audio file with the player console displayed at the top of the page, and inserting and playing a video in a Web page.

Code Review

ALIGN attribute	In the IMG element, floats an image to the left or right margin or vertically aligns it relative to a line of text.
CLEAR attribute	In the BR element, stops following text or elements from wrapping around a floating image.
HSPACE and VSPACE attributes	In the IMG or OBJECT element, these attributes add horizontal space on the left and right sides of an image or vertical space above or below an image.
BORDER attribute	In the IMG or OBJECT element, draws a border around the element; border="0" turns off the border displayed around an image link.
GIF image	CompuServe Graphics Interchange Format, an image format, which supports a color palette of up to 256 colors, transparency, and multiple frames (animation).
JPEG image	Joint Professional Experts Group image format, which supports a color palette of up to 16.3 million colors, but does not support transparency or animation.
PNG image	Portable Network Graphics image format, which supports 48-bit True Color (compared with 24-bit True Color for JPEG images). PNG images also support transparency and are slated eventually to replace GIF images on the Web. PNG images do not support animation.
EMBED element	A non-standard element introduced by Netscape, but supported by current browsers, that allows audio and video to be embedded into a Web page.
AUTOSTART attribute	In the EMBED element, causes an audio or video file to start playing automatically after the page where it is embedded is opened in a browser.
LOOP attribute	In the EMBED element, causes an audio and video file to loop indefinitely, rather than only play once.

PLUGINSPAGE attribute	In the EMBED element, indicates the URL where an appropriate plug-in player for a media file can be downloaded, which a browser can convey to a user if no plug-in player for the media file is installed.
HEIGHT and WIDTH attributes	In the EMBED or OBJECT element, these attributes specify the dimensions of the player console, but also can be used to hide the console.
OBJECT element	An element introduced in HTML 4 that is used to include objects in HTML documents, including images, audio, video, Java animations, and more.
PARAM element	In conjunction with the OBJECT element, specifies display or behavior parameters for an object.

ONLINE QUIZ

Go to this text's IRC at **www.emcp.com/** and take the online self-check quiz for this chapter.

REVIEW EXERCISES

This section provides some hands-on practice exercises to reinforce the information and material included within this and previous chapters.

Save **mercury.html** and **spacegallery.html** under new files names (**mercury_practice.html** and **spacegallery_practice.html**, for instance) and then use the new documents to practice using the elements, attributes, styles, and other features that were covered in this chapter.

1. In the first or second practice document (mercury_practice.html or spacegallery_practice.html), use any of the example images included with this chapter's example files to experiment further with floating images using the IMG element's ALIGN attribute and the BR element's CLEAR attribute.

2. Experiment with finding and downloading images from the Web. Go to NASA's Photo Gallery at **www.nasa.gov/gallery/photo/** and download several images you want to experiment with. To save an image, just right-click on it and then select to save the picture or image to your hard drive.

3. If you do not have an image viewer, use one of the links provided earlier in this chapter or in this chapter's section at the IRC for this book at **www.emcp.com/** to download an image viewer you can experiment with. Practice viewing images that are located on your computer. Practice viewing thumbnail galleries of images, if your image viewer has that capability. Practice using your image viewer to open, copy, and rename images on your computer.

4. If you do not have an image editor, use one of the links provided earlier in this chapter or in this chapter's section at the IRC for this book at **www.emcp.com/** to download an image editor you can experiment with. Practice opening, cropping, and resizing the images you downloaded from the NASA site in Exercise 2. Practice

saving the images as optimized JPEG images, by trying to choose a compression level that sets the file size as small as possible, while still preserving acceptable image quality. Experiment with adding text to photographic images and then save them as optimized GIF images.

5. Use your image editor to save smaller-sized thumbnail images of the images you have downloaded from the Web. Use the second practice document (spacegallery_practice.html) to experiment further with using thumbnail images to link with larger-sized images.

6. Use your image editor to experiment with creating your own banner images. Experiment with using different fonts, color combinations, and special effects. Experiment with saving your banner as a transparent GIF. If you created your own personal page at the end of Chapters 1 and 3, create a personalized banner image to use on your personal page. If you created a page for a club or organization, create a banner image for that page.

7. Experiment further with using different graphic rules in the second practice document. You can find additional graphic rules with this chapter's example files and in the art folder that accompanies this book's example files. The file names of graphic rules all end with "_bar." You also can search for graphic rules on the Web that you can download and use. If you have an image editor, experiment with creating your own graphic rules.

8. If you have a GIF animation editor, use it to experiment with creating GIF animations. The four button images (go1.gif, go2.gif, go3.gif, and go4.gif) that were used to create the go_anim.gif GIF animation are included with this chapter's example files and can be used to create your own GIF animation. If you have an image editor, you also can create your own images to use in a GIF animation.

9. Use any of the links provided earlier in this chapter or at this book's IRC at **www.emcp.com/** to download additional WAV, MIDI, or other audio files and practice using the EMBED and OBJECT elements to include them in Web pages. Experiment with playing audio files automatically in the background or with the player console displayed. Experiment with turning looping on or off.

10. Go to NASA's Video Gallery at **www.nasa.gov/gallery/video/** and download one or more additional videos you can use to experiment further with including videos in your Web pages.

WEB-BASED LEARNING ACTIVITIES

In this book's text, Find It icons inserted in the margin highlight the Web addresses of additional resources you might find helpful or informative. To further extend your learning using the Web, you can:

- Go back and visit any of the Web addresses highlighted in this chapter that you have not yet visited. Look for additional resources and information that add to your understanding and knowledge of the material covered in this chapter. When you find a relevant page or site with information or resources you might want to access later, add it to your Favorites (in Internet Explorer) or your Bookmarks (in Netscape or Mozilla).

- Visit this book's Internet Resource Center at **www.emcp.com/** to find additional Web addresses of resources related to the material covered in this chapter and that you can further investigate and explore.

- Further research a specific topic introduced in this chapter. For instance, do further research on using copyrighted, restricted license, and public domain image, audio, and video files in Web pages. Create a report on the topic you have chosen or team up with classmates to create a presentation.

PROJECTS

These projects can be done either in class, in a computer lab, or at home. Use the skills you have developed in this and the previous chapters to create any of the following projects.

Project 1. Add images to a page you have already created.

Add floating images, graphical rules, a banner graphic, and a navigation icon to a page you have already created, such as a personal page, a page for a club or organization, a topical page, or any other page. Incorporate lessons you learned in previous chapters, including using a document menu, return links, and colors and backgrounds, for instance. Use images downloaded from the Web or create your own images in an image editor. Optionally, incorporate audio or inline video.

If downloading images, use any of the links provided previously in the "Finding Images on the Web" section or at this book's IRC at **www.emcp.com/** to find links you can use in your page, or use Google (**www.google.com/**), AltaVista (**www.altavista.com**), or Yahoo! (**www.yahoo.com/**) to find additional sources for images you can download and use. Use an image editor to resize, crop, and optimize the images.

If creating your own images, you can create your images from scratch in an image editor or use images that you have scanned in using a scanner or imported from a digital camera. Here are some additional resources on using images from a scanner or a digital camera:

- A Few Scanning Tips by Wayne Fulton (**www.scantips.com/**)
- Scanning Tips (**www.graffiti.org/faq/scan.html**)
- A Short Course in Using Your Digital Camera (**www.shortcourses.com/using/**)
- Use Digital Camera Support to Import Photos (**www.jasc.com/tutorials/revised/pspdcs.asp**)

Visit this chapter's section at the IRC for this book at **www.emcp.com/** to find additional links to scanning and digital imaging resources on the Web.

Project 2. Create your own online gallery.

Using this chapter's online gallery example as a guide, create your own online gallery from scratch. For instance, create a gallery of vacation photos, or a gallery of other personal snapshots. If you are an artist, create a gallery of photos of your paintings, illustrations, drawings, or other artwork. If you are a photographer, create a gallery to display some of your photographic works. Use a scanner or digital camera to create the raw images you will use or create your own images in an image editor. Crop, resize, sharpen, and apply other corrections or effects to prepare your images to be displayed on the Web. Save your images as either optimized JPEGs or optimized GIFs. Save smaller-sized thumbnail versions and larger-sized versions of each image.

Project 3. Create a Web page using images.

Create any other kind of Web page from scratch that makes use of images (any kind of page you can imagine or conceive). Use images downloaded from the Web or images that you have scanned or imported from a digital camera. Optionally, incorporate audio and inline video. Apply skills learned in this chapter and any previous chapters.

CHAPTER

Working with Tables

PERFORMANCE OBJECTIVES

In this chapter, you learn to use HTML tables for a variety of purposes, including how to:
- Use the PRE element to format tabular data.
- Use the TABLE element to format tabular data in rows and columns.
- Span columns and rows within tables.
- Control the width and appearance of table columns.
- Control the appearance of row groups.
- Control the appearance of tables using styles.
- Add captions to floating figures using tables.
- Create indented icon bullet lists.
- Design a two-column layout using tables.
- Format an online resume using a table.

Tables are one of the most commonly used features of HTML. They are used in Web pages for two different purposes, one being the purpose for which they were designed, to format tabular data, and the other being to create multicolumn layouts that cannot be created using other HTML elements.

USING THE EXAMPLE FILES

If you have created a working folder for storing files you create, you will find the example files for this chapter located in the **chap05** folder within your working folder. You should save any HTML files you create in this chapter in that folder.

If you have created a working disk, you should copy the chap05 folder to your working disk from the **HTML_Examples** folder that you or your instructor downloaded from this book's Internet Resource Center (IRC), or from a CD-R disc or floppy disk provided by your instructor. You should save any HTML file you create in this chapter in the chap05 folder that you have copied to your working disk.

CASE EXAMPLE: FORMATTING A WORKSHEET

When creating published reports, it is common to include worksheet tables from spreadsheet programs. You also might want to include such data in tabular format within an HTML document.

Chandra Nichols is an assistant to the president of the Parker-Ruff Corporation, a major firm with more than $80 million in quarterly sales. She is producing the company's quarterly sales report, which provides the sales results for all the company's sales representatives. Besides creating a printed sales report in Quark Express, her boss also wants her to produce a version of the sales report for posting on the Web.

To get started working with this example:

1. In your text editor, open **salesreport_ex.html** from the chap05 folder in your working folder or working disk.
2. Save salesreport_ex.html as **salesreport.html** in the chap05 folder.
3. In your browser, open **salesreport.html** from the chap05 folder.

FORMATTING TABULAR DATA AS PREFORMATTED TEXT

The easiest way to include tabular data in a Web page is as preformatted text. In HTML, the PRE element is used to insert preformatted text into a Web page. Before the introduction of the TABLE element, the PRE element was the only way to include tabular data in a Web page.

Chandra has created the quarterly sales report as a worksheet in Microsoft Excel (see Figure 5.1). She needs to export the worksheet data from Excel so that it can be formatted and displayed using HTML. She has opened Microsoft Excel and saved her worksheet file as a space-delimited PRN (.prn) file, which preserves all the spaces within the worksheet.

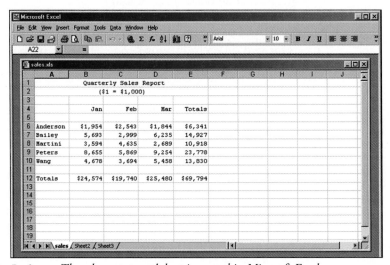

FIGURE 5.1 • *The sales report worksheet is created in Microsoft Excel.*

The PRN text file format is actually a "print" format file. It originated from Lotus 1-2-3, which provided a feature called "printing to a file." This allowed a user to save a copy of a worksheet (or range within a worksheet) as a text file with all relative spacing, as it appears in the worksheet, preserved. Then the feature was primarily used to print a worksheet on a printer connected to another computer via "sneaker net." This transportability now works just as well to import worksheet data into a Web page. In Microsoft Excel, to save your worksheet as a PRN file, select File, Save As, and then Formatted Text (Space delimited)

(*.prn) as the file type. There is nothing official or standard about the PRN file format—this is just the file extension that Lotus 1-2-3 and Excel have used when saving this type of file. Other spreadsheet programs might use different file extensions for this type of file. (For example, the Macintosh does not generally use file extensions.) An example PRN file, sales.prn, is included with the example files in the chap05 folder. This is just a regular text file that you can open directly in your text editor. To see files with file extensions other than .txt in Windows Notepad's Open dialog box, select All Files as the file type. In Excel 2000 for Windows, you cannot save a PRN file with a .txt extension—Excel will save the file as sales.txt.prn, for instance.

tip

For a quick and dirty way to transfer worksheet data to your text editor, in your spreadsheet program, click and drag to highlight the data cells you want to transfer, copy the highlighted data, and then paste it into your text editor. All the spacing will not be preserved, so you will have to insert or delete spaces to line up the columns.

action

Open **sales.prn** in your text editor and then paste it into salesreport.html as preformatted text:

1. Run a second copy of your text editor and open **sales.prn** from the chap05 folder in your working folder. (If you are using a text editor that lets you open multiple file windows, just open **sales.prn** in a separate window.)
2. If the data columns are out of alignment, it is because a proportional font is being used to display text in your text editor. To specify that a monospaced font is to be used to display text in Notepad for Windows, click and drag to highlight the contents of the file, and then select Edit, Set Font, and choose Fixedsys as the font. In SimpleText on the Macintosh, highlight the contents of the file, select Font, and choose Courier or Courier New as the font.
3. Insert five spaces at the start of each line to indent the text lines from the left margin. Add an additional space following each item in the month columns in each row, to further space them out horizontally.
4. Insert three additional spaces at the start of the first two lines (by keying or pasting them) to re-position them horizontally relative to the following data rows.
5. In the first data row ("Anderson…"), delete a space in front of each $ sign and then insert a space following each $ sign. The result should appear similar to the following:

```
            Quarterly Sales Report
                ($1 = $1,000)


              Jan        Feb        Mar       Totals

   Anderson  $ 1,954   $ 2,543   $ 1,844   $ 6,341
   Bailey      5,693     2,999     6,235    14,927
   Martini     3,594     4,635     2,689    10,918
   Peters      8,655     5,869     9,254    23,778
   Wang        4,678     3,694     5,458    13,830

   Totals    $24,574   $19,740   $25,480   $69,794
```

6. Click and drag with the mouse cursor to highlight the contents of sales.prn, and then copy it (Ctrl+C in Windows or Command+C on the Macintosh).

7. Switch to the text editor window that contains salesreport.html. Scroll down to and highlight **[Insert worksheet file here.]**, and then paste in the text that you copied in the previous step (Ctrl+V in Windows or Command+V on the Macintosh), as shown in the following example:

```
<p>At Parker-Ruff, we have one of the top firms in our field in
the country and this sales report only reinforces that. We rank
in the top tier of firms in our field, with gross annual sales
of over $250 million. We trail only three other firms, all of
which have much larger sales forces and have been competing in
the field for longer periods of time. In the all-important
category of earnings as a percentage of gross sales, we are
actually the leader, which shows that we both try harder and
can do more with less. With current sales growth at over 20
percent per quarter, we project that Parker-Ruff will be the
leader in gross sales inside of two years. The following table
shows sales figures for the quarter, broken down by individual
sales representatives and monthly sales figures:</p>
```

```
                    Quarterly Sales Report
                        ($1 = $1,000)


                    Jan        Feb        Mar      Totals

    Anderson      $ 1,954    $ 2,543    $ 1,844    $ 6,341
    Bailey          5,693      2,999      6,235     14,927
    Martini         3,594      4,635      2,689     10,918
    Peters          8,655      5,869      9,254     23,778
    Wang            4,678      3,694      5,458     13,830


    Totals       $24,574    $19,740    $25,480    $69,794
```

```
<p>We are proud of what we have accomplished. We have a
superior product line, a top-notch sales program, and a great
crew of sales representatives. Congratulations on another
outstanding quarter! We look forward to seeing even higher
results in the remaining quarters!</p>
```

8. Nest the sales report data inside a PRE element, as shown in the following (see Figure 5.2):

```
<pre>
                    Quarterly Sales Report
                        ($1 = $1,000)


                    Jan        Feb        Mar      Totals

    Anderson      $ 1,954    $ 2,543    $ 1,844    $ 6,341
    Bailey          5,693      2,999      6,235     14,927
    Martini         3,594      4,635      2,689     10,918
    Peters          8,655      5,869      9,254     23,778
    Wang            4,678      3,694      5,458     13,830


    Totals       $24,574    $19,740    $25,480    $69,794
</pre>
```

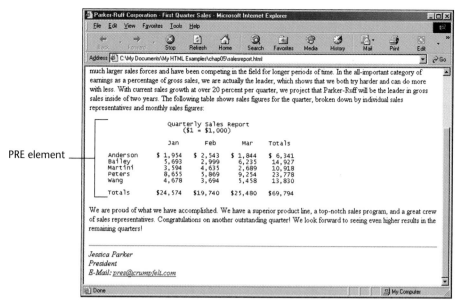

PRE element

Inside the browser window (Parker-Ruff Corporation - First Quarter Sales - Microsoft Internet Explorer), the preformatted text reads:

```
much larger sales forces and have been competing in the field for longer periods of time. In the all-important category of
earnings as a percentage of gross sales, we are actually the leader, which shows that we both try harder and can do more
with less. With current sales growth at over 20 percent per quarter, we project that Parker-Ruff will be the leader in gross
sales inside of two years. The following table shows sales figures for the quarter, broken down by individual sales
representatives and monthly sales figures:

                 Quarterly Sales Report
                      ($1 = $1,000)

                   Jan        Feb        Mar       Totals

       Anderson  $ 1,954    $ 2,543    $ 1,844    $ 6,341
       Bailey      5,693      2,999      6,235     14,927
       Martini     3,594      4,635      2,689     10,918
       Peters      8,655      5,869      9,254     23,778
       Wang        4,678      3,694      5,458     13,830

       Totals    $24,574    $19,740    $25,480    $69,794

We are proud of what we have accomplished. We have a superior product line, a top-notch sales program, and a great crew
of sales representatives. Congratulations on another outstanding quarter! We look forward to seeing even higher results in the
remaining quarters!


Jessica Parker
President
E-Mail: pres@crumpfelt.com
```

FIGURE 5.2 • *For text nested inside a PRE element, hard returns and multiple spaces are shown, rather than ignored.*

Only inline elements can be nested inside the PRE element, such as the I, B, EM, STRONG, and FONT elements. You can even insert a hypertext link using the A element inside the PRE element. You cannot, however, insert IMG, OBJECT, BIG, SMALL, SUB, or SUP elements inside the PRE element. For instance, you could use the B element to bold the top two lines in the worksheet and the FONT element to make the Totals row red.

Use inline elements to vary the display of the data worksheet:

1. Use the B element to bold the first two lines:

```
<b>Quarterly Sales Report</b>
    <b>($1 = $1,000)</b>
```

2. Use the FONT element to apply a red color to the bottom line (see Figure 5.3):

```
    Wang           4,678       3,694       5,458      13,830
<font color="red">
    Totals        $24,574     $19,740     $25,480     $69,794
</font>
</pre>
```

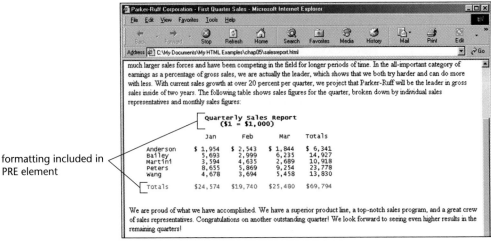

formatting included in PRE element

FIGURE 5.3 • *The B and FONT elements are used to apply bolding and a red color to the preformatted text.*

You cannot apply the B element to text included in the data columns because that alters the character width of the text. For instance, if you applied bolding to the bottom row, as well as a red color, the monthly totals would no longer line up with the text columns.

FORMATTING TABULAR DATA USING AN HTML TABLE

Another way to include tabular data in a Web page is to use the TABLE element. The TABLE element lets you format tabular data in cells that are arranged in rows and columns. The TABLE element gives you much more control over the appearance of tabular data than the PRE element.

NOTE

You also can save an Excel worksheet as an HTML file. Excel tries to duplicate the appearance and layout of your worksheet, including fonts, column widths, and so on. In doing so, however, Excel produces a large amount of both XML and HTML code, often referred to as "spaghetti code." It also includes some doubtful coding, such as setting font sizes and column widths in points, which should never be used in Web pages. By exporting your worksheet as a PRN file, you not only create a file that is many times smaller than an Excel-generated HTML file, you also maintain control over the final appearance of your worksheet because you will be doing all the formatting.

Creating the Basic Table

The TABLE element is used in conjunction with the CAPTION, TR (Table Row), TH (Table Heading), and TD (Table Data) elements. The TABLE element brackets everything that is contained within the table, the CAPTION element brackets the table caption, and the TR element brackets each table row. The TH element defines table cells that function as column and row headings, whereas the TD element defines table cells that contain data.

 Use the TABLE element to format the quarterly sales report:

1. Delete the PRE, B, and FONT elements you added in the previous example, and then nest the table text inside a TABLE element (just leave any blank lines as they are, since they are only displayed when nested in a PRE element):

```
<table>
<pre>

                    <b>Quarterly Sales Report</b>
                      <b>($1 = $1,000)</b>

                  Jan        Feb        Mar      Totals

      Anderson    $ 1,954    $ 2,543    $ 1,844    $ 6,341
      Bailey        5,693      2,999      6,235     14,927
      Martini       3,594      4,635      2,689     10,918
      Peters        8,655      5,869      9,254     23,778
      Wang          4,678      3,694      5,458     13,830
<font color="red">
      Totals      $24,574    $19,740    $25,480    $69,794
</font>
</pre>
</table>
```

2. Delete the spaces at the start of the first two lines, nest the first two lines inside a CAPTION element, and insert a BR element at the end of the first line:

```
<table>
<caption>Quarterly Sales Report<br>
($1 = $1,000)</caption>
```

3. Delete the five spaces at the start of each line and nest the lines inside of TR elements to define them as table rows:

```
<tr>              Jan        Feb        Mar      Totals</tr>

<tr>Anderson    $ 1,954    $ 2,543    $ 1,844    $ 6,341</tr>
<tr>Bailey        5,693      2,999      6,235     14,927</tr>
<tr>Martini       3,594      4,635      2,689     10,918</tr>
<tr>Peters        8,655      5,869      9,254     23,778</tr>
<tr>Wang          4,678      3,694      5,458     13,830</tr>

<tr>Totals      $24,574    $19,740    $25,480    $69,794</tr>
</table>
```

4. Use TH and TD elements to tag the remaining table items, defining them as either table heading cells or table data cells (delete any more than one space between the elements; see Figure 5.4):

```
<tr><th></th> <th>Jan</th> <th>Feb</th> <th>Mar</th>
<th>Totals</th></tr>


<tr><th>Anderson</th> <td>$ 1,954</td> <td>$ 2,543</td> <td>$
1,844</td> <td>$ 6,341</td></tr>
<tr><th>Bailey</th> <td>5,693</td> <td>2,999</td> <td>6,235</td>
<td>14,927</td></tr>
```

```
<tr><th>Martini</th> <td>3,594</td> <td>4,635</td>
<td>2,689</td> <td>10,918</td></tr>
<tr><th>Peters</th> <td>8,655</td> <td>5,869</td> <td>9,254</td>
<td>23,778</td></tr>
<tr><th>Wang</th> <td>4,678</td> <td>3,694</td> <td>5,458</td>
<td>13,830</td></tr>

<tr><th>Totals</th> <td>$24,574</td> <td>$19,740</td>
<td>$25,480</td> <td>$69,794</td></tr>
</table>
```

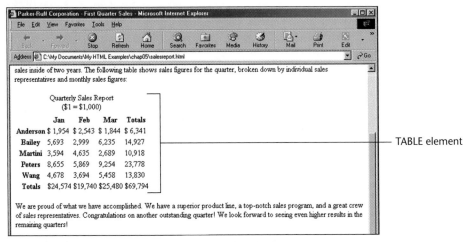

TABLE element

FIGURE 5.4 • *The tabular data is formatted in rows and columns.*

Although the table is not very impressive at this point, you will make it look more presentable in the following sections.

tip

Although you should first learn how to build tables from scratch, a number of utilities are available for Windows and the Macintosh that automate the creation of tables and convert comma-delimited files (which most spreadsheet and database programs should be able to save) into HTML tables. A filter is also available from Microsoft that removes Office-specific markup from documents saved in HTML format in Microsoft Excel 2000 and Word 2000. For links to these resources, see the section for this chapter at this book's IRC at **www.emcp.com/**.

Controlling the Table Border

The TABLE element's BORDER attribute draws a border around the table and its cells. Adding a border can help delineate the different parts of the table and make it easier for you to see them.

Add a one-pixel border around the table and its cells (see Figure 5.5):

```
<table border="1">
```

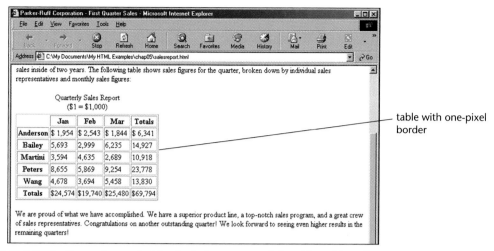

FIGURE 5.5 • *A one-pixel border is drawn around the table and its cells.*

Increasing the border size only increases the size of the border around the table, giving it a 3-D look, but the borders around the table cells remain unchanged.

Increase the size of the border to six pixels (see Figure 5.6):

```
<table border="6">
```

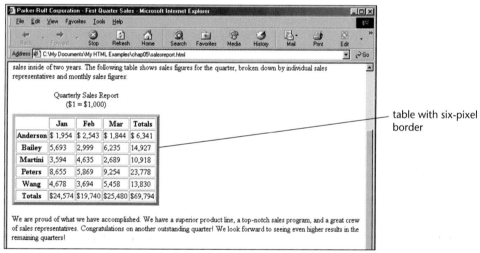

FIGURE 5.6 • *Increasing the border value only changes the style and increases the size of the outside border; the inner borders remain unchanged.*

Controlling Spacing and Padding

The TABLE element's CELLPADDING and CELLSPACING attributes let you control the amount of padding displayed inside the cells and the amount of space displayed between the cells.

Add five pixels of padding and spacing to the table (see Figure 5.7):

```
<table border="6" cellpadding="5" cellspacing="5">
```

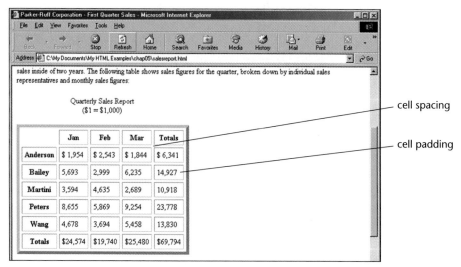

sales inside of two years. The following table shows sales figures for the quarter, broken down by individual sales representatives and monthly sales figures:

cell spacing

cell padding

Quarterly Sales Report
($1 = $1,000)

	Jan	Feb	Mar	Totals
Anderson	$ 1,954	$ 2,543	$ 1,844	$ 6,341
Bailey	5,693	2,999	6,235	14,927
Martini	3,594	4,635	2,689	10,918
Peters	8,655	5,869	9,254	23,778
Wang	4,678	3,694	5,458	13,830
Totals	$24,574	$19,740	$25,480	$69,794

FIGURE 5.7 • *Padding and spacing are added to the table's cells.*

Some browsers, such as Internet Explorer 6 for Windows, for example, apply padding and spacing to both the table caption and the body of the table. Other browsers, including Internet Explorer 5 for the Macintosh and the Mozilla browser, however, apply padding and spacing only to the body of the table, not to the table caption. The only workaround for this is to use a style to set bottom-padding and bottom-margin values for the CAPTION element.

Use an inline style to set a bottom-padding value and a bottom-margin value for the CAPTION element, which will cause all browsers that recognize styles to add vertical spacing beneath the CAPTION element:

```
<caption style="margin-bottom: 10px; padding-bottom:
10px">Quarterly Sales Report<br>
($1 = $1,000)</caption>
```

This does not produce absolutely uniform results, but at least ensures that browsers display vertical separation between the caption and the table body. The Mozilla browser applies both the bottom-margin and bottom-padding values, inserting 20 pixels of vertical spacing between the caption and the table body. Internet Explorer 6 for Windows applies only the bottom-padding value, ignoring the bottom-margin value, while Internet Explorer 5 for the Macintosh applies only the bottom-margin value, ignoring the bottom-padding value.

According to the HTML 4 specifications, you also can use the ALIGN attribute to align a table caption above and below a table, as well as on the left and right sides of a table. Current browsers should all support using **align="bottom"** to align a table caption beneath a table, but no browsers support aligning a caption along the left or right sides of a table. Instead, **align="left"** or **align="right"** causes nested text to be left-aligned or right-aligned within the caption box. Because the ALIGN attribute for the CAPTION element is also deprecated, you should not expect the recommended usage to be implemented in future browsers.

You might notice that the empty TH cell in the first table row does not have a border drawn around it. In this case, that is the desired result, but in other situations, you might want an empty table cell to have a border. The solution is to insert an invisible non-breaking space character, ` `, in the table cell, which causes a border to be drawn around the otherwise empty cell.

Setting Table Width and Alignment

The TABLE element's WIDTH and ALIGN attributes let you control the table's width and horizontal alignment.

action

Set the table to a width of 85 percent and center it (see Figure 5.8):

```
<table border="6" cellpadding="5" cellspacing="5" width="85%"
align="center">
```

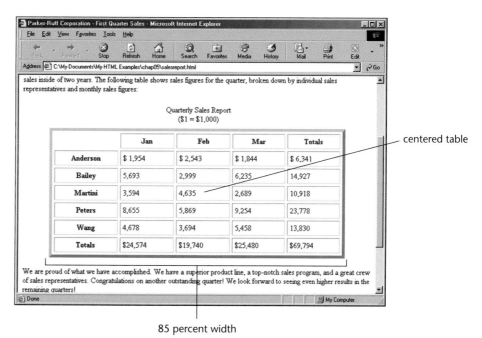

FIGURE 5.8 • *The table is centered and set to an 85 percent width.*

The WIDTH attribute can be set using a percentage or a numerical value. A percentage value sets the width of the table to a percentage of the browser window. For instance, if you set the browser width to 100 percent, the table will always be as wide as the browser window.

The ALIGN attribute sets the horizontal alignment of the table and can take a value of **center**, **left**, or **right**. Center-alignment works the same way as in the heading-level and paragraph elements. Left-alignment and right-alignment, on the other hand, work similarly to the IMG element, with the table floating to the left or right margin and following text or elements flowing around the table. As with the IMG element, the BR element's CLEAR attribute can be used to stop following text or elements from flowing around a table.

Center-aligning the table, however, causes the caption to be displayed off-center in Netscape 6. The only workaround for this problem is to use styles to center the caption. Alternatively, you can just leave the caption displaying off-center in Netscape, since it is only that one browser that does this.

Insert the following style properties to cause Netscape 6 to center the caption:

```
<caption style="margin-bottom: 10px; padding-bottom: 10px;
margin-left: auto; margin-right: auto">Quarterly Sales
Report<br>
($1 = $1,000)</caption>
```

Horizontally Aligning Cell Contents

The ALIGN attribute can be used in the TR, TH, and TD elements to horizontally align cell contents. By default, the content of TH elements is center-aligned and the content of TD elements is left-aligned, although either can inherit a horizontal-alignment setting from the TR element.

Use the ALIGN attribute to right-align the table's data rows (see Figure 5.9):

```
<tr align="right"><th>Anderson</th> <td>$ 1,954</td> <td>$
2,543</td> <td>$ 1,844</td> <td>$ 6,341</td></tr>
<tr align="right"><th>Bailey</th> <td>5,693</td> <td>2,999</td>
<td>6,235</td> <td>14,927</td></tr>
<tr align="right"><th>Martini</th> <td>3,594</td> <td>4,635</td>
<td>2,689</td> <td>10,918</td></tr>
<tr align="right"><th>Peters</th> <td>8,655</td> <td>5,869</td>
<td>9,254</td> <td>23,778</td></tr>
<tr align="right"><th>Wang</th> <td>4,678</td> <td>3,694</td>
<td>5,458</td> <td>13,830</td></tr>

<tr align="right"><th>Totals</th> <td>$24,574</td>
<td>$19,740</td> <td>$25,480</td> <td>$69,794</td></tr>
```

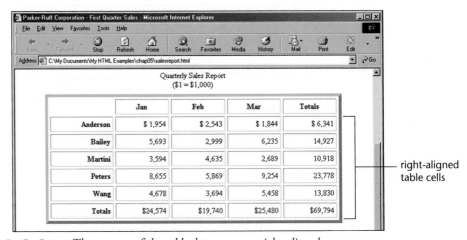

FIGURE 5.9 • *The contents of the table data rows are right-aligned.*

Setting Column Widths

The WIDTH attribute can be used in the TH or TD elements to set the width of a column. The attribute only needs to be inserted in one cell in a column to set the width of all cells within that column.

Set the width of the first cell in the second row to a width equal to 18 percent of the table width (see Figure 5.10):

```
<tr align="right"><th width="18%">Anderson</th> <td>$ 1,954</td>
<td>$ 2,543</td> <td>$ 1,844</td> <td>$ 6,341</td></tr>
```

18 percent
column width

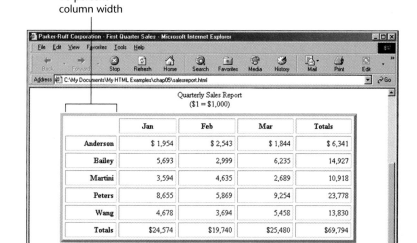

FIGURE 5.10 • *The first column is set to a width that is 18 percent of the table width.*

You also could use the WIDTH attribute in the first cell in the first row to set the column width. It was set in the first cell in the second row, however, because you will be deleting the first cell in the first row in the next section, "Spanning Columns and Rows."

In a table without any WIDTH attributes set in the TABLE, TH, or TD elements, column widths are determined by the width of the column content. If a WIDTH attribute is only set in the TABLE element, most browsers apportion column widths equally so their sum is equal to the table width.

Because there are five columns, without any width settings, each column is equal to 20 percent of the table width. For current browsers, with a percentage width set for the table as a whole, reducing the width of one column (to 18 percent, in this case) causes the widths of the remaining columns to be increased by an equal amount necessary to keep the total width of the table at 85 percent (of the browser's viewport).

For some earlier browsers, such as Netscape Navigator 4, setting a width for only a single column causes the remaining columns to be displayed with unequal widths. To fix that, you need to set the same width value for each of the remaining columns.

Set a percentage width for each of the remaining columns to make sure that the other columns display at equal widths in Netscape Navigator 4:

```
<tr align="right"><th width="18%">Anderson</th> <td
width="20%">$ 1,954</td> <td width="20%">$ 2,543</td> <td
width="20%">$ 1,844</td> <td width="20%">$ 6,341</td></tr>
```

You might notice that percentage widths of the columns do not add up to 100 percent. That is because Netscape Navigator 4 does not include the spacing between cells when computing column width, although Internet Explorer does. The main consideration is that the sum of the percentage amounts do not exceed 100 percent.

Although not included in this example, you also can use the HEIGHT attribute to set the height of cells within a row. For instance, to increase the first row to a height of 65 pixels, you just need to insert **height="65"** in any TH (or TD) element within that row.

Spanning Columns and Rows

The COLSPAN and ROWSPAN attributes can be used in TH and TD elements to create table cells that span multiple columns or rows.

Add a row to the example table that includes a cell that spans three columns (see Figure 5.11):

```
<tr><th></th> <th colspan="3">Monthly Sales
Figures</th><th></th></tr>
<tr><th></th> <th>Jan</th> <th>Feb</th> <th>Mar</th>
<th>Totals</th></tr>
```

cell spanning
three columns

FIGURE 5.11 • *The "Monthly Sales Figures" cell spans three columns.*

Because the remainder of the table has five columns (five TD elements in each row), the COLSPAN value should not exceed the number of available columns. In the previous example row, two regular TH elements, each representing one column, and one spanned TH element that spans three columns, add up to five columns.

Use the ROWSPAN element to create table cells in the upper-left and upper-right corners of that table that span two rows:

1. Because they are going to be spanned, delete the first and last TH elements in the second row:

```
<tr><th></th> <th colspan="3">Monthly Sales
Figures</th><th></th></tr>
<tr><th></th> <th>Jan</th> <th>Feb</th> <th>Mar</th>
<th>Totals</th></tr>
```

2. Key **Sales Reps** as the content of the first cell and **Totals** as the content of the last cell in the first row. Use the ROWSPAN attribute in the first and last cells of that row to cause those cells to span two rows (see Figure 5.12):

```
<tr><th rowspan="2">Sales Reps</th> <th colspan="3">Monthly
Sales Figures</th><th rowspan="2">Totals</th></tr>
<tr><th>Jan</th> <th>Feb</th> <th>Mar</th></tr>
```

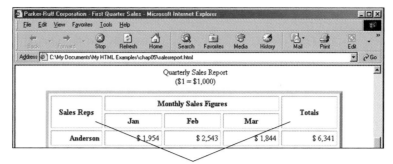

cells spanning two rows

FIGURE 5.12 • *The "Sales Reps" and "Totals" cells are spanning two rows.*

Vertically Aligning Cell Contents

By default, the contents of table cells are vertically aligned with the middle of the cell. The VALIGN attribute lets you vertically align the contents of table cells with the top, middle, or bottom of a cell, or along a common baseline.

Use the VALIGN attribute to vertically align the contents of the "Sales Reps" and "Totals" cells with the bottom of the cells (see Figure 5.13):

```
<tr><th rowspan="2" valign="bottom">Sales Reps</th> <th
colspan="3">Monthly Sales Figures</th><th rowspan="2"
valign="bottom">Totals</th></tr>
```

bottom-aligned cell contents

FIGURE 5.13 • *The contents of the "Sales Reps" and "Totals" cells are bottom-aligned.*

In addition to the **top**, **middle**, and **bottom** values, the VALIGN attribute also can take a **baseline** value, which causes text strings in different cells in a row to be aligned along their baselines.

USING HTML TO CONTROL TABLE APPEARANCE

There are a number of ways to control the appearance of tables by using HTML alone. For instance, you can use the FONT element to set font characteristics (sizes, colors, and faces) inside table cells and use the BGCOLOR and BACKGROUND attributes in various elements to control background colors and background images within tables.

Save the current file twice, so you can use it to experiment with setting table display characteristics using HTML attributes, and then to do the same thing using styles:

1. In your text editor, save any changes you have made to **salesreport.html** (File, Save).
2. Resave salesreport.html as **salesreport2.html** in the chap05 folder. (Later, you will return to salesreport.html and use it to experiment with using styles with tables.)
3. Open **salesreport2.html** in your browser.

Controlling Font Characteristics

You cannot bracket a table with a FONT element to change the font or color of text included in a table cell. A FONT element must be inserted inside each cell in which a change in font or color is desired.

Use the FONT and B element to change the appearance of text within the table:

1. Change the appearance of the caption and text in the first table row by using the FONT element:

```
<caption style="margin-bottom: 10px; padding-bottom: 10px;
margin-left: auto; margin-right: auto"><font size="4">Quarterly
Sales Report</font><br>
($1 = $1,000)</caption>

<tr><th rowspan="2" valign="bottom">Sales Reps</th> <th
colspan="3"><font color="blue" face="Arial, Helvetica">Monthly Sales
Figures</font></th><th rowspan="2" valign="bottom">Totals</th></tr>
<tr><th>Jan</th> <th>Feb</th> <th>Mar</th></tr>
```

2. Change the appearance of the bottom row of totals by using the FONT and B elements (see Figure 5.14):

```
<tr align="right"><th>Totals</th> <td><font color="red"
face="Arial, Helvetica"><b>$24,574</b></font></td> <td><font
color="red" face="Arial, Helvetica"><b>$19,740</b></font></td>
<td><font color="red" face="Arial,
Helvetica"><b>$25,480</b></font></td> <td><font color="red"
face="Arial, Helvetica"><b>$69,794</b></font></td></tr>
```

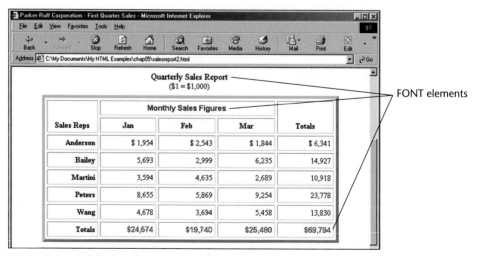

FIGURE 5.14 • *The font characteristics of the caption, top row, and bottom row are changed.*

Displaying a Background Color behind the Table

The BGCOLOR attribute lets you control the background color of the table, rows, or cells. It works exactly the same way as in the BODY element. You insert the BGCOLOR attribute in the TABLE element to display a background color behind the whole table.

action

Use the BGCOLOR attribute to assign a light blue color (one of the Web-safe colors) to the table background (see Figure 5.15):

```
<table border="6" cellpadding="5" cellspacing="5" width="85%"
align="center" bgcolor="#ccffff">
```

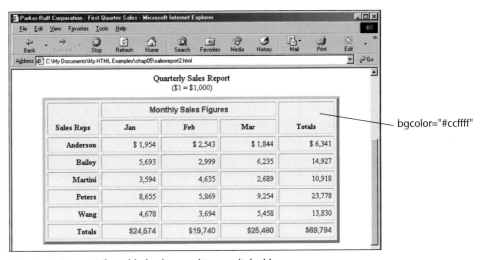

FIGURE 5.15 • *The table background is now light blue.*

Although current browsers all handle this as shown in Figure 5.15, earlier browsers vary in how they display a background color set for the whole table. Internet Explorer 4, for instance, displays the background color behind the caption, as well. Netscape Navigator 4 displays the background color only behind the table cells, but not behind the spacing between the cells (see Figure 5.16).

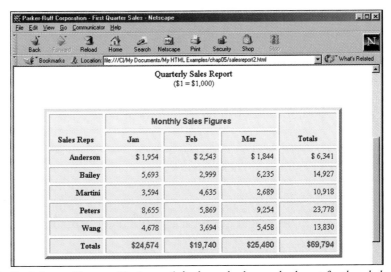

FIGURE 5.16 • *Netscape Navigator 4 displays a background color set for the whole table only behind the table cells, but not behind the spacing between the cells.*

The only workaround for this is to turn off the spacing between the cells, while increasing the padding to maintain the same table dimensions.

Eliminate the spacing between the table's cells and increase the padding within the table's cells to eight pixels (see Figure 5.17):

```
<table border="6" cellpadding="8" cellspacing="0" width="85%"
align="center" bgcolor="#ccffff">
```

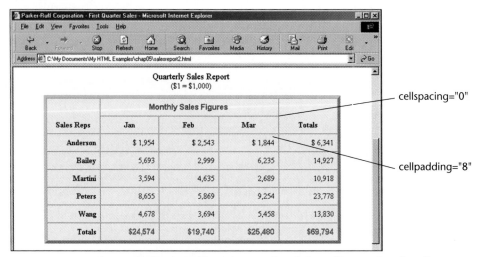

FIGURE 5.17 • *The spacing between cells is eliminated and the padding within the cells in increased to eight pixels.*

The eight-pixel padding amount roughly equals the previous padding and spacing amount, in that the spacing between cells was shared.

The table now displays the same in Netscape Navigator 4 as it does in current browsers. To cater to an older browser that is only being used by a small percentage of users, another alternative is to use the Web Standard Project's Invisible Object Method, which was demonstrated in Chapter 3, *Working with Fonts, Colors, and Backgrounds* (in the "Compatibility Issues with Font Sizes Using Ems" section). This method alerts users of Netscape Navigator 4 that they can access your page using that browser, but that your page will look better if viewed using a browser that supports current Web standards.

Displaying Background Colors behind Rows and Cells

You insert the BGCOLOR attribute in the TR, TH, or TD elements to display background colors behind table rows or table cells.

Use different background colors to highlight the different parts of the table:
1. Copy and then paste a second copy of the table below the current table. In the following steps, you will be working in the second table (the one you pasted in).
2. Set a light green background color behind the first two rows:

```
<tr bgcolor="#ccffcc"><th rowspan="2" valign="bottom">Sales
Reps</th> <th colspan="3"><font color="blue" face="Arial,
Helvetica">Monthly Sales Figures</font></th><th rowspan="2"
valign="bottom">Totals</th></tr>
<tr bgcolor="#ccffcc"><th>Jan</th> <th>Feb</th> <th>Mar</th></tr>
```

3. Set a light yellow color behind the row heading cells that contain the last names of the sales reps:

```
<tr align="right"><th bgcolor="#ffffcc" width="18%">Anderson</th>
<td width="20%">$ 1,954</td> <td width="20%">$ 2,543</td> <td
width="20%">$ 1,844</td> <td width="20%">$ 6,341</td></tr>
<tr align="right"><th bgcolor="#ffffcc">Bailey</th> <td>5,693</td>
<td>2,999</td> <td>6,235</td> <td>14,927</td></tr>
<tr align="right"><th bgcolor="#ffffcc">Martini</th>
<td>3,594</td> <td>4,635</td> <td>2,689</td> <td>10,918</td></tr>
<tr align="right"><th bgcolor="#ffffcc">Peters</th> <td>8,655</td>
<td>5,869</td> <td>9,254</td> <td>23,778</td></tr>
<tr align="right"><th bgcolor="#ffffcc">Wang</th> <td>4,678</td>
<td>3,694</td> <td>5,458</td> <td>13,830</td></tr>
```

4. Set a light pink background color behind the bottom row in the table (see Figure 5.18):

```
<tr bgcolor="#ffcccc" align="right"><th>Totals</th> <td><font
color="red" face="Arial, Helvetica"><b>$24,574</b></font></td>
<td><font color="red" face="Arial,
Helvetica"><b>$19,740</b></font></td> <td><font color="red"
face="Arial, Helvetica"><b>$25,480</b></font></td> <td><font
color="red" face="Arial,
Helvetica"><b>$69,794</b></font></td></tr>
</table>
```

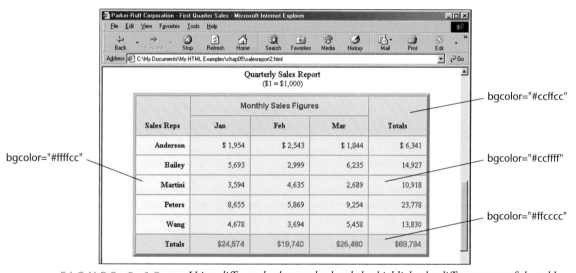

FIGURE 5.18 • *Using different background colors helps highlight the different parts of the table.*

Displaying Background Images in Tables

The BACKGROUND attribute can be used to display background images in tables. You should be aware, however, that the BACKGROUND attribute is not part of the HTML 4 standard, although all current browsers and many earlier browsers support it. An example background image, back_clouds.jpg, is included with this chapter's example files in the chap05 folder.

With current browsers, any background colors set in the TR, TH, or TD elements take precedence over a background image set in the TABLE element. Therefore, if you want to display a background image behind the whole table, you need to delete any background colors (other than transparent) that are set in the TR, TH, or TD elements.

Go back to the first table (the one without the BGCOLOR attributes in the rows and cells) and set a background image for the table (see Figure 5.19):

```
<table border="6" cellpadding="8" cellspacing="0" width="85%"
align="center" bgcolor="#ccffff" background="back_clouds.jpg">
```

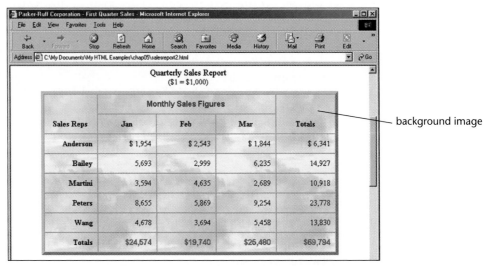

FIGURE 5.19 • *A background image can give a table a dramatic look.*

Because the BACKGROUND attribute is not a standard attribute for the TABLE element, you should expect some variability in how it displays in browsers. Current browsers all display it the same, as shown in Figure 5.19, but one earlier browser, Netscape Navigator 4, displays the background image individually behind each table cell, rather than tiling it behind the whole table. As with a background color, a background image in Netscape 4 is only displayed behind the table cells, but not behind the spacing between the cells.

Whenever displaying a background image in a table, you also should specify a background color that resembles the color of your background image. That way, if users are surfing with the display of images turned off, they will still see your background color. This is especially important when displaying light text against a dark background image because with the display of images turned off, a visitor could end up seeing (or not seeing) white text against a white background, for instance.

USING STYLES TO CONTROL TABLE APPEARANCE

The use of styles provides much more control over the appearance of tables than can be achieved through HTML alone. Styles are also much more efficient than using the FONT element to control table appearance. You have to insert the FONT element inside of each and every table cell where you want it to have effect, but a single entry in a style sheet can change the formatting of every table cell.

The use of styles to format tables also provides for better accessibility, in that they separate the presentation of the table from its content and organization. A nonvisual browser, for instance, can easily ignore any presentation features defined by styles to concentrate on conveying the table's content and organization.

A number of table elements were introduced as part of HTML 4, which require the use of styles to provide visual formatting. By themselves, the TBODY, THEAD, TFOOT, COL, and COLGROUP elements have no visual formatting, but can be used in conjunction with styles to format row groups and column groups in tables.

The disadvantage of using styles to format tables is that many earlier browsers either do not understand styles or poorly implement them. Even among current browsers, the style features supported and how some style features are implemented varies.

NOTE — The purpose of this section is to demonstrate how certain HTML 4 features and elements, in conjunction with styles, can be used to provide more control over the appearance of tables. This section is not intended to provide an in-depth understanding of the use of styles in general. For links to resources that cover the use of styles in more depth, see Chapter 3's section at the IRC for this book at **www.emcp.com/**.

NOTE — Because of variability in how different browsers implement the use of styles to control the display of tables, you should use Internet Explorer 5.5 or 6 for Windows, Internet Explorer 5 for the Macintosh, Mozilla 1.0, or any higher version of these browsers, to do the following example. You can use Netscape 6 and Opera 6 browsers to do the example, but the result you see in your browser might not exactly match what is shown in the figures.

action — Return to the copy of your example file that you saved earlier to do the following style examples:

1. Reopen **salesreport.html** in your text editor from the chap05 folder.
2. Save salesreport.html as **salesreport3.html** in the chap05 folder and open it in your browser.

Alerting Netscape 4 Users

Netscape Navigator 4 has poor support for styles. When using styles to control the appearance of tables, you need to be aware that the results might not look perfect in Netscape 4. One option to deal with users of Netscape 4 is to use the Web Standards Project's Invisible Object Method, which was covered in Chapter 3, *Working with Fonts, Colors, and Backgrounds*.

action — Set up the page to display an object that will be hidden from users of current browsers, but will alert users of Netscape 4 and other earlier browsers that they need to upgrade their browsers:

```
<style type="text/css">
.oops { display: none; }
</style>
</head>
<body>
<iframe class="oops">
<center><font size="5" color="red">This site will look much
better in a browser that supports
```

```
<a href="http://www.webstandards.org/upgrade/" title="Download a
browser that complies with Web standards."> Web
standards</a>,<br>but it is accessible to any browser or Internet
device.</font>
</center>
<hr>
</iframe>

<h1 align="center">Parker-Ruff Corporation Quarterly Sales</h1>
<h2 align="center">First Quarter Sales</h2>
```

Changing Fonts and Colors

You can use styles to easily change fonts, colors, and backgrounds used in a table.

Create a style sheet to transform the appearance of the table:

1. Create a style sheet that assigns fonts and colors to the table's contents (see Figure 5.20):

```
<title>Parker-Ruff Corporation - First Quarter Sales</title>
<style type="text/css">
.oops { display: none; }
table { color: #330000; background: #ffffcc; }
caption { color: black; background: transparent; }
th { font-family: Arial, Helvetica, sans-serif; }
</style>
</head>
```

background and foreground colors set by styles

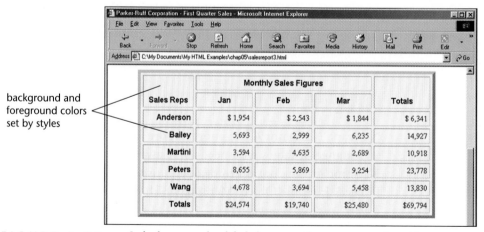

FIGURE 5.20 • *Styles let you make global changes to the appearance of a table.*

2. Use a style to add a background image to the table (see Figure 5.21):

```
<style type="text/css">
table { color: #330000; background: #ffffcc
url("back_marblebeige.jpg"); }
```

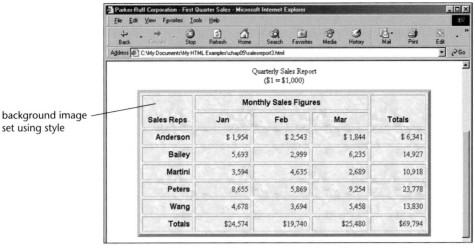

FIGURE 5.21 • *A background image gives a table a whole new look.*

Controlling the Appearance of Row Groups

The TBODY, THEAD, and TFOOT elements are HTML 4 elements that let you set different display characteristics for groups of rows within a table. By themselves, these elements have no visual formatting; you must use these elements in conjunction with styles to produce any visual result.

Use the TBODY, THEAD, and TFOOT elements to create separate display characteristics for the body, head, and foot of the table:

1. Add THEAD, TBODY, and TFOOT elements to the table to define table head, body, and foot groups of rows:

```
<table border="6" cellpadding="5" cellspacing="5" width="85%"
align="center">
<caption style="margin-bottom: 10px; padding-bottom: 10px; margin-
left: auto; margin-right: auto">Quarterly Sales Report<br>
($1 = $1,000)</caption>
<thead>
<tr><th rowspan="2" valign="bottom">Sales Reps</th> <th
colspan="3">Monthly Sales Figures</th><th rowspan="2"
valign="bottom">Totals</th></tr>
<tr><th>Jan</th> <th>Feb</th> <th>Mar</th></tr>
</thead>
<tbody>
<tr align="right"><th width="18%">Anderson</th> <td width="20%">$
1,954</td> <td width="20%">$ 2,543</td> <td width="20%">$
1,844</td> <td width="20%">$ 6,341</td></tr>
<tr align="right"><th>Bailey</th> <td>5,693</td> <td>2,999</td>
<td>6,235</td> <td>14,927</td></tr>
<tr align="right"><th>Martini</th> <td>3,594</td> <td>4,635</td>
<td>2,689</td> <td>10,918</td></tr>
<tr align="right"><th>Peters</th> <td>8,655</td> <td>5,869</td>
<td>9,254</td> <td>23,778</td></tr>
<tr align="right"><th>Wang</th> <td>4,678</td> <td>3,694</td>
<td>5,458</td> <td>13,830</td></tr>
<tr align="right"><th>Totals</th> <td>$24,574</b></td>
<td>$19,740</b></td> <td>$25,480</b></td>
<td>$69,794</b></td></tr>
</tbody>
```

```
<tfoot>
<tr><td colspan="5">All sales amounts are stated at $1 per
$1,000.</td></tr>
</tfoot>
</table>
```

2. Create styles to control the display of the table's head, body, and foot sections (see Figure 5.22):

```
th { font-family: Arial, Helvetica, sans-serif; }
thead { color: #330000; background: #ffff99
url("back_sandstone.jpg"); }
tbody { color: #990000; background: transparent; }
tfoot { color: #330000; background: #ffff99
url("back_goldrock.jpg"); font-weight: bold; text-align: center; }
</style>
```

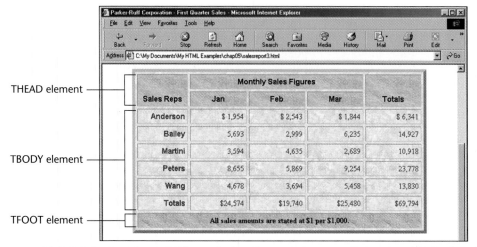

THEAD element

TBODY element

TFOOT element

F I G U R E   5 . 2 2   •   *Different display characteristics are applied to the table's head, body, and foot.*

The TBODY element can be optionally left out. Any table cells not included in a THEAD or TFOOT element will be formatted using style properties assigned to the TBODY element in the style sheet.

You should be aware, however, that current browsers vary in how they display background properties set for these row group elements. Both Internet Explorer 6 for Windows and Mozilla 1 display background properties only behind the table cells in a row group, whereas Internet Explorer 5 for the Macintosh and Netscape 6 display background properties behind both the table cells and the spacing between table cells within a row group. The only way to get all these browsers to display a relatively similar result when applying background properties to row groups is to turn off the spacing between the table's cells as shown in the following section.

Turning Off Spacing between Cells

Earlier, in the salesreport2.html example, you eliminated the spacing between table cells by setting a `cellspacing="0"` attribute in the TABLE element, while increasing the padding amount within the cells by setting a `cellpadding="8"` attribute. The same result can be achieved using styles and without using the CELLSPACING or CELL-PADDING attributes.

Use styles to eliminate the spacing between the table cells and set a black one-pixel border between the cells:

1. Remove the cell padding and cell spacing currently set in the TABLE element:

```
<table border="6" cellpadding="5" cellspacing="5" width="85%"
align="center">
```

2. Collapse the spacing between the table cells:

```
table { border-collapse: collapse; border-spacing: 0; color:
#330000; background: #ffffcc url("back_marblebeige.jpg"); }
caption { color: black; background: transparent; }
```

3. For the TH and TD elements, set eight pixels of padding and set a one-pixel black border to be drawn around the table cells (see Figure 5.23):

```
th { font-family: Arial, Helvetica, sans-serif; }
th, td { padding: 8px; border: 1px solid black; }
```

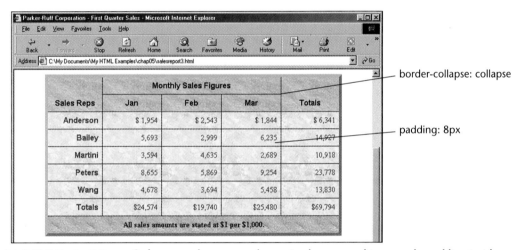

FIGURE 5.23 • *Styles are used to remove the spacing between and increase the padding inside the table cells.*

Netscape 6 does not recognize the **border-collapse: collapse** property (which is a CSS2 property), but does collapse the borders if a **border-spacing: 0** property is included.

The default setting for tables is **border-collapse: separate**. As long as that setting is active, each cell has its own separate border. To set a specific amount of spacing around the border of a cell, set the border-spacing property to the amount of spacing you want between cell borders (**border-spacing: 6px**, for instance).

Internet Explorer 5 for the Macintosh does not recognize the border-spacing property. To make sure that spacing set between cell borders is also displayed in that browser, include a corresponding CELLSPACING attribute in the TABLE element.

Controlling the Appearance of Columns

You also can control the appearance of columns using styles. You can do this by assigning table cells to a class, to which style properties can be applied, or by setting a contextual style (applying style properties to elements only within certain contexts, such as to TH elements located inside a TBODY element).

Assign separate display characteristics to the "Sales Reps" column and the "Totals" column:

1. Assign the "Totals" column to a class, so a style can be applied to it:

```
<tr align="right"><th width="18%">Anderson</th> <td
width="20%">$ 1,954</td> <td width="20%">$ 2,543</td> <td
width="20%">$ 1,844</td> <td class="totalcol" width="20%">$
6,341</td></tr>
<tr align="right"><th>Bailey</th> <td>5,693</td> <td>2,999</td>
<td>6,235</td> <td class="totalcol">14,927</td></tr>
<tr align="right"><th>Martini</th> <td>3,594</td> <td>4,635</td>
<td>2,689</td> <td class="totalcol">10,918</td></tr>
<tr align="right"><th>Peters</th> <td>8,655</td> <td>5,869</td>
<td>9,254</td> <td class="totalcol">23,778</td></tr>
<tr align="right"><th>Wang</th> <td>4,678</td> <td>3,694</td>
<td>5,458</td> <td class="totalcol">13,830</td></tr>

<tr align="right"><th>Totals</th> <td>$24,574</td>
<td>$19,740</td> <td>$25,480</td> <td
class="totalcol">$69,794</td></tr>
```

2. Define styles that apply formatting to the "Sales Reps" and "Totals" columns (see Figure 5.24):

```
tbody th { color: #ffffcc; background: #330066
url("back_blueslate.jpg"); }
tbody td.totalcol { font-weight: bold; color: navy; background:
#990000 url("back_paper.jpg"); }
</style>
```

column formatted using contextual style: tbody th...

column formatted using class selector: class="totalcol"

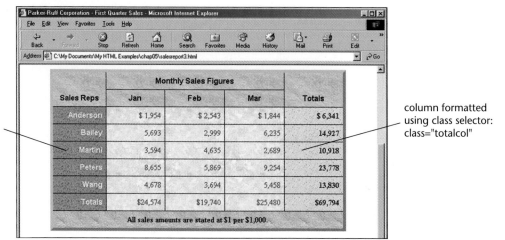

FIGURE 5.24 • *Styles are used to set the display characteristics of the "Sales Reps" and "Totals" columns.*

Two additional HTML elements, the COLGROUP and COL elements, can be used in conjunction with styles to control the appearance of column groups and individual columns. However, because support for these elements among current browsers is either inconsistent or nonexistent, you should stick to specifying column formatting using the methods shown in the previous example.

An example file, salesreport_colgroups.html, that demonstrates using the COLGROUP and COL elements is included with the other example files for this chapter. To see how these elements are used in an HTML file, open the example file in your text editor. If you are using Internet Explorer 6 for Windows or Netscape 6, or higher versions of these browsers, you can open and view the example file in your browser, although the results will vary depending on the browser you use. Neither Mozilla 1 nor Opera 6 support these elements, however.

SETTING DISPLAY CHARACTERISTICS OF SPECIFIC ROWS AND CELLS You also can apply display characteristics to specific rows and cells within the table.

Include specific cells or rows within classes and then create styles that apply display characteristics to those classes:

1. If **salesreport3.html** is not currently open in your text editor and browser, reopen it.
2. Assign classes to the first row's second TH element, to the second row's TR element, and to the next to last row's TR element:

```
<thead>
<tr class="toprow"><th rowspan="2" valign="bottom">Sales Reps</th>
<th colspan="3">Monthly Sales Figures</th><th rowspan="2"
valign="bottom">Totals</th></tr>
<tr class="months"><th>Jan</th> <th>Feb</th> <th>Mar</th></tr>
</thead>

[...]

<tr class="totalrow" align="right"><th>Totals</th>
<td>$24,574</b></td> <td>$19,740</b></td> <td>$25,480</b></td> <td
class="totalcol">$69,794</b></td></tr>
</tbody>
```

3. Create three styles that set display characteristics for the three classes:

```
.toprow { color: #003399; background: transparent
url("back_marblegreen.jpg"); }
.months th { font-weight: bold; color: #003300; background:
#336600 url("back_lightbrown.jpg"); }
.totalrow td { font-weight: bold; color: #ffcc33; background:
#990000 url("back_redstone.jpg"); }
</style>
```

4. Create an additional style that sets a separate format for the grand total cell (see Figure 5.25):

```
tr.totalrow td.totalcol { font-family: Arial, Geneva, Helvetica,
sans-serif; font-size: 1.1em; font-weight: bold; color: #ccff99;
background: #990000 url("back_bluestone2.jpg"); }
</style>
```

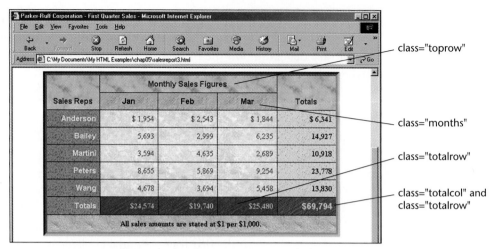

class="toprow"

class="months"

class="totalrow"

class="totalcol" and
class="totalrow"

FIGURE 5.25 • *Different display characteristics are applied to elements within the table that are assigned to specific classes.*

ADDING BORDERS TO THE TABLE Using styles, you can add a variety of different styles of borders to HTML elements.

Add borders above the first row in the table body, above the "Totals" row, and around the table:

1. Assign a class to the first row in the table body section:

```
<tbody>
<tr class="firstrow" align="right"><th width="18%">Anderson</th>
<td width="20%">$ 1,954</td> <td width="20%">$ 2,543</td> <td
width="20%">$ 1,844</td> <td class="totalcol" width="20%">$
6,341</td></tr>
```

2. Create the styles that draw the borders (see Figure 5.26):

```
.firstrow th, .firstrow td { border-top: #33ccff 6px ridge; }
.totalrow th, .totalrow td { border-top: #33cc99 6px ridge; }
</style>
```

3. Set a style to draw a border around the table (see Figure 5.26):

```
table { border: 8px #ffcc00 inset; border-collapse: collapse;
border-spacing: 0; color: #330000; background: #ffffcc
url("back_marblebeige.jpg"); }
```

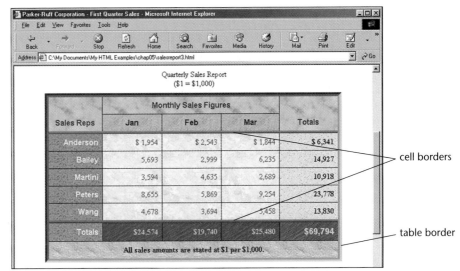

FIGURE 5.26 • *Borders are drawn above the "Anderson" and "Totals" rows in the table, and around the table as a whole.*

You can apply a variety of border styles to a table (or any other block element). The borderstyles.html example file is included with this chapter's example files, which you can open in your browser (see Figure 5.27).

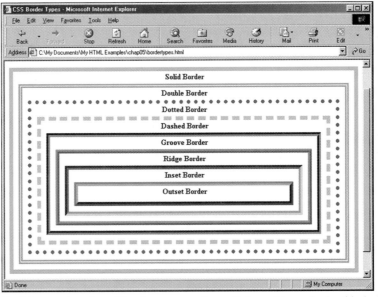

FIGURE 5.27 • *A variety of border types can be applied to tables and other block elements.*

Be aware, however, that Figure 5.27 shows the interpretation of one browser (Internet Explorer 6 for Windows) of how the different border styles should be displayed. Other browsers might display many of these border styles differently, as they are free to do, because the W3C only specifies the names for these border styles, but not how they should be displayed.

CASE EXAMPLE: CREATING FLOATING FIGURE CAPTIONS

In the previous chapter, you created a report on the history of the Mercury space program that used floating images to illustrate the narrative. By using tables, you also can include figure captions with the images.

Shirley Johnson has decided that creating figure captions for the images in her report on the Mercury space program will make them more informative.

Prepare to get started with this example by following these steps:
1. In your text editor, open **mercuryfigs_ex.html** from the chap05 folder in your working folder or working disk.
2. Save mercuryfigs_ex.html as **mercuryfigs.html** in the chap05 folder.
3. Run your browser and open **mercuryfigs.html** from the chap05 folder.

With a non-floating image, you just have to insert a BR element immediately following the IMG element to display following text as a caption beneath the image. That will not work, however, if the image is floating on the left or right margin because text following a BR element would still flow around, rather than being displayed below, the image.

To display a text caption below a floating image, you need to unfloat the image and then insert it inside a floating table. In the floating table, the image is displayed in the top row, while the caption is displayed in the bottom row.

Add a caption to the first floating image:
1. Delete the ALIGN and HSPACE attributes from the IMG element and nest the image inside of a left-aligned (or floating) table:

```
<p><table align="left"><tr><td>
<img src="atlas_mercury.jpg" align="left" hspace="10" alt="Atlas
rocket with Mercury spacecraft" width="200" height="272">
</td></tr>
</table>
The Atlas rocket launch vehicle, which lifted John Glenn into
orbit, began being used following World War II.
```

2. Set the width of the table to 215 pixels, add a second row to the table that contains a caption for the figure, and add a figure reference to the page's text (see Figure 5.28):

```
<p><table align="left" width="215"><tr><td>
<img src="atlas_mercury.jpg" alt="Atlas rocket with Mercury
spacecraft" width="200" height="272">
</td></tr>
<tr><td><font color="aqua"><small>Figure 1. <i>Atlas rocket with
Mercury spacecraft<i></small></font></td></tr>
</table>
The Atlas rocket launch vehicle (see Figure 1), which lifted
John Glenn into orbit, began being used following World War II.
```

horizontal spacing

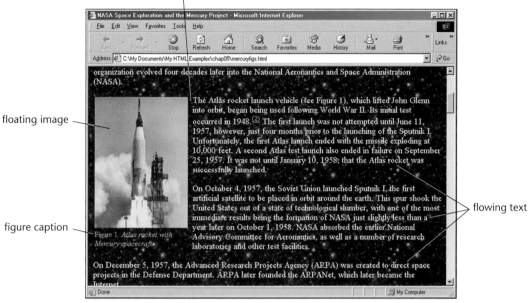

floating image

flowing text

figure caption

FIGURE 5.28 • *Adding captions to floating images can make them more informative.*

The addition of the `width="215"` attribute to the TABLE element is important. If not included, the width of the caption text determines the width of the table, which could exceed the width of the image. The value of **215** is derived from the width of the image (200 pixels) and the desired amount of horizontal spacing (15 pixels) that separates the table's content from the text flowing around its right side.

Setting the table's width to be greater than the width of its content only works for adding horizontal spacing to the right of a left-aligned table, since it relies on the default left-alignment of the table's content. To add horizontal spacing only to the left side of a right-aligned table, one option is to insert a new table column (`<td rowspan="2" width="15">`, for instance) to the left of the current table column:

```
<p><table align="right" width="215"><tr><td rowspan="2"
width="15"></td><td>
```

Another option is to use a style to set a left or right margin for the table. For instance, the following sets a 5-pixel right margin for a left-aligned table:

```
<p>table align="left" width="200" style="margin-right:
5px"><tr><td>
```

practice

Using the figure caption you just created for Figure 1 as a guide, create figure captions (Figure 2, Figure 3, and so on) for the remaining images in the report. Use the content of the ALT attribute as the caption text (or write your own caption). For left-aligned images, add horizontal spacing to the right side of the table by setting the width of the table to be greater than the width of the image it contains. For right-aligned images, add horizontal spacing to the left side of the table by inserting an additional column (in the form of a row-spanned cell) at the start (left side) of the table. In either case, set the table width to be equal to the width of the image, plus the width of any horizontal spacing you want to add to the right or left side of the table. Insert figure references that point to the figures at appropriate places within the text.

CASE EXAMPLE: CREATING INDENTED ICON LINK LISTS

In previous chapters, you created bulleted link lists simply by using the UL and LI elements. You will notice on the Web, however, many instances in which bulleted lists are created using graphical bullet icons.

While surfing the Web, Johnny Watson has noticed that many sites make use of colorful graphical bullet icons when presenting lists. He decided that he wants to do the same in his personal page to add more color and visual appeal. Johnny removed the DIV, UL, and LI elements he used previously, nested his list of link items in a P element, added descriptions to the link list items in his page, and added BR elements where he wants line breaks.

Creating an Icon Link List Using a Table

A better, although somewhat more complicated, way to create an indented icon link list is to use a table.

Prepare to work with this example by following these steps:
1. Open **watson4_ex.html** in your text editor.
2. Save watson4_ex.html as **watson4.html** in the chap05 folder.
3. Open **watson4.html** in your browser from the chap05 folder.

You create an indented icon link list using a table by creating a two-column table, with the bullet icon inserted in the cells of the first column and the link text and descriptions inserted in the second column. An example icon bullet image, goldball.gif, is included with this chapter's example files.

Use a table to create an indented icon line list:
1. Create a two-column table, with the bullet icons nested in the first column and the links and link descriptions nested in the second column:

```
<table>
<tr valign="top"><td width="30">
<img src="goldball.gif" height="15" vspace="3" width="15" alt="*">
</td><td>
<a href="mybio.html">My biography</a> - Read about where I'm
from, my family history, my interests and involvements, the
accomplishments I'm most proud of, and my future plans.
</td></tr>
<tr valign="top"><td>
<p><img src="goldball.gif" height="15" vspace="3" width="15"
alt="*">
</td><td>
<a href="myresume.html">My resume</a> - Look here for details
about my studies, work experience, community involvements, and
awards and honors.
</td></tr>
<tr valign="top"><td>
<img src="goldball.gif" height="15" vspace="3" width="15" alt="*">
</td><td>
```

```
<a href="http://www.usatoday.com/sports/scores.htm">Get the latest
sports scores</a> - Learn how your favorite local sports team did
the night before and read other sports stories from around the
nation.
</td></tr>
<tr valign="top"><td>
<img src="goldball.gif" height="15" vspace="3" width="15" alt="*">
</td><td>
<a href="http://www.about-house-plants.com/">Get indoor gardening
tips and advice</a> - Learn how to deal with pests and other
problems that plague your indoor plants.
</td></tr>
<tr valign="top"><td>
<img src="goldball.gif" height="15" vspace="3" width="15" alt="*">
</td><td>
<a href="http://www.blank.com/jshmoe/">My friend Joe's site</a> -
Joe is into trading baseball and football cards. He's got a great
collection. Check it out!
</td></tr>
<tr valign="top"><td>
<img src="goldball.gif" height="15" vspace="3" width="15" alt="*">
</td><td>
<a href="http://www.wherever.com/jdoe/homepage.html">My friend
Jane's site</a> - Jane is a very talented photographer. She's put
up a gallery of photos from her recent trip to Olympic National
Park in Washington state. Don't miss it!<br><br>
</td></tr>
</table>
```

2. Reduce the width of the table and center it on the page:

```
<table width="85%" align="center">
```

3. Edit the style sheet so that text in the TD element will display at the same size as the paragraph text (see Figure 5.29):

```
p, td, blockquote, li, address { font-size: 1.1em; }
```

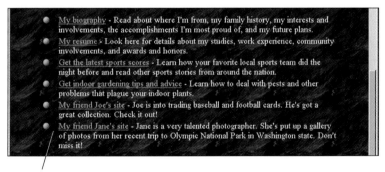

indent created using
table columns

FIGURE 5.29 • *It is easy to indent and center an icon link list created using a two-column table.*

The primary disadvantage of using tables to create indented icon link lists is that they tend to be somewhat labor-intensive to create and maintain, especially if you have a lot of list items. They also are less efficient and consume more bytes than the other methods for creating an indented icon link list.

Creating an Icon Link List Using Styles

You also can create indented icon link lists using styles.

Prepare to work with this example by following these steps:
1. Re-open **watson4_ex.html** in your text editor.
2. Save watson4_ex.html as **watson5.html** in the chap05 folder.
3. Open **watson5.html** in your browser from the chap05 folder.

You use the **list-style-image** style property to specify a bullet image to be displayed in an unordered list. This example uses another icon bullet image, blueball.gif, which is included with this chapter's example files.

Create an indented icon link list using a style:
1. Use the UL and LI elements to set up the list of links and descriptions as an unordered list:

```
<ul>
<li><a href="mybio.html">My biography</a> - Read about where I'm
from, my family history, my interests and involvements, the
accomplishments I'm most proud of, and my future plans.
<li><a href="myresume.html">My resume</a> - Look here for
details about my studies, work experience, community
involvements, and awards and honors.
<li><a href="http://www.usatoday.com/sports/scores.htm">Get the
latest sports scores</a> - Learn how your favorite local sports
team did the night before and read other sports stories from
around the nation.
<li><a href="http://www.about-house-plants.com/">Get indoor
gardening tips and advice</a> - Learn how to deal with pests
and other problems that plague your indoor plants.
<li><a href="http://www.blank.com/jshmoe/">My friend Joe's
site</a> - Joe is into trading baseball and football cards. He's
got a great collection. Check it out!
<li><a href="http://www.wherever.com/jdoe/homepage.html">My
friend Jane's site</a> - Jane is a very talented photographer.
She's put up a gallery of photos from her recent trip to
Olympic National Park in Washington state. Don't miss it!
</ul>
```

2. Edit the style sheet to assign a bullet icon image to be displayed in the list and add additional formatting (see Figure 5.30):

```
ul { list-style-image: url(blueball.gif); }
ul li { padding-left: 15px; margin-left: 15px; margin-right:
15px; padding-right: 15px; }
</style>
```

bullet icon created
using a style

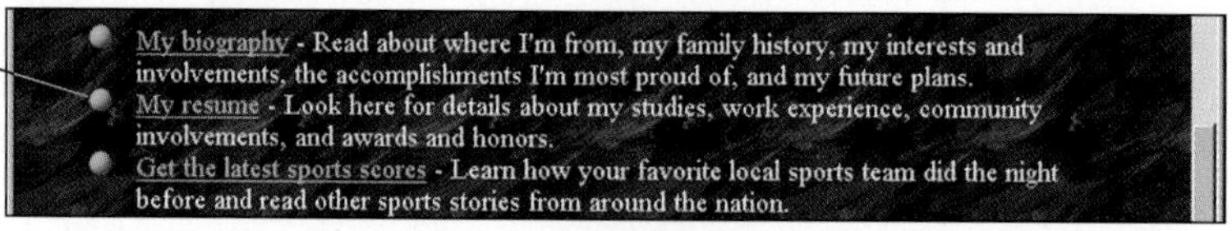

FIGURE 5.30 • *You also can create an indented icon link list using styles.*

The primary disadvantage of using styles to create indented icon link lists is that many earlier browsers either do not support styles or do not support the `list-style-image` style property. Such browsers, however, will simply display the list as a regular unordered list, so using this feature does degrade gracefully in earlier browsers. There is also no immediate way to adjust the vertical positioning of the bullet icon; to adjust the bullet icon down a couple of pixels, you need to add a couple of pixels at the top of the image in your image editor. An advantage of using styles to create indented icon link lists is they are much easier to create and maintain and are much more efficient than using either left-aligned bullet icons or a table.

Creating an Icon Link List Using Floating Bullet Icons

A third way to create an indented icon link list is to use floating bullet icons.

Prepare to work with this example by following these steps:
1. Open **watson4_ex.html** in your text editor.
2. Save watson4_ex.html as **watson6.html** in the chap05 folder.
3. Open **watson6.html** in your browser from the chap05 folder.

This method uses the IMG element's ALIGN attribute in conjunction with the HSPACE and VSPACE attributes to create an indented icon link list. An example icon bullet image, redball.gif, is included with this chapter's example files.

Create an indented icon link list using the IMG element's ALIGN attribute (see Figure 5.31):

```
<p><img src="redball.gif" align="left" vspace="4" hspace="15"
height="15" width="15" alt="*"><a href="mybio.html">My
biography</a> - Read about where I'm from, my family history, my
interests and involvements, the accomplishments I'm most proud
of, and my future plans.<br clear="left">
<img src="redball.gif" align="left" vspace="4" hspace="15"
height="15" width="15" alt="*"><a href="myresume.html">My
resume</a> - Look here for details about my studies, work
experience, community involvements, and awards and honors.<br
clear="left">
<img src="redball.gif" align="left" vspace="4" hspace="15"
height="15" width="15" alt="*"><a
href="http://www.usatoday.com/sports/scores.htm">Get the latest
sports scores</a> - Learn how your favorite local sports team did
the night before and read other sports stories from around the
nation.<br clear="left">
<img src="redball.gif" align="left" vspace="4" hspace="15"
height="15" width="15" alt="*"><a href="http://www.about-house-
plants.com/">Get indoor gardening tips and advice</a> - Learn how
to deal with pests and other problems that plague your indoor
plants.<br clear="left">
<img src="redball.gif" align="left" vspace="4" hspace="15"
height="15" width="15" alt="*"><a
href="http://www.blank.com/jshmoe/">My friend Joe's site</a> - Joe
is into trading baseball and football cards. He's got a great
collection. Check it out!<br clear="left">
```

```
<img src="redball.gif" align="left" vspace="4" hspace="15"
height="15" width="15" alt="*"><a
href="http://www.wherever.com/jdoe/homepage.html">My friend Jane's
site</a> - Jane is a very talented photographer. She's put up a
gallery of photos from her recent trip to Olympic National Park
in Washington state. Don't miss it!<br clear="left"></p>
```

indent created using floating bullet icons

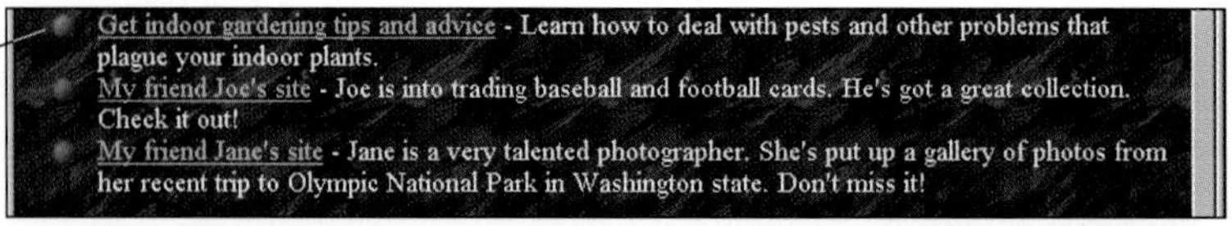

FIGURE 5.31 • *An indented icon link list can be created using floating bullet icons.*

In this example, the ALIGN attribute floats the bullet icon to the left margin, the HSPACE attribute sets horizontal spacing on both sides of the bullet icon, and the VSPACE attribute sets vertical spacing above and below the bullet icon. The VSPACE attribute causes the indent by extending the height of the bullet icon beyond the height of the text line, which causes the second text line to be indented, rather than wrap to the left margin.

The primary advantage of using this method is that it is simpler to implement than using a table. There are some disadvantages to creating an icon bullet list using this method, however. You are limited to only two indented lines of text; a third line of text wraps to the left margin. Remember that a two-line description in a maximized browser window running at 800×600-pixel resolution might be a three-line description in a browser running at 640×600-pixel resolution. The other disadvantage is that browsers vary somewhat in how they align the bullet icon with the following text line.

CASE EXAMPLE: FORMATTING AN ONLINE RESUME

A common type of HTML document that many people want to create is an online resume. Having an attractive resume online can be a real asset in landing that dream job.

Kristine Kochanski has been the controller of a medium-sized corporation for more than five years. She believes she is ready to step into a management position and has launched a job search because the opportunities for further advancement at her current firm are limited.

Kristine has decided that creating an online resume will help in her job search. She has already written her resume and done the initial HTML formatting. She has been studying using HTML tables, however, and has decided to use them to finalize the formatting of her resume. For instance, one of the changes she wants to implement is to use tables to format the dates and following paragraphs as hanging paragraphs.

Prepare to work with this example by following these steps:
1. Open **resume_ex.html** in your text editor.
2. Save resume_ex.html as **resume.html** in the chap05 folder.
3. Open **resume.html** in your browser from the chap05 folder (see Figure 5.32).

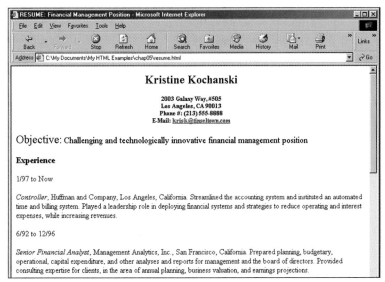

Initially, the layout is not very efficient and it does not look much like a resume. An HTML table can be used to create a more efficient layout that also looks much more like a resume.

action

Create an online resume using a table:

1. Use a two-column HTML table and COLSPAN attributes to create the resume layout:

```
<table width="97%" cellpadding="3" cellspacing="3">
<tr><td colspan="2" height="15"></td></tr>
<tr valign="baseline"><th width="112" align="right">
<p><font size="5">Objective:</font></th>
<td><font size="4">Challenging and technologically innovative
financial management position</font></p>
</td></tr>
<tr><th colspan="2"><h3>Experience</h3></h2>
<hr></th></tr>
<tr valign="top">
<p><th width="115" align="right">1/97 to Now </th>
<p><td><i>Controller</i>, Huffman and Company, Los Angeles,
California. Streamlined the accounting system and instituted an
automated time and billing system. Played a leadership role in
deploying financial systems and strategies to reduce operating
and interest expenses, while increasing revenues.</td>
</tr>
<tr valign="top">
<p><th align="right">6/92 to 12/96 </th>
<p><td><i>Senior Financial Analyst</i>, Management Analytics,
Inc., San Francisco, California. Prepared planning, budgetary,
operational, capital expenditure, and other analyses and reports
for management and the board of directors. Provided consulting
expertise for clients, in the area of annual planning, business
valuation, and earnings projections.</td>
</tr>
<tr valign="top">
<p><th align="right">2/86 to 5/92 </th>
```

```
<p><td><i>Financial Analyst</i>, D. Lister and Associates, Portland,
Oregon. Applied statistical methodologies in performing financial
business analyses. Constructed business simulations and models to
help anticipate business trends, clarify relations with strategic
partners, and highlight potential threats from competitors.</td>
</tr>
<tr><th colspan="2"><h2><h3>Education and Training</h3></h2>
<hr></th></tr>
<tr valign="top">
<p><th align="right">9/84 to 6/86 </th>
<p><td><i>Master of Business Administration</i>, with
concentrations in Technology/Innovation Management and Finance,
University of Colorado at Boulder.</td>
</tr>
<tr valign="top">
<p><th align="right">9/80 to 6/84 </th>
<p><td><i>Bachelor of Arts</i>, Business Administration,
University of Colorado at Boulder.</td>
</tr>
<tr><th colspan="2"><h2><h3>Certifications and
Memberships</h3></h2>
<hr></th></tr>
<tr valign="top">
<p><td colspan="2" align="center"><i>Certified Public Accountant
(CPA)</i>, San Francisco, California.<br>
<i>Personal Financial Planning (PFP)</i>, Portland, Oregon.<br>
<i>American Association of Financial Planners, senior member</i>,
Portland, Oregon.</td>
</tr>
</table>
<p align="center">References available upon request.</p>
```

2. Create a style sheet to control the spacing of the H2 and H5 elements and set a
   different font for the H2, H5, and TH elements (see Figure 5.33):

```
<style type="text/css">
h2, h5 { margin-top: 10px; margin-bottom: 0; padding: 0; }
h2, h5, th { font-family: Arial, Geneva, Helvetica, sans-serif; }
</style>
</head>
```

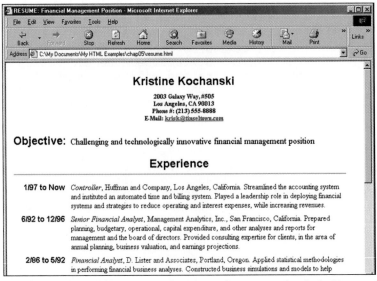

FIGURE 5.33 • *Using tables, you can create an online resume that looks like a real resume.*

Most of the techniques applied in creating the online resume layout have been used in previous examples in this chapter. One feature that is new in this example is the use of the **valign="baseline"** attribute in the "Objective" table row. Because the text strings in the two table cells in the row are differently sized (in Size 5 and Size 4 font sizes), this attribute causes the text strings to be vertically aligned along their baselines.

A nonbreaking space character (** **) is inserted following the dates to create more separation between the two table columns without having to globally increase the padding or spacing in the table.

Browsers are inconsistent in how they display block elements nested inside table cells. When a block element is nested inside a table cell, Internet Explorer does not display the vertical spacing that is normally added above a block element, but the Mozilla and Netscape browsers do. The result can be very different vertical spacing within the page if block elements are nested inside table cells, depending upon which browser is used to view the page. The solution to this problem in the example is to create a style sheet to specify the margin and padding space to be added in above block elements that are nested inside table cells, which will cause Internet Explorer, Mozilla, and Netscape 6 to add the same amount of vertical spacing above the nested block elements.

CASE EXAMPLE: CREATING A TWO-COLUMN LAYOUT

A common use for tables is to create a two-column Web page, with a menu or table of contents in a sidebar column and the main content of the page in the other column.

Shirley Johnson has decided that she wants to format her report on the Mercury space program in two columns, with a table of contents in a sidebar column.

Prepare to work with this example by following these steps:
1. Save (File, Save) any changes to **mercuryfigs.html**. If you have closed your text editor, reopen **mercuryfigs.html**. (If you have not yet created mercuryfigs.html, go back to "Case Example: Creating Floating Figure Captions" and do that case example first.)
2. Save mercuryfigs.html as **mercurycols.html** in the chap05 folder.
3. Open **mercurycols.html** in your browser from the chap05 folder.

The most basic layout you can do with tables is to create a two-column layout, with a sidebar column on the left side and a main content column on the right side. The method for doing this involves setting a width of 100 percent for the whole table, while setting the sidebar column within the table to a fixed pixel width. That way, the table as a whole can expand or contract along with the browser window, while the sidebar column remains the same width.

Create a two-column table with the content of the page in the second column (see Figure 5.34):

```
<body text="white" link="#99ff99" vlink="#99ff99" alink="yellow"
bgcolor="black" background="starcluster.jpg">

<table width="100%" border="1" cellpadding="5" cellspacing="0">
```

```
<tr><td width="150" valign="top" class="side">

</td>
<td class="main">

<a name="top"></a>
<h1 align="center">NASA Space Exploration<br>and the Mercury
Project</h1>

[...]

</td></tr>
</table>
</body>
```

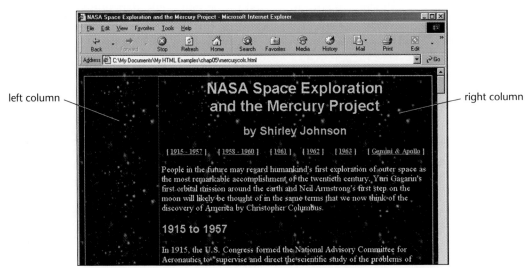

left column   right column

FIGURE 5.34 • *A basic two-column layout is created, with the main content of the page in the right column.*

Using a Spacer Image

Some earlier browsers, such as Netscape 4, do not recognize using the WIDTH attribute to set the width of a column if the width of the content is less than that specified by the WIDTH attribute. A solution to this is to use a "spacer" image, which is a totally transparent single-pixel GIF image that can be resized to force the desired column width. An example image, spacer.gif, is included with this chapter's example files.

Use a spacer image to force the first column to be 150 pixels wide in all browsers:

```
<tr><td width="150" valign="top" class="side">
<p><img src="spacer.gif" height="1" width="140"></p>
```

The width of the spacer image is set to 140 pixels because the 5 pixels of cell padding is set on both the left and right sides of the cell. Thus, the image's width of 140 pixels and the 10 pixels of cell padding equal 150 pixels.

NOTE For links to additional resources on the Web that discuss how spacer images work and how they can be used to create a variety of different Web designs, see this chapter's section at this book's IRC at **www.emcp.com/**.

Creating a Sidebar Menu

To create a sidebar menu, you just need to create a link list in the left column that jumps to the section headings in the right column.

Add a sidebar menu to the left column:

1. Click and drag to highlight the menu in the second column and then cut it (Ctrl+X in Windows or Command+X on the Macintosh):

```
<a name="top"></a>
<h1 align="center">NASA Space Exploration<br>and the Mercury
Project</h1>
<h2 align="center">by Shirley Johnson</h2>

<p align="center" class="menu"><b>
[ <a href="#sect1">1915 - 1957</a>
]     
[ <a href="#sect2">1958 - 1960</a>
]     
[ <a href="#sect3">1961</a> ]     
[ <a href="#sect4">1962</a> ]     
[ <a href="#sect5">1963</a> ]     
[ <a href="#sect3">Gemini & Apollo</a> ]</b></p>
```

2. In the first column, paste in the menu codes and text (Ctrl+V in Windows or Command+V on the Macintosh), and then delete everything except the P element and the hypertext links, so the result looks like this:

```
<table width="100%" border="1" cellpadding="5" cellspacing="0">
<tr><td width="150" valign="top" class="side">
<p align="center" class="menu"><b>
<a href="#sect1">1915 - 1957</a>
<a href="#sect2">1958 - 1960</a>
<a href="#sect3">1961</a>
<a href="#sect4">1962</a>
<a href="#sect5">1963</a>
<a href="#sect3">Gemini & Apollo</a></b></p>
<p><img src="spacer.gif" height="1" width="140"></p>
</td>
```

3. Add a heading, remove the center-alignment from the P element that you pasted in, and then set the links up so they are all in their own paragraphs (see Figure 5.35):

```
<table width="100%" border="1" cellpadding="5" cellspacing="0">
<tr><td width="150" valign="top" class="side">
<h4>Menu:</h4>
<p align="center" class="menu"><b>
<a href="#sect1">1915 - 1957</a></b></p>
<p class="menu"><b>
```

```
<a href="#sect2">1958 - 1960</a></b></p>
<p class="menu"><b>
<a href="#sect3">1961</a></b></p>
<p class="menu"><b>
<a href="#sect4">1962</a></b></p>
<p class="menu"><b>
<a href="#sect5">1963</a></b></p>
<p class="menu"><b>
<a href="#sect3">Gemini & Apollo</a></b></p>
<p class="menu"><img src="spacer.gif" height="1"
width="140"></p>
</td>
```

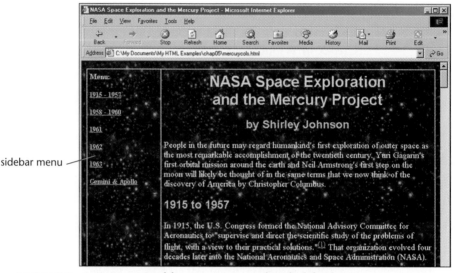

sidebar menu

FIGURE 5.35 • *A sidebar menu is inserted in the left column.*

Varying the Padding Amounts

When creating a two-column layout, sometimes the amount of padding set in the TABLE element can be too much for the sidebar column, but too little for the main body column.

One way to vary padding amounts is to nest a second table inside the main body column and use its TABLE element to set increased padding for the main body column, while decreasing the padding for the sidebar column.

Turn off the padding in the table and then nest another table inside of its main body column:

1. Turn off padding in the table:

```
<table width="100%" border="1" cellpadding="0" cellspacing="0">
```

2. Nest another table inside the first table's main body column, with 10 pixels of padding set:

```
<td class="main">
<table width="100%" border="0" cellpadding="10">
<tr><td>
<a name="top"></a>
<h1 align="center">NASA Space Exploration<br>and the Mercury
Project</h1>
```

```
<h2 align="center">by Shirley Johnson</h2>

[...]

</td></tr>
</table>
</td></tr>
</table>
</body>
```

3. Set display characteristics for the H4 heading and increase the size of the sidebar menu's font (see Figure 5.36):

```
h1, h2, h3, h4 { font-family: Arial, Geneva, Helvetica, sans-
serif; }
h1 { color: #99ffff; background: transparent; }
h2 { color: #ffcc00; background: transparent; }
h3 { color: #ccccff; background: transparent; }
h4 { font-size: 1.25em; margin-top: 15px; color: #ffcc00;
background: transparent; }
.menu { color: yellow; background: transparent; font-size: 1.1em; }
```

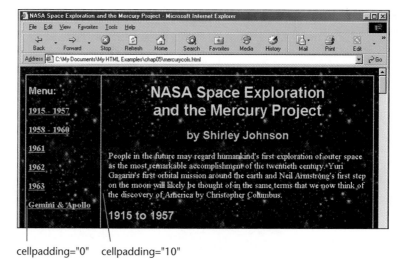

cellpadding="0"   cellpadding="10"

FIGURE 5.36 • *Nesting one table within another table is one way to vary the amount of padding.*

Web pages commonly feature designs involving several levels of nested tables. Web publishing programs often create these types of designs. Although nothing in the HTML specifications forbids creating Web pages with several levels of nested tables, such pages are often difficult to edit and maintain, and can waste bandwidth. They also make it more difficult for someone using a nonvisual browser to access a page because multiple levels of nested tables make understanding the structure and order of precedence of information within a document much more difficult, if not impossible.

Therefore, although you should not necessarily avoid using nested HTML tables, since there is really no good alternative to them if you want to achieve certain design results, you should try to limit the number of nested tables you use in a page.

On the other hand, some Web designers believe that HTML tables should not be used at all for creating layouts because that violates the intended purpose of tables, which is to format tabular data, and can make it more difficult for nonvisual browsers to access and present the information in a Web page. Currently, however, if you want to create multicolumn page layouts that can be reliably viewed with the vast majority of graphical browsers in use, the only way is to use tables. Eventually, page layout will likely be done much more frequently using Cascading Style Sheets (CSS), after browsers become entirely compliant with the second level of CSS (CSS2) and older browsers are gradually phased out of use.

Creating a Seamless Table Layout

In the current layout, the table is separated by margin space between it and the edge of the browser window. That space is actually the default page margin that the browser inserts.

REMOVING THE PAGE MARGINS No standard set of attributes can be used to remove the page margin set by a browser. To achieve this result, you need to use an assortment of nonstandard attributes.

Use a mixture of nonstandard HTML attributes to turn off the page border (see Figure 5.37):

```
<body text="white" link="#99ff99" vlink="#99ff99" alink="yellow"
bgcolor="black" background="starcluster.jpg" marginheight="0"
marginwidth="0" topmargin="0" leftmargin="0">
```

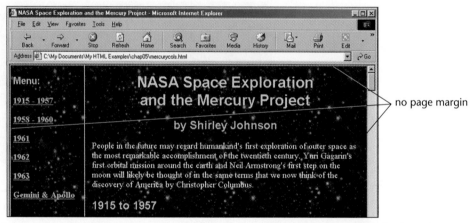

FIGURE 5.37 • *The page margin is turned off using an assortment of nonstandard attributes.*

ADDING A SEAMLESS BACKGROUND If you include a background color in the sidebar column, you no longer need the table border to show the separation between the columns.

Turn off the table borders and set a background color in the sidebar column (see Figure 5.38):

```
<table width="100%" border="0" cellpadding="5" cellspacing="0">
<tr><td width="150" valign="top" class="side" bgcolor="#660000">
```

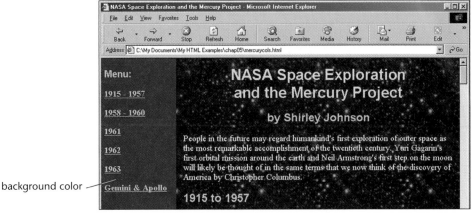

FIGURE 5.38 • *The table borders are turned off and a background color is displayed behind the sidebar column.*

You also can add a background image to the sidebar column. A special background image, back_nebula.jpg, is included with the example files. This background image was created from a NASA photograph of the star nebula and is sized so that it will only tile vertically, but not horizontally, within the sidebar column.

Add a background image, **back_nebula.jpg**, to the sidebar column that is sized to tile only vertically (see Figure 5.39):

```
<tr><td width="150" valign="top" class="side" bgcolor="#660000"
background="back_nebula.jpg">
```

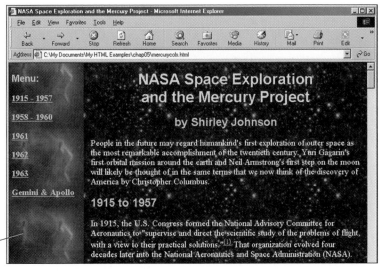

FIGURE 5.39 • *A background image, sized to tile only vertically, is displayed behind the sidebar column.*

GETTING THE ROLLOVER LINKS TO WORK The only problem now is that the rollover links do not work because they are nested inside a table, instead of within the page body. To fix the problem, you need to edit the rollover styles to target the links' positions within a table cell.

Edit the rollover link styles to target their locations inside a table cell (see Figure 5.40):

```
td a.return { color: #ffcc00; background: transparent; font-size:
0.9em; }
td a:link { color: #99ff99; background: transparent; }
td a:visited { color: #99ff99; background: transparent; }
td a:hover { color: maroon; background: #ffcc00; text-decoration:
none; }
td a:active { color: #99ff99; background: transparent; }
```

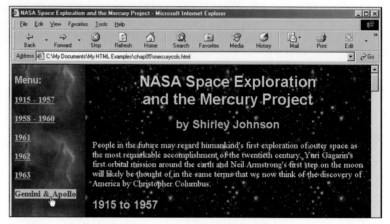

FIGURE 5.40 • *Rollover links are set up in the sidebar column.*

CHAPTER SUMMARY

You should now be familiar with creating tables in HTML documents, including using the PRE element and the TABLE element to format tabular data, creating floating figures with captions, formatting indented icon link lists, creating an online resume with hanging paragraphs, and designing a two-column Web page layout. You should be familiar with adding captions to tables, defining table heading and table data cells, controlling table borders, setting padding within and spacing outside of cells, setting the table width and horizontal alignment, horizontally and vertically aligning cell contents, setting column widths, spanning columns and rows, and controlling font characteristics and backgrounds in tables. You should also be familiar with formatting row groups in tables using HTML 4's TBODY, THEAD, and TFOOT elements in conjunction with CSS styles, as well as with formatting column groups using styles.

Code Review

TABLE element	Defines a table (data arranged in rows and columns) in HTML.
CAPTION element	Specifies a caption that can be displayed above or below a table.
TR element	Defines a row of cells in a table.
TH element	Defines a table heading cell, which can function as either a column heading or a row heading.
TD element	Defines a table data cell.
BORDER attribute	In the TABLE element, draws a border around the table and between the table cells.
CELLPADDING attribute	Specifies the amount of padding that is displayed inside a table's cells.
CELLSPACING attribute	Specifies the amount of spacing that is displayed between a table's cells.
WIDTH attribute	In the TABLE element, specifies the width of the table, either in pixels or as a percentage of the width of the browser window. In a TH or TD element, specifies the width of a column, either in pixels or as a percentage of the width of the table.
ALIGN attribute	In the TABLE element, either centers or floats the table to the left or right margin (with following text or other elements flowing around the table). In the TR, TH, or TD elements, it horizontally aligns nested text or other elements.
COLSPAN element	Causes a table cell (TH or TD element) to span more than one column.
ROWSPAN element	Causes a table cell (TH or TD element) to span more than one table row.
VALIGN attribute	In the TR, TH, and TD elements, vertically aligns nested text or elements with the top, middle, or bottom of a table cell.
TBODY, THEAD, and TFOOT elements	Allow the application of style properties to row groups within a table.
list-style-image property	A style property that specifies an image to be displayed as an icon bullet in an unordered list.

ONLINE QUIZ

Go to this text's IRC at **www.emcp.com/** and take the online self-check quiz for this chapter.

REVIEW EXERCISES

This section provides some hands-on practice exercises to reinforce the information and material included within this and previous chapters.

You can use any of the example files that you created in this chapter to further practice features or methods covered in this chapter. To practice with an example file, save it under a new name (as **salesreport_practice.html**, for instance), so you will not overwrite your original example file.

1. If you have access to Microsoft Excel or another spreadsheet program that can save a space-delimited text file (PRN file), practice saving a PRN file, opening it in your text editor, copying it, and then pasting it into an HTML file. You can create your own worksheet file to practice with, or you can use a worksheet file you have already created. Your spreadsheet program might also have sample worksheet files you can practice with.

2. Practice using the TABLE, CAPTION, TR, TH, and TD elements to format table data, using many of the features covered in this chapter. Focus on the features that control the structural formatting of a table, rather than its appearance, including setting a border, controlling spacing and padding, setting column widths, spanning columns and rows, vertically and horizontally aligning cell contents, and so on. Use **worksheet_ex.html** to get started, saving it under a new name, or you can create your own HTML file from scratch.

3. Practice using HTML attributes to control the appearance of HTML tables, including specifying font sizes, colors, and faces, and setting background colors and background images.

4. Practice using style properties to control the appearance of HTML tables, including controlling padding, spacing, and borders, assigning display characteristics to rows and columns, setting background colors and background images, and setting borders both within and around the table.

5. Experiment further with creating floating figure captions. For instance, instead of using a two-row table, experiment nesting the figure caption in a CAPTION element displayed underneath the table. Use **mercuryfigs_ex.html** to get started, saving it under a new name, or you can create your own HTML file from scratch. Look for images to experiment with in the chap05 folder, or you can copy additional images from the chap04 folder.

6. Experiment further with creating indented icon link lists, using each of the three methods covered in the chapter. Use **watson4_ex.html** to get started, saving it under a new name, or you can create an HTML file from scratch. Look for additional bullet icon images with this chapter's example files that you can practice with.

7. Experiment further with creating a two-column layout. For instance, instead of creating a layout with a sidebar menu on the left, create a layout with a sidebar menu on the right of the page. Use the **mercuryfigs.html** example file you created in this chapter, saving it under a different name, or any other HTML file you have created.

WEB-BASED LEARNING ACTIVITIES

In this book's text, Find It icons inserted in the margin highlight the Web addresses of additional resources you might find helpful or informative. To further extend your learning using the Web, you can:

- Go back and visit any of the Web addresses highlighted in this chapter that you have not yet visited. Look for additional resources and information that add to your understanding and knowledge of the material covered in this chapter. When you find a relevant page or site with information or resources you might want to access later, add it to your Favorites (in Internet Explorer) or your Bookmarks (in Netscape or Mozilla).
- Visit this book's IRC at **www.emcp.com/** to find additional Web addresses of resources related to the material covered in this chapter that you can further investigate and explore.
- Research a specific topic introduced in this chapter. For instance, you can research table utilities for converting and generating tables, or research different ways in which tables can be used in Web pages. Compile your research into a report that can be shared with your fellow students. You also can team up with other students to create a class presentation on a particular topic.

PROJECTS

These projects can be done in class, in a computer lab, or at home. Use the skills you have developed in this and the previous chapters to create any of the following projects.

Project 1. Incorporate tabular data into a Web page.

Take the lessons learned in this chapter and apply them in incorporating an HTML table or tables for formatting tabular data into a Web page you have already created or that you create from scratch. This can be a personal page, a topical page, an online paper, or any other page you have created or can create that can profit from the inclusion of tabular data. Focus more on the organized and structured presentation of data than on the esthetic appearance of the tables.

Project 2. Coordinate the design of a table or tables with the overall design of a Web page using HTML attributes.

Take the lessons learned in this chapter and apply them to incorporating the design of an HTML table with the overall design of a Web page, using HTML attributes. Use a Web page you have already created or that you create from scratch. In this project, focus on using HTML attributes to create a consistent overall look for the page by making use of fonts, colors, and backgrounds.

Project 3. Coordinate the design of a table or tables with the overall design of a Web page using styles.

Take the lessons learned in this chapter and apply them to incorporating the design of an HTML table with the overall design of a Web page, using CSS styles. Use a Web page you have already created or that you create from scratch. In this project, focus on using styles to create a consistent overall look for the page by making use of fonts, colors, and backgrounds. Use the Invisible Object Method to warn Netscape 4 users that they need to upgrade their browsers or the DOM Sniff method to redirect Netscape users to a browser upgrade page (see Chapter 3 for instructions). While creating your design, be sure to test your page in more than one browser (in Mozilla and Opera, for instance, in addition to Internet Explorer).

Project 4. Incorporate floating figures with captions into an online paper.

Take the lessons learned in this chapter and apply them in incorporating floating figures with captions into an online paper you have already created or that you create from scratch. Be sure to include HEIGHT, WIDTH, and ALT attributes in the IMG elements. Use either a two-row table or a one-row table with a bottom-aligned CAPTION element to create the figure captions.

Project 5. Incorporate an icon link list into a Web page.

Take the lessons learned in this chapter and apply them in incorporating an icon link list into a Web page that you have already created or that you create from scratch. Use any of the three methods for creating indented icon link lists covered in this chapter. Select the bullet icon so that it is coordinated with the overall look and color scheme of your page. Use any of the bullet icons included with this chapter's example files or look in the Art folder that accompanies this book's example files for additional bullet icons you can use. You also can look online for sources of bullet icons that you can download and use.

Project 6. Create a Web page that uses a two-column layout.

Take the lessons learned in this chapter and apply them in formatting a Web page that uses a two-column layout. Use a Web page you have already created or that you create from scratch. Create a sidebar menu that uses rollover links. Include return links that jump back to the top of the page at the end of sections in the page. Use any of the techniques covered in this chapter, such as eliminating page margins and creating a seamless table layout. If using background images, use any of the background images included in this chapter, or copy background images included in other chapter folders or in the Art folder that accompanies this book's example files. You also can look online for additional sources of background images. If you have access to Paint Shop Pro, you can experiment with creating your own seamless background patterns (select an area within any image and then choose Selections, and Convert to Seamless Pattern).

Project 7. Format an online resume using a table.

Take the lessons learned in this chapter and apply them in formatting an online resume for yourself or a friend that uses a table to create a side-by-side format (with dates in one column and following text in a second column). Use the text for a resume you have already created or that you create from scratch. Experiment with more than one way of organizing and laying out a resume, discovering solutions and methods using tables, HTML attributes, and/or styles to achieve a desired layout or organization. If using styles, be sure to also use the DOM Sniff or Invisible Object Method for shielding or warning users of earlier browsers with poor support for CSS.

CHAPTER

6

Working with Multi-Page Web Sites

PERFORMANCE OBJECTIVES

In this chapter, you will learn to perform various tasks involved in creating and publishing multi-page Web sites, including how to:

- Use frames to create a multi-windowed Web site.
- Create two-row, two-column, and combination row-column framed Web sites.
- Control the appearance of a framed site using an external style sheet.
- Use relative URLs to link to files in multiple folders.
- Validate your page's HTML and CSS.
- Publish your Web page files using FTP.

Until now in this book, you mostly have been working with single HTML documents. Web design involves more than just creating single Web pages. A Web site can be composed of many documents and files organized into separate folders. Creating, publishing, and maintaining more complex Web sites presents a unique set of opportunities and challenges.

USING THE EXAMPLE FILES

If you have created a working folder for storing files you create, you will find the example files for this chapter located in the **chap06** folder within your working folder. Save any HTML files you create in this chapter in that folder.

  If you have created a working disk, copy the chap06 folder to your working disk from the **HTML_Examples** folder that you or your instructor downloaded from this book's Internet Resource Center (IRC) or from a CD-R disc or floppy disk provided by your instructor. Save any HTML file you create in this chapter in the chap06 folder that you have copied to your working disk.

CASE EXAMPLE: CREATING A FRAMED WEB SITE

A popular way to present a multi-page Web site is to use frames. HTML frames allow you to create a multi-windowed page, with individual pages displayed in the window frames.

Arturo Rodriguez is a graphic designer and printer working for a full-service printing firm, A-Plus Printers. Because Arturo is in charge of designing Web sites for customers, his boss has given him the task of creating a new Web site for the company that can effectively market its services and serve its customers online over the Web.

Arturo has decided to redesign the A-Plus Printers site to take advantage of a two-column layout using frames.

CREATING FRAME PAGE LAYOUTS

Frames were originally introduced by Netscape and have been included since HTML 4. All current graphical browsers support using frames. By using frames, you can create a wide variety of different multi-column, multi-row, and combination column-and-row layouts. Unlike tables, frame layouts can include separate windows (or *frames*) within which scrollable content can be displayed.

Creating a Two-Column Frame Page

You can arrange frames in columns or rows. In this case, you create a basic frames layout that uses two columns, with a sidebar menu in one column and the main content of the page in the other column.

CREATING THE FRAMESET PAGE A frameset page is a page that includes the instructions for laying out frames. The pages that are displayed in the frames are already created for you. A starter page, framestart_ex.html, has also been created that you will use to start creating the different frame page examples in this chapter.

To start working with this example:
1. Open **framestart_ex.html** in your text editor.
2. Save framestart_ex.html as **twocol_frame.html** in the chap06 folder in your working folder or disk.
3. Open **twocol_frame.html** in your Web browser.

A frameset page is created using the FRAMESET and FRAME elements. A frameset page does not contain any displayable content, but only pointers to the pages (or other files) to be displayed in the individual frames. In a frameset page, the FRAMESET element replaces the BODY element.

Create a frameset page that creates a two-column Web page, with a sidebar menu in the left column and the main content of the page in the right column:
1. Add a FRAMESET element that specifies a two-column layout, with a 150-pixel wide column on the left and a column on the right that will expand to fill the page:

```
<!DOCTYPE HTML PUBLIC "-//W3C//DTD HTML 4.01 Frameset//EN"
 "http://www.w3.org/TR/html4/frameset.dtd">
<html>
<head>
<meta http-equiv="Content-Type" content="text/html; charset=ISO-
8859-1">
```

```
<title>A-Plus Printers: Serving All Your Printing Needs Since
1975</title>
</head>
<frameset cols="150,*">
</frameset>
</html>
```

2. Use the FRAME element to define the frames that compose the columns and point to the documents to be displayed in them:

```
<frameset cols="150,*">
  <frame src="sidebar.html">
  <frame src="main.html" name="main">
</frameset>
```

3. Save **twocol_frame.html** (File, Save) and open it in your browser (see Figure 6.1).

sidebar.html

main.html ("main" frame)

FIGURE 6.1 • *The A-Plus Printers page is displayed in a two-column format.*

4. Click on the Design/Layout link in the left sidebar (see Figure 6.2).

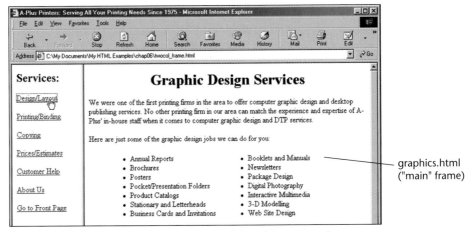

graphics.html ("main" frame)

FIGURE 6.2 • *The graphics.html page is displayed in the main window.*

5. Click on the Go to Front Page link in the left sidebar to return to the site's front page.

When displaying a frameset page in a browser, only the title defined in the frameset page will be displayed in the browser's title bar. Any titles defined for pages displayed within frames will not be displayed, unless the pages are opened as standalone pages.

In Figures 6.1 and 6.2, the "sidebar" frame is not displaying scroll bars. Scroll bars will be displayed, however, if the content of the "sidebar" frame extends below the bottom of the browser window.

UNDERSTANDING THE SIDEBAR PAGE You have just activated two links whose functions are key to creating an effective navigation scheme using frames.

Open and review the sidebar page codes:

1. Open **sidebar.html** in your text editor:

```
<!DOCTYPE HTML PUBLIC "-//W3C//DTD HTML 4.01 Transitional//EN">
<html>
<head>
<meta http-equiv="Content-Type" content="text/html; charset=ISO-8859-1">
<title>A-Plus Printers</title>
</head>
<body>
<h2>Services:</h2>
<p><a href="graphics.html" target="main">Design/Layout</a></p>
<p><a href="printing.html" target="main">Printing/Binding</a></p>
<p><a href="copying.html" target="main">Copying</a></p>
<p><a href="prices.html" target="main">Prices/Estimates</a></p>
<p><a href="service.html" target="main">Customer Help</a></p>
<p><a href="about.html" target="main">About Us</a></p>
<p><a href="main.html" target="main">Go to Front Page</a>
</body>
</html>
```

2. With sidebar.html open in your text editor, use the following pointers to review the content of the page.

Notice that a foreshortened DocType declaration, **<!DOCTYPE HTML PUBLIC "-//W3C//DTD HTML 4.01 Transitional//EN">**, is inserted at the top of the sidebar.html. A foreshortened, rather than a full, DocType declaration is used to get around a bug in Internet Explorer 6 for Windows, which inserts unnecessary horizontal scroll bars in frame windows when vertical scroll bars are also displayed. This only happens, however, when Internet Explorer 6 for Windows, using DocType switching, invokes standards mode, but not when it invokes quirks mode. A foreshortened "frameset" DocType declaration (without the URL to the W3C DTD file) causes Internet Explorer 6 (and any other browser that does DocType swtching) to revert to quirks mode (also called "bugwards compatibility mode"). In doing this, however, you need to be aware that you cannot include features in the page that will not display properly if standards mode is not invoked. Later in this chapter, in "Using Styles with Multi-Page Web Sites," you will work with an example where standards mode must be invoked for the page to display properly in Internet Explorer 6 (or later versions), even though the page is included within a frame in which scrolling is not turned off.

A couple of features of this file are key to its definition and operation:

- The **target="main"** attributes in the links target the "main" window as the location in which the objects of the links should be displayed. This corresponds to the **name="main"** that you applied to the second FRAME element in your frameset file. This combination of attributes allows you to click on a link in one frame to cause a file to be displayed in another frame. Without a TARGET attribute, the object of the link is displayed in the same frame as the linking file.

- The last link allows the user to redisplay the site's front page, main.html, in the main frame window.

Creating a sidebar frame on the left side of the page is only one way to lay out a framed page. You could just as easily position the sidebar frame on the right side of the page, for instance, simply by switching the positions of the FRAME elements in the frameset page.

NOTE ———— Only the graphics.html subpage has been fully developed for this example. Dummy files have been created for the other subpages (printing.html, copying.html, service.html, and about.html).

Creating a Two-Row Frame Page

Another common way to lay out a framed page is by using two rows, with the top row containing a menu running along the top of the page. Because the previous left-side frame was referred to as a sidebar frame, this kind of frame is called a topbar frame.

CREATING THE FRAMESET PAGE As with creating a two-column frame page, you need to create a frameset page that specifies a two-row layout. To get started, you will be using the same starter page, framestart_ex.html, you used in creating the previous example.

action

To start working with this example:
1. Open **framestart_ex.html** in your text editor.
2. Save framestart_ex.html as **tworow_frame.html** in the chap06 folder in your working folder or disk.
3. Open **tworow_frame.html** in your Web browser.

You create a two-row frame page in the same way you created a two-column frame page, except you specify the layout using the ROWS attribute, rather than the COLS attribute.

action

Create a two-row frame layout:
1. Define a two-row frame layout containing a top row with a height of 25 pixels and a bottom row that expands to vertically fill the page. Make the first frame row link to topbar.html and the second frame row link to main.html (see Figure 6.3):

```
</head>
<frameset rows="25,*">
   <frame src="topbar.html" scrolling="no" marginheight="0">
   <frame src="main.html" name="main">
</frameset>
</html>
```

topbar.html

main.html

FIGURE 6.3 • *The A-Plus Printers page is displayed in a two-row format.*

2. Click the Design link in the topbar frame (see Figure 6.4).

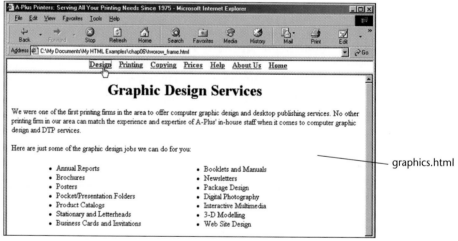

graphics.html

FIGURE 6.4 • *Clicking the Design link in the topbar frame causes the graphics.html file to be displayed in the main frame.*

This example differs from the previous example in the following ways:
*   The `rows="25,*"` attribute in the FRAMESET element specifies that the following nested FRAME elements define horizontal rows, rather than vertical columns. It sets the height of the first row to 25 pixels and uses the wildcard character ("*") to set the second row to expand to fill the browser window. You also can set the height of a row using a percentage value (`rows="15%,*"`, for instance).
*   The `scrolling="no"` attribute in the first FRAME element turns off any scroll bars that might be displayed in the frame window.
*   The `marginheight="0"` attribute in the first FRAME element sets the top and bottom margins of the frame to 0, so that the content of the frame (topbar.html) will fit vertically within the frame. To set a positive height for the top and bottom margins in pixels, just specify an integer value.

UNDERSTANDING THE TOPBAR PAGE You have just activated two links whose functions are key to creating an effective navigation scheme using frames.

Open and review the topbar page codes:

1. Open **topbar.html** in your text editor:

```
<!DOCTYPE HTML PUBLIC "-//W3C//DTD HTML 4.01 Transitional//EN"
 "http://www.w3.org/TR/html4/loose.dtd">
<html>
<head>
<meta http-equiv="Content-Type" content="text/html; charset=ISO-
8859-1">
<title>A-Plus Printers</title>
</head>
<body>
<p align="center" style="margin-top: 0"><b>
<a href="graphics.html"
target="main">Design</a>   
<a href="printing.html"
target="main">Printing</a>   
<a href="copying.html"
target="main">Copying</a>   
<a href="prices.html" target="main">Prices</a>   
<a href="service.html" target="main">Help</a>   
<a href="about.html" target="main">About
Us</a>   
<a href="main.html" target="main">Home</a></b>
</body>
</html>
```

2. With topbar.html open in your text editor, use the following pointers to review the content of the page.

A number of features of this file are key to its definition and operation:

- The document includes a full DocType declaration, which triggers standards mode in Internet Explorer 6 (and other browsers that do DocType switching). Because the scroll bars have been turned off for the frame, you do not have to worry about Internet Explorer 6's scroll bar bug.
- The P element that contains the menu links includes a `style="margin-top: 0"` inline style to turn off the top margin that the Mozilla and Netscape 6 browsers insert when an element is the first element in a frame. (Internet Explorer does not display top margin spacing for the first element in a frame.)
- The topbar menu links are arranged horizontally in a centered paragraph, with three non-breaking space characters (`   `) separating the links.
- The `target="main"` attributes work the same way as in the sidebar file, causing the linked files to be displayed in the "main" frame.
- The last link allows the user to redisplay the site's front page, main.html, in the "main" frame.

Creating a Frame Page with Columns and Rows

For a more complex frame layout, you can create a layout that contains both columns and rows by nesting one frameset element within another.

CREATING THE FRAMESET PAGE For this example, you will start out using the two-column frame page layout you created previously. If you have not yet done that example, you should go back and do it first, before trying to do this example.

To start working with this example:
1. Reopen **twocol_frame.html** in your text editor.
2. Save twocol_frame.html as **combo_frame.html** in the chap06 folder in your working folder or disk.
3. Open **combo_frame.html** in your Web browser.

You create a combination row-column frame layout by nesting one FRAMESET element inside of another FRAMESET element, with the first defining the rows and the second defining the columns.

Create a combination frame layout that uses both rows and columns:
1. Create a frameset layout that nests one frameset element (that specifies columns) inside another frameset element (that specifies rows) (see Figure 6.5):

```
</head>
<frameset rows="85,*">
  <frame src="topbanner.html" scrolling="no" marginheight="0">
  <frameset cols="150,*">
    <frame src="sidebar2.html">
    <frame src="main2.html" name="main">
  </frameset>
</frameset>
</html>
```

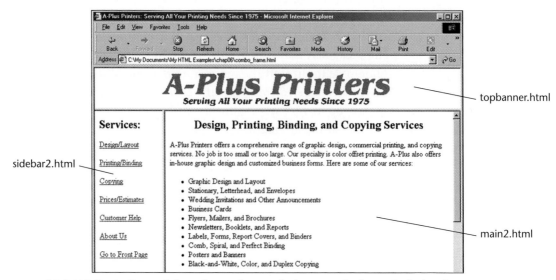

FIGURE 6.5 • *A frame layout that uses both rows and columns is displayed.*

2. Click on the Design/Layout link in the sidebar (see Figure 6.6).

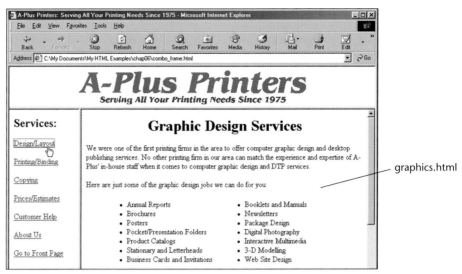

FIGURE 6.6 • *Clicking on the Design/Layout link causes the graphics.html file to be displayed in the "main" window.*

The following are the main features of this example:

- The outside FRAMESET element defines an initial two-row layout, with the top row set to a height of 85 pixels and the bottom row set to expand to fill the page.
- The first FRAME element defines the first row in the outside frameset. It links to a topbanner.html file that contains the A-Plus Printers' banner image. It also turns off scrolling and sets the top margin to 0, as in the previous example.
- The inside FRAMESET element forms the second row in the outside frameset. It defines a two-column layout that is nested inside of the outside frameset's bottom row.

UNDERSTANDING THE FRAMED PAGES The inside frameset links to two new files, sidebar2.html and main2.html, included with the example files. The sidebar2.html file differs from sidebar.html only in the "Go to Front Page" link, which links to main2.html, rather than main.html. The main2.html file differs from main.html only in that the banner image at the top of the page has been deleted.

The topbanner.html file is similar to the topbar.html file from the two-row frame layout example.

Open and review the content of the topbanner page:

1. Open **topbanner.html** in your text editor:

```
<!DOCTYPE HTML PUBLIC "-//W3C//DTD HTML 4.01 Transitional//EN"
  "http://www.w3.org/TR/html4/loose.dtd">
<html>
<head>
<meta http-equiv="Content-Type" content="text/html; charset=ISO-
8859-1">
<title>A-Plus Printers</title>
</head>
<body>
<p align="center" style="margin-top: 5px">
```

```
<a href="combo_frame.html" target="_top"><img src="aplusbanner.gif"
height="75" width="500" alt="A-Plus Printers banner image"
border="0"></p>
</body>
</html>
```

2. With topbanner.html open in your text editor, use the following pointers to review the content of the page.

A number of features of this file are key to its definition and operation:

- As in topbar.html, a full DocType declaration is included. Because scrolling is turned off in the frame in which this document is displayed, you do not need to worry about Internet Explorer 6 for Windows' scroll bar bug.
- The banner image is centered by nesting it in a centered paragraph. The inline style in the P element sets its top margin to five pixels. This setting also enforces the same top margin height in both Internet Explorer and the Netscape 6/Mozilla 1 browsers (otherwise, Internet Explorer 6 does not insert a top margin, but Netscape 6 and Mozilla 1 do insert a top margin for the P element).
- The banner image is set up as an image link by nesting it inside a hypertext link that causes the combo_frame.html frameset page to be displayed in the top-level browser window (by including **target="_top"** in the A element) if the image is clicked on.
- The border that was drawn around the banner image in the previous examples has been turned off (**border="0"**).

The main advantages of this layout is that the banner image remains visible in the browser window at all times, instead of scrolling off the screen if inserted at the top of page in the main frame.

NOTE

You can create a "grid" layout by combining the ROWS and COLS attributes in the same FRAMESET element. For instance, to split the browser window into four equally sized frames, just create the following FRAMESET element:

```
<frameset cols="50%,50%" rows="50%,50%">
  <frame src="filename1.html" name="upperleft">
  <frame src="filename2.html" name="upperright">
  <frame src="filename3.html" name="lowerleft">
  <frame src="filename4.html" name="lowerright">
</frameset>
```

Substitute the actual file names of the pages you want to display in the grid. To increase the number of cells within the grid, just increase the number of columns and/or rows, reapportioning the percentages accordingly.

USING A NESTED FRAMESET FILE A variation on using a nested FRAMESET element is to use a nested frameset file. You do this by first creating two frameset files, with the first defining two rows, for instance, and the second defining two columns. You then link the second FRAME element in the two-row frameset to the two-column frameset. The advantage of this is that you can name the FRAME element that links to the nested frameset file, whereas you cannot name a nested FRAMESET element. You can then create a series of frameset files (containing more than one frame) that can be swapped in and out using the name of the linking FRAME element. The disadvantage of this is that you have to create and maintain at least one additional file.

Understanding Pros and Cons of Using Frames

Frames were originally introduced by Netscape and have only been a standard part of HTML since HTML 4. Both positives and negatives are involved in using frames. If you want to use frames in designing Web sites, you need to understand the possible negatives and some of the solutions that can at least partially overcome those negatives.

WHY USE FRAMES? You might choose to use frames in a Web site for a number of positive reasons:

- Multi-column and multi-row layouts can be easily created.
- The presentation of content, such as sidebar menus, masthead banners, and so on, remain fixed and visible, while other content can scroll within the page.
- If done right, frames can help create a consistent and easy-to-use navigation system because sidebar, topbar, or bottombar menus remain visible and accessible at all times.
- Creating and maintaining a more complex multi-page Web site can be more efficient and manageable because the HTML code for presenting repeating page elements, such as banners and menus, needs only to be created once and requires only a single update if a change is necessary.

WHY NOT USE FRAMES? Frames also present a number of drawbacks that you need to be aware of before deciding whether to use frames in a Web site:

- Some earlier browsers do not understand frames. Internet Explorer 2, for instance, which is the default browser for Windows NT 4, does not understand frames.
- Search engines and directories may not list a frameset page, because it does not contain any content that can be indexed.
- Search engines and directories may not list pages that are linked to in a frameset page, because most search engines' robots do not follow frame page links (set using the FRAME element's SRC attribute).
- It is difficult to bookmark a page that is linked to within a frame. For instance, if a user clicks on the Design/Layout link in the current example's sidebar menu to display graphics.html in the main window, he cannot bookmark that specific page simply by clicking on the Favorites or Bookmark button. Instead, only the initial frameset page (showing main.html) is bookmarked. To bookmark a particular page, users have to know to right-click on the page's background and select Add to Favorites (in Internet Explorer) or Bookmark This Page (in Netscape or Mozilla).
- If a Web author does not use TARGET attributes with external links (either intentionally or unintentionally), any external pages that are linked to will be displayed within a frame in the site's frameset, which also makes it impossible to bookmark the external page without right-clicking on the page's background. Most users do not know that they can open a framed page within its own window, because the procedures for doing this are not obvious—a Netscape 6 user needs to right-click on the page's background and select Open Frame in New Window, whereas an Internet Explorer 6 user needs to right-click on the page's background, select Properties, copy the page's address, and paste the address in the Address box.

There have been a number of lawsuits over Web sites deep-linking into another site's commercial content. This is generally done using frames; the other site's page is displayed in a frame within the linking site. Including another person's page or site within your own frame is generally frowned upon on the Web and might even be illegal if the content you are framing within your site is copyrighted. When linking to an external Web site from a framed page, you should *always* include a `target="_top"` or `target="_blank"` attribute in the link's A element to open the page in the top-level browser window or in a new browser window.

If you decide to link to a page that is deep within another's site, you also should include a link to the site's front page, especially if the identity of the page's parent site is neither obvious nor easy to navigate to. You should avoid linking directly to "printer-ready" pages, because doing so will likely bypass advertising that might be present on the regular version of the page.

See this chapter's section at the IRC for this book at **www.emcp.com/** for additional links to resources on the Web that discuss ethical, legal, and free speech issues involved in linking and deep-linking.

- Although content within a framed Web page—such as menus, banners, or advertising—can remain fixed and always visible, this is at the expense of the amount of space available for viewing the scrollable content of the page.
- A multi-page framed Web site can take longer to download and display than a single page because multiple pages must be downloaded.

A question that is often asked is whether an author should link to external pages (pages external to your site) from within a framed page using a `target="_top"` or a `target="_blank"` attribute. The first attribute causes the external page to be displayed in the top-level browser window, replacing the current window. The second attribute causes the external page to be displayed in a new browser window, with the current window remaining open in the background. Designers creating commercial Web sites often opt to use `target="_blank"` when linking to external pages because they are concerned that if they use `target="_top"`, a potential customer might go away and never come back. If, however, your site is informational, rather than commercial, using `target="_top"` is friendlier to visitors to your site because it does not force them to open a second browser window when they might not want to.

Using META Elements in Frame Pages

The META element allows you to provide a description and a list of keywords that search engines and directories can use in indexing and listing a framed Web site.

Use the META element to add a description and a list of keywords to the combo_frame.html frameset page:

1. If necessary, open **combo_frame.html** in your text editor and your browser.
2. In your text editor, add a description and a list of keywords:

```
<title>A-Plus Printers: Serving All Your Printing Needs Since
1975</title>
<meta name="description" content="A-Plus Printers offers a
comprehensive range of graphic design, commercial printing, and
copying services. We specialize in one-color, two-color, and
full-color offset printing, as well as embossing, binding,
laminating, and more."
```

```
<meta name="keywords" content="printer, printing, printing
services, service bureau, offset printing, 3-color, 4-color,
perfect binding, spiral binding, comb binding, linotype,
prepress, graphic design, flyers, brochures, newsletters,
booklets, banners, reports, posters, invitations"
</head>
```

When creating META element descriptions and keyword lists, you should be aware that including descriptions or keywords lists that do not correspond to the actual content of your page or site is considered spamming and may result in your page or site being penalized by receiving a lower search ranking (or no ranking).

Because the META element has been abused by Web site promoters trying to get a higher ranking in search response lists, some search engines and directories no longer use META element descriptions and keyword lists to index and list a page or site. For that reason, you should not rely upon the META element alone to provide content for a framed page. The following section details another way to include positive content within a framed page.

Using the NOFRAMES Element

The NOFRAMES element is included in HTML ostensibly to enable you to provide content to browsers that do not recognize framed pages. Perhaps even more importantly, however, you can also use the NOFRAMES element to provide content and links that search engine robots and spiders can index and follow.

CREATING A SIMPLE NOFRAMES ELEMENT The simplest way to use the NOFRAMES element is to alert users of browsers that do not support frames and provide them with an alternative means to view the content of your site. An efficient way to do this is to link to your main content page, and then link to the rest of the pages in your site through that page.

Use the NOFRAMES element to provide a means for users of browsers that do not understand frames and for search engine robots to access the content of your site:

1. If not already open, open **combo_frame.html** in your text editor.
2. Save combo_frame.html as **combo_frame2.html** in the chap06 folder.
3. Add a NOFRAMES element to the combo_frame2.html file:

```
<frameset rows="85,*">
  <frame src="topbanner.html" scrolling="no" marginheight="0">
  <frameset cols="150,*">
    <frame src="sidebar2.html">
    <frame src="main2.html" name="main">
  </frameset>
<noframes>
<h3>A frames-compatible browser is required to view this page.
Please visit the <a href="main.html">non-frames version</a> of
this site.</h3>
</noframes>
</frameset>
```

The NOFRAMES element may be nested inside the top-level FRAMESET element. A browser that recognizes frames will ignore the content of the NOFRAMES element, while a browser that does not recognize frames will ignore the FRAMESET and FRAMES elements, seeing only the NOFRAMES content (which is the only positive content in the page). This example has two primary characteristics:

- Search engines' robots can also follow the NOFRAMES link to access the rest of your site. As long as the page linked through the NOFRAMES link contains links to other pages in your site, search engine robots will also be able to find and index those other pages, as well.
- The link to the "non-frames version," in this instance actually links to the site's main page, main.html. Linking directly to your site's main content page (or front page) allows you to avoid having to create an entire separate page (or site) simply to service a rapidly diminishing body of users (users using non-frames-compatible browsers).
- You can use HTML elements within the NOFRAMES element to control how the content will be presented to users of browsers that do not recognize frames. You even can include a BODY element within the NOFRAMES element to assign a background color or background image to the NOFRAMES content.

MAKING SURE PAGES IN FRAMES CAN STAND ALONE If the page linked to through the NOFRAMES link does not link to any other pages, a search engine robot will not be able to index any more than just that one page. If you want other pages in your site to be indexed and listed, you should make sure that links also are included in the linked page that let search engine robots access the rest of your site.

A search engine robot cannot index the rest of your site if your framed pages are not linked together. Instead of simply relying on a sidebar (or topbar) menu to provide links to the other pages in your site, you should also include links in your other pages, so they can stand alone as link nodes in your site.

With all the content pages of your site linked together (with none standing apart unlinked to any other page), a search engine might index and list any page within your site. Visitors are not limited to simply visiting your site through your front door, in other words. They can "beam in" at any point within your site.

NOTE

Clients sometimes instruct Web designers that they want visitors to only access their site through the front page, so they can maximize revenue from ads that are displayed there. There is, however, no way to do this other than setting up password protection and forcing visitors to log in before accessing pages within your site. Having to log in, however, will probably drive away more visitors from your site's front door, so to speak, than you will have gained from diverting them from other pages.

A much better idea is to embrace the idea that every page in your site is potentially a front page. Every content page in your site should be designed to stand on its own, as a separate and independent page. By attracting visitors to many pages within your site, you can attract more "traffic" than if you try to attract visitors only to a single page.

action

Add a navigation menu to the bottom of your site's content pages:
1. Open **topbar.html** in your text editor and copy everything inside the BODY element.
2. Open **main2.html** in your text editor and paste the codes and text you copied in Step 1 in the location shown here:

```
<p align="center" style="margin-top: 0"><b><a href="graphics.html"
target="main">Design</a>   
<a href="printing.html" target="main">Printing</a>   
<a href="copying.html" target="main">Copying</a>   
<a href="prices.html" target="main">Prices</a>   
<a href="service.html" target="main">Help</a>   
<a href="about.html" target="main">About Us</a>   
<a href="main.html" target="main">Home</a></b></p>
<hr>
<address>
```

3. Edit the menu you just pasted in so it references the name of your site's front page:

```
<a href="main2.html" target="main">Home</a></b></p>
```

4. Repeat Steps 2 and 3 with the graphics.html page, adding a navigation menu at the bottom of that page, as well.

Figure 6.7 shows the navigation menu displayed at the bottom of the main2.html front page.

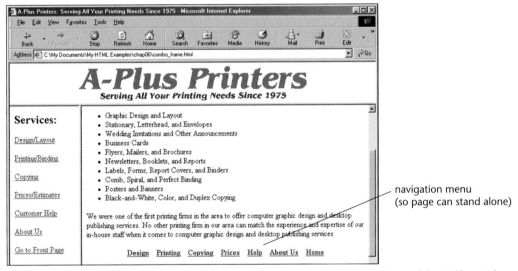

FIGURE 6.7 • *A navigation menu at the bottom of a framed page lets it stand by itself, outside of the frameset, as a standalone Web page.*

CREATING A MORE COMPLEX NOFRAMES ELEMENT   You can do more than just include a link in the NOFRAMES element to another page in your site. You can include the codes for an entire page, including a BODY element, within the NOFRAMES element. Then this embedded page also can contain links to other pages in your site.

BREAKING UP A FRAMED SITE INTO MULTIPLE FRAMESETS   One way to overcome the problem of users not being able to bookmark separate pages within a framed site is to create additional frameset files for each of the major sections in your site. Then, instead of linking to the front pages for those sections, you can link to the framesets instead. For instance, the following is an example of a sidebar menu file that links to frameset files rather than to the individual section pages:

```
<h2>Services:</h2>
<p><a href="graphics_frame.html" target="_top">Design/Layout</a></p>
<p><a href="printing_frame.html"
target="_top">Printing/Binding</a></p>
<p><a href="copying_frame.html" target="_top">Copying</a></p>
<p><a href="prices_frame.html"
target="_top">Prices/Estimates</a></p>
<p><a href="service_frame.html" target="_top">Customer Help</a></p>
<p><a href="about_frame.html" target="_top">About Us</a></p>
<p><a href="combo_frame.html" target="_top">Go to Front Page</a>
```

Notice that instead of targeting the "main" frame, the links in this example use a target="_top" attribute to display the linked page in the top-level browser window.

Each of these additional frameset files is almost identical to the combo_frame.html file, for instance, except that instead of linking to the main.html in the "main" frame, they link instead to graphics.html, printing.html, copying.html, prices.html, service.html, and about.html, respectively, in their "main" frames.

The advantage of doing it this way is that a user can bookmark and return later to any of the main sections in your site. The disadvantage is that you have to create and maintain an additional file (the frameset file) for each of your site's main sections.

USING STYLES WITH MULTI-PAGE WEB SITES

By creating an external style sheet file, you can control the look and feel of an entire site from a single file. This can make changing and updating the appearance and design of a site much easier than if you are using an internal style sheet or HTML FONT elements to add colors, fonts, and backgrounds to your pages.

To get started with this example, do the following:

1. Open **combo_frame2.html** in your text editor and save it as **combo_frame4.html**.
2. In your text editor, edit **combo_frame4.html** so that it points to different files (you will be saving these files shortly):

```
<frameset rows="85,*">
  <frame src="topbanner2.html" scrolling="no" marginheight="0">
  <frameset cols="150,*">
    <frame src="sidebar3.html" marginheight="0" marginwidth="10px">
    <frame src="main3.html" name="main">
  </frameset>
<noframes>
<h3>A frames-compatible browser is required to view this page.
Please visit the <a href="main.html">non-frames version</a> of
this site.</h3>
</noframes>
</frameset>
```

Setting Up the Files to Be Styled

Before you create an external style sheet to control the appearance of your site's pages, you need to prepare the files to be displayed.

SETTING UP THE TOP BANNER FILE To set up the top banner file, you need to link the file to the external style sheet you will be creating, assign the BODY element to a class so styles can be applied to it, and repoint the top banner image link so it links to combo_frames4.html.

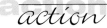

Set up the top banner file:
1. Open **topbanner.html** in your text editor and save it as **topbanner2.html**.
2. Edit **topbanner2.html** so it matches what is shown here:

```
<!DOCTYPE HTML PUBLIC "-//W3C//DTD HTML 4.01 Transitional//EN"
 "http://www.w3.org/TR/html4/loose.dtd">
<html>
<head>
<meta http-equiv="Content-Type" content="text/html; charset=ISO-
8859-1">
<title>A-Plus Printers</title>
<link rel="stylesheet" type="text/css" href="aplus.css">
</head>
<body class="topbanner">
<p align="center" style="margin-top: 5px">
<a href="combo_frame4.html" target="_top"><img src="aplusbanner.gif"
height="75" width="500" alt="A-Plus Printers banner image"
border="0"></p>
</body>
</html>
```

The LINK element defines the relationship, or link, between a document or other object and the current document. In this case, the relationship is of an external style sheet that is linked to the current document. The REL attribute defines the relationship (`rel="stylesheet"`) and the TYPE attribute specifies that the linked file is a CSS style sheet (the same attribute value used in the STYLE element to embed a style sheet). The HREF attribute specifies the URL of the link.

You also can include both a linked style sheet (using the LINK element) and an embedded style sheet (using the STYLE element) within the same HTML file. Styles in an embedded style sheet take precedence over the same styles included in a linked style sheet.

Another way to attach an external style sheet to an HTML file is to use CSS' @import at-rule. For instance, in browsers that support this, the following example achieves the same result as using the LINK element to link to an external style sheet:

```
<style type="text/css">
@import { url("aplus.css"); }
</style>
```

Linking to an external style sheet in this fashion also has the added side benefit of excluding Netscape Navigator 4, Internet Explorer 3, and many other early browsers with poor support for styles from accessing the style sheet. At least one early version of Netscape Navigator 4, however, crashes when it encounters an @import at-rule in a style sheet.

You also can shield Netscape Navigator 4 users accessing a style sheet by using a LINK element with a MEDIA attribute:

```
<link rel="stylesheet" media="all" type="text/css" href="aplus.css">
```

This works because Navigator 4 recognizes a LINK element containing a `media="screen"` attribute, but not if it contains any other form of the MEDIA attribute.

You can combine this method with use of the @import at-rule method to avoid the problem of early versions of Navigator 4 crashing when encountering an @import at-rule. Using a LINK element with a `media="all"` attribute to link to an external style sheet blocks all Navigator 4 users from accessing the style sheet. An @import at-rule can then be included in the external style sheet that links to a second external style sheet, thus blocking any other browsers (such as Internet Explorer 3, for instance) that do not recognize the @import at-rule from accessing that style sheet.

NOTE

The MEDIA attribute can be applied to both the LINK and STYLE elements to define styles used only for printing a document. For instance, the following LINK element links to a style sheet that will be used to specify how the Web page should be printed:

```
<link rel="stylesheet" media="print" type="text/css"
href="print.css">
```

When creating a style sheet specifically for printing a document, it is okay to use absolute measurements (points, inches, or centimeters, for instance), because the dimensions of the output media are generally known (an 8.5 × 11-inch piece of paper). You can also specify black text against a white background where light text against a dark background will cause problems when printing.

Styles can be targeted to other media types, as well. For additional information on using styles to specify a media-specific presentation, see this chapter's section at the IRC for this book at **www.emcp.com/**.

SETTING UP THE SIDEBAR FILE To set up the sidebar file to be styled, you need to add a link to the external style sheet you will be creating and assign the BODY element to a class so that styles can be applied to it.

action

Set up the sidebar file:
1. Open **sidebar3_ex.html** and save it as **sidebar3.html**.
2. Edit **sidebar3.html** so it matches what is shown here:

```
<!DOCTYPE HTML PUBLIC "-//W3C//DTD HTML 4.01 Transitional//EN"
 "http://www.w3.org/TR/html4/loose.dtd">
<html>
<head>
<meta http-equiv="Content-Type" content="text/html; charset=ISO-
8859-1">
<title>A-Plus Printers</title>
<link rel="stylesheet" type="text/css" href="aplus.css">
</head>
<body class="sidebar">
<div class="side">
<p><a href="graphics2.html" target="main">Design</a></p>
<p><a href="printing2.html" target="main">Printing</a></p>
<p><a href="copying2.html" target="main">Copying</a></p>
<p><a href="prices2.html" target="main">Prices</a></p>
<p><a href="service2.html" target="main">Help</a></p>
<p><a href="about2.html" target="main">About Us</a></p>
```

```
<p><a href="main3.html" target="main">Home</a></p>
</div>
</body>
</html>
```

Notice that a full DocType declaration is included in this version of the sidebar file, rather than the foreshortened DocType that was included previously. The foreshortened DocType declaration was used to get around the horizontal scroll bar bug in Internet Explorer 6, by triggering quirks mode in that browser. The reason you cannot do the same in this case will be explained after you have created the external style sheet file.

SETTING UP THE MAIN FRAME FILE To set up the main frame file to be styled, you need to add a link to the external style sheet you will be creating and assign the BODY element to a class so that styles can be applied to it.

Set up the main frame file:
1. Open **main2.html** in your text editor and save it as **main3.html**.
2. Edit **main3.html** so it matches what is shown here:

```
<!DOCTYPE HTML PUBLIC "-//W3C//DTD HTML 4.01 Transitional//EN">
<html>
<head>
<meta http-equiv="Content-Type" content="text/html; charset=ISO-
8859-1">
<title>A-Plus Printers</title>
<link rel="stylesheet" type="text/css" href="aplus.css">
</head>
<body class="mainframe">
<h2 align="center">Design, Printing, Binding, and Copying
Services</h2>

[...]

<p align="center" style="margin-top: 0"><b>
<a href="graphics2.html" target="main">Design</a>   
<a href="printing2.html"
target="main">Printing</a>   
<a href="copying2.html" target="main">Copying</a>   
<a href="prices2.html" target="main">Prices</a>   
<a href="service2.html" target="main">Help</a>   
<a href="about2.html" target="main">About Us</a>   
<a href="main3.html" target="main">Home</a></b></p>

<hr>
<address>
<b>A-Plus Printers</b><br>
Toll-Free Phone #: 1-800-000-0000<br>
E-Mail: <a href="mailto:info@aplusprint.com">info@aplusprint.com</a>
</address>
</body>
</html>
```

SETTING UP THE OTHER MAIN FRAME FILES To set up the graphics.html file to be styled, you need to add a link to the external style sheet you will be creating and assign the BODY element to a class so that styles can be applied to it.

Set up the graphics file:

1. Open **graphics.html** in your text editor and save it as **graphics2.html** in the chap06 folder.
2. Edit **graphics2.html** so it matches what is shown here:

```
<!DOCTYPE HTML PUBLIC "-//W3C//DTD HTML 4.01 Transitional//EN">
<html>
<head>
<meta http-equiv="Content-Type" content="text/html; charset=ISO-
8859-1">
<title>A-Plus Printers: Graphic Design and Desktop Publishing
Services</title>
<link rel="stylesheet" type="text/css" href="aplus.css">
</head>

<body class="mainframe">
<h1 align="center">Graphic Design Services</h3>

[...]

<p align="center" style="margin-top: 0"><b>
<a href="graphics2.html" target="main">Design</a>   
<a href="printing2.html"
target="main">Printing</a>   
<a href="copying2.html" target="main">Copying</a>   
<a href="prices2.html" target="main">Prices</a>   
<a href="service2.html" target="main">Help</a>   
<a href="about2.html" target="main">About Us</a>   
<a href="main3.html" target="main">Home</a></b></p>
<hr>
<address>
<b>A-Plus Printers</b><br>
Toll-Free Phone #: 1-800-000-0000<br>
E-Mail: <a href="mailto:info@aplusprint.com">info@aplusprint.com</a>
</address>
</body>
</html>
```

The remaining files—printing2.html, copying2.html, prices2.html, service2.html, and about2.html—have not been fully developed for this example, but exist as dummy files with the other example files.

Creating the External Style Sheet

By creating a single style sheet, you can control the appearance of all the files included in the A-Plus Printers site. An external style sheet is just a regular text file with the same styles listed in it that would otherwise be listed inside the STYLE element, if the styles were embedded within an HTML file. External style sheet files should be saved with a ".css" file extension.

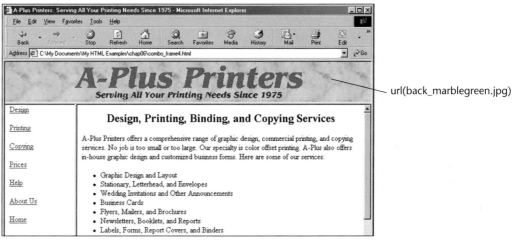

action

Create the external style sheet:
1. Open a blank window within your text editor.
2. Save your blank file as **aplus.css** in the chap06 folder.

STYLING THE TOP BANNER FILE   You have already prepared the top banner file to be styled, so all you have to do is add the appropriate styles to the aplus.css style sheet file.

action

Edit and save the style sheet file and open the frameset file in your browser:
1. Add the following styles to the aplus.css style sheet file:

```
/* Top Banner Styles */

body.topbanner { color: navy; background: #fc9
url(back_marblegreen.jpg); }
```

2. Save the style sheet (File, Save) and then open the frameset file (**combo_frame4.html**) in your browser (see Figure 6.8).

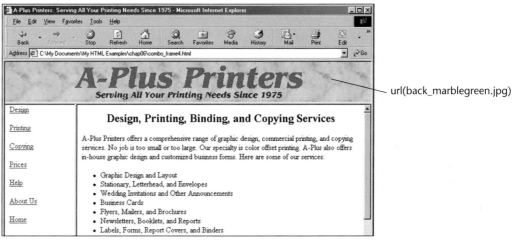

FIGURE 6 . 8 • *The linked style sheet causes a background image to be displayed in the page (topbanner2.html) in the top frame.*

The **body.topbanner** style applies the specified properties only to a BODY element belonging to the "topbanner" class.

STYLING THE SIDEBAR FILE   You have already prepared the sidebar file to be styled, so all you have to do is add the appropriate styles to the aplus.css style sheet file.

action

Edit and resave the style sheet file and refresh the frameset file in your browser:
1. Add the following styles to the aplus.css style sheet file:

```
/* Top Banner Styles */
body.topbanner { color: navy; background: #fc9
url(back_marblegreen.jpg); }

/* Sidebar styles */
body.sidebar { color: yellow; background: teal
url(back_turquoise.jpg); }
```

```
div.side { margin-left: 10px; margin-top: 15px; }
div.side a, div.side a:link, div.side a:visited, div.side
a:active { color: #fc0; text-decoration: none; font-family:
'Comic Sans MS', Arial, Helvetica, sans-serif; font-size: 18px; }
div.side a:hover { color: yellow; text-decoration: underline; }
```

2. Save the style sheet (File, Save) and then refresh the frameset file (**combo_frames4.html**) in your browser (see Figure 6.9).

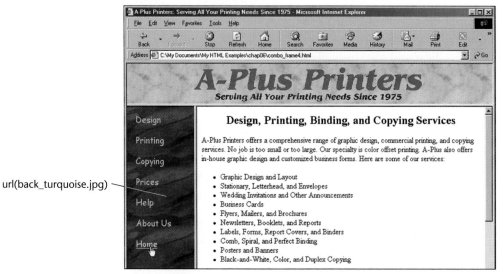

FIGURE 6.9 • *The linked style sheet causes a background image and rollover links to be displayed in the page (sidebar2.html) in left sidebar frame.*

The **body.sidebar** style applies the specified properties only to a BODY element belonging to the "sidebar" class. The **div.side** style sets the left and top margins for nested elements. The following selector is a group of contextual selectors that assign properties to the A element and the a:link, a:visited, and a:active pseudo-elements. Because these are contextual selectors, the properties are assigned only to links that are nested inside the "side" DIV element.

In this example, foreshortened color codes are used. For instance **#fc0** is the same as **#ffcc00**. This only works in CSS, however, and not in HTML.

STYLING THE MAIN FRAME FILE You have already prepared the files to be styled that will be displayed in the "main" frame.

Edit and resave the style sheet file and refresh the frameset file in your browser:

1. Add the following styles to the aplus.css style sheet file:

```
/* Top Banner Styles */
body.topbanner { color: navy; background: #fc9
url(back_marblegreen.jpg); }


/* Sidebar styles */
body.sidebar { color: yellow; background: teal
url(back_turquoise.jpg); }
div.side { margin-left: 10px; margin-top: 15px; }
div.side a, div.side a:link, div.side a:visited, div.side a:active
{ color: #fc0; text-decoration: none; font-family: 'Comic Sans
MS', Arial, Helvetica, sans-serif; font-size: 18px; }
```

```
div.side a:hover { color: yellow; text-decoration: underline; }

/* Main Frame Styles */

body.mainframe { color: #630; background: #ff9
url(back_parch.jpg); margin-top: 8px; }

h1, h2, h3 { font-family: Arial, Helvetica, sans-serif; color:
#fc0; background: #069; padding: 3px; border: 4px #f90 outset;
margin-top: 0; }
p, li, address { font-family: Arial, Helvetica, sans-serif;
font-size: 1.1em; }

li { list-style-image: url(smblueball.gif); font-size: 95%;
font-weight: bold; padding-left: -15px; margin-left: -15px;
color: #369; background: transparent; }

table { width: 100%; }
td { width: 45%; padding-left: 0; margin: 0; }
```

2. Save the style sheet (File, Save) and then refresh the frameset file (**combo_frames4.html**) in your browser (see Figure 6.10).

FIGURE 6.10 • *The linked style sheet determines the formatting of the page (main3.html) displayed in the right ("main") frame.*

NOTE

In the previous code example, negative margin-left and padding-left properties are applied to the LI element. List items are indented in from the left margin by default, but some browsers, such as Internet Explorer and Opera, set this using a left margin, while others, such as Netscape and Mozilla, set this using left padding. Internet Explorer and Opera recognize the **margin-left: -15px** property, while Netscape and Mozilla ignore it. Netscape and Mozilla recognize the **padding-left: -15px** property, while Internet Explorer and Opera ignore it.

If you want to increase how far the list items are indented, you need to apply positive margin-left and padding-left property values, but to the UL (or OL) element, rather than the LI element.

Note, however, that if you validate this using the W3C CSS Validator, you will get an error report that a negative padding-left value is not allowed for the LI element. This is an example in which valid CSS coding will not work the same in all major browsers, so you have to make adjustments. To get the style sheet to validate, however, you will have to remove the negative padding-left property.

3. In your browser, click on the Design link in the sidebar to display graphics2.html in the main frame window (see Figure 6.11).

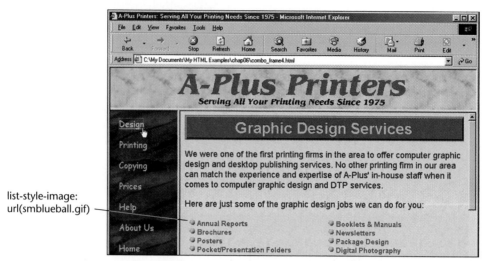

list-style-image: url(smblueball.gif)

FIGURE 6.11 • *Clicking on the Design link in the sidebar menu causes graphics.html to be displayed in the main frame.*

In this example, a group selector assigns the same properties to the H1, H2, and H3 elements. The main3.html file contains an H2 element and the graphics2.html element contains an H1 element. The group selector sets a sans serif font (Arial or Helvetica); defines foreground and background colors; sets three pixels of padding; and specifies the color, width, and style of a border to be drawn around the element. The result is a boxed element, as shown previously in Figures 6.10, 6.11, and 6.12.

Adding Rollover Buttons

Earlier you created rollover links that change their appearance when the mouse pointer is passed over them. In the following example, you will be adding rollover buttons to the sidebar menu.

Edit the sidebar section of the style sheet as shown below, save it, and then refresh your browser's display (see Figure 6.12):

```
/* Sidebar styles */
body.sidebar { color: yellow; background: teal
url(back_turquoise.jpg); }
div.side { margin-left: 8px; margin-top: 10px; }
div.side a, div.side a:link, div.side a:visited, div.side
a:active { display: block; padding: 2px; border: 4px #f90 outset;
margin-bottom: 5px; background: #069; color: #fc0; text-
decoration: none; font-family: 'Comic Sans MS', Arial, Helvetica,
sans-serif; font-size: 18px; }

/* Start Box Model Hacks - Required for Internet Explorer 5.5 */
div.side a, div.side a:link, div.side a:visited, div.side a:active
{ width: 112px; voice-family: "\"}\""; voice-family: inherit;
width: 100px; }
```

```
html>body div.side a { width: 100px; }

div.side a:hover { color: #c00; background: #fc6; font-size:
20px; padding: 2px 4px; border: 2px #3c9 outset; width: 112px;
voice-family: "\"}\""; voice-family: inherit; width: 100px; }
html>body div.side a { width: 100px; }
/* End Box Model Hacks */

div.side p { margin: 0; padding: 0; }
```

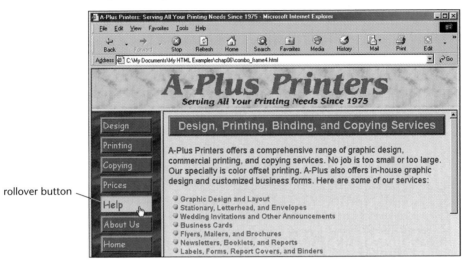

FIGURE 6.12 • *The linked style sheet causes rollover buttons to be displayed in the left sidebar frame.*

This example sets padding, border, and width values for the A element and the anchor pseudo-elements that control the appearance of unvisited, visited, active, and hover links. Internet Explorer 5 and 5.5 for Windows, however, incorrectly implement the CSS box model, by including any specified padding or border widths within the total width for the element. The correct implementation is to consider the width of an element to be independent of any padding or border widths. The result is that elements that have a specific width, set along with border, and/or padding values, will be displayed at a shorter width than in browsers that, correctly, do not calculate padding and border widths as part of the element width. When creating button links, the difference in width can be critical, in that a shorter element width in Internet Explorer 5.5 could end up not providing enough space for the button text. On the other hand, a longer element width in Netscape 6, Mozilla, and Opera, could end up exceeding the available width of the sidebar frame.

The solution to this is the *box model hack*, which was developed by Tantek Çelik, a leader of the Internet Explorer development team at Microsoft. The box model hack takes advantage of an Internet Explorer 5.5 for Windows parsing error to fool it into displaying the correct element width. In the code example, the start and end of the box model hack section are marked by CSS comments (/* and */). Here is how the box model hack works:

1. The **width: 112px;** property sets the element width for Internet Explorer 5.5 for Windows.
2. The **voice-family: "\"}\"";** **voice-family: inherit;** style properties cause Internet Explorer 5.5 for Windows to stop parsing the style rule (this is the parsing error).
3. The following **width: 100px;** property resets the element width to a width that is equal to the width set earlier for Internet Explorer 5.5 for Windows, but minus

the border and padding amounts (8 pixels of padding and 4 pixels of borders, or 12 pixels in total). This width is read by browsers that do not have the parsing error that Internet Explorer 5.5 for Windows has.

4. The following style rule, `html>body div.side a { width: 100px; }`, is necessary for Opera 5, which has the same parsing error as Internet Explorer 5.5 for Windows, but correctly implements the CSS box model. The style uses a CSS2 style selector, which is not recognized by Internet Explorer 5.5 for Windows, but is recognized by Opera 5, to reset the element width to 100 pixels for Opera 5.

To see Tantek Çelik's own explanation of the box model hack, see **www.tantek.com/CSS/Examples/boxmodelhack.html**.

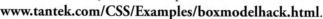

TROUBLE *spot* — One possible problem arises when using the box model hack in a framed page. Earlier, you were advised to use a foreshortened DocType declaration to force Internet Explorer 6 for Windows to go into quirks mode to overcome the horizontal scroll bug that is present in that browser when it is running in standards mode. Unfortunately, although running in quirks mode also causes Internet Explorer 6 for Windows to reduplicate the same incorrect implementation of the CSS box model that is present in Internet Explorer 5.5 for Windows, it does not reduplicate the parsing error that makes the box model hack possible. Therefore, to ensure that the rollover buttons are the same width in all CSS1-supporting browsers, it is necessary to include a full DocType declaration to trigger standards mode, even if that might result in unnecessary horizontal scroll bars being displayed for the frame in Internet Explorer 6 for Windows.

USING RELATIVE URLS

Until now, you have been working with examples that utilize files that are all located in the same folder. When working with a more complex Web site with many files, using a single folder can become cumbersome. To make working with a more complex Web site easier, you can organize it into separate folders. These can include separate folders for the different parts of a project, for instance. If creating an online manual or multi-part report, you could break out the different parts into separate folders. You also can create a separate images folder to store images that are reused in the different parts of your project. For instance, Arturo Rodriguez might decide to organize his A-Plus Printers project as shown in Figure 6.13.

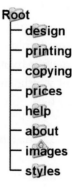

FIGURE 6.13 • *A complex Web site can be easier to work with and maintain if it is organized into multiple folders.*

You create links between two files located in different folders within your site by using a *relative URL*. A relative URL states the location of a linked object relative to the location of the linking file. You should always use relative URLs when linking between files that are internal to your own site. The same relative URL will work equally well both when creating your site on your local machine and after you have published your site to the Web. You also can easily move a site that uses relative URLs from one Web server to another, without having to fix a single internal link, but if you had used absolute URLs to link to files internal to your own site, you would need to fix every single internal link in your site.

You have actually been using relative URLs all along in this book—using only the name of file to link to it is the simplest form of a relative URL (because the linked and linking files are in the same folder, no other path information is required to create the link).

Reorganizing the A-Plus Printers Site

Before you can experiment with using relative URLs, you need to reorganize the last A-Plus Printers example you created into multiple folders.

In this section, you will be asked to create folders and then move files into those folders. The tools and steps required to perform these tasks vary according to the tool being used and the platform (Windows, Macintosh, or UNIX) that you are working on. If you need additional assistance creating folders and copying or moving files, ask your instructor for assistance.

WORKING WITH FILES AND FOLDERS IN WINDOWS Use My Computer or Windows Explorer to create new folders and copy or move files between folders.
- **Create a new folder.** In My Computer or Windows Explorer, select File, New, and Folder. In Windows Explorer, just key the folder name and press Enter. In My Computer, scroll down until you see the New Folder folder, click on the "New Folder" folder name, and then after a short delay, click on it again to highlight it (double-clicking will open the folder, which is not what you want). Then, just key the name of the folder and press the Enter key.
- **Copy or move a file.** In My Computer or Windows Explorer, right-click on the file and select Copy or Cut. Then right-click on the folder to which you want to copy or move the file, and select Paste. To copy or move multiple files between folders, first select them by clicking on them while holding down the Ctrl key, and then copy or move them the same way you do with a single file.

WORKING WITH FILES AND FOLDERS ON THE MACINTOSH Use the Finder to create new folders and copy or move files between folders.
- **Create a new folder.** Open the folder where you want to create the new folder and then select File, and New Folder. Key the name of the folder and press the Enter key.
- **Copy or move a file.** Hold down the Option key if copying the file (but not if you are moving the file), and then click and drag the file to drop it on the open folder or the icon for the folder into which you want to copy or move the file. To copy or move multiple files between folders, first select them by holding down the Shift key while clicking on the files, and then copy or move them the same way you do with a single file.

Even though both Windows and the Macintosh allow it, you should never include spaces in the names of folders or files you will be publishing to the Web, since doing so will likely result in broken links or pages not displaying. That is because UNIX does not allow spaces in the names of folders or files and most Web servers are still running UNIX.

Create a folder structure for the A-Plus Printers site and move the project's files into their appropriate folders:

1. In Windows, run Windows Explorer or open My Computer from the Desktop. On the Macintosh, if the Finder is not in the foreground, click the Applications menu in the upper-right corner and select the Finder.
2. In Windows Explorer, My Computer, or the Finder, open the chap06 folder (in your working folder or your working disk).
3. In the chap06 folder, create a new folder, keying **design** as the folder name. Do the same to create a **printing**, an **images**, and a **styles** folder.
4. Move the **graphics2.html** file into the design folder you just created. Move the **printing2.html** file into the printing folder.
5. Move the **aplus.css** style sheet file into the styles folder you just created.
6. Copy the following images into the images folder you just created: **aplusbanner.gif**, **back_marblegreen.jpg**, **back_turquoise.jpg**, **back_parch.jpg**, and **smblueball.gif**.

Shortcut: Click the Start button, select Run, key **explorer**, and press Enter to run Windows Explorer.

Creating the Relative URLs

Now that you have re-organized the A-Plus Printers site, you need to edit any of the files that need to use relative URLs to link to files in their new locations. You do not need to change the links in the frameset file, combo_frames4.html, because the files it links to are all still located in the root folder, but you do need to edit the HTML files that are linked to from the frameset file.

EDITING THE TOP BANNER FILE The top banner file, topbanner2.html, links to the style sheet file, aplus.css, and to the banner image, aplusbanner.gif, both of which have been moved to separate folders.

Open **topbanner2.html** in your text editor and edit it as follows (save the file when done):

```
<link rel="stylesheet" type="text/css" href="styles/aplus.css">
</head>
<body class="topbanner">
<p align="center" style="margin-top: 5px">
<a href="combo_frame4.html" target="_top"><img
src="images/aplusbanner.gif" height="75" width="500" alt="A-Plus
Printers banner image" border="0"></p>
```

The **images/aplusbanner.gif** relative URL creates a link from the topbanner2.html file, located in the root folder (the chap06 folder), to the aplusbanner.gif file, which is now located in the images folder that is inside the root folder.

A common error when creating relative URLs that link to files located in the child folder (or subfolder) of the linking file's folder is to insert a forward slash at the start of the URL: **/images/aplusbanner.gif**. Another common error is to use a backward slash, instead of a forward slash, in the URL: **images\aplusbanner.gif**. Earlier versions of Internet Explorer let you get away with committing both of these errors, while Internet Explorer 6 lets you get away with using backward slashes in URLs. Other browsers, however, will not complete the links if these errors are made.

EDITING THE SIDEBAR FILE The sidebar file, sidebar3.html, links to the style sheet file, aplus.css, and to the Graphic Design page, graphics2.html, both of which have been moved to separate folders.

action

Open **sidebar3.html** in your text editor and edit it as follows (save the file when done):

```
<link rel="stylesheet" type="text/css" href="styles/aplus.css">
</head>
<body class="sidebar">

<div class="side">
<p><a href="design/graphics2.html" target="main">Design</a></p>
<p><a href="printing/printing2.html"
target="main">Printing</a></p>
<p><a href="copying/copying2.html" target="main">Copying</a></p>
<p><a href="prices/prices2.html" target="main">Prices</a></p>
<p><a href="help/service2.html" target="main">Help</a></p>
<p><a href="about/about2.html" target="main">About Us</a></p>
<p><a href="main3.html" target="main">Home</a></p>
</div>
```

Other than graphics2.html and main3.html, you have not worked with the other files linked to in the sidebar file and have not created the folders that these links now point to. You will have a chance to work with these files and folders later, however, when doing the Review Exercises for this chapter. For the sake of illustrating how relative URLs work, you will just be using graphics2.html and main3.html.

EDITING THE MAIN FILE The initial "main" frame file you have been working with, main3.html, also links to the style sheet file, as well as to the graphics and printing files that have been moved.

Open **main3.html** in your text editor and edit it as follows (save the file when done):

```
<title>A-Plus Printers</title>
<link rel="stylesheet" type="text/css" href="styles/aplus.css">
</head>

[...]

<p align="center" style="margin-top: 0"><b>
<a href="design/graphics2.html"
target="main">Design</a>   
<a href="printing/printing2.html"
```

```
target="main">Printing</a>   
<a href="copying/copying2.html"
target="main">Copying</a>   
<a href="prices/prices2.html"
target="main">Prices</a>   
<a href="help/service2.html"
target="main">Help</a>   
<a href="about/about2.html" target="main">About
Us</a>   
<a href="main3.html" target="main">Home</a></b></p>
```

EDITING THE GRAPHICS DESIGN FILE The initial graphics design file you have
been working with, graphics2.html, also links to the style sheet file, as well as to the main
and printing files.

Open **graphics2.html** in your text editor from the design folder (in the chap06 folder)
and edit it as follows (save the file when done):

```
<title>A-Plus Printers: Graphic Design and Desktop Publishing
Services</title>
<link rel="stylesheet" type="text/css" href="../styles/aplus.css">
</head>

[...]

<p align="center" style="margin-top: 0"><b>
<a href="../design/graphics2.html"
target="main">Design</a>   
<a href="../printing/printing2.html"
target="main">Printing</a>   
<a href="../copying/copying2.html"
target="main">Copying</a>   
<a href="../prices/prices2.html"
target="main">Prices</a>   
<a href="../help/service2.html"
target="main">Help</a>   
<a href="../about/about2.html" target="main">About
Us</a>   
<a href="../main3.html" target="main">Home</a></b></p>
```

In this case, the relative URLs need to connect a linking file located in a subfolder of
the chap06 folder (the design folder) with linked files that are located in other subfolders
of the chap06 folder (the design and printing folders, for example). In the relative URL,
../design/graphics2.html, the **../** part steps back one level up the folder tree
(to the parent folder, which in this case is the chap06 folder), while the remainder,
design/graphics2.html, steps one level back down the folder tree (to the design folder,
which is a child folder of the chap06 folder). The design and printing folders referenced
in the preceding example also can be called "sibling" folders, because they share the same
parent folder (while folders sharing the same grandparent folder can be referred to as
"cousins").

EDITING THE STYLE SHEET FILE The style sheet file that is linked to by all the
previous files has been relocated to the styles folder. It also links to a number of background images have been relocated to the images folder.

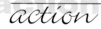

Open **aplus.css** in your text editor from the styles folder (in the chap06 folder) and edit it as follows (save the file when done):

```
/* Top Banner Styles */

body.topbanner { color: navy; background: #fc9
url(../images/back_marblegreen.jpg); }

/* Sidebar styles */
body.sidebar { color: yellow; background: teal
url(../images/back_turquoise.jpg); }

[...]

/* Main Frame Styles */

body.mainframe { color: #630; background: #ff9
url(../images/back_parch.jpg); margin-top: 8px; }

[...]

li { list-style-image: url(../images/smblueball.gif); font-size:
95%; font-weight: bold; padding-left: -15px; margin-left: -15px;
color: #369; background: transparent; }
```

Testing the Reorganized Site

You have now created subfolders (the design, printing, images, and styles folders) within the root folder (the chap06 folder) and transferred files from the root folder to each of those subfolders. You have edited all the files included in the example (all files appending from the combo_frames4.html frameset file) to repoint the links to the new locations of the linked files using relative URLs. You can now test the reorganized site.

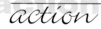

Test the reorganized site:
1. Open **combo_frame4.html** in your browser. All the background images that have been copied to the images folder should be displayed.
2. Click the Design button link in the sidebar menu. The graphics design file, graphics2.html, which has been moved to the design folder, should be displayed. (The background image, which has been copied to the images folder, should also be displayed.)
3. Click the Printing button link in the sidebar menu. The printing file, printing2.html, which has been moved to the printing folder, should be displayed. (*Note: this is a dummy file, which is why it is in black and white.*)
4. Click the Home button link in the sidebar menu. The main file, main3.html, should now be redisplayed in the main frame window.

If any of these links do not work correctly, double-check to make sure that you have copied or moved all the required files to the new folders you have created. Open the file in which the link is not working and double-check the URL to make sure it matches both the folder name and file name to which it is linking.

You should now have understanding and practical experience of working with at least the most commonly used forms of relative URLs. See Table 6.1 for additional examples of using relative URLs. All of the URLs shown in Table 6.1 assume a base URL of www.server.com/folder/project1/.

TABLE 6.1 • *Examples of Different Relative URLs*

Relative URLs	Absolute URL Equivalents
images/back.jpg	www.server.com/folder/project1/images/back.jpg
../project2/index.html	www.server.com/folder/project2/index.html
../../folder2/project-a/	www.server.com/folder2/project-a/
chap1/tbls/tbl1.html	www.server.com/folder/project1/chap1/tbls/tbl1.html
main.html	www.server.com/folder/pdroject1/main.html
./index2.html	www.server.com/folder/project1/index2.html
./	www.server.com/folder/project1/

Note: A double period followed by a forward slash (../) indicates the parent folder of the base folder, while a single period followed by a forward slash (./) indicates the current folder (or base folder). A double period and forward slash repeated twice (../../) indicates the grandparent folder of the current folder.

Creating Seamless Frames

A common question about creating framed Web sites is how to create seamless frames. The FRAMEBORDER attribute can be used in the FRAME element to turn the display of frame borders off and on (by specifying **0** or **1** as the value), but this attribute does not eliminate the space (or "seam") between the frames. You cannot, in fact, create seamless frames by using standard HTML. However, a collection of non-standard HTML attributes can be used that has the effect of eliminating the seams between frames in all the major browsers, at least, with some of the attributes working in some browsers, and some working in other browsers.

Apply a collection of non-standard HTML attributes to the top-level frameset element to turn off the display of the frame borders and eliminate the spaces ("seams") between the frames:

1. If it is not already open in your text editor, open **combo_frame4.html** and then resave it as **combo_frame5.html**.
2. Edit **combo_frame5.html** to create a seamless frame layout (see Figure 6.14):

```
<frameset rows="85,*" border="0" spacing="0" frameborder="0"
framespacing="0">
```

FIGURE 6.14 • *A collection of non-standard HTML attributes must be used to create a seamless frame layout.*

Controlling Frame Borders Using Styles

You also can use styles to control the display of borders in frame pages. You can do this simply by applying inline styles to the FRAMESET or FRAME elements that you want to style.

action

Use inline styles in combo_frame5.html to set a top border for the nested frameset and a left border for the main frame:

```
<frameset rows="85,*" border="0" spacing="0" frameborder="0"
framespacing="0">
  <frame src="topbanner2.html" scrolling="no" marginheight="0">
  <frameset cols="150,*" style="border-top: 5px ridge lime">
    <frame src="sidebar3.html" marginheight="0" marginwidth="10px">
    <frame src="main3.html" name="main" style="border-left: 5px
ridge lime">
  </frameset>
```

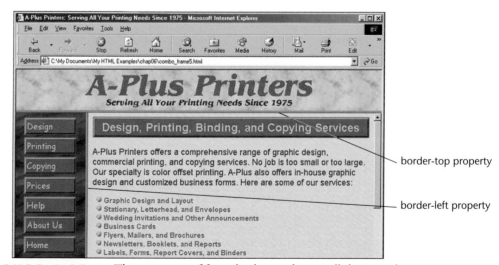

FIGURE 6.15 • *The appearance of frame borders can be controlled using styles.*

VALIDATING YOUR WEB PAGES

To make sure that a Web page includes only valid HTML codes, you can use an online HTML Validator. Validating your page is also one way to help make sure that your page will display correctly in current browsers. An HTML Validator checks your page for compatibility to the version and definition of HTML that is declared in your page's DocType declaration. If you have declared your page to be in conformance with the transitional definition of HTML 4.01, then an HTML Validator tests your page for conformance to the transitional HTML 4.01 DTD (Document Type Definition). The main online HTML Validators are discussed below.

Using the W3C HTML Validation Service

Because the W3C is in charge of defining the official recommended standard for HTML, you should start with its validation service when validating your page. The W3C HTML Validator can check the validity of both HTML and XHTML pages. You can go directly to the W3C HTML Validator at the URL given in the previous bulleted list, or you can go to the W3C home page at **www.w3.org/** and click on the HTML Validator link in the sidebar menu.

You can validate a page in two different ways. You can validate a page you have already published to the Web or you can upload a page to be validated.

UPLOADING AN HTML FILE TO BE VALIDATED To upload an HTML file to be validated, you need to specify the path on your computer on which the file you want to validate is located.

action

Validate the main3.html file:

1. In your browser, go to the W3C HTML Validation service at **validator.w3.org/**.
2. Scroll down on the page and click the "Upload Files" link.
3. Click the Browse button and navigate to the chap06 folder in your working folder or working disk. Double-click on main3.html (see Figure 6.16).

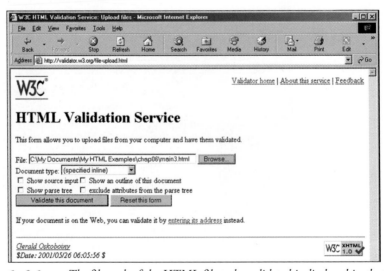

FIGURE 6.16 • *The file path of the HTML file to be validated is displayed in the File box.*

4. Because you have included a DocType declaration in your document, leave "(specified inline)" selected in the Document type box. Leave the check boxes all unchecked.

5. Click the Validate this document button. As long as you have not introduced any errors on your own, you should see a page with the "No errors found!" message displayed (see Figure 6.17).

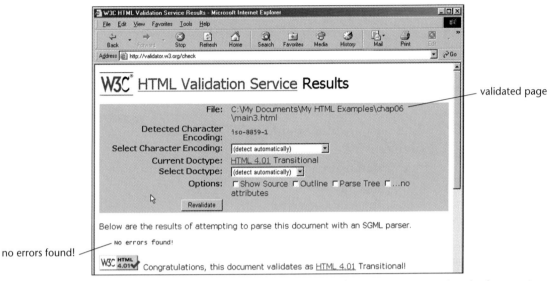

FIGURE 6.17 • *If no errors are found, the W3C validation service reports that the document's HTML is valid (for HTML 4.01 Transitional).*

If errors are found in your page, see the following section, "Correcting Errors," for pointers on interpreting error messages. The error message (or messages) should give you a good idea of what the error is. Correct your HTML code and then try to validate your page again.

6. Scroll down and click and drag to copy the HTML code you can include in your page to show that it includes only valid HTML 4.01 code.

7. Open **main3.html** in your text editor and paste in the code you just copied as shown in the following example:

```
</address>
<p>
<a href="http://validator.w3.org/check/referer"><img border="0"
src="http://www.w3.org/Icons/valid-html401" alt="Valid HTML 4.01!"
height="31" width="88"></a>
</p>
</body>
</html>
```

8. Open **combo_frame4.html** in your Web browser and scroll the page (main3.html) displayed in the main window to display the bottom of the page. If you are connected to the Internet, you will see the W3C validation icon displayed below the page's address block (see Figure 6.18).

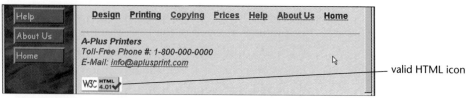

valid HTML icon

FIGURE 6.18 • *The W3C validation icon is displayed at the bottom of the main3.html page.*

CORRECTING ERRORS Of course, not every HTML file you validate is going to check out as completely valid. If any errors are reported, you need to correct the errors before you can identify your page as valid.

action

Add some errors to your HTML file, validate it, correct the reported errors, and then revalidate it:

1. Open **main3.html** in your text editor. Resave the file as **mainerror.html** in the chap06 folder.
2. Introduce some errors into the file and delete the HTML validation icon you added previously (resave the file when done):

```
<body class="mainframe">
<h2 align="center">Design, Printing, Binding, and Copying
Services</h3>

[...]

<address>
<b>A-Plus Printers</b><br>
Toll-Free Phone #: 1-800-000-0000<br>
E-Mail: <a href="mailto:info@aplusprint.com">info@aplusprint.com</a>
</address>
<p>
<a href="http://validator.w3.org/check/referer"><img border="0"
src="http://www.w3.org/Icons/valid-html401" alt="Valid HTML 4.01!"
height="31" width="88"></a>
</p>
</body>
```

3. In your browser, go back to the W3C HTML validation service at **validator.w3.org/**. Scroll down and click the "Upload Files" link. Click the Browse button, navigate to the chap06 folder in your working folder or working disk, and double-click on **mainerror.html**.
4. Click the Validate this document button. Instead of reporting that your document is a valid HTML 4.01 document, the W3C HTML Validator reports a series of errors (see Figure 6.19).

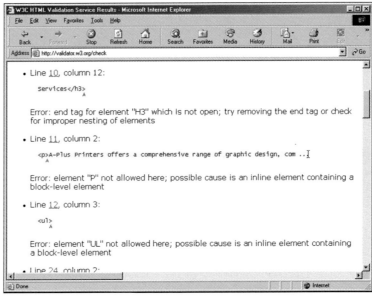

- Line 10, column 12:

    Services</h3>
                ^

    Error: end tag for element "H3" which is not open; try removing the end tag or check for improper nesting of elements

- Line 11, column 2:

    <p>A-Plus Printers offers a comprehensive range of graphic design, com ..Ị
     ^

    Error: element "P" not allowed here; possible cause is an inline element containing a block-level element

- Line 12, column 3:

    <ul>
      ^

    Error: element "UL" not allowed here; possible cause is an inline element containing a block-level element

- Line 24, column 2:

FIGURE 6.19 • *If your HTML file contains errors, the W3C HTML Validator provides a report of the errors it has found.*

The W3C error report actually includes more errors than your page actually contains because one error can trigger the reporting of additional errors. When the first error is corrected, the following errors are also corrected. For instance, the first error reported (Line 10, column 12) is for the **</h3>** end tag, which does not match the preceding **<h2>** start tag. Because of that error, the W3C HTML Validator reports errors for all the following block elements (for each instance of the following P, UL, HR, and ADDRESS elements) in the page, because it sees them as being nested inside of the H2 element (which is not allowed).

Toward the bottom of the error report, you will see the two other errors you introduced, which were the missing **</a>** and **</address>** tags, as well as the **<h2>** start tag that is missing a corresponding **</h2>** end tag:

```
Error: end tag for "A" omitted; possible causes include a missing
end tag, improper nesting of elements, or use of an element where
it is not allowed
```

and

```
Error: end tag for "ADDRESS" omitted; possible causes include a
missing end tag, improper nesting of elements, or use of an
element where it is not allowed
```

and

```
Error: end tag for "H2" omitted; possible causes include a missing
end tag, improper nesting of elements, or use of an element where
it is not allowed
```

In other words, just a few errors in an HTML file can generate the reporting of many other errors. A simple missing end tag for a block element caused all other following block elements to be reported as errors.

Correct the errors you added to the mainerror.html document and, following the previous examples of validating an HTML document as a guide, revalidate your document at the W3C HTML validation service.

Using Other Validators

You can use other validators to check the validity of your HTML and CSS documents. For links to HTML validators, CSS validators, and link checkers, see this chapter's section at the IRC for this book at **www.emcp.com/**.

NOTE

A number of other utilities are available that can be used to check HTML files, such as the Weblint utility and the CSE HTML Validator. In the strict sense, these are not actually HTML Validators (regardless of the CSE utility's name), in that they do not check the validity of your document against the official DTD for the definition and version of HTML you are using. These utilities are, more correctly, termed as style checkers—they might provide useful feedback about your HTML file, but do not actually test to determine whether your file's HTML is valid.

PUBLISHING WEB SITES

After you have planned and developed a Web page or site, you will want to publish it to the Web. The primary way of doing that is to use an FTP program to transfer your Web page files to your folder located on a Web server.

Finding a Web Host

Many options are available for finding a Web host for your Web pages:

- **Web space through your school.** Your school might provide you with free Web space on its Web server. The primary drawback of this is that you will lose the Web space when you graduate or leave.
- **Web space through your dial-up provider.** The dial-up provider you use to connect to the Internet also might provide you with free Web space. The amount of free space provided can vary, from 1 MB to 10 MB.
- **Web space through a free Web space provider.** There are also many providers of free Web space. Generally, these sorts of Web space accounts require that you display a banner or pop-up window with advertising when your Web pages are opened.
- **Web space through a for-pay Web space provider.** To gain access to more features, additional e-mail addresses, domain name registration, and higher traffic and space allotments, you can sign up for an account with a for-pay Web space provider. Costs run anywhere from $10 to $30 a month, depending on the account and its features.
- **Web space through a reseller account.** A reseller account allows you to resell Web space accounts. This can be handy, for instance, if you want to both design and manage Web sites for clients; by using a reseller account, you also can sell Web space, domain registration, and other Web services to your design clients.

For additional information on finding the right Web host for your Web pages, as well as links to resources for finding free and budget Web space providers, see this chapter's section at the IRC for this book at **www.emcp.com/**.

Understanding What You Need to Know

To transfer files from your local computer to your Web space folder on a remote Web server, you need or might need to know the following:

- **Host name (server name or Web address).** This is usually the name of the Web server on which your Web site folder is located (srv3.myhost.net, for instance). Some providers also let you use the Web address of your site, which might be different from the server name (www.myhost.net/~myfolder/, for instance).

- **Host type.** In most cases, you should not need to know this, but can specify that the host type should be automatically detected (if asked for this information). If that does not work, your Web server might require that you identify the specific host type you are trying to connect to. Your Web space provider will need to provide that information, or you can just experiment with the different available options in your FTP program until you find the right one.

- **User name.** If you are using Web space provided by your dial-up provider, this will be the same user name you use to log on the Internet. If you are using Web space provided by a separate provider, you need to use the user name assigned to you by that provider. Your user name is case-sensitive.

- **Password.** If you are using Web space provided by your dial-up provider, this will be the same password you use to log on to the Internet. If you are using Web space provided by a separate provider, you need to use the password assigned to you by that provider. Your password is case-sensitive.

- **Initial remote folder.** This is not required to connect to your Web space folder, but can specify that a particular folder, other than the root folder, be connected to. Web space folders are often organized into separate folders, one of which contains all the files and folders that are included in your Web site and into which you need to publish your Web page files. This folder can be named as **www**, **web**, or anything that your server administrator has decided to name this folder. By specifying that folder as your initial remote folder, you will go directly to it when you connect to your site.

- **Firewall settings.** If your computer is located behind a firewall, you might need to specify additional information, such as the name or IP address of your firewall and your user name and password. To set these settings, in WS_FTP, for instance, click the Connect button and then click the Firewall tab. Generally, this should not affect you in uploading files to a remote server, but might stop you from downloading files to your local computer. Check with your server administrator if you need to specify these additional settings.

 FTPplanet at **www.ftpplanet.com**/ provides a number of tutorials for using WS_FTP LE for Windows to connect to your folder through various services that provide free Web space, including AOL, GeoCities, Angelfire, Tripod, Hometown, Bizland, FortuneCity, and V3space. The tutorials include what you need to specify as the host name in each case, which can easily be adapted for use with FTP programs other than WS_FTP LE. For additional FTP resources and tools, see this chapter's section at the IRC for this book at **www.ecmp.com**/.

Using an FTP Program

You can use many FTP programs to publish your Web page files to the Web. For links to where you can download FTP programs that are available for your platform, see this chapter's section at this book's IRC at **www.emcp.com/**. The following are some general tips for using an FTP program to connect to your Web space folder:

- You should uncheck any Anonymous check box or other option. An anonymous log-on is only done when a user name and password are not required.

- You usually can select to save your password, which will save you from having to retype it each time you connect. Realize, however, that your password will be saved on your local computer in an unencrypted form. If you are creating an e-commerce site or a site containing trade secrets, for instance, you would not want to save the password to access that site. If just creating a personal Web site, however, there is not much risk in saving your password.

- When transferring files, it is important to transfer them in the right format. You will need to transfer two types of files: ASCII files and binary files. ASCII files are any text files you want to transfer, including HTML (.html), CSS (.css), and JavaScript (.js) files. Binary files include any non-text files you want to transfer, including image, video, and audio files, for instance. If you transfer an ASCII text file as a binary file (or a binary file as an ASCII text file), it might not display properly.

- Although FTP programs give you the option of editing the HTML files located on your Web server, you should only make edit changes to the HTML files located on your local machine. If you directly edit the HTML files on your remote folder and your Web server crashes, you could lose all your edits. If you edit only on your local machine, after republishing your site, any changes you have made will be present on both your local machine and on your remote Web server.

- Some FTP programs include an "auto" feature that can be chosen when transferring Web page files. This is generally used when batch transferring all the contents of a folder, which can contain both ASCII and binary files. However, you might need to specify the file extensions for some ASCII text files, or they might be transferred as binary files. In WS_FTP, for instance, after connecting to your Web site, you can select Options and click the Extensions tab to specify the file extensions of ASCII text files (.htm, .html, .css, .js, .txt, and .xml).

- Some FTP programs also let you automatically convert file names to all lowercase. If you follow a policy of always naming files using all lowercase characters, this can be a handy way to insure that your link URLs and the file names they link to agree (file names on UNIX servers are case-sensitive). Windows, for instance, has a tendency to want to capitalize the first letter in file names, so selecting this option can guard against such file names sneaking through. To set this in WS_FTP, for instance, after connecting to your Web site, select Options and check the Force Lowercase Remote Names check box.

The spelling of file names referenced in links to local files within your own site should exactly match the actual file names, including all uppercase and lowercase characters. That is because file names are case-sensitive on UNIX computers and most Web servers still run some variant of UNIX. If after publishing your Web site's files to a Web server you find that links are suddenly no longer working that worked fine on your local machine, the most likely reason is that the file name referenced in the link URL does not exactly match the actual file name.

CHAPTER SUMMARY

You should now be familiar with creating multi-page Web sites using frames, understand the pros and cons of using frames, and know how to overcome some of the negatives associated with using frames. You also should understand how to create an external style sheet that can control the appearance of all the pages within a Web site, as well as how to use relative URLs to organize a multi-page Web site into multiple folders. Lastly, you should be familiar with the different Web hosting options, how to find out more about Web hosting options, and what you need to know to publish your Web pages to a Web server using an FTP program.

Code Review

FRAMESET element	Specifies a set of frames (or frameset), in columns or rows, and the files to be displayed in them.
COLS or ROWS attribute	In a FRAMESET element, specifies the number of columns or rows that are included in a frameset.
FRAME element	Defines a frame within a frameset, including specifying the file to be displayed in the frame, the name of the frame, vertical and horizontal margins, and whether borders and scrolling are turned off or on.
SCROLLING attribute	In the FRAME element, turns scrolling within the frame off (0) or on (1).
MARGINHEIGHT and MARGINWIDTH attributes	In the FRAME element, these attributes set the amount of vertical or horizontal margin spacing, in pixels, surrounding the content of a frame.
NAME attribute	Provides a name for a frame, so it can be targeted in a link.
TARGET attribute	In the A element (hypertext link), targets the name of a frame, so the link's object can be displayed in the targeted frame.
LINK element	In the HEAD element, defines the relationship of a linked file to the current document.
REL and TYPE attributes	In the LINK element, `rel="stylesheet"` declares that the link functions as a style sheet in relation to the current document and the `type="text/css"` specifies that the style sheet is a CSS style sheet.
display property	Specifies the type of element to be displayed (block, inline, list item, or none). This property can be used to specify that an inline element should be treated as a block element, so margins can be applied to it, for instance.
box model hack	A sequence of style codes that tricks Internet Explorer 5.5 for Windows to apply the correct width to a block element that also includes borders and padding.
list-style-image property	Specifies a bullet icon image to be displayed as the bullet in a bulleted list.
border property	Draws a border around an element in a variety of different styles (solid, double, dotted, dashed, groove, ridge, inset, and outset).

| padding property | Controls the amount of padding that is displayed between an element's content and its border. |
| margin property | Controls the amount of margin spacing that is displayed outside of an element's border. |

ONLINE QUIZ

Go to this text's IRC at **www.emcp.com/** and take the online self-check quiz for this chapter.

REVIEW EXERCISES

This section provides some hands-on practice exercises to reinforce the information and material included within this and previous chapters.

You can use any of the example files that you created in this chapter to further practice features or methods covered in this chapter. Because this chapter used example files that are linked together by name, to further practice with these files, make a copy of the whole chap06 folder, naming it as chap06_practice, for instance. If you are using a working disk, you can just copy the chap06 folder to another floppy disk and use that disk for further practice.

To copy the chap06 folder in Windows' My Computer or Windows Explorer, just right-click on the folder and select Copy, and then right-click in the background of your working folder or working disk and select Paste. Click on the name of the Copy of chap06 folder, click on it again, and then key **chap06_practice** as the new folder name.

On the Macintosh, in the Finder, just hold down the Option key, and click and drag the chap06 folder to create a copy. Then click on the "chap06 copy" folder name and key **chap06_practice** as the new folder name.

1. Working in the chap06_practice folder, experiment further with creating different kinds of frameset layouts. For instance, create a layout using a right sidebar frame or a bottom menu frame. Use any of the other example HTML files as the content of the frames, or create your own HTML pages to display in the frames. Experiment with using percentages to set frame widths and heights and then resize the browser window up or down to see what happens to percentage widths and heights in those situations.

2. Experiment further with creating frameset layouts that use both columns and rows. Copy and rename the **combo_frame4.html** frameset file (as **combo_frame4_2.html**, for instance). Revise the frameset layout so that the top-level FRAMESET element defines two columns, with the first column containing the sidebar menu file and the second column containing a nested FRAMESET element defining two rows. In the nested FRAMESET, set the first row as containing the top banner frame file and the second row as containing the main frame file.

3. The chapter explained how to create a grid layout by specifying both rows and columns in the same FRAMESET element. Create your own frameset from scratch to experiment with creating grid layouts. For the content of the frames, use any of the other HTML files in the folder. You also can experiment with linking to images as the content of frames within a grid layout. You can use any images you want to experiment doing this, or you can use any of the images that are included with the Chapter 4 example files (in chap04).

4. Experiment working with the aplus.css external style sheet file to specify different colors, backgrounds, or other formatting characteristics for the files linked to in by the combo_frame4.html frameset file. See Chapter 3, *Working with Fonts, Colors and Backgrounds*, to review specifying colors using hexadecimal RGB codes. For links to where you can find color charts, wheels, and pickers on the Web, see Chapter 3's section at the IRC for this book at **www.emcp.com/**.

Experiment with assigning different background images in the aplus.css style sheet file. Coordinate the color scheme you are using with the background image, or vice versa. Use any of the other background images included with this chapter's example files. You also can find additional background images in the **art** folder that is included with this book's example files. You also can download background images from the Web or you can create your own background images. For links to image-viewing utilities that you can download and use, see Chapter 4's section at the IRC for this book at **www.emcp.com/**.

5. In the aplus.css style sheet file, experiment with creating different looks for the rollover button menu. Experiment setting different foreground and background colors, as well as different border colors, for the non-hover links (a:link, a:visited, and a:active) and the hover links (a:hover). Coordinate these colors with the color scheme for the site as a whole and with any background images you are displaying. When you have created a whole new look for the framed site that you are happy with, ask at least two other classmates for their opinions of your choices.

6. Experiment further with using inline styles to control the appearance of frame borders. Try setting different border widths, styles, and colors.

WEB-BASED LEARNING ACTIVITIES

In this book's text, Find It icons inserted in the margin highlight the Web addresses of additional resources you might find helpful or informative. To further extend your learning using the Web, you can:

- Go back and visit any of the Web addresses highlighted in this chapter that you have not yet visited. Look for additional resources and information that add to your understanding and knowledge of the material covered in this chapter. When you find a relevant page or site with information or resources you might want to access later, add it to your Favorites (in Internet Explorer) or your Bookmarks (in Netscape or Mozilla).

- Visit this book's Internet Resource Center at **www.emcp.com** to find additional Web addresses of resources related to the material covered in this chapter that you can further investigate and explore.

- Further research a specific topic introduced in this chapter. For instance, you can research issues involved with deep-linking with pages in other sites, especially when displayed within a site's own frames. Debate the pros and cons of the copyright and free speech issues that are involved with deep-linking.

  You might also further research the pros and cons of using frames in Web pages. Look for examples on the Web that show both effective and ineffective uses of frames.

  You also can research the availability of free and inexpensive Web hosting options. Find at least five sources of free Web space and five sources of inexpensive Web space ($15/month or less). Compare the features offered by each, including space and traffic allowances, e-mail addresses, domain name registration, and other services.

Sign up for a free Web space account and practice publishing a Web page to the Web space folder it provides.

You also can research available FTP programs for your platform. Download several FTP programs from the Web. If you have signed up for a couple of free Web space accounts, experiment using different FTP programs to publish a Web page to the Web. Compare the user interfaces, ease of use, and features.

Compile your research into a report that can be shared with your fellow students. You also can team up with other students to create a class presentation on a particular topic.

PROJECTS

These projects can be done in class, in a computer lab, or at home. Use the skills you have developed in this and the previous chapters to create any of the following projects.

Project 1. Create your own two-column or two-row framed Web site.

Take the lessons learned in this and previous chapters and apply them in creating your own two-column or two-row framed Web site:

- If you have already created a personal, topical, or other Web page that contains multiple sections, you can copy and save those sections as separate files and use them as the basis for creating content pages for a framed Web site. Create a sidebar or top bar menu file that accesses the content pages included in your site. Use any of the lessons you have learned in this book's chapters in creating the menu and content pages for your site.
- You can plan, write, and create a multi-page Web site using frames from scratch based on any topic of your choice. Create a sidebar or top bar menu file that accesses the content pages included in your site.

Keep it relatively simple starting out. Get a working multi-page framed Web site working first, before you spend a lot of time designing the individual pages. After you create a starter site, save a backup copy of it, and then use it as the base for experimenting with different designs and looks. With one version, for instance, create the appearance and design of the site entirely using HTML elements and attributes, without using styles. With another version, use styles to control the appearance and design of your site.

Project 2. Use an existing Web site as an example for creating a two-column or two-row framed Web site.

Look for an example of a multi-page framed Web site on the Web and use it as an example for creating your own two-column or two-row framed Web site.

For instance, to find examples of Web sites in specific categories, go to Yahoo! at **www.yahoo.com** and do a search on a keyword or key phrase of your choice. To find examples of computer consulting sites, for instance, do a search on "computer consultants." Feel free to browse any of Yahoo!'s categories to find an interesting example of the kind of Web site you would like to create.

Do not simply copy the text of the example site, but use the content of the example site as the basis for (and providing information and data for) writing your own content pages. If you have access to an image editor, create your own top banner or other graphics. If you want to publish the site on the Web (as opposed to simply creating it for practice on your own local computer), be sure to ask permission from the author or owner before using any graphics from the example Web site.

Project 3. Create a framed Web site that uses both rows and columns.

If you have done one of the first two projects, expand it to incorporate both rows and columns. Use an image editor to create your own top banner image, for instance, or you can use styles to create "styled" top banner text (using colors, borders, padding, and a background, for instance). Experiment with different layouts that combine a menu (left sidebar, right sidebar, topbar, or bottombar), a top banner frame, and a main content frame.

Project 4. Experiment with other frame schemes.

Take the lessons learned in this and previous chapters and apply them in experimenting with frame layouts (or schemes) not specifically covered in this chapter. For instance, create a layout that features the following:
- A topbar (or bottombar) menu that links to multiple frameset pages. This menu functions as a navigation bar for your whole site.
- Content pages with subsections that are marked with destination anchors (that can be jumped to using jump links).
- Sidebar menu pages for each of the content pages that use jump links (using fragment identifiers) to jump to subsections within the content pages.
- A main frameset page that links to the topbar (or bottombar) menu page, the first sidebar menu page, and the first content page. This frameset should be linked to from your topbar (or bottombar) menu through a "Home" or similar link, with a `target="_top"` attribute included in the link to cause the linked frameset file to be displayed in the top-level browser window.
- Use the first frameset page as a model for creating additional frameset pages that link to the topbar (or bottombar) menu page, as well as to each of the other sidebar menu/content page combinations you have created. These framesets should be linked to from your topbar (or bottombar) menu through the other menu link options, with `target="_top"` attributes included in the links to cause the linked frameset files to be displayed in the top-level browser window.

Project 5. Publish a Web page or site on the Web.

Using the lessons learned in this chapter, as well as any additional resources at this chapter's section in the IRC for this book at **www.emcp.com/**, validate and publish a Web page or Web site of your own creation on the Web:
- Choose any Web page or site that you have created and that you want to present to the rest of the world over the Web. If you have not yet finalized a page or site that you want to publish, do that first.
- Decide which kind of Web space account you want to use to publish your page or site. If you have Web space through your school that you want to use, but do not know how to access it, check with your system administrator, network support, or your instructor to find out what you need to do. You also can use free Web space provided by your home dial-up provider or by any other provider of free Web space. See this chapter's section at the IRC for this book at **www.emcp.com/** for links to additional resources that can help you find a provider of free Web space.

- Before publishing your site, validate your HTML files using the W3C HTML Validator. Correct any errors that are reported. When your pages are reported as valid, include valid HTML 4.01 icons at the bottom of your content pages.
- If you are using embedded style sheets or an external style sheet in your Web page or site, validate your style sheet using the W3C CSS Validator. Correct any errors that are reported. When your style sheet or sheets are reported as valid, include valid CSS icons at the bottom of your content pages.
- Publish your page or site to the Web. If you are publishing to your Web space folder on a school Web server, you might be able to simply copy and paste your Web page files into your Web space folder (ask your system administrator, network support, or your instructor for details of what you need to do). If you are publishing to Web space provided by your dial-up provider or another free provider, you might be able to use the provider's wizard or control panel to transfer your Web page files.

  You also can use an FTP program to publish your Web page files—see this chapter's section at the IRC for this book at **www.emcp.com/** for links to FTP guides and tutorials. For tutorials on how to use WS_FTP LE to connect to the many major free Web space providers (AOL, Angelfire, GeoCities, and so on), see FTPplanet at **www.ftpplanet.com/**). You also can check the support pages provided by the provider of your free Web space for details of how you need to configure your FTP software to connect to its server.
- After successfully validating and publishing a page or site to the Web, ask at least three classmates to critique your page's design, usability, and general attractiveness. Elicit other responses from friends or family members.
- Using the feedback provided by classmates, friends, and family, further refine the design and appearance of your site. Revalidate its pages and style sheets and then republish it to the Web.
- After you have created, published, and finalized your site, see this chapter's section at the IRC for additional resources on how to register your site at the major search engines and directories and how to promote your site. Be sure to include a mailto link to your e-mail address (use a free Web-mail address to protect against getting spammed), so you can receive feedback from visitors to your page or site.

7

Working with Forms

PERFORMANCE OBJECTIVES

In this chapter, you will learn how to create user-input forms, including how to:
- Create mailto and CGI forms.
- Create text boxes.
- Create radio buttons and check boxes.
- Create unfolding list menus.
- Create multi-line text area boxes.
- Handle form responses.
- Design form layouts.

Forms provide you with a means to gather information and data from visitors to a Web page. Forms can be as simple as a text area box that lets visitors send you a message or as complex as a survey or questionnaire that lets visitors fill out text boxes and select radio buttons, check boxes, and options from pull-down menus. You can gather information for your own use or you can format the data for presentation on the Web.

USING THE EXAMPLE FILES

If you have created a working folder for storing files you create, you will find the example files for this chapter located in the **chap07** folder within your working folder. Save any HTML files you create in this chapter in that folder.

If you have created a working disk, copy the chap07 folder to your working disk from the **HTML_Examples** folder that you or your instructor downloaded from this book's Internet Resource Center (IRC), or from a CD-R disc or floppy disk provided by your instructor. Save any HTML file you create in this chapter in the chap07 folder that you have copied to your working disk.

USING MAILTO AND CGI FORMS

You can include two basic kinds of forms in your Web pages: mailto and CGI forms. A mailto form uses a mailto URL to send form responses to your e-mail addresses. A CGI form uses a CGI script to process form responses, either saving them to a folder on your server or forwarding them to your e-mail address.

Mailto forms are easier to set up and test, but many users may not be able to use a mailto form. To use a mailto form, a user needs to be running one of the following:

- Any version of Netscape Navigator 2, 3, or 4 with Netscape's mail program (Netscape Messenger in Navigator 4) configured to send mail.
- Internet Explorer 4 with Internet Mail designated as the mail program and configured to send mail.
- Internet Explorer 5 or 5.5 with Outlook Express designated as the mail program and configured to send mail.

Many users, however, use browsers and/or mail programs that will not let them use a mailto form, including Netscape 4 users who have designated a mail program other than Messenger, Internet Explorer 4 users who have designated a mail program other than Internet Mail, and Internet Explorer 5 users who have designated a mail program other than Outlook Express. No version of the Opera browser supports sending mailto form responses. Internet Explorer 6, Netscape 6, and Mozilla 1, or later versions of those browsers, also do not support using sending mailto forms responses. In other words, users of the most current browsers will not be able to use mailto forms.

Users of mail systems that do not use SMTP (outgoing mail) servers are also not able to use a mailto form. For instance, if you are sending mail through AOL's mail system, you cannot use a mailto form. If you are using your local area network's (LAN) mail system to send mail, you also might not be able to use a mailto form.

For these reasons, if your browser/e-mail client combination allows the sending of mailto form responses, you should use a mailto form only to practice submitting and receiving form responses on your local computer. Mailto forms should not be published to the Web. Always publish forms to the Web as CGI forms. In the "Creating CGI Forms" section of this chapter, you learn how to create and use CGI forms.

Later in this chapter, you learn how to configure Internet Explorer 5 and 5.5 to send mailto forms, in case you are using either of those browsers, so you can use either of them to test sending and receiving mailto form responses, if you wish. You also learn what you need to know and do to create CGI forms and enable them in your Web pages.

CASE EXAMPLE: CREATING A SUBMISSION FORM

You can use a form to gather data from visitors to your page or site and then republish it on the Web.

Roger Yang is a computer science student who is taking a class in Web design. Through research, he found a bewildering array of Web hosting options. For a project to be completed for his class, he has decided to create a Web site that organizes different Web hosting options according to key features and characteristics. He has even registered a domain name, BestHosts.org, for his site. As part of that project, he has decided to create a user-input form that Web hosting companies can use to submit their Web hosting plans to be displayed on his site.

CREATING A FORM

In this section, you will create an HTML form containing a text area box, text boxes, radio buttons, check boxes, and pull-down lists. A starter page, hostsubmit_ex.html, also has been created for you that you will use to get started creating the example form for this chapter.

To start working with this example:

1. Open **hostsubmit_ex.html** in your text editor from the chap07 folder.
2. Save hostsubmit_ex.html as **hostsubmit.html** in the chap07 folder in your working folder or disk.
3. Open **hostsubmit.html** in your Web browser.

Starting the Form

The FORM element is used to create a user-input form in HTML. All other form elements are nested inside the FORM element.

Add a FORM element set to post the form response to a mailto e-mail address:

```
<h2 align="center">BestHosts.org</h2>
<h1 align="center">Web Hosting Plans - Submission Form</h1>
<p>To submit a hosting plan to be published on my Web Hosting
Plans page, fill out and submit the following form. This form
posts the responses to a mailto e-mail address, so not everyone
will be able to use this form. If you cannot use this form, send
the details of your hosting plan directly to <a
href="mailto:hostplans@besthosts.org">hostplans@besthosts.org</a>.
</p>

<form action="mailto:hosts@besthosts.org" method="post">
</form>
</body>
```

The ACTION attribute specifies the URL to which the form response is to be sent. This particular attribute specifies that the form data should be sent to a mailto e-mail address. A CGI form would specify the URL of a CGI script as the value of the ACTION attribute.

The METHOD attribute specifies the method to be used to transfer the form data when it is submitted. The METHOD attribute has two possible values: **post** and **get**. The post method sends the form response as an attachment to the post request that is included in the HTTP header; the get method sends the response as appended to the URL specified by the ACTION attribute. With the get method, a limit of 1,024 to 2,000 characters can be sent in a form response (the actual total number depends on the server being used). Because of the limit on the number of characters that can be sent, the get method is generally used only to send queries to and get responses from a CGI script. When submitting form data, however, you should always use the post method, not the get method.

You will notice that an introductory paragraph alerts users that they might not be able to use a mailto form and gives them an alternative means to submit their data. Because not everyone can use a mailto form, you should always provide an alternative means for submitting the form data whenever you use a mailto form.

Creating Input Controls

The INPUT element lets you specify a variety of different input controls you can add to a form, including text boxes, radio buttons, check boxes, and pull-down lists.

CREATING TEXT BOXES The INPUT element's `type="text"` attribute specifies a text box to be added to the form.

Add text boxes for specifying the provider's name, phone number, Web address, and e-mail address (see Figure 7.1):

```
<form action="mailto:hosts@besthosts.org" method="post">
<p>Provider: <input type="text" name="Provider" size="40"> Phone
#: <input type="text" name="Phone_Number" size="40"></p>
<p>Web Address: <input type="text" name="URL" size="40"> E-Mail:
<input type="text" name="EMail" size="40"></p>
<p>Plan Name: <input type="text" name="PlanName" size="30">
Setup Fee: <input type="text" name="Setup_Fee" size="15" value="$">
Monthly Fee: <input type="text" name="Monthly_Fee" size="15"
value="$"></p>
</form>
```

FIGURE 7.1 • *Four text box input controls are added to the form.*

The NAME attribute names the text field. NAME attribute values should not include spaces (use underscores instead). Each text box input control should have a unique name. When the form response data is submitted, the text keyed in the text box will be associated with the name of the text box field. If two text box input controls have the same name, the second text box's data will overwrite the first text box's data when the form is submitted.

The SIZE attribute specifies the width of the text box, according to text characters (not pixels). This attribute, however, only sets the width of the text box; it does not delimit the amount of text that can be entered in a text box. To delimit the amount of text that can be entered in a text box, use a MAXLENGTH attribute, which limits the total number of characters that can be entered in a text box to the specified value. For instance, `maxlength="40"` would limit input to a total of 40 characters. You might want to do this, for instance, if you plan on importing the form responses into a database with length limits set on specific fields.

The VALUE attribute specifies an initial value to be displayed within a text box.

CREATING RADIO BUTTONS The INPUT element's `type="radio"` attribute specifies a radio button option to be added to the form. Only one button from a group of radio buttons can be selected. The term *radio button* actually comes from car radios, which as a safety feature used push buttons for selecting radio stations. In this older radio style, pushing one button would pop up any other button that had been pushed previously.

action

Add a group of radio buttons that allows a user to specify the type of host plan being submitted (see Figure 7.2):

```
<p>Plan Name: <input type="text" name="PlanName" size="30">
Setup Fee: <input type="text" name="Setup_Fee" size="15"
value="$">
Monthly Fee: <input type="text" name="Monthly_Fee" size="15"
value="$"></p>

<p>Plan Type:
<input type="radio" name="PlanType" value="Non-Virtual Host"
checked>Non-Virtual Host Plan  
<input type="radio" name="PlanType" value="Basic Virtual
Host">Basic Virtual Host Plan  
<input type="radio" name="PlanType" value="Advanced Virtual
Host">Advanced Virtual Host Plan  
<input type="radio" name="PlanType" value="Reseller">Reseller
Plan  
</p>
</form>
```

FIGURE 7.2 • *A group of radio button options is added to the form.*

Notice that a CHECKED attribute is included in the first radio button INPUT element. It specifies that the radio button should initially be selected. In the absence of a CHECKED attribute, none of the radio buttons will be selected initially. The same attribute can be used with check boxes (covered in the next section) to specify that a check box should initially be checked.

Unlike with text boxes, notice that the NAME attribute in each radio button input control specifies the same name. The NAME attribute, in this case, defines a group of radio button controls.

The VALUE attribute specifies the value to be submitted with the form response data if a radio button is selected (the data value will be associated with the name of the radio button input control group).

CREATING CHECK BOXES The INPUT element's `type="checkbox"` attribute specifies a check box option to be added to the form. Unlike with radio buttons, multiple check boxes from a group of check boxes can be selected at the same time.

Add a group of check boxes to the form (see Figure 7.3):

```
<input type="radio" name="PlanType" value="Reseller">Reseller
Plan  
</p>
<p>Basic Features Included:</p>
<p><input type="checkbox" name="Basic_Features" value="stock CGI
scripts">stock CGI scripts  
<input type="checkbox" name="Basic_Features" value="FTP
upload">FTP upload  
<input type="checkbox" name="Basic_Features" value="extra e-mail
addresses">multiple e-mail addresses  
<input type="checkbox" name="Basic_Features" value="access
reports">access reports  
<input type="checkbox" name="Basic_Features" value="free domain
name registration">free domain name registration  </p>
</form>
```

Plan Type: ⦿ Non-Virtual Host Plan ○ Basic Virtual Host Plan ○ Advanced Virtual Host Plan ○ Reseller Plan   ——— check boxes

Basic Features Included:

☐ stock CGI scripts ☐ FTP upload ☐ multiple e-mail addresses ☐ access reports ☐ free domain name registration

FIGURE 7.3 • *A group of check boxes is added to the form.*

Unlike with text boxes, notice that the NAME attribute in each check box input control specifies the same name. The NAME attribute, in this case, defines a group of check box input controls.

The VALUE attribute specifies the value to be submitted with the form response data if a check box is selected (the data value will be associated with the name of the check box input control group). If more than one check box is selected, a comma-separated list of selected values is returned.

USING OTHER INPUT CONTROLS You can use a number of additional input controls in forms, including hidden, password, file, submit, reset, image, and button input controls. Examples will be shown later in this chapter of using the hidden, submit, reset, and image input controls. The password input control works like the text input control, but displays text that is keyed as a series of asterisks. You might, for instance, use a password input control to ask for a credit card number in a secure form. The file input control allows you to create a box where the name of a file to be uploaded can be specified. The button input control allows you to create a push button that can activate a JavaScript script, for instance.

Creating List Menus

The SELECT and OPTION elements are used to include a pull-down menu in a form that lets users select from a list of options.

Add a pull-down menu to the form (see Figure 7.4):

```
<input type="radio" name="PlanType" value="Reseller">Reseller
Plan  </p>
<p>Server Type:
<select name="ServerType">
  <option selected>Unix/Linux-Based Server
  <option>Windows-Based Server
  <option>Macintosh-Based Server
  <option>Other Server</select>
</p>
<p>Basic Features Included:</p>
```

list menu

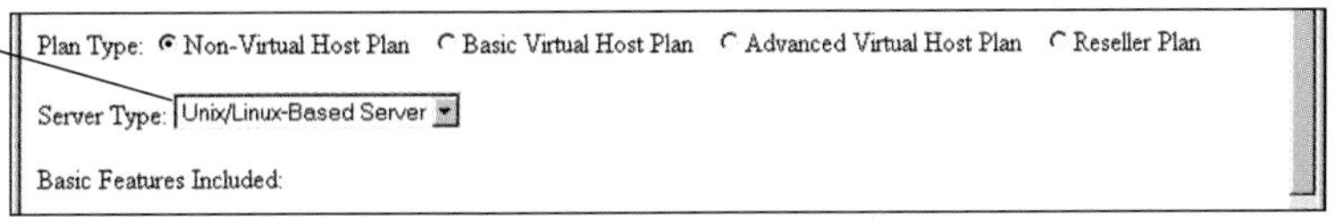

FIGURE 7.4 • *A pull-down list is displayed folded when it is included in a form.*

When you click on a pull-down list, the list options drop down (or pop-up), as shown in Figure 7.5.

list menu (unfolded)

FIGURE 7.5 • *When a pull-down list is clicked, it unfolds to display the options.*

SETTING THE SIZE OF A LIST MENU By default, a list menu only displays one option. You can use the SELECT element's SIZE attribute to specify the number of options that will be displayed initially in a list menu. For instance, to set all four options to be displayed, set a size of 4:

```
<select name="ServerType" size="4">
```

SPECIFYING OPTION VALUES By default, the text following the selected OPTION element in a list menu is sent with the form response data. You can use the OPTION element's VALUE attribute, however, to specify alternative data values that you want to have sent. This allows you to display more descriptive text as your options, for instance, while sending more abbreviated text as data in the form response:

```
<select name="ServerType">
  <option value="unix" selected>Unix/Linux-Based Server
  <option value="win">Windows-Based Server
  <option value="mac">Macintosh-Based Server
  <option value="other">Other Server
</select>
```

ENABLING MULTIPLE SELECTIONS IN A LIST MENU Normally, a user only can select one item from a list menu. The SELECT element's MULTIPLE attribute specifies that users can select multiple options from a list menu, either by holding down the Ctrl key to select separate options or by holding down the Shift key to select a range of options.

For this to be practical, you need to preface the list menu with some kind of notice indicating that multiple options can be selected and instructing the user how to do it.

```
<p>Server Type (hold down CTRL or SHIFT to select multiple
options):
<select name="ServerType">
  <option value="unix" selected>Unix/Linux-Based Server
  <option value="win">Windows-Based Server
  <option value="mac">Macintosh-Based Server
  <option value="other">Other Server
</select>
```

Creating Text Area Boxes

The TEXTAREA element creates a multi-line text box. Text area boxes are often used to allow users to provide comments or expand on their previous selections.

Add a text area box that is 8 lines high and 75 characters wide (see Figure 7.6):

```
<input type="checkbox" name="Basic_Features" value="free domain
name registration">free domain name registration  </p>
<p>Added Comments:</p>
<p><textarea name="Comments" rows="8" cols="75"></textarea></p>
</form>
```

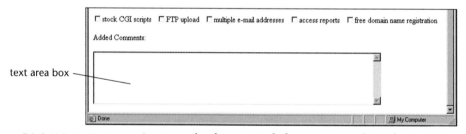

text area box —

FIGURE 7.6 • *A text area box lets users include comments within a form.*

Creating Control Buttons

After you have created the elements of your form, you need to provide a means for the user to submit or reset the form.

CREATING SUBMIT AND RESET BUTTONS Two additional input controls, the Submit button and the Reset button, allow users to submit or reset the form.

Add Submit and Reset buttons to the form (see Figure 7.7):

```
<p><textarea name="Comments" rows="8" cols="75"></textarea></p>

<p><input type="submit" value="Submit"> <input type="reset"
value="Reset"></p>
</form>
```

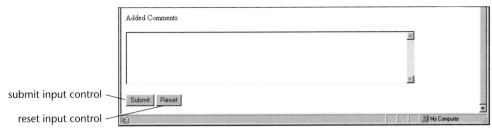

submit input control

reset input control

FIGURE 7.7 • *Buttons are added that allow users to submit or reset the form.*

The VALUE attribute specifies the label for the button. This can be whatever you want, as long as it conveys the action of the button when it is clicked. For instance, you could just as easily specify **Submit Form** and **Submit Button** as the value of these attributes. When a user clicks on the Submit button, the form is submitted to the URL specified by the FORM element's ACTION attribute.

CREATING AN IMAGE BUTTON Alternatively, you can use an image as a Submit button. An example Submit button image, submit.gif, is included with this chapter's example files. For this example, you will be including both a Submit button and a Submit image button in the same form for testing purposes; in normal practice, however, you would use one or the other, not both, in a form.

Add a Submit image button to the form (see Figure 7.8):

```
<p><input type="submit" value="Submit"> <input type="reset"
value="Reset"></p>
<p><input type="image" src="submit.gif" alt="Submit Form Button"
border="0"></p>
```

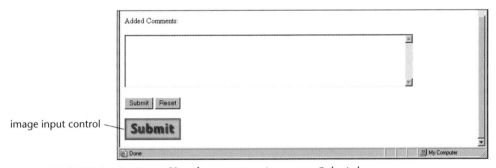

image input control

FIGURE 7.8 • *You also can use an image as a Submit button.*

USING THE BUTTON ELEMENT HTML 4 includes an additional element, the BUTTON element, that is supposed to work the same way as a Submit button created using the INPUT element, except with richer rendering possibilities. The main problem with using the BUTTON element is that few browsers support it and it does not degrade gracefully in browsers that do not support it, because users of such browsers are left with no way to submit the form. The BUTTON element is supported by Internet Explorer 5.5 for Windows and Internet Explorer 5 for the Macintosh, but not by the Netscape or Mozilla browsers.

Create Submit and Reset buttons using the BUTTON element (see Figure 7.9):

```
<p><input type="image" src="submit.gif" alt="Submit Form Button"
border="0"></p>
<p><button name="submit" value="submit" type="submit">
  <font size="4" color="green">Submit</font>
</button>  
<button name="reset" type="reset">
  <font size="4" color="maroon">Reset</font>
</button></p>
</form>
```

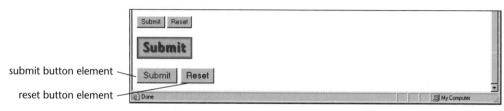

submit button element

reset button element

FIGURE 7.9 • *Submit and Reset buttons created with the BUTTON element are more flexible, but are supported by fewer browsers.*

You also can use a style to set the formatting of the BUTTON element, including specifying a background image for the button. An example background image, back_marblebeige2.jpg, is included with the example files for this chapter.

Create a style that defines the visual formatting of the BUTTON element (see Figure 7.10):

```
<style type="text/css">
button { font-size: 1.25em; font-weight: bold; background:
#ffffcc url(back_marblebeige2.jpg); width: 5em; }
</style>
</head>
```

styled button elements

FIGURE 7.10 • *A style can be used to control the visual appearance of BUTTON elements.*

Because few browsers support the BUTTON element and it degrades ungracefully in browsers that do not support it, it is probably best to avoid using it, at least until more browsers support it. Use the INPUT element, instead, to create Submit and Reset buttons for forms.

Testing the Form

Now that you have created a form, you can test it. Depending on your browser/mail program combination and configuration, you might not be able to actually submit and retrieve a form response. You can, however, test all the elements of the form and make sure the Submit and Reset buttons are working properly.

FILLING IN THE TEXT BOXES The top of the form contains a series of text boxes. You can move from one text field to another by pressing the Tab key.

Test the form you have just created:
1. With hostsubmit.html open in your browser, key **XYZ Hosting Company** in the Provider text box.
2. Press Tab to get to the Phone # text box and key **(212) 555-8743**.
3. Press Tab to get to the Web Address text box and key **http://www.xyzhosting.com/**.
4. Press Tab to get to the E-Mail text box and key **info@xyzhosting.com**.
5. Press Tab to get to the Plan Name text box and key **ABC Host Plan**.
6. Press Tab to get to the Setup Fee text box and key **$10.00**.
7. Press Tab to get to the Monthly Fee text box (see Figure 7.11) and key **$12.95**.

FIGURE 7.11 • *The form's text boxes are filled in.*

SELECTING A RADIO BUTTON The next section of the form contains a group of radio buttons. You can select only one radio button out of a group.

Click on the Basic Virtual Host Plan radio button to select the Plan Type (see Figure 7.12). Notice that the Non-Virtual Host Plan radio button, which was selected previously, is no longer selected.

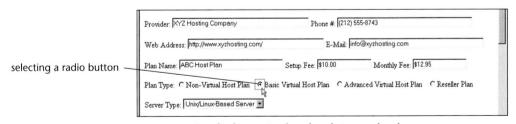

FIGURE 7.12 • *A radio button is selected to designate the plan type.*

SELECTING A LIST MENU OPTION The next line of the form contains a list menu that lets a user specify a server type.

Click on the Server Type list box to unfold it and select the Windows-Based Server option (see Figure 7.13).

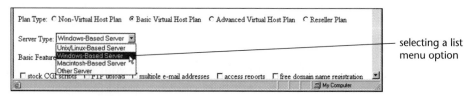

selecting a list menu option

FIGURE 7.13 • *The Windows-Based Server option is selected from the list box.*

SELECTING CHECK BOXES The next section of the form contains a series of check boxes. Unlike radio buttons, you can select multiple check boxes within a check box group.

In the Basic Features Included group of check boxes, click on the first, second, and fourth check boxes (stock CGI scripts, FTP upload, and access reports) to select them, while leaving the other two check boxes unchecked (see Figure 7.14).

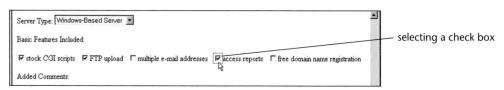

selecting a check box

FIGURE 7.14 • *You can select multiple check boxes in a group of check boxes.*

FILLING IN THE TEXT AREA BOX You cannot key more than one line of text in a text box, but you can key multiple lines of text in a text area box.

In the Added Comments text area box, key: **Same day e-mail support. 30-day money back guarantee. Redundant T3 connections to the Internet backbone.** (See Figure 7.15.)

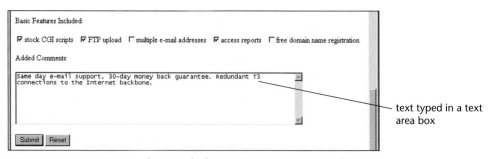

text typed in a text area box

FIGURE 7.15 • *You can key a multi-line comment in a text area box.*

TESTING THE SUBMIT AND RESET BUTTONS The current form has three kinds of Submit buttons and two kinds of Reset buttons. In a normal form, you only have one set of these buttons.

NOTE ——— To successfully use the Submit buttons to send mailto form responses, you must use Netscape 4, Internet Explorer 4 with Internet Mail as your mail program, or Internet Explorer 5 or 5.5 with Outlook Express as your mail program. If using Internet Explorer 6 or later versions, you can test using the Submit button, but you will not be able to actually send a mailto form response.

action

Test the Submit and Reset buttons:

1. Click the gray Submit button. Internet Explorer 5.5 (with Outlook Express designated as the mail program) displays a pop-up box alerting you that the form is being sent via e-mail and asking you if you want to continue (see Figure 7.16). Just click Cancel at this point.

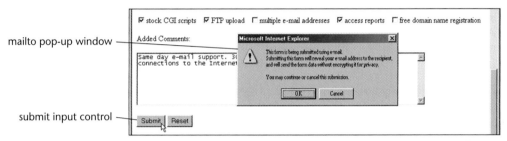

mailto pop-up window

submit input control

FIGURE 7.16 • *When submitting a mailto form, Internet Explorer alerts the user that the form is being sent by e-mail.*

2. Click the Submit image button. You should get the same pop-up box shown in Figure 7.16, if using Internet Explorer 6 (with Outlook Express). Click Cancel.

3. Click the green Submit button (the bottom Submit button). If using Internet Explorer 6 (with Outlook Express), you should see the same pop-up box as in Steps 1 and 2. Click Cancel.

4. Click the first Reset button (in the first line of buttons). You will see that the form has reverted to its original state, with none of the fields filled out.

5. Key any text in the Added Comments text area box. Click the maroon Reset button (on the bottom line of buttons). You will see that the form has reverted to its original state, with none of the fields filled out.

Setting the Tabbing Order

Users can move from one form element to the next by pressing the Tab key. Normally, the tabbing order is the same as the order in which the form elements are inserted in the document. By using the TABINDEX attribute, however, you can set a different tabbing order. The following elements accept the TABINDEX attribute: A, AREA, BUTTON, INPUT, OBJECT, SELECT, and TEXTAREA. Not all of these are form elements, but they would normally be included in the tabbing order.

The TABINDEX attribute takes a value from 0 to 32,767. The element with the lowest TABINDEX value is tabbed to first, the one with the second-lowest value is tabbed to second, and so on. The following example uses the TABINDEX value to reorder the tabbing order:

```
<p>Provider: <input type="text" name="Provider" size="40"
tabindex="1"> Phone #: <input type="text" name="Phone_Number"
size="40" tabindex="3"></p>
```

```
<p>Web Address: <input type="text" name="URL" size="40"
tabindex="2"> E-Mail: <input type="text" name="EMail" size="40"
tabindex="4"></p>
```

SENDING AND RECEIVING MAILTO FORM RESPONSES

As was stressed at the start of this chapter, many users cannot use a mailto form. For that reason, you should use a mailto form only to test sending and receiving form responses on your local computer, but not for soliciting responses from the Web. If you decide to publish a mailto form to the Web, you should always alert users that they might not be able to use the form and provide them with a link to your e-mail address, so they can submit data or provide feedback by sending you an e-mail. When including your e-mail address in the form, be sure to display your e-mail address as the link text, because some users also cannot use a mailto e-mail address (although more people can use mailto e-mail addresses than can use mailto forms) and will need to copy and paste your e-mail address into their mail programs.

Setting Up Your Browser to Send Mailto Forms

Only some browsers can send mailto form responses. The following sections provide details about using mailto forms with the Netscape, Mozilla, and Internet Explorer browsers.

USING MAILTO FORMS WITH NETSCAPE AND MOZILLA To send mailto form responses in Netscape 2, 3, or 4, you only need to have Netscape's mail client (Netscape Messenger in Netscape 4) configured to send mail. If you can send an e-mail message by clicking on a mailto link, you also should be able to send a mailto form response.

Netscape 6 (or higher) and Mozilla 1, however, do not support sending mailto form responses. Clicking on the Submit button pops up a correctly addressed blank message composition window, but without the form response data attached. If sent, the recipient would receive a blank e-mail message.

tip

One option is to download and install a copy of Netscape Communicator 4 (which includes Netscape Navigator 4 and Messenger 4) and use it to test submitting and receiving mailto form responses on your local computer. You can download and install a version of Netscape Communicator 4 for Windows, Macintosh, or UNIX at **wp.netscape.com/download/archive.html**. To get it to work, you will need to configure Netscape Messenger to send mail by specifying the outgoing (SMTP) mail server you are using.

USING MAILTO FORMS WITH INTERNET EXPLORER The most recent versions of Internet Explorer (Version 6 and higher) do not support sending mailto form responses, even if you have Outlook Express specified as your mail client and have configured it properly to send e-mail. To send mailto form responses, you must use Internet Explorer 4 (with Internet Mail installed as your mail client and configured to send mail) or Internet Explorer 5 or 5.5 (with Outlook Express installed and designated as your mail client and configured to send mail). If using Exchange or Outlook (not Express) as your mail client with Internet Explorer 5 or 5.5, you will not be able to send mailto form responses.

Internet Explorer 5 or 5.5 for Windows. If you are using Internet Explorer 5 or 5.5 for Windows as your browser, designate Outlook Express as your mail program in Internet Explorer 5 or 5.5 for Windows:

1. In Internet Explorer, select Tools and Internet Options.
2. Click the Programs tab. Make sure that Outlook Express is specified in the E-mail field (see Figure 7.17). Click OK.

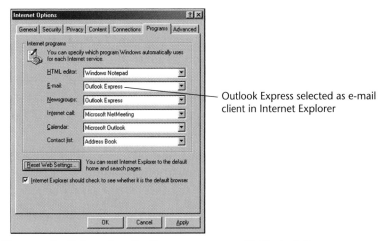

Outlook Express selected as e-mail client in Internet Explorer

FIGURE 7.17 • *To use mailto links and mailto forms, you must specify Outlook Express as your mail program in Internet Explorer 6.*

If you are using Internet Explorer 5 for the Macintosh, you can specify separately the outgoing mail server (SMTP host) you are using to send mail.

Internet Explorer 5 for the Macintosh. Specify an outgoing mail server to be used when sending mailto form responses:

1. In Internet Explorer, select Edit and Preferences.
2. Scroll down to the bottom of the left panel. Expand the E-mail option, if it is not already expanded.
3. Under E-mail, click on the General option. The outgoing mail server for the e-mail account provided by your dial-up provider should be displayed in the SMTP host box. (If the SMTP host is empty or specifies an inactive mail server, you will not be able to send mailto form responses.)

NOTE

It is important to stress that posting form responses to a mailto URL is not provided for in the official HTML or XHTML specifications. When using the FORM element's ACTION attribute, the HTML 4.01 specification states the following: "User agent behavior for a value other than an HTTP URI is undefined." This means that how a particular browser handles (or does not handle) posting mailto form data depends entirely upon the individual browser. The HTML 4 and XHTML 1 standards do not require that browsers support mailto forms.

Sending Mailto Form Responses

If you are using one of the browsers specified as supporting mailto forms and have properly configured it and your mail program, you should be able to send a mailto form response. If, however, your connection to the Internet does not use a standard POP3 e-mail facility (if connecting through AOL or a school LAN, for instance), you probably will not be able to send a mailto form response. If you have an alternative means to connect to the Internet (such as your home Internet account), you can try using that to test this.

If you are not using a browser that supports sending and receiving mailto forms or have difficulty configuring a browser that does, skip ahead to the next section, "Creating CGI Forms."

Set up the example form to send a mailto form response to your e-mail address and then send a form response to that address:

1. If it is not already open in your text editor, open **hostsubmit.html** in your text editor.
2. Revise the FORM element's ACTION attribute to refer to your e-mail address:

```
<form action="mailto:type your e-mail address here" method="post">
```

3. Comment out the additional Submit and Reset buttons (otherwise, the content of the BUTTON element will be sent as form data):

```
<p><input type="submit" value="Submit"> <input type="reset"
value="Reset"></p>
<!--
<p><input type="image" src="submit.gif" alt="Submit Form Button"
border="0"></p>
<p><button name="submit" value="submit" type="submit">
    <font size="4" color="green">Submit</font></button>  
<button name="reset" type="reset">
    <font size="4" color="maroon">Reset</font></button>
</p>
-->
```

4. Save the form (File, Save) and then open (or refresh) it in your browser.
5. Fill out text fields (using whatever text you like), select radio buttons, and select check boxes.
6. Click on the Submit button (the one in the first line).
7. If alerted that the form is being sent via e-mail, click OK. If further alerted that a program is trying to use Outlook Express to send an e-mail message on your behalf, just click the Send button.

Receiving Mailto Form Responses

If you have successfully sent a mailto form response to yourself, you will find a message in your e-mail account's inbox containing the form response. How this message is displayed and how the form response is accessed depends upon the browser that sent the form response and on the mail program being used to access it:

• A form response sent using Netscape 4 is displayed with a subject heading of "Form posted from Mozilla." Do not confuse this with the Mozilla browser (which cannot send mailto form responses). A form response sent using Internet Explorer 4, 5, or 5.5 is displayed with a subject heading of "Form posted from Microsoft Internet Explorer."
• To view form response data sent by Netscape 4, open the form message and then click on the Part 1 link.

- For a form response sent by Internet Explorer, click on the attachment (POST-DATA.ATT) and save it as a file (as **testresponse.txt**, for instance) to your hard drive or floppy disk. Figure 7.18 shows a fictional form response that has been saved and opened in Notepad.

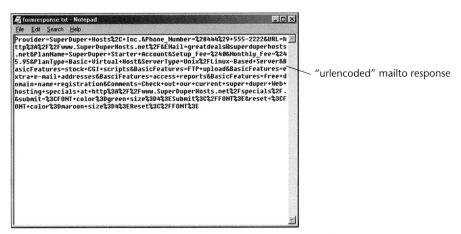

"urlencoded" mailto response

FIGURE 7.18 • *A mailto form response is opened in Windows Notepad.*

DECIPHERING MAILTO FORM RESPONSES As you will notice in Figure 7.18, mailto form data is not sent in a format that is easy for a person to read. That is because the default content type for mailto form responses (referred to as a *urlencoded* content type) substitutes control codes for any spaces, hard returns, and commas, for instance. To send mailto form responses in a format that is friendly to humans, you must change the content type for the form response.

Change the content type of the form data and then resend and receive the form data:
1. If not already open, open **hostsubmit.html** in your text editor. Edit the FORM element to change the content type, as shown here:

```
<form action="mailto:your e-mail address" method="post"
enctype="text/plain">
```

2. Save the file (File, Save) and open (or refresh) it in your browser. Fill out the form and click the Submit button to send a form response to your e-mail address.
3. In your mail program, open the form response. Now, instead of the POSTDATA.ATT attachment, you will see the form data displayed in the message body in a format that is easy for a person to read (see Figure 7.19).

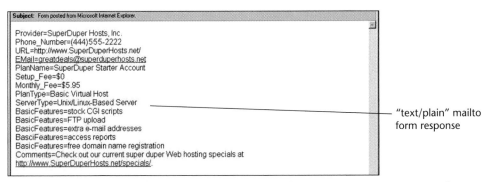

"text/plain" mailto form response

FIGURE 7.19 • *By setting the content type of a mailto form response, you get a response that is much more easily read by a human being.*

USING MAILTO FORM UTILITIES   Various utilities also are available on the Web that process mailto form responses. Besides converting form responses into text format, such utilities might also translate mailto form responses into comma-delimited format so they can be easily imported into a database or spreadsheet program. For links to where you can find mailto form utilities you can download and try out, see this chapter's section at the IRC for this book at **www.emcp.com/**.

CREATING CGI FORMS

To create a form that everyone can use, you need to create a CGI form. A CGI form uses a program or script located on the Web server, generally referred to as a *CGI script*, to process and direct form responses. Many Web hosts provide a stock form-processing CGI script that you can use. If your Web host does not provide a stock form-processing CGI script and does not allow you to install your own CGI scripts, you will not be able to use a CGI form, at least not a form using a CGI script hosted by your Web host. There are, however, services that provide remotely hosted form-processing CGI scripts that you can use instead, usually in exchange for allowing them to display advertising along with the form submission confirmation.

NOTE The acronym, CGI, stands for Common Gateway Interface and refers to the standard means by which a client-side application, such as a Web browser, can communicate and interface with a server-side program or script that is located on a Web server. The term, CGI script, refers to any script or program that can be executed over the Web from a Web server.

Setting Up a CGI Form

The following includes a hypothetical example of setting up a CGI form. In real life, the ACTION attribute value will vary according to what your Web host requires, which can be different, depending upon the location and name of the script being used.

Resave your example form file (to preserve the mailto form example) and set up your form as a CGI form:

1. In your text editor, save any changes to **hostsubmit.html** (File, Save) and then resave it as **hostsubmit2.html** in the chap07 folder in your working folder or working disk.
2. Open **hostsubmit2.html** in your browser.
3. In your text editor, edit **hostsubmit2.html** so it matches what is shown here:

```
<form action="/cgi-bin/FormMail.pl" method="post"
enctype="text/plain">
<p><input type="hidden" name="recipient" value="type your email
address here"></p>
```

This is just one example of linking a form-processing CGI script. A different CGI script might be required by your Web host, so check first with your Web host to see which CGI script they provide (if they provide one). The hidden input control that follows the FORM element specifies the e-mail address to which form responses should be sent. Other form-processing CGI scripts might require a slightly different hidden input control to specify this, using a different NAME value, for instance, but they should be relatively similar to what is shown here.

CGI scripts can be written in any programming or scripting language available on the Web server. Many CGI scripts are written using Perl, which is a programming language commonly available on UNIX servers, but they also can be written using other languages, such as C or C++, Visual Basic, AppleScript, TCL, ASP, and the UNIX shell, for instance.

NOTE

Some Web authors use a CGI form instead of a mailto link to provide visitors with a means to provide feedback. This has the advantage of hiding your e-mail address from spam robots that roam the Web looking for e-mail addresses in Web pages.

Setting Up and Configuring a Form-Processing CGI Script

To use CGI scripts, your Web host must allow the use of at least stock CGI scripts that they provide for you. A Web host also might allow you to create and add your own custom CGI scripts to your site. On a Windows server or Macintosh server, you can install CGI scripts in any folder. On a UNIX server, however, most Web hosts that support the use of custom CGI scripts set up a *personal cgi-bin* folder that is part of your site's folder structure. In that folder, you can add or create CGI scripts, as well as assign permissions.

If your site is hosted on a UNIX or Linux server, before you can use a CGI script in your personal cgi-bin folder, you must set the access permissions for it. If you do not, users might not be able to access the CGI script over the Web.

Most Web servers on the Web are running under UNIX. For that reason, the following instructions are for using Telnet or FTP to set access permissions on a UNIX (or Linux) server. If your Web host's server is running under Windows or on a Macintosh, see their technical support notes for information on what you need to do to install and configure CGI scripts on those platforms.

USING TELNET TO SET PERMISSIONS FOR A CGI SCRIPT You can use a telnet program to log on to your Web hosting account, if your account allows you to do this. See this chapter's section at the IRC for this book at **www.emcp.com/** for links to telnet programs you can download and try. To use a telnet program to set permissions for a CGI script, you would do something similar to the following:

1. Run the telnet program and specify the name of the server on which your Web site folders are located (sv2.someserver.com, for instance) to connect to it.
2. After connecting to your server, you should be prompted to log in. Key your user name and press Enter, and then key your password and press Enter.
3. To see your current position, key **pwd** and press Enter. You might see something like /users/vhome/*username* (with *username* standing for your user name).
4. A personal cgi-bin folder is usually directly off the root folder. To change to your personal cgi-bin folder, key **cd cgi-bin** and press Enter.
5. To set the permissions for the CGI script, key **chmod 755 FormMail.pl** (FormMail.pl is a CGI script written in Perl; substitute a different name for the CGI script if your form-processing script is named differently), and press Enter.
6. Key **logout** and press Enter to end and close the telnet session.

USING AN FTP PROGRAM TO SET CGI SCRIPT PERMISSIONS You also might be able to use an FTP program to set CGI script permissions on a UNIX or Linux server. Using an FTP program was covered in Chapter 6, *Creating Multi-Page Web Sites*; to find freeware and shareware FTP programs you can download and use, see that chapter's section at the IRC for this book at **www.emcp.com/**.

For instance, if your site is located on a UNIX server, following are steps you can follow to use WS_FTP LE for Windows to set CGI script permissions:

1. Run WS_FTP LE and connect to your Web hosting account.
2. Change to your cgi-bin folder—if you have set up WS_FTP LE to automatically open your Web site folder, you will need to first change to the parent folder (your site's root folder) and then change to your cgi-bin folder.
3. Right-click on the CGI script (FormMail.pl, for instance), select FTP Commands, and then select SITE.

The name of the form-processing CGI script that is used on your site's server may be different from the CGI script shown in Step 3. Check your Web host's support pages for information on which CGI script is used on your server.

4. Key **chmod 755 FormMail.pl** and press Enter (substitute the actual name of the CGI script you want to set permissions for).
5. Click Close and then click Exit.

UNDERSTANDING THE CHMOD NUMBER The CHMOD (Change Mode) command is used to set access permissions for the owner, the group, and all others. The number, 755, used to set the permissions for the FormMail.pl script is not nearly as arcane as it might appear. Rather than a three-digit number, it actually represents three separate numbers: 7, 5, and 5. The first number sets permissions for the owner, the second for the group, and the third for everyone else.

You are the owner, of course. The group is either everyone logged onto the server or a more restrictive listing of individuals who are assigned permission to access the file by the server administrator. Everyone else refers to the users on the Web who will visit your site and make use of the form. Table 7.1 shows how these access numbers are derived.

TABLE 7.1 • *How CHMOD Permission Numbers Are Derived*

Access Permission	Owner	Group	World
Read (4 = yes; 0 = no)	4	4	4
Write (2 = yes; 0 = no)	2	0	0
Execute (1 = yes; 0 = no)	1	1	1
CHMOD Number	7	5	5

Thus, as shown in Table 7.1, if you want the owner to have read, write, and execute permissions for a file, you need to assign a value of 7 (or 4 + 2 + 1) in the first number. On the other hand, if you do want group members or others to have permission to read and execute a file, but not to write to that file, you need to assign a value of 5 (4 + 0 + 1) in the second two numbers, with the full resulting CHMOD value thus being 755.

Sending and Receiving CGI Form Responses

Unlike a mailto form, you cannot test submitting CGI form responses on your local computer without accessing a Web host's server, since a CGI script needs to be located on a Web server for you to be able to access it. If you have access to a form-processing CGI script located on the Web, you can access it on your local computer by specifying an absolute URL for the script. If using a relative URL, however, you need to first publish your form to the Web before you can test it.

When you submit a mailto form, if your browser/mail program combination and configuration supports using mailto forms, a pop-up window alerts you that you are sending a form via e-mail. When you submit a CGI form, the CGI script on the server generates an HTML page that confirms that the form response has been sent. Figure 7.20 shows a form response confirmation page generated by the FormMail CGI script.

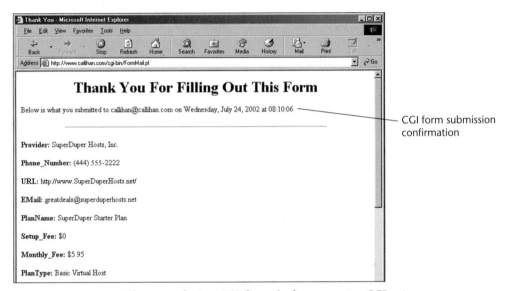

FIGURE 7.20 • *When you submit a CGI form, the form-processing CGI script generates a page confirming that the form response has been sent to the recipient's e-mail address.*

When you receive the form response in your inbox, the form response data is generally included in the body of the message. Figure 7.21 shows an example of a CGI form response.

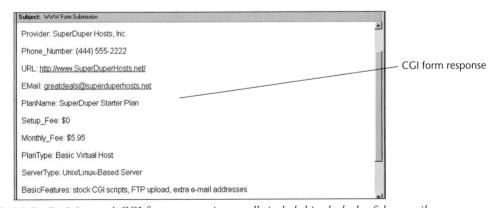

FIGURE 7.21 • *A CGI form response is generally included in the body of the e-mail message.*

NOTE

Everyone does not have the capability to run CGI forms on their sites. Many free Web space accounts, for instance, do not provide any form-processing CGI script that you can use and do not allow you to add your own. You also might not want to go to the trouble of telneting to your server to set permissions for the CGI script provided by your Web hosting company.

An alternative is to use a remotely hosted form-processing CGI script. Many companies let you use their form-processing CGI script free, in return for posting advertising on the confirmation page that is displayed after a form is submitted. See this chapter's section at the IRC for this book at **www.emcp.com/** for links to free services that provide remotely hosted form-processing CGI scripts.

DESIGNING FORMS

Until now in this chapter, you focused on using the different form elements and attributes, as well as understanding how to use, submit, and receive form responses. You also can design and format your forms further so they are more attractive and easier to read.

Using the PRE Element with Forms

You can use the PRE element to horizontally align text fields and other form elements.

Use the PRE element to horizontally align text fields and other form elements:
1. Re-open **hostsubmit.html** in your text editor and save it as **hostsubmit3.html**. Open **hostsubmit3.html** in your browser.
2. Edit **hostsubmit3.html** so it matches what is shown here (insert spaces where "·" characters are displayed).

```
<pre>Provider:·····<input type="text" name="Provider" size="40"
tabindex="1">··Phone #:···<input type="text" name="Phone_Number"
size="30">
</pre>

<pre>Web Address:···<input type="text" name="URL"
size="40">··E-Mail:····<input type="text" name="EMail" size="30">
</pre>

<pre>Plan Name:·····<input type="text" name="PlanName"
size="30">··Setup Fee:·<input type="text" name="Setup_Fee"
size="10" value="$">··Monthly Fee:·<input type="text"
name="Monthly_Fee" size="10" value="$"></pre>

<pre>Plan Type:····<input type="radio" name="PlanType"
value="Non-Virtual Host" checked>Non-Virtual Host
Plan·······<input type="radio" name="PlanType" value="Basic
Virtual Host">Basic Virtual Host Plan
·············<input type="radio" name="PlanType" value="Advanced
Virtual Host">Advanced Virtual Host Plan··<input type="radio"
name="PlanType" value="Reseller">Reseller Plan</pre>

<pre>Server Type:···<select name="ServerType">
  <option selected>Unix/Linux-Based Server
  <option>Windows-Based Server
  <option>Macintosh-Based Server
```

```
      <option>Other Server
</select>
</pre>

<pre>Basic Features Included:

· · · · · · · · · · · · ·<input type="checkbox" name="Basic_Features"
value="stock CGI scripts">stock CGI scripts· ·<input
type="checkbox" name="Basic_Features" value="FTP upload">FTP
upload· ·<input type="checkbox" name="Basic_Features" value="extra
e-mail addresses">multiple e-mail addresses
· · · · · · · · · · · · ·<input type="checkbox" name="Basic_Features"
value="access reports">access reports· · · · ·<input type="checkbox"
name="Basic_Features" value="free domain name registration">free
domain name registration</pre>

<pre>Added Comments:

· · · · · · · · · · · · ·<textarea name="Comments" rows="8"
cols="75"></textarea></pre>

<pre>· · · · · · · · · · · · ·<input type="submit" value="Submit">· ·<input
type="reset" value="Reset"></pre>
```

Do not add additional hard returns inside of the PRE elements in the preceding example. When using the PRE element to align input controls in a form, you need to be aware that any hard returns nested inside of the PRE element will be displayed when the page is viewed in a browser.

3. Save your file (File, Save) and refresh the display of the form in your browser. Compare the horizontal spacing of your form with that shown in Figure 7.22.

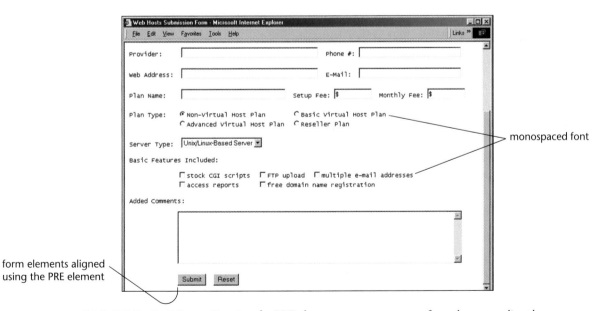

FIGURE 7.22 • *By using the PRE element, you can space out form elements to line them up vertically.*

Using Colors and Backgrounds with Forms

Using colors and backgrounds with forms can help make forms more attractive, as well as provide additional contrast between form element backgrounds (which stay white) and a background color or background image.

Specify text and background colors in the BODY element (see Figure 7.23):

```
<body bgcolor="#ccccff" text="#660000">
```

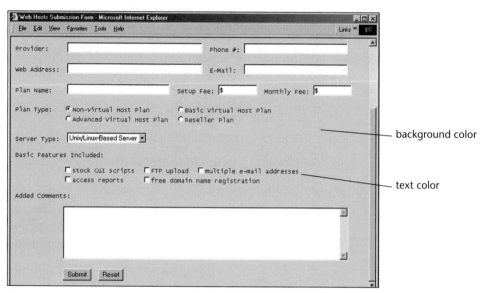

FIGURE 7.23 • *Setting text and background colors can improve the visual appeal of a form, as well as provide increased contrast between form elements and the page's background.*

Using Tables with Forms

The primary disadvantage of using the PRE element is that the form text has to be displayed in a monospaced font—otherwise, you cannot space out the input elements to line them up vertically. Alternatively, you can use a table to vertically line up elements within in a form.

Format a form using tables:

1. Re-open **hostsubmit.html** in your text editor and save it as **hostsubmit4.html**. Open **hostsubmit4.html** in your browser.
2. To create visual appeal and add contrast, set background, text, and link colors:

```
<body bgcolor="navy" text="white" link="aqua" vlink="silver"
alink="blue">
```

3. Edit **hostsubmit4.html** so that it matches what is shown here (see Figure 7.24):

```
<table width="100%"><tr valign="bottom">
<td width="13%" height="20">Provider:</td> <td><input
type="text" name="Provider" size="40"></td>
<td>Phone #:</td> <td><input type="text" name="Phone_Number"
size="35"></td>
</tr><tr valign="bottom" height="35">
```

```
<td>Web Address:</td><td><input type="text" name="URL"
size="40"></td>
<td>E-Mail:</td><td><input type="text" name="EMail" size="35"></td>
</tr></table>

<table width="100%"><tr valign="bottom" height="35">
<td width="13%">Plan Name:</td> <td><input type="text"
name="PlanName" size="30">
  Setup Fee: <input type="text" name="Setup_Fee"
size="15" value="$">
  Monthly Fee: <input type="text" name="Monthly_Fee"
size="15" value="$"></td></tr></table>

<table width="100%"><tr valign="bottom" height="35">
<td width="13%">Plan Type:</td> <td><input type="radio"
name="PlanType" value="Non-Virtual Host" checked>Non-Virtual
Host Plan  <input type="radio" name="PlanType"
value="Basic Virtual Host">Basic Virtual Host Plan  
<input type="radio" name="PlanType" value="Advanced Virtual
Host">Advanced Virtual Host Plan  
<input type="radio" name="PlanType" value="Reseller">Reseller
Plan</td></tr></table>

<table width="100%"><tr valign="bottom" height="35">
<td width="13%">Server Type:</td>
<td><select name="ServerType">
  <option selected>Unix/Linux-Based Server
  <option>Windows-Based Server
  <option>Macintosh-Based Server
  <option>Other Server
</select></td></tr></table>

<table width="100%"><tr valign="bottom" height="50">
<td width="13%">Basic Features Included:</td>
<td><input type="checkbox" name="Basic_Features" value="stock
CGI scripts">stock CGI scripts  
<input type="checkbox" name="Basic_Features" value="FTP
upload">FTP upload  
<input type="checkbox" name="Basic_Features" value="extra e-mail
addresses">multiple e-mail addresses  <input
type="checkbox" name="Basic_Features" value="access
reports">access reports<br>

<input type="checkbox" name="Basic_Features" value="free domain
name registration">free domain name registration</td>
</tr></table>

<table width="100%"><tr height="10">
<td></td></tr>
<tr valign="top">
<td width="13%">Added Comments:</td>
<td><textarea name="Comments" rows="8"
cols="77"></textarea></td>
</tr></table>

<table width="100%"><tr valign="bottom" height="35">
<td width="13%"></td><td><input type="submit" value="Submit">
<input type="reset" value="Reset"></td>
</tr></table>
</form>
```

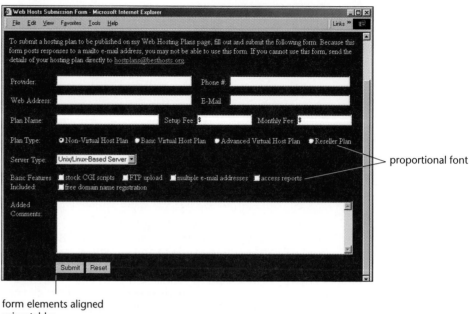

proportional font

form elements aligned
using tables

FIGURE 7.24 • *You also can use tables to vertically align table elements.*

As was previously noted, you need to be aware when displaying light text against a dark background that users can have difficulty printing such a page, which in many browsers will print as light text against a white background (or, even worse, as white text against a white background). If you believe a user might want to print a completed form, you should format it with dark text against a light or white background.

USING JAVASCRIPT WITH FORMS

Straight HTML forms do not give you much control over the data that a user enters into a form or how the form interacts with the user. JavaScript scripts enable you to include much more interactivity and intelligence in your forms. The following are some of the things that JavaScript lets you do with forms:

- Check that an input field is not blank.
- Check that an integer value (rather than an alphanumeric text string) has been keyed in a field.
- Check that an integer value between a minimum and a maximum value (between 1 and 6, for instance) has been keyed in a field.
- Check that an e-mail address has been keyed in a field requesting an e-mail address.
- Check that a valid phone number has been keyed in a field requesting a phone number.
- Check that a valid postal code has been keyed in a field requesting a ZIP or other postal code.
- Perform calculations on numerical values that have been keyed or selected in input fields. For instance, you might want to total the cost of items selected in an order form, calculate the sales tax, add shipping and handling, and then display the total amount.
- Check that text entered in a text area box does not exceed a set number of characters. Although you can use the MAXLENGTH attribute to limit the number of

characters that can be keyed in a text box, it cannot be used to do the same thing in a text area box.
- Create a button element (using an INPUT element with a `type="button"` attribute that performs an action when the button is clicked).
- Set other actions to be performed in response to user actions.
- Create drop-down menus that allow users to jump to different pages or other objects in your site.
- Redirect users to a confirmation page after submitting a mailto form (which normally provides confirmation that the form data has actually been sent).

This is just a sampling of how you can use JavaScript to add versatility and functionality to forms. For links to resources, guides, and tutorials that can help you learn more about using JavaScript in forms, see this chapter's section in the IRC for this book at **www.emcp.com/**.

CHAPTER SUMMARY

You should now be familiar with how to create all the different form elements, including text boxes, radio button groups, check box groups, pull-down list menus, multi-line text area boxes, and various kinds of Submit and Reset buttons. You gained practical experience using the PRE element and tables to create horizontally aligned form layouts, and learned how to use colors and backgrounds with forms. You should be conversant in the differences between mailto forms and CGI forms and understand the pros and cons of using one or the other. You might have gained experience sending and receiving form responses. You also should be aware of the role that JavaScript can play in validating forms and extending their functionality.

Code Review

FORM element	Defines a user-input form in an HTML file.
ACTION attribute	In the FORM element, specifies the URL to which form data is to be submitted.
METHOD attribute	In the FORM element, specifies the method of submitting the form. Possible values are **post** and **get**, with the first being the more usual method for submitting online form data.
INPUT element	Defines a range of user input controls, including text boxes, radio buttons, check boxes, and more.
`type="text"`	In the INPUT element, specifies that an input control is a text box.
SIZE attribute	In a text box input control, specifies the width of the text box in characters. Text entered in a text box can exceed the size of the box.
MAXLENGTH attribute	In a text box input control, specifies a maximum number of characters that can be keyed.
`type="radio"`	In the INPUT element, specifies that an input control is a radio button.
`type="checkbox"`	In the INPUT element, specifies that an input control is a check box.
`type="password"`	In the INPUT element, specifies that an input control allows the entry of a password. Text keyed in a password box is displayed as a series of asterisks.
SELECT and OPTION elements	The SELECT element defines a list menu (or selection list), while the OPTION element defines the individual options for the menu.
MULTIPLE attribute	In the SELECT element, specifies that multiple list options can be selected (otherwise, only one option can be selected).
TEXTAREA element	Defines a text area box, which allows users to key in multi-line comments.
ROWS and COLS attributes	In the TEXTAREA element, defines the dimensions of a text area box. The ROWS attribute value specifies the number of text lines that are included in the box and the COLS attribute specifies the width of the box in text characters (not pixels).

`type="submit"`	In the INPUT element, specifies that an input control is a Submit button.
`type="reset"`	In the INPUT element, specifies that an input control is a Reset button.
`type="image"`	In the INPUT element, specifies that an input control is an image button. Image buttons function identically to Submit buttons.
BUTTON element	An HTML 4 element that can define a Submit button or a Reset button. BUTTON element Submit and Reset buttons function identically to input control Submit and Reset buttons, except that they can be more richly rendered.
TABINDEX attribute	Resets the tabbing order for elements, including the A, AREA, BUTTON, INPUT, OBJECT, SELECT, and TEXTAREA elements.
mailto form	A form that posts form responses to a mailto e-mail address. Not supported by all browsers.
CGI form	A form that posts form responses to a CGI script on a Web server. The CGI script can either store responses in a file or database on the server or forward them to an e-mail address.
`type="hidden"`	In the INPUT element, specifies that an input control is a hidden control, which passes a value when the form is submitted, but is not displayed in the form. In CGI forms, a hidden control is often used to specify the URL of a CGI script.
chmod 755 *filename*	UNIX command used to set permissions for a CGI script file, so it can be accessed over the Web.

ONLINE QUIZ

Go to this text's IRC at **www.emcp.com/** and take the online self-check quiz for this chapter.

REVIEW EXERCISES

This section provides some hands-on practice exercises to reinforce the information and material included within this and previous chapters.

You can use any of the example files that you created in this chapter to further practice features or methods covered in this chapter. To save the original versions of these files for future reference, save them under another name, such as hostsubmit_practice.html in the chap07 folder in your working folder or disk, before using them for practice.

1. Save **hostsubmit.html** under a new name (**hostsubmit_practice.html**, for instance) and practice creating additional text boxes. For instance, under the line including the Plan Name, Setup Fee, and Monthly Fee text boxes, create two more lines containing the following text boxes:

1st text box (1st line):

    lead-in text = Web Space:
    name = Space
    size = 40

2nd text box (1st line)

    lead-in text = Extra Space:
    name = Extra_Space
    size = 35

3rd text box (2nd line):

    lead-in text = Traffic:
    name = Traffic
    size = 40

4th text box (2nd line):

    lead-in text = Extra Traffic:
    name = Extra_Traffic
    size = 35

2. Still working with hostsubmit_practice.html, practice further creating a second radio button group following the Plan Type radio button group you already created:

Lead-in text = Advanced Payment Discounts?

1st radio button:

    name = Pay_Discount
    value = Y
    following text = Yes

2nd radio button:

    name = Pay_Discount
    value = N
    following text = No

3. Still working with hostsubmit_practice.html, practice further creating a second pull-down menu list on the same line following the Server Type menu list you have already created:

Lead-in text = Connection Type:

Name = ConnectType

1st list menu option:

    text = Multiple DS-3 Connections

2nd list menu option:

    text = Single DS-3 Connection

3rd list menu option:

    text = Other

4. Still working with hostsubmit_practice.html, practice further creating a second group of check boxes following the Basic Features Included check box group you have already created:

Lead-in text = Other Features Included:

1st check box:

    name = Other_Features
    value = custom CGI scripts
    following text = custom CGI scripts

2nd check box:

    name = Other_Features
    value = autoresponders
    following text = autoresponders

3rd check box:

    name = Other_Features
    value = shell account
    following text = shell account

4th check box:

    name = Other_Features
    value = access logs
    following text = access logs

5th check box:

    name = Other_Features
    value = RealMedia
    following text = RealMedia

6th check box:

    name = Other_Features
    value = FrontPage Extensions
    following text = FrontPage Extensions

7th check box:

    name = Other_Features
    value = password protected folders
    following text = password protected folders

8th check box:

    name = Other_Features
    value = database/MySQL
    following text = database/MySQL

9th check box:

    name = Other_Features
    value = Cold Fusion
    following text = Cold Fusion

10th check box:

    name = Other_Features
    value = PHP
    following text = PHP

11th check box:

    name = Other_Features
    value = ASP
    following text = ASP

12th check box:

    name = Other_Features
    value = multiple domain hosting
    following text = multiple domain hosting

13th check box:

    name = Other_Features
    value = shopping cart
    following text = shopping cart

14th check box:

    name = Other_Features
    value = 24/7 phone support
    following text = 24/7 phone support

5. If your browser supports sending mailto form responses, further test sending form responses directly to your e-mail address. Use your mail program to open and receive form responses. Experiment with sending form responses using both the "urlencoded" (the default) and "text/plain" content types.

6. If you have access to a Web space account that provides a forms-processing CGI script, check the support area to find out the URL of the forms-processing CGI script and what you need to do to call it in your form. If the CGI forms-processing script is located on a UNIX or LINUX server in a personal cgi-bin folder that has been created for you, following the instructions provided earlier in this chapter, telnet to your server, change to your personal cgi-bin folder, and then key **chmod 755 *scriptname*** and press Enter to set the access permissions for your forms-processing CGI script.

7. As a continuation of the previous review exercise, after you set the access permissions for your forms-processing CGI script, do further research to see which hidden input controls you need to include in your form to instruct the forms-processing CGI script to forward form responses to your e-mail address. Open **hostsubmit2.html** and save it as **hostsubmit2_practice.html** and edit it to post form responses to the forms-processing CGI script on your server. After editing your form, publish it to your Web site folder and test submitting CGI form responses in your browser and receiving them in your e-mail program.

8. If you have a Web space account but it does not provide access to a forms-processing CGI script, see this chapter's section at the IRC for this book at **www.emcp.com/** to find services that provide remotely hosted forms-processing CGI scripts. Sign up for a service and follow its instructions to edit your form (hostsubmit2_practice.html) to use the service's forms-processing script to send form responses to your e-mail address. Publish the page with your form to your Web site and test sending and receiving form responses using the remotely hosted forms-processing CGI script.

9. Open **hostsubmit3.html** in your text editor and resave it as **hostsubmit3_practice.html**. Practice setting different text, link, and background colors in combination with your form. To refresh your memory about setting text, link, and background colors in Web pages, see Chapter 3, *Working with Fonts, Colors, and Backgrounds*. Try out several color schemes to find the color scheme you think works best with your form. When you find the color scheme you like, ask at least two classmates to critique your color choices.

10. Still working with hostsubmit3_practice.html, rearrange the organization and layout of the form, while still using the PRE element to allow the spacing and horizontal alignment of form elements. Create an entirely different layout from the current layout. Adjust text box sizes (widths) to fit your layout.

11. Reopen **hostsubmit1_practice.html** in your text editor and resave it as **hostsubmit4_practice.html**. In a separate text editor window, open **hostsubmit4.html**. Using hostsubmit4.html as a reference, use HTML tables in hostsubmit4_practice.html to create a layout design for your form. In hostsubmit4_practice.html, create a different table layout than that used in hostsubmit4.html, incorporating the new text boxes, radio buttons, list menu, and check boxes you created earlier in this section into your layout design.

WEB-BASED LEARNING ACTIVITIES

In this book's text, Find It icons inserted in the margin highlight the Web addresses of additional resources you might find helpful or informative. To further extend your learning using the Web, you can:

- Visit this book's IRC at **www.emcp.com/** to find additional Web addresses of resources related to the material covered in this chapter that you can further investigate and explore. When you find a relevant page or site with information or resources you may want to access later, add it to your Favorites (in Internet Explorer) or your Bookmarks (in Netscape or Mozilla).

- Further research a specific topic introduced in this chapter. For instance, you can further research the pros and cons of using mailto and CGI forms. You also can research services that provide remotely hosted forms-processing CGI scripts. Another topic you can research is the use of JavaScript scripts with forms.

Compile the results of your research into a report that can be shared with your fellow students. You also can team up with other students to create a class presentation or demonstration.

- Use Yahoo! at **www.yahoo.com/** to look for examples of how forms are used on the Web. Look for different form designs and different functions that forms are performing. Find at least six different form examples on the Web that you think demonstrate the effective design and use of forms. Save the examples you find as bookmarks or favorites, so you can use them as a reference later in conceptualizing and designing your own forms.

PROJECTS

These projects can be done in class, in a computer lab, or at home. Use the skills you have developed in this and the previous chapters to create any of the following projects.

Project 1. Conceptualize and design a user feedback form.

For any page that you have created for yourself or for any of the fictional case example scenarios that you have worked with so far in this book, conceptualize and design a user feedback form from scratch that allows users to fill out a form to send you feedback. For instance, create a user feedback form for the page on NASA Space Exploration that you created in Chapter 4 that asks visitors their opinions about space exploration, whether money should be spent on space exploration, whether human beings should go to Mars, and so on. Include a text area box that lets a visitor provide a longer comment.

Create a user feedback form for any other page, whether as part of a fictional case example scenario or for a personal, topical, or other page that you have created for yourself.

Project 2. Create a survey form.

Create a form that surveys visitors' opinions about a particular topic, issue, or event. This can be on any topic or subject matter, so be creative and come up with something different that you think would elicit a relatively broad response. For instance, you might create a survey asking visitors what they ate (or drank) for breakfast. You can create a survey of opinions about global warming. You can create a survey of what visitors think about recent movies, asking them to rank them on a scale from 1 to 5 in different categories, for instance. Or, you can create a survey form on any other topic or subject you can conceive.

Project 3. Create an order form.

Look on the Web for examples of order forms that allow visitors to order products or services. Save examples you find as bookmarks or favorites and use them as guides in conceptualizing and designing an order form of your own. For instance, you might create an order form that allows visitors to order a range of different size and color "widgets." You can have options for ordering 2-inch, 5-inch, and 10-inch widgets in orange, green, and purple colors.

Project 4. Create a product registration form.

When people buy a product, they are increasingly asked to register the product online. This is not just for software products, but can be for non-software products, as well.

Use Yahoo! at **www.yahoo.com/** to search for examples of product registration forms. Save good examples you find as bookmarks or favorites and then use them as guides in creating a fictional product registration form from scratch. This could be for a software product, a video camera, a car stereo, a foot massager, or just about anything. Try to make it realistic. Ask for the customer's first name, last name, title, company name, address, city, state, ZIP code, country, product name, model number, date purchased, use of the product (work, entertainment, education, or other, for instance), and any comments about the product.

Project 5. Create a dating service form.

Imagine that you are running a dating service, Lonely Hearts Unlimited. Create a form that allows people looking for dates to describe their interests, likes and dislikes, favorite things to do, favorite music, ambitions, what they are looking for in a date or partner, and so on. Make liberal use of radio buttons, check boxes, and list menus to elicit responses to an array of different kinds of questions. Have fun with it. Be creative.

Project 6. Create a form for a site of your own.

Create a form for a site that you have already created for yourself, or design a site from scratch that includes a form. This can be any kind of form you care to design (totally open-ended). Decide whether you are going to use a mailto or a CGI form. If using a CGI form, you will need access to a forms-processing CGI script on your Web host's server or from a service that provides remotely hosted forms-processing CGI scripts. When satisfied with the form, publish the form to the Web. If you do not have Web space where you can publish your site, look in Chapter 6's section at the IRC for this book for links to Web hosting resources on the Web, including information and guidance in finding a free Web space provider.

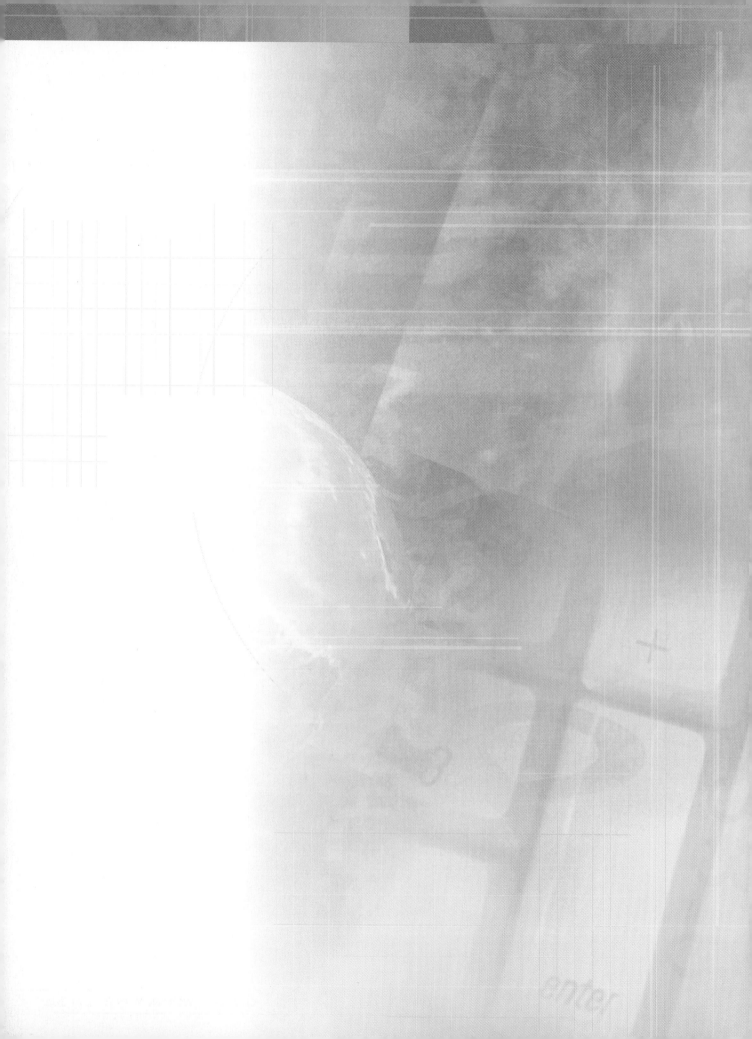

TEAM PROJECT
HTML Essentials

For this project, you will participate as a member of a team, cooperating with others in planning, preparing, creating, and publishing a multi-page Web site. Remember, it is not just the performance of the team that matters, but also your performance as a member of the team. Learning how to cooperate, communicate, and coordinate is just as important as learning how to code a page or design a graphic.

1. BRAINSTORM TOPICS, AUDIENCES, AND OBJECTIVES

With your teammates, brainstorm the kinds of topics, audiences, and objectives you might want to target. Come up with at least six topics for possible projects (with each teammate suggesting at least two topics). For each project topic, define the audience you want to address, and the goal you want to achieve by addressing that audience with the topic. Try to come to a consensus on the topic, target audience, and objective.

If you have difficulties coming up with ideas or cannot agree on a topic, audience, and objective, use Yahoo! at **www.yahoo.com/**, Google at **www.google.com/**, or any other search engine to search for sites that can suggest ideas to you.

After choosing the topic you want to cover or address through your project, further refine your understanding of your project as a team by asking and coming up with answers to the following questions:

- Why do you want to do the project? What about the project has value and significance?
- Who do you most want to do the project for? Who is the target audience of the project or what are the characteristics of the audience that will most likely be interested in the project's topic and subject matter?
- What result or results do you hope to achieve through your project? This brings together both your own impetus to do the project (why it is of value for you) and the value the project will have for your intended audience.
- How are you going to implement your project to achieve the ends you want to achieve? Think here of more specific functions and features you can implement to achieve your desired results.

2. SUBMIT YOUR PROJECT PROPOSAL FOR APPROVAL

Condense your answers to the why, who, what, and how questions into a mission statement for your project. Try to incorporate everything that is most relevant about your project in a single concise statement. Following your mission statement, include further information about your project. Include the topic of the project, the audience you will be addressing, the goals you hope to achieve, and the methods and techniques you plan to implement to achieve those goals. Keep it to less than one page, double-spaced. Be sure to share responsibility for formulating and creating this proposal.

Submit this proposal to your instructor for approval.

3. CREATE AN OUTLINE

Break down your approved project into parts. Create an outline of your site's planned content that is at least two levels deep, with the first level signifying the major branching subpages within your project's site and the second level signifying major section headings within those pages. After creating your outline, you should have a good idea of what the content of your site will be and how it will be organized.

4. ESTABLISH LAYOUT AND NAVIGATION SCHEMES

Discuss which layout and navigation schemes are appropriate and best suited for your project. Decide whether to lay out your site using regular pages, tables, or frames. Come to a team consensus on the layout scheme you want to implement. Determine the navigation scheme you will be using, whether using a link menu, a left sidebar menu, a right sidebar menu, or a topbar menu, for instance. Following are some basic types of navigation schemes:

- A link menu on a front page that jumps to subpages, with return links then jumping back to the main page's link menu.
- A navigation menu at the top and/or bottom of each page that provides access to the other main pages within the site.
- A sidebar or topbar menu using tables, which jumps to subpages that also have sidebar or topbar menus.
- A sidebar, topbar, or bottombar menu using frames, which jumps to subpages displayed within a targeted frame (the "main" frame, for instance). The menu links also can jump to additional frameset pages, so those pages can be added to a visitor's Favorites or Bookmarks.

5. CREATE A STORYBOARD

A storyboard is a kind of cartoon of your site, showing how your site's pages are ordered and related to each other. A Web site can be organized in many ways. Creating a pictorial representation of your site helps clarify the major relationships that exist between the different parts of your site. For instance, you might draw up a diagram of your site that shows it as:

- A linear series of pages, like the chapters of a book (similar to the cars of a train).
- A top-down hierarchy, in what is usually referred to as a tree structure.
- A hub and wheel, with the start or front page in the middle and the subpages arrayed around the hub like the rim of a wheel.
- A non-linear, non-hierarchical, distributed arrangement, such as a triangle, square, star, or other pattern, with three, four, five, or more co-equal entrance points. Each entrance point can highlight a significant aspect of the topic being covered or presented, without any one being foremost over the others.

Explore at least two of these options and discuss the merit of each one within your team. Then select the best model for your project.

6. DRAW A MAP

To visualize the dynamic relationships that can be achieved using hypertext links to create navigation schemes, you can draw a map of your site that shows how its pages are linked together. This is similar to creating a storyboard, except you are not outlining the order of precedence of your site's pages, but delineating the links that exist between them, outside the outward organization and structure of your site. Remember, any page can link to any other page in your site. By drawing out the links between pages, you might see ways in which pages are related to each other that you had not realized before. Look for ways to creatively cross-link your pages.

7. ESTABLISH A COLOR SCHEME

Experiment with different text, link, and background colors to establish an appropriate and effective color scheme for your project. Pay attention to legibility and accessibility when choosing color combinations. Optionally, incorporate a background image into your color scheme. Come to a team consensus on the color scheme you want to implement.

8. DEFINE RESPONSIBILITIES

Responsibilities for creating the site should be shared coequally among team members. When you start to actually create your project, however, you will need to agree on who will be responsible for which tasks. You can allocate responsibilities in a project in a couple of ways:
- Individual team members might be responsible for creating different parts of the site, but within the shared vision, layout scheme, and color scheme the team members have agreed on.
- Team members can divide up responsibilities relative to the capabilities and strengths of each member. If one team member is a visual artist, for instance, she might take a leadership role in creating and preparing graphic images that will be used in the project; if one team member is a writer, he might take a leadership role in composing and writing copy for the project.

No matter how responsibilities are assigned, it is important that each team member gain experience in all aspects of creating the project. Taking a leadership role for a particular area does not mean excluding others from participating in that area.

9. SET A TIME LINE

After agreeing on the responsibilities for the different tasks that need to be completed to finalize the project, determine the order in which those tasks need to be completed, to the best of your ability. Set a time line detailing milestones (along with their respective target dates) that everyone included within your group agrees with and that need to be achieved to complete the project. Be prepared to renegotiate these agreements, if necessary, as work on the project progresses, to take into account exigencies, problems, or changes to the project that might impact the time line. Pay close attention to those aspects of the project that must be completed first, before work on other aspects of the project can begin. In planning and executing the project, you also need to take into account any overall due date that your instructor has set for the project.

10. BUILD THE SITE

Begin building the site, considering the time line and assignment dates provided by your instructor. Some of the tasks that might need to be performed include:
- Finding or creating buttons, bars, balls, and background images to give the project a cohesive visual look.
- Creating a banner image and/or logo image for the project site.
- Writing textual copy for the site. The text that composes the content of the site is just as important as any other aspect of the site.
- Create a starter template that establishes the basic look and feel for the site's pages, which each team member can then adapt for the pages he or she is working on.
- Scan, resize, color-correct, or optimize photographic or other images you want to use in the project's site.

11. TEST AND TROUBLESHOOT

All team members should participate in testing and troubleshooting the project's site. Test the project's site in several browsers. For instance, you can test your project's site in the most recent Internet Explorer, Netscape, Mozilla, and Opera browsers. You also can test your project's site for backward compatibility in a version of Netscape Navigator 4.

When you run into problems, you might have to selectively comment out code to isolate the problem code. If you are not able to get a code to work across browsers, you should consider not using the code.

Validate your site's pages using the W3C HTML Validation Service at **validator.w3.org/**. If you are using Cascading Styles Sheets in your project, also validate your site's style sheets using the W3C CSS Validation Service at **jigsaw.w3.org/css-validator/**.

12. PUBLISH TO THE WEB

Using Web space provided by your school or by another provider of free Web space, publish your project's site so it can be viewed over the Web. Get suggestions, comments, and other feedback from fellow classmates on how you can improve your site. Make revisions to your site that incorporate positive changes suggested by your fellow classmates.

Submit your site to search engines so you can get feedback and comments from visitors to your site who are not fellow classmates.

13. CRITIQUE YOUR WORK

Write a self-critique of your participation in the team project. List some of the important lessons you learned while doing the project. Spell out where you think you performed well and where you think you performed less well, detailing some of the reasons that determined your performance. Point out areas in which you feel you need to improve and what you need to work on in order to improve.

Include a critique of your team's performance. Evaluate your team's ability to communicate, work cooperatively, complete assigned responsibilities in a timely and satisfactory manner, and any other factors you believe made either a positive or negative contribution to completing the project in a satisfactory fashion.

As part of your critique, indicate whether the site fulfilled the approved mission statement and support your evaluation with examples. Report your recommendations for improving or further enhancing the site developed by your team.

APPENDIX A

HTML Quick Reference

This HTML quick reference consists of two parts. The first part includes a listing in alphabetical order of all of the standard elements of HTML 4.01 and their most commonly used attributes. The second part covers generic and other attributes that are applied to many elements.

Elements and attributes that were first standardized in HTML 3.2 and HTML 4.0 are marked with "3.2" and "4.0." All recent browsers should support HTML 3.2 elements and attributes. Use of HTML 4.0 elements and attributes requires more care, however, because some HTML 4.0 elements and attributes are widely supported, but others are currently only supported by a few browsers or not at all.

HTML ELEMENTS

A (Anchor)   Type: Inline/Container   Content: Inline

Attributes		
	name="*destination anchor name*"	See note
	href="*URL and/or fragment identifier*"	See note
	target="*frame name*"	Optional

Note: Either NAME or HREF is required.

Example

```
<a href="http://www.somesite.com/somedir/somepage.html">Go to my
page.</a>
```

ABBR (Abbreviation) (4.0)   Type: Inline/Container   Content: Inline

Specifies the expanded form of an abbreviation. If the letters of a shortened expression are individually pronounced, such as ABC, FBI, BBC, NCAA, NAACP, WWW, CSS, and so on, it is an abbreviation.

Attributes   title="*expanded term*"

Example
```
<p>J. Edgar Hoover was the first Director of the <abbr
title="Federal Bureau of Investigation">FBI</abbr>.
```

ACRONYM (4.0)
Type: Inline/Container   **Content:** Inline

Specifies the expanded form of an acronym. If the shortened expression is pronounced as a word, such as NATO, CERN, radar, laser, SOHO, SCUBA, and so on, it is an acronym.

Attributes   `title="expanded term"`

Example
```
<p>The World Wide Web was invented by Tim Berners-Lee at <acronym
title="Conseil European pour la Recherche Nucleaire/European
Organization for Nuclear Research">CERN</acronym>.</p>
```

ADDRESS
Type: Inline/Container   **Content:** Inline

Identifies the author/owner of a Web page, along with a means to contact or provide feedback, such as a link to a contact page.

Note: The ALIGN attribute is not a legal attribute for the ADDRESS element, although many browsers recognize it. Block elements are not allowed within the ADDRESS element (although browsers do not care).

Example
```
<address>
Roger Dodger<br>
E-mail: <a href="mailto:rogdodg@blutto.com">rogdodg@blutto.com</a>
</address>
```

APPLET (3.2) (Deprecated)
Type: Inline/Container   **Content:** Inline

Inserts a Java applet inline within an HTML document.

Attributes

`code="applet class file"`	See Note
`object="applet class resource"` (4.0)	See Note
`alt="alternative text description"`	Recommended
`codebase="URL"`	Optional
`archive="comma-delimited list of URLs"` (4.0)	Optional
`width="n|n%"`	Optional
`height="n|n%"`	Optional
`name="applet name"`	Optional
`align="top|middle|bottom|left|right|center"`	Optional
`hspace="n"`	Optional
`vspace="n"`	Optional

Note: Either CODE or OBJECT is required. If both are present, they must reference the same applet class file name.

PARAM (3.2) (Deprecated in APPLET)
Type: Inline/Empty   **Content:** N/A

When nested inside an APPLET element, passes parameters to a Java applet. Also can be nested inside an OBJECT element. *See also* OBJECT.

Attributes

`name="parameter name"`	Required
`value="parameter value"`	Required

Note: The NAME attribute value must start with a letter (A–Z or a–z), with the remainder of the value composed of letters, numbers, hyphens, or periods.

AREA (3.2)

See MAP.

B (Bold)
Type: Inline/Container   **Content:** Inline

Specifies that nested text should be bolded. *See also* EM (Emphasis), STRONG (Strong Emphasis), and I (Italic).

Example
```
<p>It is <b>important</b> that assignments be turned in on time.</p>
```

BASE

See HEAD.

BASEFONT (3.2) (Deprecated)
Type: Inline/Empty   **Content:** N/A

Sets font characteristics for following text. BASEFONT is not implemented in many recent browsers and should be avoided. *See also* FONT.

Attributes
```
size="1|2|3|4|5|6|7"                          Optional
color="color name|RGB color code" (4.0)       Optional
face="font name|font name list" (4.0)         Optional
```

BDO (4.0)
Type: Inline/Container   **Content:** Inline

Changes the direction in which nested text is displayed.

Attributes
```
dir="LTR|RTL"                                 Required
lang="language code"                          Optional
```

BIG (3.2)
Type: Inline/Container   **Content:** Inline

Increases the size of nested text by one font size. The sizes correspond to the seven font sizes that can be set with the FONT and BASEFONT elements. *See also* SMALL.

Example
```
<p>In case of a fire alarm, walk, don't run, to the nearest
<big>Exit</big> sign.</p>
```

BLOCKQUOTE
Type: Block/Container   **Content:** Block/SCRIPT

Displays a long quotation as an indented block.

Attributes
```
cite="URL"                                    Optional
```

Example
```
<p>When starting a chess game, one should keep in mind the following
basic principles, enumerated by the great American Grandmaster,
Frank J. Marshall, in his book, <em>Chess Step by Step</em>:
<blockquote>
```

```
<p>In selecting a Sphere of Action, always move the pieces where
they will command the greatest number of squares, have the greatest
freedom of action, where they cannot be readily attacked or driven
away, and where they will restrict or delay the opponent's
development.</p>
</blockquote>
```

BODY

Type: Container   **Content:** Block

In a non-frameset page, one of two elements (along with HEAD) that is nested directly inside the
HTML element. Both the start tag and end tag are optional in HTML 4.01.

Attributes		
	text="*color name|RGB color code*" (Deprecated)	Optional
	link="*color name|RGB color code*" (Deprecated)	Optional
	vlink="*color name|RGB color code*" (Deprecated)	Optional
	alink="*color name|RGB color code*" (Deprecated)	Optional
	bgcolor="*color name|RGB color code*" (Deprecated)	Optional
	background="*image URL*" (Deprecated)	Optional

Example
```
<body text="navy" link="red" vlink="#666600" alink="#666600"
bgcolor="#ffffcc" background="images/back_light.jpg">
```

BR (Break)

Type: Inline/Empty   **Content:** N/A

Causes a line break to be displayed.

Attributes   clear="left|right|all" (Deprecated)   Optional

Note: The CLEAR attribute causes text flowing around a floating image to move down until the left,
right, or both margins are clear (not obstructed by the floating image).

Example
```
<h2>From "Auguries of Innocence" by William Blake:</h2>
<blockquote>
<p>To see a World in a Grain of Sand<br>
And a Heaven in a Wild Flower,<br>
Hold Infinity in the palm of your hand<br>
And Eternity in an hour.</p>
</blockquote>
```

BUTTON (4.0)

See FORM.

CAPTION (3.2)

See TABLE.

CENTER (3.2) (Deprecated)

Type: Block/Container   **Content:** Block/Inline

Centers nested text or elements horizontally on the page. In HTML 3.2 and HTML 4, the CENTER
element is equivalent to a DIV element with an **align="center"** attribute set.

| *Example* | ```
<center>
<h2>Announcement:</h2>
<p>You can sign up for volunteer positions starting on Friday at
8:00 a.m.</p>
</center>
``` |
|---|---|

CITE
Type: Inline/Container **Content:** Inline

Indicates that nested text is a citation of a source. Text nested in the CITE element is generally displayed in italics. EM or I can be used to achieve the same effect.

Example
```
<p>"There is no safe trusting to dictionaries and definitions," as
Charles Lamb stressed, in "Popular Fallacies," <cite>Essays of
Elia</cite>.
```

CODE (Computer Code)
Type: Inline/Container **Content:** Inline

Indicates that nested text is a fragment of computer (or program) code. Text nested in the CODE element is generally displayed in a monospaced font. The TT (Teletype Text) element can alternatively be used to format computer code.

Example
```
<p>Start by declaring a variable that sets a starting value for the
count: <code>var count = 1;</code>.</p>
```

COL (Column) (4.0)

See Table.

COLGROUP (Column Group) (4.0)

See Table.

DD (Definition Data)

See DL (Definition List).

DEL (Delete) (4.0)
Type: Inline/Container **Content:** Inline

Marks nested text as a deletion. In browsers that support this element, nested text is generally displayed as strikeout text (with a line drawn through it). STRIKE and S also can be used to display strikeout text, with STRIKE being the most widely supported. *See also* INS (Insert).

Example
```
<h1><del>My </del>Frequently Asked Questions Page</h1>
```

DFN (Definition) (3.2)
Type: Inline/Container **Content:** Inline

Marks nested text as the defining instance of a term. Nested text is generally displayed in italics, but some earlier browsers might bold it.
```

Example
```
<p>JavaScript is an <dfn>object-oriented</dfn> scripting language,
which means that when you work with JavaScript, you are primarily
involved in defining and manipulating objects.</p>
```

DIR (Directory List) (Deprecated)   **Type:** Block/Container   **Content:** Block

The DIR element was originally intended for displaying multi-column directory lists, but this was never implemented in browsers. The UL element produces exactly the same result in all browsers and should be used instead. *See also* UL (Unordered List).

DIV (Division) (3.2)   **Type:** Block/Container   **Content:** Inline/Block

Marks a division within a document (a document division).

Attributes   align="**left**|right|center|justify" (Deprecated)   Optional

Note: The ALIGN attribute is the only HTML formatting that can be applied to a DIV element. All other formatting must be applied using an inline style (using the STYLE attribute), an embedded style sheet (the STYLE element), or an externally linked style sheet (using the LINK element).

Example
```
<div align="center">
<h1>Causes of the American Revolution</h1>
<h2>by William Jefferson</h2>
</div>
```

DL (Definition List)   **Type:** Block/Container   **Content:** Block

Designates that nested text is a definition list (or glossary). Nested DT (Definition Term) and DD (Definition Data) elements designate the terms and definitions.

Attributes   compact (Deprecated)   Optional

Note: The COMPACT attribute is a hint to a browser that a definition list can be displayed in a more compact way. Browsers that support this, such as Internet Explorer 6, for instance, display the DT and DD elements on the same line, as long as the DT text does not include more than four characters. Most browsers, however, ignore the COMPACT element, so it is best avoided.

DT (Definition Term)   **Type:** Block/Container   **Content:** Inline

Designates nested text as a term in a definition list. The end tag is optional.

DD (Definition Data)   **Type:** Block/Container   **Content:** Inline/Block

Designates nested text as a definition in a definition list. The DD element is generally indented in from the left margin. The end tag is optional.

Example
```
<dl>
<dt>crippleware
<dd>A form of shareware software program in which one or more key
functions have been crippled.
<dt>demoware
<dd>A form of shareware software program that is distributed for
demonstration purposes only, usually with an evaluation period,
```

```
                        after which the software stops functioning.
                        </dl>
```

EM (Emphasis)   **Type:** Inline/Container   **Content:** Inline

Marks nested text as emphasized, which is displayed in italics in all browsers. Alternatively, the I (Italics) element can be used to achieve the same result. *See also* STRONG (Strong Emphasis), I (Italic), and B (Bold).

Example
```
<p>When moving, it is very <em>important</em> to submit a Change of
Address form at the post office.</p>
```

FIELDSET (4.0)

See FORM.

FONT (3.2) (Deprecated)   **Type:** Inline/Container   **Content:** Inline

Designates font characteristics, including size, color, and face, that are to be applied to nested text.

Attributes
```
size="n[1|2|3|4|5|6|7] or +n|-n"                    See Note
color="color name|RGB color code"                  Optional
face="font name|font name list"                    Optional
```

Note: The default font size is equivalent to `size="3"`, unless it has been reset by a preceding BASE-FONT element or a bracketing FONT element. A + or - sign preceding the size number designates a font size that is relative to the default font size.

Example
```
<h1><font size="7" color="blue" face="Arial">Upcoming
Schedule</font></h1>
```

FORM   **Type:** Block/Container   **Content:** Block

Designates that nested elements are part of a form.

Attributes
```
action="URL"                                       Required
method="get|post"                                  Optional
enctype="content type"                             Optional
```

Note: ACTION attribute should specify an HTTP URL; behavior of user agents resulting from use of non-HTTP URLs (such as a mailto URL) is undefined. For user-input forms, use the **post** value with the METHOD attribute.

INPUT   **Type:** Inline/Empty   **Content:** N/A

Defines various input controls that can be included in forms, including text boxes, radio buttons, check boxes, and more.

Attributes
```
type="text|password|checkbox|radio|submit
      |reset|file|hidden|image|button"             See Note
name="control name"                                See Note
value="initial value"                              See Note
```

```
              size="n"                                              See Note
              maxlength="n"                                         See Note
              checked                                               See Note
              src="URL"                                             See Note
```

Note: The TYPE attribute is optional when creating text boxes, but required when creating other input controls. When submitted, values input by the user are associated with the NAME attribute value. The VALUE attribute is required for check boxes and radio buttons, but optional otherwise. The SIZE and MAXLENGTH attribute number specifies the width in character spaces for text box and password input controls, but in pixels for other input controls. The CHECKED attribute is recognized only for radio button and check box controls. The SRC attribute, specifying the location of an image, is required only when creating an image input control.

Example

```
<form action="http://www.mysite.com/cgi-bin/sendform.pl"
method="post">
<p><input type="hidden" name="recipient" value="bonzo@bedtime.com">
First Name/Initial: <input type="text" name="FirstName"
size="30"><br>
Last Name: <input type="text" name="LastName" size="30"><br>
Gender: <input type="radio" name="Sex" value="Male"> <input
type="radio" name="Sex" value="Female">
Allergies: <input type="checkbox" name="Allergies" value="Food">
<input type="checkbox" name="Allergies" value="Pets"> <input
type="checkbox" name="Allergies" value="Trees/Plants"> <input
type="checkbox" name="Allergies" value="Molds/Fungi"> <input
type="checkbox" name="Allergies" value="Chemicals"><p>
<p><input type="submit" value="Submit"> <input type="reset"
value="Reset"></p>
</form>
```

SELECT   **Type:** Inline/Container   **Content:** OPTGROUP/OPTION

Creates a list menu, in combination with the OPTION element and, optionally, the OPTGROUP element.

Attributes
```
          name="control name"                                 Optional
          size="n"                                            Optional
          multiple                                            Optional
          disabled                                            Optional
```

Note: The SIZE attribute value specifies the number of visible rows (options) that will be displayed; the default value is **1**. MULTIPLE allows the selection of multiple options.

OPTION (Required in SELECT)   **Type:** Inline/Container   **Content:** Inline

Specifies an option in a list menu (required in the SELECT option). The end tag is optional.

Attributes
```
          selected                                            Optional
          value="initial value"                               Optional
          label="option label" (4.0)                          Optional
```

Note: The VALUE attribute specifies the initial value for an option; otherwise, the option value defaults to the OPTION element's content. The LABEL attribute is supposed to specify a label for an option, but this attribute is not widely supported; otherwise, the option label defaults to the OPTION element's content.

Example
```
<select name="menu">
<option selected>Eenie</option>
<option>Meenie</option>
<option>Minie</option>
<option>Moe</option>
</select>
```

TEXTAREA   **Type:** Inline/Container   **Content:** Text

Creates a multi-line text input box.

Attributes

name="*control name*"	Optional
rows="*n*"	Required
cols="*n*"	Required
disabled	Optional
readonly	Optional

Note: Browsers should display text nested within the element, if there is any, as its initial value.

Example
```
<textarea name="comment" rows="20" cols="80">
Type your comment here.
</textarea>
```

OPTGROUP (4.0) (Optional in SELECT)   **Type:** Inline/Container   **Content:** Inline

Specifies a group of options to be displayed in a list menu.

Attributes

label="*option group label*"	Required
disabled	Optional

Example
```
<select name="Foods" size="13" multiple>
<optgroup label="Breakfast">
    <option value="cereal">Cold Cereal w/Milk</option>
    <option value="bacon">Bacon and Eggs</option>
    <option value="fruit">Fresh Fruit</option>
</optgroup>
<optgroup label="Lunch">
    <option value="bologna">Bologna w/Cheese Sandwich</option>
    <option value="soup">Soup w/Salad</option>
    <option value="peanut">Peanut Butter Sandwich</option>
</optgroup>
<optgroup label="Dinner">
    <option value="steak">Steak w/Potatoes</option>
    <option value="fish">Broiled Fish w/Rice</option>
    <option value="chicken">Fried Chicken w/Fries</option>
    <option value="vegetable">Vegetable Tempura</option>
</optgroup>
</select>
```

BUTTON (4.0)   **Type:** Inline/Container   **Content:** Inline

This alternative to using the INPUT element to create Submit and Reset buttons has richer rendering possibilities. Also can be used to create push buttons that trigger scripts.

Attributes

type="**submit**|reset|button"	Optional
name="*control-name*"	Optional

```
               value="initial value"                               Optional
               tabindex="n"                                         Optional
               accesskey="character"                                Optional
               disabled                                             Optional
```

Note: The button label is provided by the text nested inside the BUTTON element; if an image is nested inside the BUTTON element, it is displayed as the button.

Example
```
<p><button type="submit" name="submit" value="submit">
  <font size="5" color="red">Submit</font></button>  
<button name="reset" type="reset">
  <font size="5" color="purple">Reset</font></button></p>
```

LABEL (4.0)   **Type:** Inline/Container   **Content:** Inline

Associates a label with a form control.

Attributes   for="control ID"   Optional

Note: Although visual browsers do nothing with the LABEL element, its use can help non-visual browsers and screen readers identify the purpose and function of a form control. This can be especially useful when using a table to lay out form controls in which the text identifying the control's purpose and function is located in a separate table cell. The FOR value references the ID value of the associated form control.

Example
```
<tr>
<th><label for="fname">First Name/Initial:</label></th>
<td><input name="first" id="fname"></td>
</tr>
```

FIELDSET (4.0)   **Type:** Block/Container   **Content:** Inline/Block

In conjunction with the LEGEND element, specifies a set of thematically related form controls and labels.

LEGEND (4.0)   **Type:** Container   **Content:** Inline

In conjunction with the FIELDSET element, provides a legend for a set of thematically related form controls.

Example
```
<fieldset>
<legend>Academic Interests</legend>
<input type="checkbox" name="Interest" value="arts"> Arts
<input type="checkbox" name="Interest" value="science"> Science
<input type="checkbox" name="Interest" value="business"> Business
</fieldset>
```

FRAME (4.0)

See FRAMESET.

BASE | Type: Empty | Content: N/A

Specifies the absolute URL for the document that acts as a base for resolving relative URLs.

| *Attributes* | href="*URL*" | Required |

Example
```
<head><title>John Peters' Political Science Site</title>
<base href="http://www.somewhere.com/peters/polysci/index.html">
</head>
<body>
<p align="center">Visit John Peter's <a href="../index.html">Home
Page</a></p>
<hr>
```

Note: Because of the BASE URL, the relative URL in the BODY element correlates to an absolute URL of http://www.somewhere.com/peters/index.html.

ISINDEX (Deprecated) | Type: Empty | Content: N/A

Creates a one-line text-input control. The W3C recommends that Web authors use the INPUT element to create text-input controls.

| *Attributes* | prompt="*prompt string*" | Optional |

LINK | Type: Empty | Content: N/A

Defines a link in the HEAD element. A primary use for the LINK element is to link to external style sheets.

Attributes	type="*content-type*"	Optional
	rel="*link-type*"	Optional
	rev="*link-type*"	Optional
	href="*URL*"	Optional
	media="*media-descriptor*" (4.0)	Optional

Note: REL and REV can be used in combination with HREF to specify forward and reverse links. TYPE can be used in combination with HREF to specify a link to an external style sheet (**type="text/css"**). When linking to an external style sheet, MEDIA can be used to target a linked style sheet for a particular media. Because Netscape Navigator 4 ignores any LINK element with a MEDIA attribute other than **screen** set, the LINK element's MEDIA attribute can be used to block Netscape 4 users from accessing an external style sheet. Current allowable values for MEDIA include screen (the default), all, print, projection, handheld, tv, tty, aural, braille, and embossed.

Example
```
<head><title>Peter Locke's Political Science Site</title>
<link href="mystyles.css" rel="stylesheet" type="text/css"
media="all">
```

META | Type: Empty | Content: N/A

Specifies meta-information about the document.

Attributes	name="*meta-data identifier*"	See Note
	http-equiv="refresh"	See Note
	content="*meta-data data*"	Required

Note: Either NAME or HTTP-EQUIV is required.

Example
```
<head><title>John Peters' Political Science Site</title>
<meta name="description" content="Opinions and discussion of
political science, including the theory of representative government,
political constitutions, popular sovereignty, and other topics.">
<meta name="keywords" content="political science, polysci, politics,
constitution, civil rights, free speech, bill of rights, inalienable
rights, liberty">
</head>
```

or

```
<meta http-equiv="refresh"
content="3;url="http://www.somewhere.com/peters/polysci/index.html">
```

STYLE (3.2)   **Type:** Container   **Content:** Style Codes

Embeds a style sheet in the document's HEAD element. Multiple STYLE elements can be embedded.

Attributes
`type="content-type"` (4.0)	Required
`media="media-descriptor"` (4.0)	Optional

Note: Only CSS style sheets can be used with HTML documents, so **`type="text/css"`** is always set for the STYLE element in HTML documents. In XHTML, however, other style sheet languages can be used, such as XSL, for instance. The MEDIA attribute allows the creation of style sheets that target specific media; current allowable values include **screen** (the default), **all**, **print**, **projection**, **handheld**, **tv**, **tty**, **aural**, **braille**, and **embossed**. This allows the embedding of a style sheet that will only be used when printing the document. Because only recent browsers support the MEDIA attribute, STYLE elements with a MEDIA attribute value other than **all** should precede any other STYLE elements in the HEAD element. Similar to the SCRIPT element, comment codes (`<!--` and `-->`) can be used to shield the content of the STYLE element from browsers that do not support it; style-aware browsers will ignore the comment codes.

Example
```
<head><title>Peter Locke's Political Science Site</title>
<style type="text/css">
<!--
h1, h2, h3 { color: blue; background: transparent; }
p { font-family: Arial, Helvetica, sans-serif; }
-->
</style>
```

HR (Horizontal Rule)   **Type:** Block/Empty   **Content:** N/A

Draws a horizontal rule across the page.

Attributes
`size="n"` (Deprecated)	Optional
`width="n|n%"` (Deprecated)	Optional
`align="left|center|right"` (Deprecated)	Optional
`noshade`	Optional

Note: SIZE specifies the height of the rule in pixels. ALIGN horizontally aligns the rule within the browser window, if WIDTH is set to a value of less than **100%** or a pixel-width is set that is less than the width of the browser window. NOSHADE turns off the 3-D shading for rules that is otherwise generally displayed by browsers.

Example	`<hr size="5" width="75%" align="center" noshade>`

HTML
Type: Container   **Content:** HEAD elements, BODY, FRAMESET

The top-level element in an HTML document. HTML 4.01 requires that a DocType declaration specifying the document's HTML conformance be inserted above the HTML element.

Example
```
<!DOCTYPE HTML PUBLIC "-//W3C//DTD HTML 4.01 Transitional//EN"
 "http://www.w3.org/TR/html4/loose.dtd">
<html>
All other elements in the document are nested here.
</html>
```

I (Italic)
Type: Inline/Container   **Content:** Inline

Causes nested text to be displayed in italics.

Example
```
<p>One of my favorite books is <i>The Brothers Karamazov</i> by
Fyodor Dostoevsky.</p>
```

IFRAME (Inline Frame) (4.0)
Type: Inline/Container   **Content:** Inline

Creates an inline windowed frame within a Web page.

Attributes		
`src="URL"`	Required
`width="n"`	Optional
`height="n"`	Optional
`align="bottom|middle|top|left|right"`	Optional
`name="frame name"`	Optional
`marginheight="n"`	Optional
`marginwidth="n"`	Optional
`scrolling="auto|yes|no"`	Optional
`frameborder="1	0"`	Optional
`longdesc="URL"`	Optional

Note: Netscape 4 does not support inline frames. Content can be included in the IFRAME element to alert users of browsers that do not recognize the IFRAME element. NAME allows the targeting of an inline frame by a link using the TARGET attribute. The **left** and **right** values for the ALIGN attribute float the inline frame at the left or right margins, with following text flowing around the other side of the inline frame.

Example
```
<p><iframe src="insert.html" align="top" width="200" height="100">
[Note: This page uses inline frames, which is a feature not
supported by your browser. To find out how to upgrade to a browser
that supports current Web standards, see the <a
href="http://www.webstandards.org/upgrade/">Web Standard Project's
Browser Upgrade Campaign</a>.]
</iframe></p>
```

IMG (Image)
Type: Inline/Empty   **Content:** N/A

Inserts an image inline within a Web page.

Attributes	src="*URL*"	Required
	alt="*alternate text*"	Required
	height="*n*	*n%*"	Recommended
	width="*n*	*n%*"	Recommended
	align="**bottom**|middle|top|left|right"	
	(3.2) Deprecated	Optional
	hspace="*n*" (3.2) Deprecated	Optional
	vspace="*n*" (3.2) Deprecated	Optional
	name="*image name*"	Optional
	usemap="*#mapname*	*URL*"	Optional
	border="1|0"	Optional

Note: ALIGN with **left** or **right** set floats the image on the left or right margin with following text or elements flowing around the other side of the image. VSPACE and HSPACE are used with floating images to add vertical horizontal spacing outside the image. NAME allows the image to be targeted by a script. USEMAP links the image with the name of a client-side image map and is only used in conjunction with a fragment identifier that points to the NAME attribute of a MAP element or the URL of an external HTML file containing the associated MAP element. BORDER can turn the image border off (**border="0"**) when the image is an image link (nested inside the A element).

Example   `<p align="center"><img src="mybanner.jpg" alt="Banner image" height="125" width="175"></p>`

INPUT

See FORM.

INS (Insert) (4.0)   **Type:** Inline/Container   **Content:** Inline

Marks nested text as an insertion. In browsers that support this element, nested text is generally displayed as underlined. INS can be used in combination with DEL (Delete) to display insertions and deletions in an HTML document. *See also* DEL (Delete).

| *Attributes* | cite="*URL*" | Optional |

Note: CITE can link to an HTML file providing details about why the document was revised, who revised it, when it was revised, and so on. No browser currently supports CITE.

Example   `<h1><del>My </del><ins>Most </ins>Frequently Asked Questions Page</h1>`

ISINDEX

See HEAD.

KBD (Keyboard)   **Type:** Inline/Container   **Content:** Inline

Can be used to indicate keyboard input. Text nested in the KBD element is generally displayed in a monospaced font. To distinguish KBD from the other monospaced text elements, it can be nested inside of (or bracket) a B (Bold) element.

Example   `<p>At the prompt, key <b><kbd>newuser</kbd></b> and press the Enter key.</p>`

LABEL (4.0)

See FORM.

LEGEND (4.0)

See FORM.

LI (List Item)

See OL (Ordered List) *or* UL (Unordered List).

LINK

See HEAD.

MAP (Client-Side Image Map) (3.2)   **Type:** Inline/Container   **Content:** Block/AREA

In conjunction with the AREA element, defines a client-side image map.

Attributes   `name="mapname"`   Required

Note: In NAME, *mapname* must match (including uppercase and lowercase letters) the pointer included in the USEMAP attribute (**usemap="#mapname"**) of the IMG element being used for the image map.

AREA (3.2)   **Type:** Inline/Empty   **Content:** N/A

Defines an area within a client-side image map that functions as a hotspot link.

Attributes   `shape="`**rect**`|circle|poly|default"`   Optional
                 `coords="coordinates"`   Optional
                 `href="URL"`   Optional
                 `nohref`   Optional
                 `alt="alternative text"`   Required

Example
```
<p align="center"><img src="mymap.jpg" height="135" width="450"
alt="Image Map: Navigation Menu" usemap="#mymap" border="0"></p>
<map name="mymap">
<area shape="rect" alt="Previous" coords="15,15,145,120"
href="page1.htm">
<area shape="rect" alt="Contents" coords="160,15,290,120"
href="toc.htm">
<area shape="rect" alt="Next" coords="305,15,435,120"
href="page3.htm">
<area shape="default" nohref>
</map>
```

MENU (Deprecated)

Type: Block/Container   **Content:** Block

Originally intended for specifying a single-column menu, in contrast to the DIR element, originally intended for specifying a multi-column menu. Browsers treat MENU and DIR elements exactly like UL (Unordered List) elements and the W3C recommends that Web authors use UL instead.

META (Meta Data)

See HEAD.

NOFRAMES (4.0)

See FRAMESET.

NOSCRIPT (4.0)

See SCRIPT.

OBJECT (4.0)

Type: Inline/Container   **Content:** Block/Inline

Generic mechanism for inserting inline objects into a Web page. Optionally used in conjunction with the PARAM (Parameter) element.

Attributes		
	`classid="URL"`	Optional
	`codebase="URL"`	Optional
	`codetype="content-type"`	Optional
	`data="URL"`	Optional
	`type="content-type"`	Optional
	`standby="standby message"`	Optional
	`id="objectname"`	Optional

PARAM (Parameter) (4.0)

Type: Empty   **Content:** N/A

Sets initial parameters for an object displayed by the OBJECT element.

Attributes		
	`name="parameter name"`	Required
	`value="parameter value"`	Optional
	`valuetype="`**data**`|ref|object"`	Optional
	`type="content-type"`	Optional

Note: NAME's value and case-sensitivity depends on the specific object implementation. VALUE is the value of the run-time parameter specified by NAME; the actual value is determined by the object implementation. VALUETYPE specifies the type of value being passed by the VALUE attribute; if **data**, the value is passed as a string; if **ref**, the value is passed as a URL; and if **object**, the value is passed as the ID value of the object.

Example

```
<object data="intro.wav" type="audio/wav" width="200" height="45"
vspace="5">
<param name="src" value="intro.wav">
<param name="autostart" value="true">
<param name="controller" value="true">
```

```
            <param name="loop" value="false">
            Audio introduction to site.
            </object>
```

OL (Ordered List)   **Type:** Block/Container   **Content:** Block

Creates an ordered (or numbered) list.

Attributes   type="**1**|a|A|i|I"   Optional
                start="*n*"   Optional
                compact (Deprecated)   Optional

Note: TYPE specifies the numbering system, whether Arabic (**1**), lowercase alphabetic (**a**), uppercase alphabetic (**A**), lowercase Roman (**i**), or uppercase Roman (**I**). START can specify a starting number other than **1**.

LI (with OL)   **Type:** Block/Container   **Content:** Inline/Block

Specifies a list item, within an OL element in this case. The end tag for LI is optional. See also *UL (Unordered List)*.

Attributes   type="**1**|a|A|i|I"   Optional
                value="*n*"   Optional

Note: VALUE specifies a value for the current list item. For instance, if **A** is the value of the TYPE attribute, **value="4"** corresponds to a value of D.

Example   ```
                <ol type="A">
                <li>Breakfast
                <li>Lunch
                <li>Dinner
                </ol>
                ```

## OPTGROUP (Option Group) (4.0)

*See* FORM.

## OPTION

*See* FORM.

## P (Paragraph)                                   **Type:** Block/Container    **Content:** Inline

Indicates that nested text is a paragraph. The end tag is officially optional, but should be included to avoid problems that can arise otherwise.

*Attributes*    align="left|center|right|justify" (3.2) (Deprecated) Optional

*Example*       `<p>Welcome to my home page!</p>`

## PARAM (Parameter) (3.2/4.0)

*See* APPLET *and* OBJECT.
                ```

PRE (Preformatted Text)　　　　**Type:** Block/Container　　**Content:** Inline

Specifies that nested text be treated as preformatted text, with all included spaces and hard returns displayed by the browser. Inline elements that cannot be nested in a PRE element include IMG, OBJECT, BIG, SMALL, SUB, and SUP. Text in a PRE element is generally rendered in a monospaced font.

Attributes　　`width="n"` (Deprecated)　　　　　　　　　　　　`Optional`

Example
```
<pre>
                QTR 1      QTR 2      QTR 3      QTR 4      Score
Madison State     7          14         0          3          24
Concord Tech      0          7          14         7          28
</pre>
```

Q (Quote) (4.0)　　　　**Type:** Inline/Container　　**Content:** Inline

Marks nested text as an inline quotation. Browsers that support the Q element should automatically render quotation marks delimiting the quotation. Because few browsers support the Q element (Mozilla 1 does, but Internet Explorer 6, does not) and quotations marked by the Q element do not degrade gracefully in browsers that do not support the Q element (because no quotation marks at all are displayed), the Q element probably should be avoided.

Attributes　　`cite="URL"`　　　　　　　　　　　　`Optional`
　　　　　　　　`lang="language-code"`　　　　　　`Optional`
　　　　　　　　`dir="LTR|RTL"`　　　　　　　　　　`Optional`

Note: CITE references the URL of the source of the quote. LANG specifies the language of the quotation (`lang="fr"`, if the language of the quotation is French, for instance).

S (Strike) (4.0) (Deprecated)　　　　**Type:** Inline/Container　　**Content:** Inline

Marks nested text as strikeout text, displayed with a line drawn through it. Previously proposed as part of the HTML 3.0 proposal, S (Strike) was included in HTML 4.0, but deprecated at the same time. STRIKE is more universally supported by earlier browsers and should probably be used instead.

SAMP (Sample Code)　　　　**Type:** Inline/Container　　**Content:** Inline

Marks nested text as sample code. All browsers display SAMP text in a monospaced font. The TT (Teletype Text) element can be used instead to achieve the same result.

SCRIPT (3.2)　　　　**Type:** Container　　**Content:** Script Code

Allows inclusion or linking of client-side scripts. The SCRIPT element can be inserted in either the HEAD or the BODY element.

Attribute
　　　　　`type="content type"`　　　　　　　　　　`Required`
　　　　　`language="script language"` (Deprecated)　`Optional`
　　　　　`src="URL"`　　　　　　　　　　　　　　　`Optional`

Note: TYPE identifies the MIME type of the scripting language (**text/javascript**, for instance). LANGUAGE is deprecated because it references non-standard script language identifiers. Some older browsers, however, recognize LANGUAGE, but not TYPE, in the SCRIPT element, so good practice dictates including both. Comment codes, `<!--` and `//-->`, can be used to shield browsers that are not script aware from displaying the content of the SCRIPT element. Script-aware browsers ignore the comment codes.

Example
```
<script type="text/javascript" src="mainscript.js"></script>
```
or
```
<script type="text/javascript" language="JavaScript">
<!-- start hiding script
function HiThere() {
    ident = window.prompt("Enter your name: ", "");
    alert ("Welcome to my page, "+ident+"!");
}
// end hiding script -->
</script>
```

NOSCRIPT (4.0)   Type: Container   Content: Block

Specifies content to be displayed in a browser that does not support the specified script language or is not script-aware. A script-aware browser ignores the content of the NOSCRIPT element, while a script-unaware browser displays the content of the NOSCRIPT element.

Example
```
<body>
<noscript>
<p>This page includes JavaScript scripts. Please go to the <a
href="no-js.html">non-JavaScript version</a> of this page.</p>
</noscript>
```

SELECT

See FORM.

SMALL (3.2)   Type: Inline/Container   Content: Inline

Marks text for display in a smaller font. Text is displayed in a font size that is one size smaller than the default font size, based on the seven font sizes specified by the FONT and BASEFONT elements' SIZE attribute. Nesting SMALL elements, although legal, is not recommended, because it can result in an illegible font size in some Macintosh browsers, for instance.

Example
```
<h1><big>M</big><small>y</small> <big>H</big><small>ome</small>
<big>P</big><small>age</small></h1>
```

SPAN (4.0)   Type: Inline/Container   Content: Inline

Marks a span of text, to which formatting using styles can be applied. By itself, the SPAN element has no formatting.

Example
```
<p>Registration for <span style="font-family: Arial; color: maroon;
background: transparent">Winter Quarter</span> classes will begin
on January 5.</p>
```

STRIKE (Strikeout) (3.2) (Deprecated)
Type: Inline/Container   **Content:** Inline

Marks nested text as strikeout text, displayed with a line drawn through it. STRIKE is more universally supported than either the S (Strike) or the DEL (Delete) element and should probably be used instead.

Example
```
<p>Text to be deleted is marked as <strike>strikeout</strike>.</p>
```

STRONG (Strong Emphasis)
Type: Inline/Container   **Content:** Inline

Marks nested text as strongly emphasized. Browsers display STRONG text identically to B (Bold) text. Either can be used.

Example
```
<p><strong>Note:</strong> When creating Web sites, the unexpected
is to be expected.</p>
```

STYLE (3.2)

See HEAD.

SUB (Subscript) (3.2)
Type: Inline/Container   **Content:** Inline

Marks nested text as subscripted. To allow for earlier browsers that do not support SUB, subscripted text can be enclosed inside parentheses. *See also* SUP (Superscript).

SUP (Superscript) (3.2)
Type: Inline/Container   **Content:** Inline

Marks nested text as superscripted. To allow for earlier browsers that do not support SUP, superscripted text can be enclosed inside parentheses. *See also* SUB (Subscript).

Example
```
<p>Eat Crumpies<sup>(tm)</sup>, the greatest thing since
H<sub>(2)</sub>O!</p>
```

TABLE (3.2)
Type: Block/Container   **Content:** Table Elements

Specifies that nested code is a table (arranged in columns and rows).

Attributes

`width="`*n*`|`*n%*`"`	Optional
`border="`*n*`"`	Optional
`cellpadding="`*n*`"`	Optional
`cellspacing="`*n*`"`	Optional
`align="left|center|right"`	Optional
`bgcolor="`*color name*`|`*RGB color code*`"`	Optional
`frame="void|above|below|hsides|`	
`      lhs|rhs|vsides|box|border"` (4.0)	Optional
`rules="none|groups|rows|cols|all"` (4.0)	Optional

Note: The ALIGN values of **left** and **right** have the effect of floating the table to the left or right margin and flowing following text or elements around the other side of the table. Current browsers also support the BACKGROUND attribute for specifying a background image for a table, but it is not a standard attribute, primarily due to differences in how it is implemented in browsers.

CAPTION (Table Caption)   **Type:** Block/Container   **Content:** Inline

Marks nested text as a table caption.

Attributes   `align="top|bottom|left|right"` (Deprecated)   Optional

Note: A **top** value centers the caption above the table. A **bottom** value for ALIGN causes the caption to be displayed below the table. Values of **left** and **right** left-aligns or right-aligns the caption (in the caption space) above the table.

TR (Table Row) (3.2)   **Type:** Container   **Content:** TH/TD

Delineates a row of cells in a table. The end tag is officially optional in HTML 4.01, but leaving it off might cause problems in earlier browsers.

Attributes   `align="left|center|right|justify"`   Optional
     `valign="top|middle|bottom|baseline"`   Optional

TH (Table Heading) and TD (Table Data) (3.2)   **Type:** Container   **Content:** Block/Inline

Designates a table heading (TH) or table data (TD) cell. TH content is centered and bolded, whereas TD content is left-aligned and displayed in a regular font. The end tag for TH and TD is officially optional in HTML 4.01, but leaving it off might cause problems in earlier browsers.

Attributes   `align="left|center|right|justify"`   Optional
     `valign="top|middle|bottom|baseline"`   Optional
     `colspan="n"`   Optional
     `rowspan="n"`   Optional
     `width="n|n%"` (Deprecated)   Optional
     `height="n|n%"` (Deprecated)   Optional
     `nowrap` (Deprecated)   Optional

THEAD (Table Head), TBODY (Table Body), and TFOOT (Table Foot) (4.0)   **Type:** Container   **Content:** TR

Designates the head, body, and foot sections (or row groups) in a table. These elements have no formatting, by themselves, but can have styles applied to them to control their presentation. If not present, the whole table defaults to displaying styles set for TBODY (in HTML 4, but not XHTML 1). The end tags for THEAD, TBODY, and TFOOT are optional.

Attributes   `align="left|center|right|justify"`   Optional
     `valign="top|middle|bottom|baseline"`   Optional

Example
```
<style type="text/css">
<!--
thead tr.border th { border-bottom: 1px solid black; }
tbody tr.border th, tbody tr.border td { border-bottom: 3px double
black; }
tfoot th, tfoot td { color: red; background: transparent; }
-->
</style>
</head>
<body>
<table align="center" width="450" cellspacing="0">
<thead>
<tr><th></th><th colspan="3">Semi-Annual Sales Report</th></tr>
```

```
<tr class="border" align="right"><th>Salesperson</th><th>1st
Qtr</th><th>2nd Qtr</th><th>Totals</th></tr>
</thead>
<tbody>
<tr align="right"><th>Brady</th><td>$   525,000</td>
<td>$   365,000</td><td>$   890,000
</td></tr>
<tr align="right"><th>Crawford</th><td>400,000</td><td>500,000</td>
<td>900,000</td></tr>
<tr class="border" align="right"><th>Peters</th><td>250,000</td>
<td>400,000</td><td>650,000</td></tr>
</tbody>
<tfoot>
<tr align="right"><th>Totals</th><td>$1,175,000</td><td>$1,265,000
</td><td>$2,440,000</td></tr>
</tfoot>
</table>
```

COLGROUP (Column Group) (4.0)　　　**Type:** Container　　　**Content:** COL

Designates a group of columns (specified by the COL element). The end tag is optional.

COL (Column) (4.0)　　　**Type:** Empty　　　**Content:** N/A

Example

```
<table width="75%" align="center" border="1">
<colgroup id="colg1">
  <col id="col1">
</colgroup>
<colgroup id="colg2">
  <col id="col2">
  <col id="col3">
  <col id="col4">
</colgroup>
<colgroup id="colg3">
  <col id="col5">
  <col id="col6">
  <col id="col7">
</colgroup>
```

TEXTAREA

See FORM.

TFOOT (Table Foot) (4.0)

See TABLE.

TH (Table Heading) and TD (Table Data)

See TABLE.

THEAD (Table Head) (4.0)

See TABLE.

TITLE

See HEAD.

TR (Table Row)

See TABLE.

TT (Teletype Text/Typewriter Text)   **Type:** Inline/Container   **Content:** Inline

Marks nested text to be displayed in a monospaced font.

Example   `<p>The message, <tt>Wait while downloading</tt>, is displayed.</p>`

U (Underline) (3.2)   **Type:** Inline/Container   **Content:** Inline

Marks nested text to be displayed as underlined.

Example   `<p>The commissary will be <u>closed</u> on Friday.</p>`

UL (Unordered List)   **Type:** Block/Container   **Content:** Block

Creates an unordered (or bulleted) list.

Attributes	`type="disc	circle	square"`	Optional
	`start="n"`	Optional
	`compact` (Deprecated)	Optional

Note: TYPE specifies the numbering system, whether Arabic (1), lowercase alphabetic (a), uppercase alphabetic (A), lowercase Roman (i), or uppercase Roman (I). START can specify a starting number other than 1.

LI (with OL)   **Type:** Block/Container   **Content:** Inline/Block

Specifies a list item, within an OL element in this case. The end tag for LI is optional. See also *UL (Unordered List)*.

| *Attributes* | `type="1|a|A|i|I"` | Optional |
| | `value="n"` | Optional |

Note: VALUE specifies a value for the current list item. For instance, if **A** is the value of the TYPE attribute, **value="4"** corresponds to a value of D.

Example
```
<ol type="A">
<li>Breakfast
<li>Lunch
<li>Dinner
</ol>
```

VAR (Variable)

Type: Inline/Container   **Content:** Inline

Marks nested text as a variable. The VAR element is generally displayed in italics. Alternatively, the I (Italic) and EM (Emphasis) elements can be used to achieve the same effect.

Example
```
<p>The <var>count</var> variable is incremented by one each time
the loop is executed.</p>
```

GENERIC AND OTHER ATTRIBUTES

Core Attributes

```
id="unique ID"
class="class name"
style="style properties"
```

Language Attributes (i18n)

```
lang="language code"
dir="ltr|rtl"
```

Event Handler Attributes

```
onBlur="script" (See Note 1)
onChange="script" (INPUT, SELECT, and TEXTAREA)
onClick="script" (See Note 2)
onDblClick="script" (See Note 2)
onFocus="script" (See Note 1)
onLoad="script" (BODY, FRAMESET)
onKeyDown="script" (See Note 2)
onKeyPress="script" (See Note 2)
onKeyUp="script" (See Note 2)
onMouseDown="script" (See Note 2)
onMouseUp="script" (See Note 2)
onMouseOver="script" (See Note 2)
onMouseMove="script" (See Note 2)
onMouseOut="script" (See Note 2)
onReset="script" (FORM)
onSelect="script" (INPUT, TEXTAREA)
onSubmit="script" (FORM)
onUnload="script" (BODY, FRAMESET)
```

Note 1: A, AREA, BUTTON, INPUT, LABEL, SELECT, and TEXTAREA.
Note 2: All elements, except for APPLET, BASE, BASEFONT, BDO, BR, FONT, FRAME, FRAMESET, HEAD, HTML, IFRAME, ISINDEX, META, PARAM, SCRIPT, STYLE, or TITLE.

accesskey="*character*" (A, AREA, BUTTON, INPUT, LABEL, LEGEND, and TEXTAREA)

align="**top**|bottom|left|right" (CAPTION) (Deprecated)

align="top|middle|bottom|left|right" (APPLET, FRAME, IMG, INPUT, and OBJECT)
          (Deprecated)

align="**left**|center|right|justify" (DIV, H1, H2, H3, H4, H5, H6, and P)
          (Deprecated)

align="left|center|right|justify|char" (COL, COLGROUP, TBODY, TH, THEAD, and
          TR) (Not Deprecated)

bgcolor="*color name*|*RGB color code*" (BODY, TABLE, TR, TD, and TH) (Deprecated)

border="*n*" (IMG, OBJECT, and TABLE)

charset="*character set*" (A, LINK, and SCRIPT)

class="*class name*" (All, except for BASE, BASEFONT, HEAD, HTML, META, PARAM,
          SCRIPT, STYLE, and TITLE)

dir="ltr|rtl" (All, except for APPLET, BASE, BASEFONT, BDO, BR, FRAME,
          FRAMESET, IFRAME, PARAM, and SCRIPT)

id="*unique ID*" (All, except for BASE, HEAD, HTML, META, SCRIPT, STYLE, and
          TITLE)

lang="*language code*" (All, except for APPLET, BASE, BASEFONT, BDO, BR, FRAME,
          FRAMESET, IFRAME, PARAM, and SCRIPT)

style="*style properties*" (All, except for BASE, BASEFONT, HEAD, HTML, META,
          PARAM, SCRIPT, STYLE, and TITLE)

tabindex="*n*" (A, AREA, BUTTON, INPUT, OBJECT, SELECT, and TEXTAREA)

target="*frame name*" (A, AREA, BASE, FORM, and LINK)

title="*title*" (All, except for BASE, BASEFONT, HEAD, HTML, META, PARAM,
          SCRIPT, and TITLE)

valign="top|middle|bottom|baseline" (COL, COLGROUP, TBODY, TD, TFOOT, TH,
          THEAD, and TR)

APPENDIX

B

Special Characters Chart

Because HTML documents are ASCII text documents, the number of characters that should be inserted directly from the keyboard is limited to the 128 ASCII characters. The ISO 8859-1 character set defines an additional 128 characters.

ASCII (KEYBOARD) CHARACTERS

The ASCII character set has 128 (0 through 127) positions. Positions 0 through 31 in the ASCII character set are control characters (Backspace, Tab, Cancel, and so on) that do not result in a displayable character. Positions 32 to 126 are characters that can be entered directly from the standard ASCII keyboard. Position 127 is a control character (Delete). The displayable ASCII characters run from position 32 to 126. These constitute the only characters that should be directly entered from the keyboard into an HTML document.

Keyboards for some Macintosh computers marketed in the United Kingdom substitute the British pound currency symbol (£) for the number sign (#). On those computers, press Option+3 (or Alt+3) to insert the number sign (#).

NOTE

For links to resources showing where you can learn more about the ASCII character set, as well as charts showing all of the characters that are included in the ASCII character set, see the Appendixes' section at the IRC for this book at **www.emcp.com**/.

RESERVED CHARACTERS

A number of characters are used to indicate HTML codes and, depending on the circumstance, might need to be inserted into an HTML document using their entity number or entity name.

Character	Entity Number	Entity Name	Description
"	&#034;	&quot;	quotation mark
&	&#038;	&amp;	ampersand
<	&#060;	&lt;	less-than sign
>	&#062;	&gt;	greater-than sign

When displaying a < or > character in a Web page, always insert the character using either its entity number or entity name. Generally, standalone " and & characters do not need a substitute, unless they are part of an HTML code that you want to display, as is, in a Web page.

EXTENDED CHARACTERS (UNUSED)

Positions 128 through 159 reference extended characters that are in addition to the ASCII character set. Which characters in these positions are actually available depends upon the computer system and default character set being used. In the ISO 8859-1 character set, which is the standard character set for displaying Western European languages on the Web, the positions 128 through 159 are referenced as "unused" (or not to be used in Web pages). A number of browsers on the UNIX platform ignore entity numbers for all characters within this range. The following table shows the extended Latin-1 (ISO-8859-1) character set that is used in Microsoft Windows.

Character	Entity Number	Entity Name	Description
	&#128;		unused
	&#129;		unused
‚	&#130;		single quote (low)
ƒ	&#131;	&fnof;	function of, florin
„	&#132;		double quote (low)
…	&#133;	&hellip;	horizontal ellipsis
†	&#134;	&dagger;	dagger sign
‡	&#135;	&Dagger;	double dagger sign
ˆ	&#136;		small circumflex accent
‰	&#137;	&permil;	per thousand (mille) sign
š	&#138;	&Scaron;	S-caron[*]
‹	&#139;	&lsaquo;	left single quillemet
Œ	&#140;	&OElig;	capital OE ligature
	&#141;		unused
	&#142;		unused
	&#143;		unused
	&#144;		unused
'	&#145;	&lsquo;	left single quote
'	&#146;	&rsquo;	right single quote
"	&#147;	&ldquo;	left double quote
"	&#148;	&rdquo;	right double quote
•	&#149;	&bull;	round filled bullet
–	&#150;	&ndash;	en dash
—	&#151;	&mdash;	em dash
~	&#152;	&tilde;	small tilde
™	&#153;	&trade;	trademark
š	&#154;	&scaron;	s-caron[*]
›	&#155;	&rsaquo;	right single guillemet
œ	&#156;	&oelig;	small oe ligature

[*] S-caron and s-caron characters are not available in the Macintosh's default character set.

Character	Entity Number	Entity Name	Description
	&#157;		unused
	&#158;		unused
Ÿ	&#159;	&Yuml;	Y-umlaut

SPECIAL CHARACTERS (ISO 8859-1)

The positions 160 through 255 include characters from the ISO 8859-1 (or Latin-1) character set that can be displayed in Web pages. Most of these characters are supported by most browsers.

Versions of Netscape Navigator prior to version 4 only support using the entity names for the non-breakable space, copyright, registered trademark, and the accented characters (A-gravé, c-cedilla, and so on).

Character	Entity Number	Entity Name	Description
[ ]			non-breakable space (brackets added)
¡	&#161;	&iexcl;	inverted exclamation
¢	&#162;	&cent;	cent sign
£	&#163;	&pound;	British pound sign
¤	&#164;	&curren;	currency sign
¥	&#165;	&yen;	Japanese yen sign
¦	&#166;	&brvbar;	broken vertical bar*
§	&#167;	&sect;	section sign
¨	&#168;	&uml;	umlaut
©	&#169;	&copy;	copyright symbol
ª	&#170;	&ordf;	feminine ordinal
«	&#171;	&laquo;	left double guillemet
¬	&#172;	&not;	logical not sign
-	&#173;	&shy;	soft hyphen
®	&#174;	&reg;	registered trademark
¯	&#175;	&macr;	macron accent
°	&#176;	&deg;	degree
±	&#177;	&plusmn;	plus/minus sign
²	&#178;	&sup2;	superscript 2*
³	&#179;	&sup3;	superscript 3*
´	&#180;	&acute;	acute accent
µ	&#181;	&micro;	micro sign
¶	&#182;	&para;	paragraph sign
·	&#183;	&middot;	middle dot
¸	&#184;	&cedil;	cedilla accent
¹	&#185;	&sup1;	superscript 1*
º	&#186;	&ordm;	masculine ordinal

* This character is missing from the native Macintosh character set. Internet Explorer 5 for the Macintosh substitutes the Latin-1 (ISO-8859-1) character set, so this character is displayed in that browser, but might not be displayed in other Macintosh browsers.

Character	Entity Number	Entity Name	Description
»	&#187;	&raquo;	right double guillemet
¼	&#188;	&frac14;	quarter fraction[*]
½	&#189;	&frac12;	half fraction[*]
¾	&#190;	&frac34;	three-quarter fraction[*]
¿	&#191;	&iquest;	inverted question mark
À	&#192;	&Agrave;	A-gravé
Á	&#193;	&Aacute;	A-acute
Â	&#194;	&Acirc;	A-circumflex
Ã	&#195;	&Atilde;	A-tilde
Ä	&#196;	&Auml;	A-umlaut
Å	&#197;	&Aring;	A-ring
Æ	&#198;	&AElig;	AE ligature
Ç	&#199;	&Ccedil;	C-cedilla
È	&#200;	&Egrave;	E-gravé
É	&#201;	&Eacute;	E-acute
Ê	&#202;	&Ecirc;	E-circumflex
Ë	&#203;	&Euml;	E-umlaut
Ì	&#204;	&Igrave;	I-gravé
Í	&#205;	&Iacute;	I-acute
Î	&#206;	&Icirc;	I-circumflex
Ï	&#207;	&Iuml;	I-umlaut
Ð	&#208;	&ETH;	capital Eth[*]
Ñ	&#209;	&Ntilde;	N-tilde
Ò	&#210;	&Ograve;	0-gravé
Ó	&#211;	&Oacute;	O-acute
Ô	&#212;	&Ocirc;	O-circumflex
Õ	&#213;	&Otilde;	O-tilde
Ö	&#214;	&Ouml;	O-umlaut
×	&#215;	&times;	multiplication sign[*]
Ø	&#216;	&Oslash;	O-slash
Ù	&#217;	&Ugrave;	U-gravé
Ú	&#218;	&Uacute;	U-acute
Û	&#219;	&Ucirc;	U-circumflex
Ü	&#220;	&Uuml;	U-umlaut
Ý	&#221;	&Yacute;	Y-acute[*]
Þ	&#222;	&THORN;	capital Thorn[*]
ß	&#223;	&szlig;	sharp s, sz ligature
à	&#224;	&agrave;	a-gravé
á	&#225;	&aacute;	a-acute
â	&#226;	&acirc;	a-circumflex
ã	&#227;	&atilde;	a-tilde
ä	&#228;	&auml;	a-umlaut
å	&#229;	&aring;	a-ring
æ	&#230;	&aelig;	ae ligature

[*] This character is missing from the native Macintosh character set. Internet Explorer 5 for the Macintosh substitutes the Latin-1 (ISO-8859-1) character set, so this character is displayed in that browser, but might not be displayed in other Macintosh browsers.

Character	Entity Number	Entity Name	Description
ç	ç	ç	c-cedilla
è	è	è	e-gravé
é	é	é	e-acute
ê	ê	ê	e-circumflex
ë	ë	ë	e-umlaut
ì	ì	ì	i-gravé
í	í	í	i-acute
î	î	î	i-circumflex
ï	ï	ï	i-umlaut
ð	ð	ð	small eth[*]
ñ	ñ	ñ	n-tilde
ò	ò	ò	o-gravé
ó	ó	ó	o-acute
ô	ô	ô	o-circumflex
õ	õ	õ	o-tilde
ö	ö	ö	o-umlaut
÷	÷	÷	division sign
ø	ø	ø	o-slash
ù	ù	ù	u-gravé
ú	ú	ú	u-acute
û	û	û	u-circumflex
ü	ü	ü	u-umlaut
ý	ý	ý	y-acute[*]
þ	þ	þ	small thorn[*]
ÿ	ÿ	ÿ	y-umlaut

[*] This character is missing from the native Macintosh character set. Internet Explorer 5 for the Macintosh substitutes the Latin-1 (ISO-8859-1) character set, so this character is displayed in that browser, but might not be displayed in other Macintosh browsers.

TROUBLE *spot*

Do not directly insert non-keyboard characters into an HTML file by using the Windows Character Map utility, for instance, because what displays as one character on one platform might display as another character on another platform.

HTML 4 UNICODE CHARACTERS

ISO 8859-1 provides a total of 95 characters that can be inserted into HTML documents in addition to the ASCII "keyboard" characters that also can be used. This means, however, that many characters that desktop publishers, for instance, are accustomed to including in documents are not available in the ISO 8859-1 character set.

To overcome the limited number of characters that are available in ISO 8859-1, HTML 4 supports including characters in HTML documents from the Unicode character set. Unicode 3.0 supports the inclusion of over 49,000 characters from a wide range of languages, including from the Americas, Europe, the Middle East, Africa, India, Asia, and the Pacific.

The Unicode characters shown in the following sections should be available on most recent Windows and Macintosh systems and display in most recent browsers. Other Unicode characters, however, might require additional Unicode-supporting fonts that include the characters be installed on the system.

To display most of the following Unicode characters in Netscape 4, declare the document's character set to be UTF-8:

```
<html>
<meta http-equiv="Content-Type" content="text/html; charset=UTF-8">
```

Be aware that non-keyboard characters that have been directly inserted into an HTML file, instead of being inserted using the characters' entity codes, might display entirely different characters or not display any characters at all. This is one more reason not to directly insert non-keyboard characters into an HTML file.

Latin Extended-A and Extended-B

Character	Entity Number	Entity Name	Description
Œ	&#338;	&OElig;	capital ligature OE
œ	&#339;	&oelig;	small ligature oe
Š	&#352;	&Scaron;	S-caron
š	&#353;	&scaron;	s-caron
Ÿ	&#376;	&Yuml;	Y-diaeresis
ƒ	&#402;	&fnof;	function, florin

Greek Capital Characters

Character	Entity Number	Entity Name	Description
Α	&#913;	&Alpha;	capital Alpha
Β	&#914;	&Beta;	capital Beta
Γ	&#915;	&Gamma;	capital Gamma
Δ	&#916;	&Delta;	capital Delta
Ε	&#917;	&Epsilon;	capital Epsilon
Ζ	&#918;	&Zeta;	capital Zeta
Η	&#919;	&Eta;	capital Eta
Θ	&#920;	&Theta;	capital Theta
Ι	&#921;	&Iota;	capital Iota
Κ	&#922;	&Kappa;	capital Kappa
Λ	&#923;	&Lambda;	capital Lambda
Μ	&#924;	&Mu;	capital Mu
Ν	&#925;	&Nu;	capital Nu
Ξ	&#926;	&Xi;	capital Xi
Ο	&#927;	&Omicron;	capital Omicron
Π	&#928;	&Pi;	capital Pi
Ρ	&#929;	&Rho;	capital Rho
	&#930;		unused

Character	Entity Number	Entity Name	Description
Σ	&#931;	&Sigma;	capital Sigma
Τ	&#932;	&Tau;	capital Tau
Υ	&#933;	&Upsilon;	capital Upsilon
Φ	&#934;	&Phi;	capital Phi
Χ	&#935;	&Chi;	capital Chi
Ψ	&#936;	&Psi;	capital Psi
Ω	&#937;	&Omega;	capital Omega

Greek Small Characters

Character	Entity Number	Entity Name	Description
α	&#945;	&alpha;	small alpha
β	&#946;	&beta;	small beta
γ	&#947;	&gamma;	small gamma
δ	&#948;	&delta;	small delta
ε	&#949;	&epsilon;	small epsilon
ζ	&#950;	&zeta;	small zeta
η	&#951;	&eta;	small eta
θ	&#952;	&theta;	small theta
ι	&#953;	&iota;	small iota
κ	&#954;	&kappa;	small kappa
λ	&#955;	&lambda;	small lambda
μ	&#956;	&mu;	small mu
ν	&#956;	&nu;	small nu
ξ	&#958;	&xi;	small xi
ο	&#959;	&omicron;	small omicron
π	&#960;	&pi;	small pi
ρ	&#961;	&rho;	small rho
ς	&#962;	&sigmaf;	small sigma final
σ	&#963;	&sigma;	small sigma
τ	&#964;	&tau;	small tau
υ	&#965;	&upsilon;	small upsilon
φ	&#966;	&phi;	small phi
χ	&#967;	&chi;	small chi
ψ	&#968;	&psi;	small psi
ω	&#969;	&omega;	small omega

Miscellaneous Characters and Symbols

Character	Entity Number	Entity Name	Description
–	&#8207;	&ndash;	en dash
—	&#8212;	&mdash;	em dash
'	&#8216;	&lsquo;	left single quotation mark
'	&#8217;	&rsquo;	right single quotation mark
‚	&#8218;	&sbquo;	single low-9 quotation mark
"	&#8220;	&ldquo;	left double quotation mark
"	&#8221;	&rdquo;	right double quotation mark
„	&#8222;	&bdquo;	double low-9 quotation mark
†	&#8224;	&dagger;	dagger
‡	&#8225;	&Dagger;	double dagger
•	&#8226;	&bull;	bullet
…	&#8230;	&hellip;	horizontal ellipsis
‰	&#8240;	&permil;	per mille sign
′	&#8242;	&prime;	prime, minutes, feet
″	&#8243;	&Prime;	double prime, seconds, inches
‹	&#8249;	&lsaquo;	single left angle quotation mark
›	&#8250;	&rsaquo;	single right angle quotation mark
/	&#8260;	&frasl;	fraction slash
€	&#8364;	&euro;	euro sign
™	&#8482;	&trade;	trademark
←	&#8592;	&larr;	left arrow
↑	&#8593;	&uarr;	up arrow
→	&#8594;	&rarr;	right arrow
↓	&#8595;	&darr;	down arrow
↔	&#8596;	&harr;	left-right arrow
⇒	&#8658;	&rArr;	right double arrow
⇔	&#8660;	&hArr;	left-right double arrow
∀	&#8704;	&forall;	for all
∂	&#8706;	&part;	part differential
∃	&#8707;	&exist;	there exists
∇	&#8711;	&nabla;	nabla/backward difference
∈	&#8712;	&isin;	element of (is in)
∋	&#8715;	&ni;	contains as member
∏	&#8719;	&prod;	product sign
∑	&#8721;	&sum;	n-ary summation
−	&#8722;	&minus;	minus sign
√	&#8730;	&radic;	square root/radical sign
∝	&#8733;	&prop;	proportional to
∞	&#8734;	&infin;	infinity
∠	&#8736;	&ang;	angle
∧	&#8743;	&and;	logical and
∨	&#8744;	&or;	logical or
∩	&#8745;	&cap;	intersection, cap
∪	&#8746;	&cup;	union, cup
∫	&#8747;	&int;	integral

Character	Entity Number	Entity Name	Description
∴	&#8756;	&there4;	therefore
~	&#8764;	&sim;	similar to, tilde operator
≈	&#8776;	&asymp;	asymptomatic, almost equal
≠	&#8800;	&ne;	not equal
≡	&#8801;	&equiv;	equivalent
≤	&#8804;	&le;	less than or equal
≥	&#8805;	&ge;	greater than or equal
⊂	&#8834;	&sub;	subset of
⊃	&#8835;	&sup;	superset of
⊆	&#8838;	&sube;	subset of or equal to
⊇	&#9939;	&supe;	superset of or equal to
⊕	&#8853;	&oplus;	direct sum
⊥	&#8869;	&perp;	perpendicular
◊	&#9674;	&loz;	lozenge
♠	&#9824;	&spades;	spades suit
♣	&#9827;	&clubs;	clubs suit
♥	&#9829;	&hearts;	hearts suit
♦	&#9830;	&diams;	diamonds suit

NOTE

For additional resources and information on using character sets on the Web, see the Appendixes' section at the IRC for this book at **www.emcp.com/**.

Web-Safe Colors Chart

The Web-safe color palette contains 216 colors that display without being dithered on computer systems with display adapters that are limited to 256 colors. This color palette was originally called the "Netscape palette," because Netscape originated it. The 216 colors specified should all be present on the 256-color system palettes of most computers, whether running Windows, Macintosh OS, or UNIX. The Web-safe color palette also can help make it easier to select a color, because you only have to choose between 216 colors, whereas the full True Color palette includes 16.3 million possible colors.

FFFFFF	FFFFCC	FFFF99	FFFF66	FFFF33	FFFF00
FFCCFF	FFCCCC	FFCC99	FFCC66	FFCC33	FFCC00
FF99FF	FF99CC	FF9999	FF9966	FF9933	FF9900
FF66FF	FF66CC	FF6699	FF6666	FF6633	FF6600
FF33FF	FF33CC	FF3399	FF3366	FF3333	FF3300
FF00FF	FF00CC	FF0099	FF0066	FF0033	FF0000

CCFFFF	CCFFCC	CCFF99	CCFF66	CCFF33	CCFF00
CCCCFF	CCCCCC	CCCC99	CCCC66	CCCC33	CCCC00
CC99FF	CC99CC	CC9999	CC9966	CC9933	CC9900
CC66FF	CC66CC	CC6699	CC6666	CC6633	CC6600
CC33FF	CC33CC	CC3399	CC3366	CC3333	CC3300
CC00FF	CC00CC	CC0099	CC0066	CC0033	CC0000

99FFFF	99FFCC	99FF99	99FF66	99FF33	99FF00
99CCFF	99CCCC	99CC99	99CC66	99CC33	99CC00
9999FF	9999CC	999999	999966	999933	999900
9966FF	9966CC	996699	996666	996633	996600
9933FF	9933CC	993399	993366	993333	993300
9900FF	9900CC	990099	990066	990033	990000

66FFFF	66FFCC	66FF99	66FF66	66FF33	66FF00
66CCFF	66CCCC	66CC99	66CC66	66CC33	66CC00
6699FF	6699CC	669999	669966	669933	669900
6666FF	6666CC	666699	666666	666633	666600
6633FF	6633CC	663399	663366	663333	663300
6600FF	6600CC	660099	660066	660033	660000

33FFFF	33FFCC	33FF99	33FF66	33FF33	33FF00
33CCFF	33CCCC	33CC99	33CC66	33CC33	33CC00
3399FF	3399CC	339999	339966	339933	339900
3366FF	3366CC	336699	336666	336633	336600
3333FF	3333CC	333399	333366	333333	333300
3300FF	3300CC	330099	330066	330033	330000

00FFFF	00FFCC	00FF99	00FF66	00FF33	00FF00
00CCFF	00CCCC	00CC99	00CC66	00CC33	00CC00
0099FF	0099CC	009999	009966	009933	009900
0066FF	0066CC	006699	006666	006633	006600
0033FF	0033CC	003399	003366	003333	003300
0000FF	0000CC	000099	000066	000033	000000

NOTE

For additional resources and information on using color on the Web, see the Appendixes section at the IRC for this book at www.emcp.com/.

Index

text, 96–102, 115, 116–117
Web-safe, 100–101, 148
COLS attribute, 223
COLSPAN attribute, 184
comments, HTML, 16
Common Gateway Interface. *See* CGI
compatibility issues
  audio files, 161–162
  box model hack, 245–246
  Cascading Style Sheets (CSS),
    105, 111
  external style sheets, 237–238
  font faces, 90–94
  font families, 114–115
  font size, 90, 111, 113
  frames, 231–232, 233–234
  handling older browsers,
    111–113, 115, 161–162,
    237–238
  mailto forms, 267–268
  nested tables, 212–214
  styles in tables, 190–191
  validating Web pages, 254–258
CompuServe Graphics Interchange
  Format. *See* GIF
conformance levels, HTML, 41–42
Conseil European pour la Recherche
  Nucleaire (CERN), I-7–I-8
container elements, 5–6
CONTENT attribute, 44–45
copying files, 247
copyright issues, 164–165, 232
copyright notice, 63
copyright symbol, 62–64
Courier font, 93
CSS (Cascading Style Sheets). *See
also* CSS style properties; CSS
styles
  imported, 237
  linked, 236–246
  multi-page sites, 236–246
  user-defined, 109
  validation, 243, 248
CSS style properties
  background, 118–119
  background-attachment, 120
  background-image, 120
  background-position, 120
  background-repeat, 120
  border-collapse, 195
  border-left, 253
  border-spacing, 195
  border-top, 198, 253
  color, 115, 116–117
  display, 111, 113, 144
  font-family, 114–115
  font-size, 107, 108
  list-style-image, 204–205
  margin, 262
  margin-left, 243
  margin-top, 227
  padding, 195
  padding-left, 243
  width, 245–246
CSS styles
  accessibility, *vs.* HTML, 105, 106
  box model hack, 245–246
  buttons on forms, 276
  compatibility issues, 105, 111,
    113, 190–191, 237–238
  with custom classes, 110,
    195–196
  formatting page for printing, 238
  formatting tables, 190–199
  formatting text, 107, 108, 111,
    114–115
  link styles, 117–118, 244–245
  style rules, 116
  two-column page layouts,
    224–230

D

DEL element, 51–52
deleted text
  marking, 51–52
  suppressing display of, 52
deprecation, 42, 106
description, Web page, 44–45
destination anchors, 54, 57
DIR element, 65
display property, 111, 113, 144
dithering, 100, 147
DIV element
  ALIGN attribute, 26
  vs. CENTER, 28
DocType declaration
  in FRAMESET pages, 222, 224
  in HTML documents, 41–43
DocType switching, 42–43
document menu, creating, 65–68
Document Type Definition (DTD),
  I-14
domain name, in URL, 20–21
DOM Sniff method, 111, 113
downloadable fonts, 122
DTD (Document Type Definition),
  I-14

E

elements
  case-sensitivity, 7
  defined, 5
  nesting of, 6–7, 17
  top-level, 9
  types of, 5–6
em (size unit), 108, 111, 113
e-mail address links, 32–33
EMBED element
  audio files, 157–159
  video files, 162–163
EM element, 46–48
emphasized text, 46–48
empty elements, 6
ENCTYPE attribute, 283
endnotes, 60–62
end tags, 5
entity codes, 62–64
EOT (Embedded Open Type) font,
  122
example files, downloading, 3–4
Extensible HyperText Markup
  Language. *See* XHTML
Extensible Markup Language. *See*
  XML
extensions, file. *See* file extensions

F

FACE attribute
  function of, 90–95
  generic font-family names, 94–95
FAQ page, creating, 64–73
file compression utilities, 4
file extensions, displaying, 11
file names
  case-sensitive, 23
  spaces in, 12
file names of, 11–12
file permissions, setting, 285–286
files
  copying/moving, 247
  downloading, 3–4
  saving, 11–12, 13
  uploading to a Web server,
    259–260
file transfer protocol. *See* FTP
firewalls, 259
Flash animations, 156
folders, creating, 247
FONT element
  COLOR attribute, 96–101

deprecation of, 106
  FACE attribute, 90–95
  with inline styles, 115
  inside preformatted text, 175
  inside tables, 185–186
  SIZE attribute, 86–89
@font-face at-rule, 122
font faces
  on different systems, 92–93
  embedded (downloadable), 122
  FONT element, 90–95
  serif *vs.* sans serif, 95–96
  Web resources, 93
  x-height, 94
font families
  font-family property, 114–115
  generic, in FACE attribute, 94–95
font size
  absolute, 86–87
  BASEFONT element, 90
  BIG/SMALL elements, 68–70, 89
  in ems, 108, 111, 113
  FONT element, 86–89
  inline styles, 107
  in pixels, 106–108
  in points, 113
  relative, 88–89
  SPAN element, 109–110
  in style sheets, 107, 108
  x-height, 94
font-size property, 107, 108
footnotes, 52–60
foreground color, 102
FORM element
  ACTION attribute, 269, 284
  ENCTYPE attribute, 283
  METHOD attribute, 269
forms
  aligning fields, 288–289
  CGI, 284, 287–288
  check boxes, 271–272
  colors, 290
  control buttons, 274–276
  image buttons, 275
  input controls, 269–272
  JavaScript scripts in, 292–293
  list menus, 272–274
  mailto, 267–268, 280–284
  multi-line text boxes, 274
  radio buttons, 270–271
  reset button, 274–276
  submit button, 274–276
  tabbing order, 279–280
  tables in, 290–292
  testing, 276–279
  text input fields, 270, 274
FRAME element
  FRAMEBORDER attribute, 252
  inline styles, 253
  MARGINHEIGHT attribute, 226
  MARGINWIDTH attribute, 236
  NAME attribute, 223, 225
  with nested FRAMESETs,
    228–230
  SCROLLING attribute, 226
  SRC attribute, 223
frames
  borders, 252–253
  column and row layout, 228–230
  displaying other Web sites with-
    in, 24, 232
  frameset pages, 222–223
  pros and cons, 231–232
  seamless, 252–253
  two-column layout, 222–225
  two-row layout, 225–227
"frameset" conformance, 42
FRAMESET element
  BORDER attribute, 252
  COLS attribute, 222–223

  FRAMEBORDER attribute, 252
  FRAMESPACING attribute, 252
  inline styles, 253
  nesting multiple, 228–230
  ROWS attribute, 226
  SPACING attribute, 252
FTP (file transfer protocol) pro-
  grams, 259–260, 285–286

G

generic font-family names, 94–95
Geneva font, 92, 93
GIF (CompuServe Graphics
  Interchange Format)
  animations, 154–156
  interlaced, 151
  optimized color palettes,
    148–149
  transparent images, 149–151
  when to use, 27, 146–147
Google. *See* search engines
graphic rules, 143–144
Graphics Interchange Format. *See* GIF
"grid" page layout, 230

H

H1 element
  function of, 12, 19
  and search engines, 144
H2 element, 19
HEAD element, 9
headings
  alignment, 25
  levels of, 12, 19
HEIGHT attribute
  audio/video player consoles,
    158–159, 160–161
  images, 30, 143
  table rows, 184
Helvetica font, 92, 93
hexadecimal conversion table, 99
hexadecimal RGB codes, 98–100
highlighting text, 45–49
host name, in URL, 20–21
"hover" link style, 117–118, 121–122
HREF attribute
  function of, 17
  jump links, 54
  linking external documents, 237
  return links, 55
  syntax of, 18
HR element
  ALIGN attribute, 58
  function of, 32
  NOSHADE attribute, 59
  WIDTH attribute, 57
HSPACE attribute, 132–133,
  205–206
HTML (HyperText Markup
  Language)
  form and function of, I-12–I-15
  history of, I-17–I-19
  standards, I-21
HTML documents
  comments in, 16–17
  creating, 8–9
  DocType declaration, 41–42
  editing, 40–41
  file names of, 11–12
  formatting for readability, 15–16
  hierarchy of, 9
  meta data in, 44–45
  in multiple folders, 246–252
  previewing, 13–14
  saving, 11–12, 13
  templates, 10–12
  uploading to a Web server,
    259–260
HTML element, 9